MW00333232

LIEUTENANT GENERAL JAMES LONGSTREET: INNOVATIVE MILITARY STRATEGIST

LIEUTENANT GENERAL JAMES LONGSTREET: INNOVATIVE MILITARY STRATEGIST

The Most Misunderstood Civil War General

F. GREGORY TORETTA

CASEMATE

Philadelphia & Oxford

Published in the United States of America and Great Britain in 2022 by
CASEMATE PUBLISHERS
1950 Lawrence Road, Havertown, PA 19083, USA
and
The Old Music Hall, 106–108 Cowley Road, Oxford OX4 1JE, UK

Hardback Edition: ISBN 978-1-63624-117-3
Digital Edition: ISBN 978-1-63624-118-0

A CIP record for this book is available from the British Library

Printed and bound in the United States by Integrated Books International

Typeset in India by Lapiz Digital Services, Chennai.

For a complete list of Casemate titles, please contact:

CASEMATE PUBLISHERS (US)
Telephone (610) 853-9131
Fax (610) 853-9146
Email: casemate@casematepublishers.com
www.casematepublishers.com

CASEMATE PUBLISHERS (UK)
Telephone (01865) 241249
Email: casemate-uk@casematepublishers.co.uk
www.casematepublishers.co.uk

All maps provided by Library of Congress

Contents

Acknowledgments

I wish to thank my editors, Michael D. Lewis and Stephen Spagnesi, who were very supportive with their knowledge, ability and experience and helped me write and organize this manuscript. I would also like to thank Roger Williams, who advised me and provided me with a list of good editors for historical works. My special thanks to Shelley Glick in the research department of the Briarcliff Manor Public Library for her tireless efforts to obtain material to help me write the book. I want to thank Kelly Wooten of the Rare Book, Manuscript, and Special Collections Library of Duke University for providing me copies of the Longstreet Papers. Thanks to my wife, Joan, who encouraged me with her love and devotion in my many hours of writing. I wish to acknowledge my sons, Philip, George, and Stephen, who helped me with computer problems and purchased a new computer when the old one crashed so I could finish the manuscript. I also wish to acknowledge my indebtedness to the Library of Congress for obtaining copies of the Wigfall Papers.

Civil War Timeline

November 6, 1860	Abraham Lincoln is elected 16th president of the United States, the first Republican president in the nation who represents a party that opposes the spread of slavery in the territories of the United States.
December 17, 1860	The first Secession convention meets in Columbia, South Carolina.
December 20, 1860	South Carolina secedes from the Union.
January, 1861	Six additional southern states secede from the Union.
February 8–9, 1861	The southern states that seceded create a government at Montgomery, Alabama, and the Confederate States of America are formed.
February 18, 1861	Jefferson Davis is appointed the first president of the Confederate States of America at Montgomery, Alabama, a position he will hold until elections can be arranged.
March 4, 1861	Abraham Lincoln is inaugurated as the 16th president of the United States in Washington, D.C.
April 12, 1861	Southern forces fire upon Fort Sumter, South Carolina. The Civil War has formally begun.
April 15, 1861	President Lincoln issues a public declaration that an insurrection exists and calls for 75,000 militia to stop the rebellion. As a result of this call for volunteers, four additional southern states secede from the Union in the following weeks. Lincoln will respond on May 3 with an additional call for 43,000+ volunteers to serve for three years, expanding the size of the Regular army.
May 8, 1861	James Longstreet resigns his U.S. Army commission and joins the Confederate army, with the rank of Brigadier-General.
July 21, 1861	The battle of Bull Run (or First Manassas) is fought near Manassas, Virginia. The Union army under General Irwin McDowell initially succeeds in driving

back Confederate forces under General Pierre Gustav Toutant Beauregard, but the arrival of troops under General Joseph E. Johnston initiates a series of reverses that send McDowell's army in a panicked retreat to the defenses of Washington. It is here that Thomas Jonathan Jackson, a professor at VMI will receive everlasting fame as "Stonewall" Jackson.

July, 1861   To thwart the Confederate threat in northern Virginia, a series of earthworks and forts are engineered to surround the City of Washington, adding to protection already offered by active posts such as Fort Washington on the Potomac River.

August 28–29, 1861   Fort Hatteras at Cape Hatteras, North Carolina, falls to Union naval forces. This begins the first Union efforts to close southern ports along the Carolina coast.

October 7, 1861   Brigadier General James Longstreet is promoted to Major General

February 6, 1862   Surrender of Fort Henry, Tennessee. The loss of this southern fort on the Tennessee River opens the door to Union control of the river.

February 8, 1862   Battle of Roanoke Island, North Carolina. A Confederate defeat, the battle resulted in Union occupation of eastern North Carolina and control of Pamlico Sound, to be used as a Northern base for further operations against the southern coast.

February 16, 1862   Surrender of Fort Donelson, Tennessee. This primary southern fort on the Cumberland River left the river in Union hands. It was here that Union General Ulysses S. Grant gained his nickname "Unconditional Surrender."

February 22, 1862   Jefferson Davis is inaugurated as "President of the Confederate States of America."

March 7–8, 1862   Battle of Pea Ridge (Elkhorn Tavern), Arkansas. The Union victory loosened the Confederate hold on Missouri and disrupted southern control of a portion of the Mississippi River.

March 9, 1862   The naval battle between the USS *Monitor* and the CSS *Virginia* (the old USS *Merrimack*), the first "ironclads," is fought in Hampton Roads, Virginia.

April 6–7, 1862	The battle of Shiloh (Pittsburg Landing), the first major battle in Tennessee. Confederate General Albert Sidney Johnston, a veteran of the Texas War of Independence and the War with Mexico, considered to be one of the finest officers the South has, is killed on the first day of fighting. The Union victory further secures the career of Union General Ulysses S. Grant.
April 24–25, 1862	A Union fleet of gunships under Admiral David Farragut passes Confederate forts guarding the mouth of the Mississippi River. On April 25, the fleet arrives at New Orleans where they demanded the surrender of the city. Within two days the forts fall into Union hands and the mouth of the great river is under Union control.
May 25, 1862	First battle of Winchester, Virginia. After two weeks of maneuvering and battles at Cross Keys and Front Royal, General "Stonewall" Jackson attacks Union forces at Winchester and successfully drives them from the city. The victory is the culmination of his 1862 Valley Campaign.
May 31–June 1, 1862	The battle of Seven Pines near Richmond, Virginia. General Joseph Johnston, commander of the Confederate army in Virginia is wounded and replaced by Robert E. Lee who renames his command the "Army of Northern Virginia."
June 6, 1862	Battle of Memphis, Tennessee. A Union flotilla under Commodore Charles Davis successfully defeats a Confederate river force on the Mississippi River near the city, and Memphis surrenders. The Mississippi River is now in Union control except for its course west of Mississippi where the city of Vicksburg stands as the last southern stronghold on the great river.
June 25–July 1, 1862	The Seven Days' Battles before Richmond. General Lee's army attacks the "Army of the Potomac" under General George McClellan in a succession of battles beginning at Mechanicsville on June 26 and ending at Malvern Hill on July 1.
August 30–31,1862	The battle of Second Bull Run (or Second Manassas) is fought on the same ground where one year before, the Union army was defeated and sent reeling in

	retreat to Washington. Likewise, the result of this battle is a Union defeat.
September 17, 1862	The battle of Antietam (or Sharpsburg), Maryland, the bloodiest single day of the Civil War. The result of the battle ends General Lee's first invasion of the North. Following the Union victory, President Lincoln will introduce the Emancipation Proclamation, an executive order that freed every slave in the Confederate States.
October 9, 1862	Major General Longstreet is promoted to Lieutenant General.
December 13, 1862	The battle of Fredericksburg, Virginia. The Army of the Potomac, under General Ambrose Burnside, is soundly defeated by Lee's forces after a risky river crossing and sacking of the city. General Lee's army fought a defensive engagement behind intrenchments.
December 31, 1862– January 3, 1863	Battle of Stones River, Tennessee. Fought between the Union Army of the Cumberland under General William Rosecrans and the Confederate Army of Tennessee under General Braxton Bragg, the costly Union victory frees middle Tennessee from Confederate control and boosts northern morale.
January 1, 1863	The Emancipation Proclamation goes into effect. Applauded by many abolitionists, including Frederick Douglass, there are others who feel it does not go far enough to totally abolish slavery.
March 3, 1863	Conscription, or the drafting of soldiers into military service, begins in the North. It had begun in the South the year before.
April, 1863	Union forces in the east begin a new campaign in Virginia to flank Lee's Army of Northern Virginia at Fredericksburg. In the west, a Union army has begun a campaign to surround and take Vicksburg, Mississippi, the last Confederate stronghold on the Mississippi River.
May 1–4, 1863	The battle of Chancellorsville, Virginia. General Lee's greatest victory is marred by the mortal wounding of "Stonewall" Jackson, who dies on May 10. Soon after, Lee asks Jefferson Davis for permission to invade the North and take the war out of Virginia.
May 18, 1863	Siege of Vicksburg, Mississippi begins. Union forces under General Ulysses S. Grant attack Confederate

	defenses outside the city on May 19–22. If Vicksburg falls, the Mississippi River will be completely controlled by the Union.
June 9, 1863	The battle of Brandy Station, Virginia. Union cavalry forces cross the Rapidan River to attack General J. E. B. Stuart's cavalry and discover Lee's men are moving west toward the Shenandoah Valley. The largest cavalry battle of the Civil War, it also marks the beginning of the Gettysburg campaign. Meanwhile, the Union assault on Vicksburg, Mississippi, has become a siege of the city where soldiers and civilians alike suffer from constant bombardment.
June 14–15, 1863	Battle of Second Winchester, Virginia. Confederate troops under General Richard Ewell defeat Union troops under General Robert Milroy, clearing the Shenandoah Valley of Union forces.
June 28, 1863	The Gettysburg Campaign continues. Confederates pass through York and reach the bridge over the Susquehanna River at Columbia, but Union militia set fire to the bridge, denying access to the east shore. Southern cavalry skirmishes with Union militia near Harrisburg, Pennsylvania.
July 1–3, 1863	The battle of Gettysburg, Pennsylvania. The bloodiest battle of the Civil War dashes Robert E. Lee's hopes for a successful invasion of the North. General Longstreet opposed the Gettysburg campaign and the tactics in the battle.
July 4, 1863	Vicksburg, Mississippi, surrenders to the Union Army under Grant. The capture of Vicksburg gives the Union complete control of the Mississippi River, a vital supply line for the Confederate states in the west. At Gettysburg, Lee begins his retreat to Virginia.
July 13–14, 1863	Near Falling Waters, Maryland, Union troops skirmish with Lee's rearguard. That night the Army of Northern Virginia crosses the Potomac River and the Gettysburg campaign ends.
September 9, 1863	Chattanooga, Tennessee, is occupied by Union forces under General William Rosecrans whose Army of the Cumberland will soon invade northern Georgia.
September 19–20, 1863	The battle of Chickamauga, Georgia. The Union Army of the Cumberland under General William Rosecrans

is defeated and nearly routed by the Confederate Army of Tennessee commanded by General Braxton Bragg. Rosecrans' army retreats to the supply base at Chattanooga, Tennessee. General Longstreet utilizes the railroad to bring two of his divisions from Virginia to support Bragg and Longstreet is instrumental in securing a victory over the Union forces.

September–November, 1863

The Siege of Chattanooga, Tennessee. Confederate forces under Braxton Bragg surround the occupied city. General Ulysses S. Grant is assigned to command the troops there and begins immediate plans to relieve the besieged Union army.

October 9–22, 1863

Bristoe Station Campaign. In a feint toward Washington, Lee's Army of Northern Virginia marches into northern Virginia in an attempt to flank the Army of the Potomac, under General Meade. Lee successfully outmaneuvers Meade, though fails to bring him to battle or catch him in the open. An engagement at Bristoe Station, Virginia, on October 14 gives the campaign its name.

November 19, 1863

Dedication of the Soldiers' National Cemetery at Gettysburg. President Lincoln delivers the Gettysburg Address.

November 23–25, 1863

The battle for Chattanooga. Union forces break the Confederate siege of the city in successive attacks. The most notable event is the storming of Lookout Mountain on November 24 and the battle of Missionary Ridge the following day. The decisive Union victory sends the Confederate Army south into Georgia where General Bragg reorganizes his forces before resigning from command on November 30.

November 26–December 1, 1863

The Mine Run Campaign. Meade's Army of the Potomac marches against Lee's Army of Northern Virginia south of the Rapidan River, east of Orange Court House. Lee reacts and throws up a line of defenses along the banks of Mine Run Creek. After several days of probing the defenses, Meade withdraws north of the Rapidan and goes into winter quarters.

November 27–December 3, 1863

Siege of Knoxville, Tennessee. Confederate troops under General James Longstreet lay siege to the city of Knoxville held by Union forces under General

Ambrose Burnside. Longstreet finally attacks on November 30 but is repulsed with heavy losses. The arrival of Union reinforcements forces him to withdraw to Greenville, Tennessee, where his corps will spend the winter.

December 8, 1863 — Lincoln issues his Proclamation of Amnesty and Reconstruction, which would pardon those who participated in the "existing rebellion" if they take an oath to the Union.

February 14–20, 1864 — Union Capture and Occupation of Meridian, Mississippi. Union forces under William T. Sherman enter the city of Meridian, Mississippi after a successful month of campaigning through the central part of the state. The capture of this important southern town, well known for its industry and storage capabilities, severely hampers the efforts of Confederate commanders to sustain their armies in the deep south, Georgia, and west of the Mississippi River.

February 17, 1864 — First Successful Submarine Attack of the Civil War. The CSS *H. L. Hunley*, a seven-man submergible craft, attacked the USS *Housatonic* outside of Charleston, South Carolina. Struck by the submarine's torpedo, the *Housatonic* broke apart and sank, taking all but five of its crew with it. Likewise, the *Hunley* was also lost and never heard from again until discovered in 1995 at the spot where it sank after the attack.

March 2, 1864 — Ulysses S. Grant is appointed lieutenant general, a rank revived at the request of President Lincoln. Grant assumes command of all Union armies in the field the following day.

March 10, 1864 — The Red River Campaign begins. As part of an overall Union strategy to strike deep into various parts of the Confederacy, a combined force of army and navy commands under General Nathaniel Banks begin a campaign on the Red River in Louisiana.

April 8, 1864 — Battle of Sabine Crossroads or Mansfield, Louisiana, the first major battle of the Red River Campaign in Louisiana.

April 9, 1864 — Battle of Pleasant Hill, Louisiana. The Union army, under Banks, defeat the attempt by Confederate forces under General Richard Taylor to drive them out of

Louisiana. Unfortunately, the result of the campaign would be less than desired as it drew to a close in the first week of May with Confederates still in firm control of most of the state.

May 4–5, 1864   Battle of the Wilderness, Virginia, the opening battle of the "Overland Campaign" or "Wilderness Campaign." General Ulysses S. Grant, accompanying the Army of the Potomac under General Meade, issued orders for the campaign to begin on May 3. Lee responded by attacking the Union column in the dense woods and underbrush of an area known as the "Wilderness," west of Fredericksburg, Virginia. General Longstreet is gravely wounded by his own troops as he masterfully designs a series of flank and rear attacks nearly routing Grant's army which is halted after he is incapacitated.

May 7, 1864   Beginning of the Atlanta Campaign. With three Union armies under his command, General William T. Sherman marched south from Tennessee into Georgia against the Confederate Army of Tennessee under General Joseph Johnston, the objective being the city of Atlanta.

May 8–21, 1864   Battle of Spotsylvania Court House, Virginia. Lee successfully stalls Grant's drive toward Richmond.

May 11, 1864   Battle of Yellow Tavern. Six miles north of Richmond, Confederate cavalry under General J. E. B. Stuart blocked a force of Union cavalry under General Philip Sheridan. General Stuart was mortally wounded during the encounter.

May 14–15, 1864   Battle of Resaca, Georgia. General Sherman's armies are blocked at Resaca by General Johnston's Army of Tennessee. After two days of maneuvering and intense fighting, Johnston withdraws. Sherman will advance but takes precautions against ordering any further massed assaults where high casualties may occur.

June 1–3, 1864   Battle of Cold Harbor, Virginia. Relentless and bloody Union attacks fail to dislodge Lee's army from its strong line of defensive works northeast of Richmond.

June 8, 1864   Abraham Lincoln is nominated by his party for a second term as president.

June 10, 1864

Battle of Brice's Crossroads, Mississippi. In spite of being outnumbered two to one, Confederate General Nathan Bedford Forrest attacks and routes the Union command under General Samuel Sturgis.

June 15–18, 1864

Assault on Petersburg, Virginia. After withdrawing from the lines at Cold Harbor, the Army of the Potomac crossed the James River and, with the troops from the Army of the James, attacked the outer defenses of Petersburg, the primary junction for several southern railroads. After four days of bloody attacks, Grant accepts that only a siege can systematically isolate the city and cut off Confederate supplies to the capital of Richmond.

June 19, 1864

The USS *Kearsarge* sinks the Confederate raider CSS *Alabama* near Cherbourg, France.

June 27, 1864

Battle of Kennesaw Mountain, Georgia. After weeks of maneuvering and battles, Sherman's Army of the Cumberland and Army of the Tennessee smash headlong into Johnston's carefully planned defenses at Big and Little Kennesaw. Johnston remains on this line until July 2, when he retreats at the threat, being flanked by Sherman's mobile force.

July 9, 1864

Battle of Monocacy, Maryland. In an attempt to draw Union troops away from the ongoing siege of Petersburg and Richmond, a Confederate force under Jubal Early quietly moved north into Maryland. Early has made excellent progress until he reaches Frederick, Maryland, where a force of 6,000 Federal troops under General Lew Wallace, was arrayed to delay his advance. Though the battle was a Union defeat, it was also touted as "the battle that saved Washington" for it succeeded in holding back Early's march until troops could be sent to the capital's defense.

July 11–12, 1864

Attack on the Defenses of Washington. Jubal Early's troops arrive on the outskirts of Washington, D.C., and trade cannon fire with a token Union force remaining in the forts around the city. President Lincoln observes the skirmishing from Fort Stevens as reinforcements from the Army of the Potomac arrive and quickly fill in the works. Early withdraws that evening.

July 14–15, 1864	Battles near Tupelo, Mississippi. The Union defeat of Nathan Bedford Forrest secured the supply lines to Sherman's armies operating against Atlanta, Georgia.
July 17, 1864	General John Bell Hood replaces General Joseph Johnston as commander of the Army of Tennessee. This change in command signals a new Confederate strategy to thwart Sherman's campaign, though the end result will be disastrous for the southern cause.
July 20, 1864	Battle of Peachtree Creek, Georgia, the first major battle around the city of Atlanta. General Hood sends his army out of the city's defenses to attack the approaching Federal troops under George Thomas. After several hours of fierce fighting, Hood withdraws back to his own defensive works.
July 21, 1864	The battle of Atlanta. Hood's second effort to throw back Union forces under Sherman brings him heavy casualties with no positive results. General James McPherson, commander of the Union Army of the Tennessee, is killed during the fighting.
July 30, 1864	The battle of the Crater at Petersburg, Virginia. After a month of tunneling by soldiers of the 48th Pennsylvania Infantry, a massive mine exploded under a Confederate fort in the Petersburg siege lines. The infantry charge that followed was poorly coordinated and by day's end, Confederate counterattacks had driven out the Union troops and the siege lines remained unchanged.
August 5, 1864	Battle of Mobile Bay. A Union fleet under Admiral David Farragut steamed into Mobile Bay outside the city of Mobile, Alabama, defended by two strong forts and a small southern flotilla, including the formidable ironclad CSS *Tennessee*. Farragut's ships defeated the Confederate ships and bypassed the forts, capturing the important southern port.
August 18–19, 1864	Battles on the Weldon Railroad near Petersburg, Virginia. Union attempts to capture this important railroad into Petersburg were stopped by Confederate counterattacks. Despite southern efforts, the Union remained in firm possession of their gains and the railroad.
August 25, 1864	Battle of Ream's Station, near Petersburg, Virginia. A surprise Confederate counterattack briefly stopped

	Union destruction of the Weldon Railroad near Ream's Station, though failed to release the Union grip on this important supply line into Petersburg.
August 31–September 1, 1864	Battle of Jonesborough, Georgia. The final southern counterattack against Union troops outside the city of Atlanta fails.
September 1, 1864	Fall of Atlanta, Georgia. Confederate troops under General Hood evacuate the city of Atlanta. General Sherman's army occupies the city and its defenses the following day.
September 19, 1864	Third battle of Winchester, Virginia. Union forces under General Philip Sheridan attacked the Confederate army, under Jubal Early, near the city of Winchester and drove them southward, up the Shenandoah Valley.
September 22, 1864	Battle of Fisher's Hill, Virginia. The Union Army of the Shenandoah, under General Philip Sheridan, attacked Jubal Early's Confederates near Fisher's Hill, overpowering the Southerners and again forcing them to flee the battlefield. Union officers and officials in Washington believe this to be the final battle in the Shenandoah Valley.
September 29–30, 1864	Battle of Fort Harrison near Richmond, Virginia. In a sweeping assault, the Confederate stronghold known as Fort Harrison falls to the Army of the James. Confederate efforts to retake the fort fail.
October 19, 1864	The battle of Cedar Creek, Virginia. In an early-morning surprise attack, Jubal Early's Confederates successfully attack and drive troops of the Army of the Shenandoah from their camps on the banks of Cedar Creek south of Middletown, Virginia. Hearing the fight from his headquarters at Winchester, General Philip Sheridan rides southward, rallying dispirited troops who return to the battlefield. By day's end, Early's forces are put to flight. Despite several attempts to disrupt the Union advance in the coming weeks, the battle for control of the Shenandoah Valley is over.
November 8, 1864	Abraham Lincoln is re-elected president of the United States.
November 16, 1864	General Sherman's Army of Georgia begins the "March to the Sea."

November 30, 1864	Battle of Franklin, Tennessee. After a month of raiding Sherman's supply lines and attacking Union outposts. John Bell Hood's army confronts Union troops from General John Schofield's command, who they had encountered the day before near Spring Hill, Tennessee. A massive frontal assault on the well intrenched Federal line meets with disaster. Despite some taking of outside works and defenses, the toll for Hood's forces is too heavy, including the loss of six of his generals. Union troops retreat in the direction of Nashville.
December 10, 1864	Harassed only by scattered Georgia militia, Sherman's Army of Georgia arrives at Savannah, Georgia, completing the famous "March to the Sea." At Savannah, his troops will take Fort McAllister and force Confederate defenders to evacuate the city.
December 15–16, 1864	The battle of Nashville, Tennessee. The Confederate army under John Bell Hood is thoroughly defeated and the threat to Tennessee ends.
January 15, 1865	Assault and capture of Fort Fisher, North Carolina. Union occupation of this fort at the mouth of the Cape Fear River closes access to Wilmington, the last southern seaport on the east coast that was open to blockade runners and commercial shipping.
February 1, 1865	Sherman's Army leaves Savannah to march through the Carolinas.
February 17, 1865	Sherman's Army captures Columbia, South Carolina, while Confederate defenders evacuate Charleston, South Carolina.
February 22, 1865	Wilmington, N.C., falls to Union troops, closing the last important southern port on the east coast. On the same day, Joseph E. Johnston is restored to command the nearly shattered Army of the Tennessee, vice John B. Hood who resigned a month earlier.
March 4, 1865	President Abraham Lincoln is inaugurated for his second term as president in Washington, D.C.
March 16 and 19–21, 1865	The battles of Averasborough and Bentonville, North Carolina. Sherman's army is stalled in its drive northward from Fayetteville but succeeds in passing around the Confederate forces toward its object of Raleigh.

March 25, 1865	Attack on Fort Stedman, Petersburg, Virginia. Touted as "Lee's last offensive," Confederate troops under General John B. Gordon attack and briefly capture the Union fort in the Petersburg siege lines in an attempt to thwart Union plans for a late March assault. By day's end, the southerners have been thrown out and the lines remain unchanged.
April 1, 1865	The battle of Five Forks, Virginia. The Confederate defeat at Five Forks initiates General Lee's decision to abandon the Petersburg–Richmond siege lines.
April 2, 1865	The Fall of Petersburg and Richmond. General Lee abandons both cities and moves his army west in hopes of joining Confederate forces under General Johnston in North Carolina.
April 3, 1865	Union troops occupy Richmond and Petersburg, Virginia.
April 6, 1865	The battle of Sailor's Creek, Virginia. A portion of Lee's Army—almost one-third of it—is cornered along the banks of Sailor's (or "Saylor's") Creek and annihilated.
April 9, 1865	Battle of Appomattox Court House and Surrender, Appomattox Court House, Virginia. After an early-morning attempt to break through Union forces blocking the route west to Danville, Virginia, Lee seeks an audience with General Grant to discuss terms. That afternoon, in the parlor of Wilmer McLean, Lee signs the document of surrender. On April 12, the Army of Northern Virginia formally surrenders and is disbanded.
April 14, 1865	President Abraham Lincoln is assassinated by actor John Wilkes Booth at Ford's Theater in Washington, D.C. On the same day, Fort Sumter, South Carolina, is re-occupied by Union troops.
April 26, 1865	General Joseph Johnston signs the surrender document for the Confederate Army of Tennessee and miscellaneous southern troops attached to his command at Bennett's Place near Durham, North Carolina.
May 4, 1865	General Richard Taylor surrenders Confederate forces in the Department of Alabama, Mississippi, and East Louisiana.

May 10, 1865	Confederate President Jefferson Davis is captured near Irwinville, Georgia.
May 12, 1865	The final battle of the Civil War takes place at Palmito Ranch, Texas. It is a Confederate victory.
May 23, 1865	The Grand Review of the Army of the Potomac in Washington, D.C.
May 24, 1865	The Grand Review of General Sherman's Army in Washington, D.C.
May 26, 1865	General Simon Bolivar Buckner enters into terms for surrender of the Army of the Trans-Mississippi, which are agreed to on June 2, 1865. The Civil War officially ends.

Introduction

On July 3, 1863, General George Pickett's desperate charge was supposedly the high-water mark of the Confederacy on the third day of hard fighting at the battle of Gettysburg. But it was conspicuously indicative of the total failure of the thinking and planning of the Confederate government and the military men it promoted to carry out its designs. When General Robert E. Lee tendered his resignation to President Jefferson Davis of the Confederacy, he admitted his strategy was defective. Yet Lee, President Davis, and General Thomas "Stonewall" Jackson are hailed as heroes, while General James Longstreet, who General Lee put in command of this charge, was opposed to the campaign in Pennsylvania and the strategy and tactics involved, is blamed for the failure. Longstreet is one of the most misunderstood figures of the American Civil War. Although he was criticized and maligned by some of his contemporaries, and many of his biographers and Civil War historians, for his role during and after the war, he had developed a keen insight into the tactics, strategies, and complexities brought about by technological changes in weaponry, logistics, and communications.

The American Civil War is considered by many to be the first modern war. It was a war that required a different type of thinking, a leap to encompass the new tactics and strategies needed to fight this brand-new warfare. General Longstreet was among a few in the Southern cause who made this leap (others being Generals Joseph E. Johnston and P. G. T. Beauregard, to name a few) and tried new ideas to adapt to rifled muskets and cannon, trench warfare, rail transport and the telegraph, and the concept of total war, in which all civilian-associated resources and infrastructure (railroads, telegraph lines, and food supplies) are considered legitimate targets. Confederate leaders Lee, Jackson, Braxton Bragg, John B. Hood, and President Davis were among those who did not fully grasp the change.

On January 8, 1821, James Longstreet was born in the Edgefield District, South Carolina, to James and Mary Ann Dent Longstreet. James was their third son and fifth child. His grandfather William Longstreet took an interest in steam engines and constructed the first steamboat.

General Longstreet was an experienced professional soldier by the time the Civil War broke out. He graduated as a Brevetted Second Lieutenant of the infantry on July 1, 1842, from West Point, one of the best engineering schools of the 19th century and one of the world's top military institutions, where he studied under Dennis Patrick Mahan, a brilliant professor of tactics and strategy of the day. West Point is also where he developed a lifelong friendship with Ulysses S. Grant, even though they were subsequent antagonists on many Civil War battlefields.

Longstreet served on the frontier with the Fourth Infantry at Jefferson Barracks, Missouri, from the fall of 1842 to May 1844. He also gained valuable knowledge with Zachary Taylor and Winfield Scott in the Mexican conflict, 1846–1847, especially the turning movements used by Scott to defeat well-situated Mexican armies.

Longstreet fought from beginning to end in the Civil War as his autobiography, *Manassas to Appomattox,* indicates. He served with distinction in both the eastern and western theaters. His ability to command and direct troops in battle was recognized and brought him to positions of leadership. Longstreet was a pragmatic and methodical general and had a quick grasp of tactics and strategy to use during a battle. He did not smash ahead at the opposing army but tried to find the key to the situation without needlessly sacrificing his men. He showed able generalship at the battles of Gettysburg and Chickamauga. The battle of the Wilderness epitomizes his military skill and shows his ability in a crisis. His generalship was superb and had his advice been listened to, many of the battles could have decidedly been Southern victories. President Lincoln said, "Bring me Longstreet's head on a platter and the war will be over."

Yet this Southern general is not deified like Robert E. Lee and "Stonewall" Jackson, men whom he did not idolize but judged according to their abilities and flaws. There was a monument dedicated to Longstreet on July 3, 1998. An equestrian monument of Longstreet at the Gettysburg National Battlefield Park, 135 years after Gettysburg, by Robert C. Thomas and men and women of the North Carolina Division of the Sons of Confederate Veterans, who raised funds to refurbish Longstreet's image. In 2000, a nice statue was erected at his home place, funded by the Denton Hadaway Estate and arranged by the James Longstreet Chapter of the UDC. In truth, Longstreet's name has been blackened as the man who lost the battle of Gettysburg. After General Lee died on October 12, 1870, an Anti-Longstreet Faction started a campaign to discredit Longstreet. It was led by Jubal Anderson Early, one-time commander of Lee's Second Corps; Reverend William Nelson Pendleton, Lee's chief of artillery; and J. William Jones, a former chaplain in the 13th Virginia Infantry, who became editor of the *Southern Historical Society Papers* which carried much influence. They were all Virginians. General Lee had to relieve Jubal Early of command of the Second Corps late in the war, after he was badly defeated in the Shenandoah Valley. Early was the only Corps commander Lee had to dismiss. Early had hesitated on July 1 at Gettysburg to take Cemetery and Culp's Hills, which could have been decisive in the battle. Pendleton had been notoriously incompetent and failed in his capacity as artillery chief at Gettysburg. Jones was a Baptist minister, and sycophant of the worst type.

After the war, the Southern people enshrined Lee. However, there were criticisms of Lee's faults and failures that led to the loss of the battle at Gettysburg. To ingratiate themselves with the Southern people and build up Lee's reputation, the Anti-Longstreet Faction concocted a tale that Longstreet was not only to blame for losing the battle of Gettysburg but also the war itself. As Lee was no longer around to dispute their insinuations, they played fast and loose with the truth.

Longstreet was targeted and made a scapegoat because he had opposed the Gettysburg Campaign and was critical of Lee's tactics and strategy during the battle and in his writings and comments afterward. He was not a Virginian and had joined the Republican Party, promoting compromise, reconciliation, and improved race relations which were all abhorrent to the Southern people. Many of Longstreet's biographers believed the lies of the Anti-Longstreet Faction and bought into this tale of supposed treachery which bolstered Lee's image as a pure and stainless hero that Lee's biographers had popularized. Lee was idolized at Longstreet's expense.

There are some profiles of Longstreet but none have looked at him in the larger framework of the changing tactics and strategies needed to accommodate technological changes. Nor have they understood his pragmatic nature. The hope and ambition of this book is to present the generalship of Longstreet in the larger context of the military and political picture of his time and contemplate the character of the man and his military skill. It focuses on a period from May 1863 through May 1864, which exemplifies Longstreet's strategic and tactical thinking in dealing with the new technological changes. It was during this span that Longstreet made recommendations on how he thought the war should be fought in light of the new technology and the great advantage in manpower and resources the North possessed. The goal is to find the truth as good historians always strive to do. It offers no opinion as to Longstreet's desires, hopes, dreams, aspirations, or ambitions, which cannot be known, but this treatise merely presents the facts. As an historian, I feel very fortunate that General Longstreet left a valuable source of his views and perspectives in his book, *From Manassas to Appomattox*, published in 1896 which is a treasure trove of material I gleaned from to enhance my thesis. Longstreet stated his reasons for writing the book in the preface:

> The spirit in which this work has been conceived, and in which I have conscientiously labored to carry it out is one of sincerity and fairness. As an actor in, and an eyewitness of, the events of 1861–1865, I have endeavored to perform my humble share of duty in passing the materials of history to those who may give them place in the records of the nation, -not of the South nor of the North, -but in the history of the United Nation. It is with such magnified view of the responsibility of saying the truth that I have written.

In addition, there are extensive writings of participants in the Civil War, who communicate to us by means of the written word through time from which I obtained priceless quotes and insights; I have placed great emphasis on first-hand accounts by these observers. Books by Gilbert Moxley Sorrel (*Recollections of a Confederate Staff Officer*), Edward Porter Alexander (*Military Memoirs of a Confederate*), and Armistead Lindsay Long (*Memoirs of Robert E. Lee*), were especially helpful in corroborating Longstreet's accounts of events in his book. The Official Records is another font of information, furnishing communications among the parties in the conflict and official reports on military actions.

Any entity that ignores technological changes in its strategic planning does so at its own peril.

CHAPTER I

Technological Changes and Comparison of the Antagonists

Advantage North

The Confederacy had been presumptuous in taking on a war with the North despite the popular boast, "We can whip them with cornstalks!" The North was far superior in material resources and industrial capacity, but few persons foresaw the role this would play in the outcome. One who did was a former army officer William Tecumseh Sherman, later a Northern general. Sherman warned a Southern friend: "You are rushing into war with one of the most powerful, ingeniously mechanical and determined people on earth-right at your door. You are bound to fail."

First of all, the Northern states enjoyed a great advantage in population and hence had a larger manpower pool from which to draw recruits. The total population of the country was approximately 30,000,000 souls in 1861. The 23 states that remained in the Union had over 21,000,000 inhabitants, which included immigrants who tended to settle in the North so as not to compete with slave labor. The North had a pool of 4,000,000 able-bodied men to recruit from. The South, on the other hand, had 9,000,000 inhabitants but this was deceptive because 3,500,000 were Black slaves. Since the burden of the war fell upon the five and one-half million White inhabitants, they had to supply the manpower from some 690,000 eligible males. Indeed, some 350,000 men or half the available men, enlisted in the South in 1861. Thus, the North had four times more eligible recruits from which to draw combatants. The Black slaves did help the South indirectly, by serving as military laborers and as agricultural laborers, freeing a large number of Whites for military service. However, the North recruited 179,000 African-Americans into its armed forces.

Secondly, the economic potential of the North was far superior to the South's to sustain the war effort. In the North were 81 percent of the nation's factories, consisting of 110,000 plants employing 1,170,000 workers producing products worth $1,621,000,000 and representing a capital investment of $850 million. The South had 20,600 plants, 110,000 workers, producing $155 million worth of products, and capitalized at $95 million. The South's factories were, in actuality, shops that relied on hand labor and for the most part lacked mechanization. While the North was moving toward mass production and standardization of parts, the South was struggling to create an industrial base.

Thirdly, railroad transportation, started in the late 1840s and spreading across the country, greatly favored the North. This new form of transportation would be crucial in sustaining large armies in the field and moving them to vital strategic locations. In 1860, the North had 22,085 miles of railroad track compared to 8,541 miles for the South. This difference belied an even greater disparity. The Northern lines had been built by large companies and had continuous connections between distant points. The Southern lines were built by small concerns and there were gaps between lines. Many of the South's railroads ran close to land borders or the sea and were vulnerable. The Northern factories could easily replace unusable rolling stock and rails; not so the South, which had purchased much of its railroad equipment from the North or from the few large Southern ironworks capable of casting rail supplies. The war cut off supplies from the North, and the large Southern factories diverted to producing armaments. Locomotives, rolling stock, and rails, which deteriorated and became unusable, destroyed, or damaged by Northern raiders, could not be replaced. The Southern system gradually broke down and reached a state of near collapse by 1864. This situation limited rail movement in space and time for Southern armies and caused severe privation due to food shortages for the military and civilian population.

The Confederacy had precipitated a war at a time when the United States reigned as the leading firearms producer in the world, especially in techniques of mass production and standardization of parts. It was in the industrialized North that the majority of the modern arms manufacturing equipment and most of the raw materials were located. This situation was exacerbated at this critical juncture by the transformation of the musket to the rifle as standard weaponry for infantry. The weapons used by American troops up to a decade prior to the Civil War were no different than those used in Napoleon's time. The standard infantry weapon had been the flintlock smoothbore musket. This gun was loaded by tearing open a paper cartridge with one's teeth, and its contents (first the powder, then ball, and finally the paper which served as wadding) were poured down the barrel and driven home with a metal rod. The weapon was fired by a chip of flint on the weapon's cocked hammer, which when released created a spark in a shallow pan primed with gunpowder from the paper cartridge. If the powder was wet or even damp, the weapon would not fire. When it did fire (80 percent of the time), the ball was unstable in flight and had an extreme range of 250 to 300 yards and very little accuracy at any range. By 1861 the smoothbore musket was made more reliable in all weather conditions, improved by the replacement of the flintlock mechanism with a percussion cap (tiny cap-like copper casings containing a small amount of explosive such as fulminate of mercury).

The accuracy of the musket could be improved by rifling (spiral grooves scored into the bore). However, forcing a round ball down the lands and grooves of the rifled bore was difficult and time consuming, slowing the firepower of the infantry. Rifles were impractical for general infantry use. The pattern for the first general-issue rifled shoulder arm for the U.S. Army had been prepared at the U.S. Arsenal at Harpers Ferry in 1841 but suitable ammunition could not be found. This all changed in 1849 when a French Army captain named Claude A. Minie developed an ingenious solution. Minie developed a bullet made of soft lead, which was elongated with a hollow cone-shaped base. The diameter of the bullet was slightly smaller than the rifle bore, allowing it to slide down easily. The hollow base of the bullet rested on the gunpowder; when the powder was ignited, it caused the soft lead of the bullet to expand into the lands and grooves of the barrel. The spin imparted to the rifle bullet by the grooves in the rifle's bore greatly increased the bullet's accuracy in flight and range. The U.S. Army developed an improved model called the U.S. Rifle Model 1855, and later the Springfield Model 1861, using the Minie bullet. These weapons had an extreme range of half a mile or more, an effective range of 200 to 250 yards, and were lethal within 100 yards. This innovation greatly enhanced the defense because, if put in the hands of a marksman in a sheltered position, it was deadly. The rifled muzzleloader gave the entrenched defender a three-to-one advantage over offense. Several breech-loading rifles were manufactured in the North but the old idea was widely held that the percentage of hits were small—the soldiers would waste ammunition if firing too rapidly. The cavalry was the first to receive the best of the breech-loaders by the United States Ordinance Department a year or two into the war. It quickly became apparent from experience and common sense that heavy fire was extremely effective. Many believed that had the Federal infantry been armed with breech-loaders from the beginning of the conflict the war would have been over in a year.

The tactics of Napoleon were not applicable when considering this new weaponry. Napoleon threw a heavy mass of troops in close-order formations (columns) in an assault timed to break the defenders decisively. Napoleon often prepared for the infantry assault (who used the bayonet at point of impact) by sending in highly mobile artillery to "soften up" the defenders and used cavalry to take out enemy artillery. These tactics were no longer practical with the advent of the rifle. If artillerists exposed themselves at close range, the defenders, armed with rifles, would pick them off before they could do substantial damage. The rifle neutralized cavalry charges, and massed infantry assaults would come under a hail of fire from infantry and the new rifled cannon half a mile from their target, especially in open terrain. The tightly packed mass of attackers would come under such accurate fire that they would be cut to shreds before the attack hit home. If they got close, they would be hit with canister shot (metal cases containing bullets that scatter after leaving the gun) and grapeshot (three tiers of cast-iron balls arranged generally three in a tier, between four parallel iron disks connected together by a central wrought-iron pin) from smoothbore cannon, a very effective anti-personnel weapon.

Modification of tactics in the 1850s to take into account the increase in firepower by the substitution of the rifle for the musket was reflected in William J. Hardee's standard textbook, *Rifle and Light Infantry Tactics*, which advocated the attack be accelerated. However, many of the professional officers made their own adaptation based on common sense. E. Porter Alexander, Chief of Ordnance for the Confederate Army of Northern Virginia, says it best in his description of the first battle of Bull Run:

> So now, for over two hours, these lines of battle fired away at each other, across the front ridge of the plateau, neither one's fire being very murderous, as each fired mostly at random at the other's smoke. That, indeed, is the case in nearly all battles since long-range guns have come into use. It is rare that hostile lines get so near together, and are so exposed to each other's view, that men can select their targets. When this does occur, some decisive result is apt to be reached quickly. Fighting rarely consists now in marching directly upon one's enemy and shooting him down at close range. The idea is now a different one. It rather consists in making it rain projectiles all over the enemy's position. As far as possible, while so engaged, one seeks cover from the enemy's fire in return. But the party taking the offensive must necessarily make some advances. The best advance is around the enemy's flanks, where one meets less fire, and becomes opposed by smaller numbers.[1]

The shortage of rifles in the Confederate army plagued it throughout the war, and more so in the west than the east. Lack of guns caused the loss of services of 200,000 of the initial 350,000 volunteers, Secretary of War Leroy P. Walker reported in July 1861. The guns that were supplied were of the antiquated smoothbore variety. These were the comparative impressions of E. P. Alexander as he moved from his station in California to join the Confederate ranks:

> The camps near the principal Northern towns were all regiments. Those in the South were mostly of a company each. The arms of the Northern troops were generally the long-range rifled muskets. Those of the Southern troops were almost universally the old-fashioned smooth-bore muskets. The Northern troops were always neatly uniformed in blue, their camps seemed well equipped, and there was generally some visible show of military discipline about them. The Confederate uniforms were blue, gray and brown, and sometimes uniforms were lacking.[2]

How far some of the Southern leaders were removed from the impact of the new weapon can be shown by the proposal by General Thomas "Stonewall" Jackson and Governor Joseph E. Brown of Georgia to arm the soldiers with pikes. In Jackson's case Robert E. Lee actually approved the pikes and ordered the chief of ordnance, Josiah Gorgas, to send the pikes. Gorgas knew enough to send muskets instead.[3]

Although some of Napoleon's tactics were negated by the new rifle, many of his principles of military arts and science (as interpreted by Baron Antoine Henri Jomini (1779–1869), a Swiss who had served in the French army under Napoleon, in his work the *Traites des Grandes operations Militaire*) were still relevant on the Civil War battlefield and are used even today. Jomini expounded the use of interior lines especially when on the strategic or tactical offensive, the concentration of a superior force against an inferior one, and the use of the turning movement to fall on the flank and rear of the enemy, tactically or strategically, to threaten the enemy's communications and forcing him to withdraw or attack to recover his communications. Jomini's concepts were expanded upon by Henry Halleck's *Elements of Military Art* and Beauregard's *Principles and Maxims of the Art of War*, both of whom emphasized field fortifications.

Dennis Hart Mahan, the charismatic tactical instructor and founder of the Napoleon Club at West Point, taught engineering, tactics, and the art of war from 1830 to 1870. He emphasized Napoleon's strategy and the importance of entrenching and had a great impact on many Civil War officers, i.e. Halleck and Beauregard. Unfortunately for the South, Robert E. Lee was not exposed to his teachings and Thomas "Stonewall" Jackson received no benefit from them.

Given the great disparity of manpower and resources and the advent of the new rifled weapons, the Southern strategy needed to be defensive and obtain foreign intervention by Britain and France to overwhelm the Northern states. Barring that, the South had to exhaust the North and make its conquest so costly that the North would find the price not worth the prize. This required the South to conserve manpower and resources, forcing the North to attack Southern forces whenever possible in entrenched positions or use turning movements and interior lines to thwart Northern advances.

E. Porter Alexander, Chief of Ordnance for the Confederate Army of Northern Virginia, gives a vivid description of Confederate arms during the conflict:

> In its early stages we had great trouble with the endless variety of arms and calibres in use, scarcely ten percent of them being the muzzle-loading rifled musket, calibre 58, which was then the regulation arm for United States Infantry.
>
> The old smooth-bore musket, calibre 69, made up the bulk of the Confederate armament at the beginning, some of the guns, even all through 1862, being old flint-locks. But every effort was made to replace them by rifled muskets captured in battle, brought through the blockade from Europe, or manufactured at a few small arsenals which we gradually fitted up. Not until after the battle of Gettysburg was the whole army in Virginia equipped with the rifled musket.
>
> Our artillery equipment at the beginning was even more inadequate than our small-arms. Our guns were principally smoothbore 6-prs. and 12-prs. howitzers, and their ammunition was afflicted with very unreliable fuses. Our arsenals soon began to manufacture rifled guns, but they always lacked copper and brass, and the mechanical skill necessary to turn out first class ammunition. Gradually we captured Federal guns to supply most of our needs, but we were handicapped by our own ammunition until the close of the war.[4]

The South had to buy time to properly arm its forces with the rifled musket and artillery. If it stood on the defensive, it would have to cede space to gain time. Southern politicians would not allow this and clamored for protection. President

Jefferson Davis was inundated with appeals for more troops, from the Potomac to the Rio Grande. Any invasion by necessity had to be repelled or there was a threat of a loss of some political base and political pressure if the Yankees were not driven out. This situation necessitated what President Davis called his "Offensive-Defensive" plan; invasion would be met by attack and, with the range superiority of the North's rifled weapons, would induce massive casualties the South could ill afford. The only other option the South had was to conduct raids in the North to tie up the Union army in protecting vital points and create political pressure on the National government for defense. But the Confederates shouldn't have committed to battle with such a disadvantage in weaponry unless in a strong defensive position, with entrenchments inducing the Union army to attack. The tactical offensive would lead to massive casualties draining the shallow pool of recruits as a result of the new weaponry, while the defense would conserve lives, material, and resources. Many Southern generals, including James Longstreet, recognized this. President Davis, unfortunately, scattered his scarce manpower and even scarcer arms to many wide and diverse points, many of which were not even threatened. Citing Frederick the Great: "He who defends everything defends nothing." Thus, he sent barely enough men to replace what the army lost to sickness. The Southern troops were from country districts and not immune to measles and mumps as Northern troops were—many of whom lived in crowded urban conditions.

An excerpt from an English visitor around 1862 "Ten Days in Richmond" describes how the Confederate army was armed with Northern weapons captured in battle:

> Entire batteries pass down the road, with "U. S." in prominent white letters on the caissons. It is no exaggeration to say that a great part of the Confederate army has been equipped at the expense of the United States. Flint-locks and fowling pieces have been exchanged for good Minie rifles. There was, however, still so great a want of small-arms, that a considerable part of the army were armed with smooth-bore of home manufacture, loaded with a ball and three buckshot. This deficiency has, perhaps, not been altogether, a disadvantage, inasmuch as the necessity of getting to close quarters, in order to put themselves on an equality with their opponents, has in no small degree produced among the Confederates that habit of closing with the enemy which has proved so inconvenient to the Northern troops. Men who could not obtain arms have been known to fall in with the rear rank, and go into action on the chance of picking up a musket on the first opportunity.[5]

CHAPTER 2

"To Stand Behind Our Intrenched Lines"

Chancellorsville

General Robert E. Lee assumed command of what was to become the Army of Northern Virginia shortly after noon on June 1, 1862, when General Johnston had been wounded and incapacitated in the battle of Seven Pines the night before. On June 3, Lee called a conference of his division commanders to size them up. At the invitation of Lee, Longstreet rode to Lee's headquarters the day after the conference and talked privately. Four days after their meeting, Lee wrote to President Davis: "Longstreet is a Capital Soldier. His recommendations hitherto have been good, & I have confidence in him."[1] A close military and personal kinship started between Lee and Longstreet of which Brigadier General Moxley Sorrel alluded: "Longstreet was second in command and it soon became apparent that he was to be quite close to Lee."[2] Subsequently, Longstreet and Lee fought some major battles, the last being at Fredericksburg on December 13, 1862, which had been a defensive action.

To guard against a Union offensive thrust above Fredericksburg, Longstreet constructed a system of fieldworks of continuous parapets and shortened mutually supportive rifle trenches (rather than the long, open ditches with the dirt thrown forward used formerly) interspersed with battery epaulements and improved with rifle pits, when necessary, from Fredericksburg to Spotsylvania Court House, covering the upstream fords of the Rappahannock. These works, known as the "line" of the Rappahannock, were designed to block the roads and accessible terrain, holding up the enemy with a small force until other units could concentrate at the threatened point. Incorporated into the design was the innovative idea of traverses, stubby earth walls running perpendicular to the main trench wall at regular intervals, comparting the trenches and protecting the defenders from lateral blast and shrapnel flying in all directions from improved artillery shells of the Federals fired from the more accurate new rifled cannon. Traverses were an innovative construction developed by Longstreet's command and Longstreet should be credited with its development.

While Longstreet was given the task of gathering subsistence around Suffolk, Virginia, Lee was locked in combat from May 1 to 5, 1863, with Major General Joseph Hooker in the Wilderness.

Chancellorsville was a pyrrhic victory for Lee and Jackson who had a penchant for taking the tactical offensive and in some cases attacking heavily entrenched works; the Confederates sustained casualties of 1,665 killed, 9,081 wounded, and 2,018 missing, totaling 12,764, while Union casualties amounted to 1,575 killed, 9,594 wounded, and 5,676 missing in action making a total of 16,845; this amounted to 21 percent of Lee's 60,000 engaged compared to 15 percent of Hooker's 113,838.

Longstreet on Chancellorsville

Longstreet thought Lee should have proceeded as they had agreed upon previously and gave this frank and fair appraisal of the battle:

> Chancellorsville is usually accepted as General Lee's most brilliant achievement, and, considered as an independent affair, it was certainly grand. As I had no part in its active conduct, it is only apropos to this writing to consider the plan of battle as projected some four months previous, -i.e., to stand behind our intrenched lines and await the return of my troops from Suffolk.
>
> Under that plan General Lee would have had time to strengthen and improve his trenches, while Hooker was intrenching at Chancellorsville. He could have held his army solid behind his lines, where his men would have done more work on the unfinished lines in a day than in months of idle camp life.

Longstreet's plan was for Lee to take a defensive stance utilizing field fortifications and await Hooker's attack. Longstreet wanted to conserve the South's manpower and was well aware of the fact that defense is the most resourceful mode of warfare. This strategy would have mitigated Lee's casualties and exposed Hooker's army to heavy losses from the accurate long-range rifles. After the war, Union General Jacob D. Cox claimed: "One rifle in the trench was worth five in front of it." In addition, it would have bought time for Longstreet to disengage from Suffolk and join Lee's forces. Longstreet continued:

> My impression was, and is, that General Lee, standing under his trenches, would have been stronger against Hooker than he was in December against Burnside, and that he would have grown stronger every hour of delay, while Hooker would have grown weaker in morale and in confidence of his plan and the confidence of his troops. He had the interior lines for defence, while his adversary was divided by two crossings of the river, which made Lee's sixty thousand for defence about equal to the one hundred and thirteen thousand under General Hooker. By the time that the divisions of Pickett and Hood could have joined General Lee, General Hooker would have found that he must march to attack or make a retreat without battle. It seems probable that under the original plan the battle would have given fruits worthy of a general engagement. The Confederates would then have had opportunity, and have been in condition to so follow Hooker as to have compelled his retirement to Washington, and that advantage might have drawn Grant from Vicksburg; whereas General Lee was actually so crippled by his victory that he was a full month restoring his army to condition to take the field. In defensive warfare he was perfect. When the hunt was up, his combativeness was overruling.
>
> The battle as pitched and as an independent affair was brilliant, and if the war was for glory could be called successful, but, besides putting the cause upon the hazard of a die, it was crippling in resources and of future progress, while the wait of a few days would have given time

for concentration and opportunities against Hooker more effective than we experienced with Burnside at Fredericksburg. This was one of the occasions where success was not a just criterion.[3]

Indeed, recruitment was not replacing the losses sustained by the Confederates as its manpower pool was shrinking: "Well, we are getting only some 700 conscripts per month in Virginia-the largest State!" War Clerk Jones marked down in his diary on April 14, 1863, before Chancellorsville: "At this rate, how are we to replenish the ranks as they are thinned in battle? It is to be hoped the enemy will find the same difficulty in filling up their regiments, else we have rather a gloomy prospect before us."[4]

Longstreet and Lee were surely aware of the lack of replacements. Thus, Longstreet's evaluation of the battle was valid; Lee's audacity in playing long odds by going over to the offensive threatened the vitality of his army with the enormous casualties incurred and the loss of irreplaceable officers. Defensive warfare, using field fortifications to buy time for Longstreet's return, would have preserved the integrity of his command.

CHAPTER 3

"Skillful Use of Our Interior Lines"

Prelude to Gettysburg

Longstreet on Seddon

Returning from Suffolk to rejoin Lee's army, Longstreet had a meeting with James Alexander Seddon on May 6, 1863, concerning events in the west:

> Passing through Richmond, I called to report to Secretary of War Seddon, who referred to affairs in Mississippi, stating that the department was trying to collect an army at Jackson, under General Joseph E. Johnston, sufficient to push Grant away from his circling lines about Vicksburg. He spoke of the difficulty of feeding as well as collecting an army of that magnitude in Mississippi, and asked my views.
>
> The Union army under General Rosecrans was then facing the Confederate army under General Bragg in Tennessee, at Murfreesboro and Shelbyville.
>
> I thought that General Grant had better facilities for collecting supplies and reinforcements on his new lines, and suggested the only prospect of relieving Vicksburg that occurred to me was to send General Johnston and his troops about Jackson to reinforce General Bragg's army; at the same time the two divisions of my command, then marching to join General Lee, to the same point; that the commands moving on converging lines could have rapid transit and be thrown in overwhelming numbers on Rosecrans [Longstreet's West Point roommate] before he could get help, break up his army, and march for Cincinnati and the Ohio River; that Grant's was the only army that could be drawn to meet this move, and that the move must, therefore, relieve Vicksburg.
>
> It was manifest before the war was accepted that the only way to equalize the contest was by skillful use of our interior lines, and this was impressed by two years' experience that it seemed time to force it upon the Richmond authorities. But foreign intervention was the ruling idea with the President [Davis], and he preferred that as the easiest solution of all problems.
>
> The only objection offered by the Secretary was that Grant was such an obstinate fellow that he could only be induced to quit Vicksburg by terribly hard knocks.
>
> On the contrary, I claimed that he was a soldier, and would obey the calls of his government, but was not lightly to be driven from his purpose.[1]

Analytical, subtle, and deliberate, Longstreet demonstrated the depth of his generalship in this suggestion to Seddon. Longstreet, who had closely watched and was well versed about events in the west, advocated this strategy based on sound military doctrine: operate on interior lines and concentration (bringing together a larger force at one point), utilizing the new technology of the railroad, developed in the late 1840s, with its rapid, high-lift capacity to shunt troops and supplies and use the telegraph to smooth out connections. General James Longstreet subscribed to Napoleon's maxim to "converge a superior force on the critical point at the critical time." This would be not just a raid but an invasion supported logistically by the railroad.

Why Tennessee?

The question comes to mind, why Tennessee? Tennessee was an area where both armies relied on the railroad for logistic support, while in the east the North had total domination of the Atlantic coastal regions and in the west the Mississippi River and its tributaries. Major General William S. Rosecrans's army was the weakest of any of the major armies the Union were fielding, while in the east the Union presented its strongest army to defend Washington and had strongly fortified and heavily garrisoned the city's defenses. The population of Tennessee and Kentucky were friendly and supportive of the Confederate cause and would perhaps furnish recruits and supplies including partisan attacks and good intelligence. Many of the South's railroads converged in Tennessee facilitating movement. There was no railroad going North into Pennsylvania, and Lee's army had to rely on wagons moving over a long and tenuous supply line. Some historians accuse Longstreet of selfish ambition in promoting the western concentration because he wanted command of the Army of Tennessee. There is no doubt Longstreet hoped to distinguish himself as a general in command of an army in the field; it would be the special aspiration and dream of an officer of his ability, but he was perfectly content to serve under Johnston as he had indicated before. Longstreet contemplated that Johnston, as the senior general, would lead the campaign:

> With this army, General Johnston might speedily crush Rosecrans, and that he should then turn his force toward the north, and with his splendid army march through Tennessee and Kentucky, and threaten the invasion of Ohio. My idea was that, in the march through those States, the army would meet no organized obstruction; would be supplied with provisions and even reinforcements by those friendly to our cause, and would inevitably result in drawing Grant's army from Vicksburg to look after and protect his own territory.[2]

Longstreet conveyed his plan to Lee "with the freedom justified by our close personal and official relations."[3] But Lee was averse to having part of his army so far away and decided upon a plan to invade Maryland and Pennsylvania, thus, threatening Washington to obtain the same result.

The Flamboyant Senator Louis Wigfall

On May 13, Longstreet wrote a letter to Senator Louis Wigfall of the Confederate Senate Military Affairs Committee, his friend, confidant, and supporter at the time Longstreet and Lee were discussing strategy. Wigfall, like Longstreet, was born in Edgefield County, South Carolina, where he studied law. He was a flamboyant character who drank heavily and gambled extravagantly, a lifestyle which eventually led to bankruptcy. He moved to Texas in 1848 and served in the state legislature and became a United States Senator in 1859 with ardent secessionist sentiment. During the bombardment of Fort Sumter, he had himself rowed out to ask the Federal commander if he struck his flag. He was on Davis's personal staff at Montgomery and continued when the government moved to Richmond but resigned prior to the battle of First Manassas to command a Texas regiment with a commission of colonel. Subsequently, Davis promoted him to brigadier general leading a brigade. His service in the military was brief, for in February 1862, his constituents in Texas elected him to the Confederate Senate; he retained the title of general. Davis and Wigfall had a cordial relationship until the fall of 1862: Wigfall felt snubbed after he conversed with Davis about a replacement for Secretary of War George Randolph after Randolph resigned on November 15, only to find out later Davis had already decided on James A. Seddon (one of Wigfall's recommendations) prior to their meeting but was never divulged. From then on, relations between Wigfall and Davis became more and more strained as Wigfall openly criticized Davis's military policies in the Senate as detrimental to the cause and aligned himself with the opposition and "the western concentration bloc."

Longstreet intimated to Wigfall that General Lee was considering an advance into Pennsylvania which would dash any plans for a western campaign.

Longstreet envisioned if they could gather enough troops for the invasion, "We could either destroy the Yankees or bring them to terms." Seddon's plan to send help directly to Pemberton, such as his request to Lee for Pickett's division, Longstreet believed was a waste of manpower:

> As to matters in the west, I have severe doubts as to whether re-enforcements would be much good with Pemberton. We can't re-enforce strongly and it is therefore doubtful if a division or so would answer. We need all that we have and even the five thousand sent to Pemberton from Charleston. Grant seems to be a fighting man, and seems to be determined to fight. Pemberton seems not to be a fighting man. If he does not desire to fight the fewer the troops he has the better.
>
> Longstreet believed Pemberton would not take on Grant but lock his army in Vicksburg's vast intrenched camp and to give him reinforcements would lose them as well as Vicksburg which was not worth an army if it fell: "We would then be no worse cut off from the West than we are now." Longstreet's plan was contingent upon Lee taking a defensive posture in Virginia but with Lee promoting a move into Pennsylvania conditions changed, Lee was to go to Richmond to settle matters.[4]

Lee did go to Richmond, spending long hours in confidential discussions with Davis and Seddon on Friday, May 15, as to what was the best means of solving the crisis. Lee was not amenable to sending troops west as he stated to Seddon, "The adoption of your proposition is hazardous, and it becomes a question between Virginia and the Mississippi."[5] Lee pressed to go into Pennsylvania, as he explained: "I considered the problem in every possible phase and to my mind, it resolved itself into a choice of one of two things; either to retire to Richmond and stand a siege, which must ultimately have ended in surrender, or to invade Pennsylvania."[6]

Fundamentally, Lee was right about the siege, but this only happened after the Confederate armies were worn down by being the assailant. Lee's staff officer, Colonel Walter Taylor gave this reason for Lee's rationale:

> In the judgment of General Lee, it was a part of a true defensive policy to take the aggressive when good opportunity offered; and by delivering an effective blow to the enemy, not only to inflict upon him serious loss, but at the same time to thwart his designs of invasion, derange the plan of campaign contemplated by him, and thus prolong the conflict.[7]

Lee's proposal was voted favorably by Secretary of State Judah P. Benjamin, Secretary of War James A. Seddon, Secretary of the Treasury Christopher G. Memminger, Attorney General Thomas H. Watts, and Secretary of the Navy Stephen R. Mallory on Saturday, May 16. Only Postmaster General John H. Reagan voted in the negative; President Davis concurred with the majority. Reagan hailed from Texas and thought the decision a mistake, asked for another caucus on Sunday, May 17. The results were the same: five to one in favor of Lee's plan after much discussion.

Lee was leaning more heavily on Longstreet than any other general in his command. Longstreet stood pre-eminent due to his confidence, well-reasoned actions in battle, and logical, sound advice. Longstreet avowed:

> Experience during the seven days about Richmond established between General Lee and his first lieutenant relations of confidence and esteem, official and personal, which ripened into stronger ties as the mutations of war bore heavier upon us.
>
> He always invited the views of the latter in moves of strategy and general policy, not so much for the purpose of having his own views approved and confirmed as to get new light, or channels of new thought, and was more pleased when he found something that gave him new strength than with efforts to evade questions with compliments. When oppressed by severe study, he sometimes sent for me to say that he had applied himself so closely to a matter that he found his ideas running around in a circle, and was in need of help to find a tangent. Our personal relations remained as sincere after the war until politics came between us in 1867.[8]

In their discussions, Lee asked Longstreet what he thought of a Pennsylvania campaign:

> At length, while we were discussing the idea of a western forward movement, he asked me if I did not think an invasion of Maryland and Pennsylvania by his own army would accomplish the same result, and I replied that I did not see that it would, because this movement would be too hazardous, and the campaign in thoroughly United States would require more time and greater preparation than one through Tennessee and Kentucky. I soon discovered that he had determined that he would make some forward movement, and I finally assented that the Pennsylvania campaign might be brought to a successful issue if he could make it offensive in strategy, but defensive in tactics. This point was urged with great persistency. I suggested that, after piercing Pennsylvania and menacing Washington, we should choose a strong position, and force the Federals to attack us, observing that the popular clamor throughout the North would speedily force the Federal general to attempt to drive us out.

Longstreet pressed for a defensive battle which would place the onus of attack on the Federal commander:

> I recalled to him the battle of Fredericksburg as an instance of a defensive battle, when, with a few thousand men, we hurled the whole Federal army back, crippling and demoralizing it, with trifling loss to our own troops; and Chancellorsville as an instance of an offensive battle, where we dislodged the Federals, it is true, but at such a terrible sacrifice that half a dozen such victories would have ruined us. It will be remembered that Stonewall Jackson once said that "we sometimes fail to drive the enemy from a position. They always fail to drive us." I reminded him, too, of Napoleon's advice to Marmont, to whom he said, when putting him at the head of an invading army, "Select your ground, and make the enemy attack you." I recall these points, simply because I desire to have it distinctly understood that, while I first suggested to General Lee the idea of an offensive campaign, I was never persuaded to yield my argument against the Gettysburg campaign, except with the understanding that we were not to deliver an offensive battle, but to so maneuvre that the enemy would be forced attack us-or, to repeat, that our campaign should be of offensive strategy, but defensive tactics. Upon this understanding my assent was given, and General Lee, who had been kind enough to discuss the matter with me patiently, gave the order to march.[9]

An Army on Wheels

The Confederates could not remain on the defensive and hope to shift troops to meet each Federal thrust, because the Rebels would always be a step behind, while an aggressive, strategic counterstroke of converging forces utilizing interior lines could bring superiority in an engagement. Lieutenant Colonel Edward Porter Alexander favored Longstreet's plan over Lee's because any movement into Pennsylvania would only be a raid, since it lacked the logistics to sustain a long campaign and the marauding army must pull back into Virginia. Alexander believed the South had to utilize its one advantage:

> We occupied the "Interior Lines" and could reinforce from one flank to the other, across our country, more quickly then the enemy could discover and follow our movements by round-about routes. Only by such transfers of her armies could the South ever hope to face her adversaries with superior, or even with equal, numbers-by demanding double duty of her regiments, fighting battles with them alternately in the east and in the west. Here in May, 1863, was presented a rare opportunity to inaugurate what might be called an "Army on Wheels" within the Confederate lines, as distinguished from an Army of Invasion beyond them. The situation was this. Grant was investing Vicksburg with 60,000 men, and we were threatened with the loss of the Mississippi River, and of 30,000 men at Vicksburg under Pemberton. At Jackson, Miss., Johnston, with scarcely 24,000 men, was looking on and begging vainly for reenforcements.
>
> At Murfreesboro, Tenn., Bragg, with about 45,000 Confederates, confronted Rosecrans with about 84,000. Neither felt strong enough for the aggressive, and the whole spring and summer passed idly. At Knoxville were about 5,000 Confederates under Buckner, and there were also scattered brigades in southwest Va. And eastern N.C., from which reinforcements might be drawn. In this state of affairs, Longstreet, with Hood's and Pickett's divisions, arrived at Petersburg, under orders to rejoin Lee at Fredericksburg. Hooker had just been driven across the Rappahannock, and his army was soon to lose largely from the expiration of terms of service of many regiments.
>
> Nothing aggressive was probable from him for many weeks.

Longstreet and Alexander were well aware of the value of the railroad in shunting troops quickly and providing the logistics in supplying large armies in the field which was available in Tennessee. Alexander continued:

> Longstreet's veteran divisions, about 13,000 strong, could have been placed on cars at Petersburg and hurried out to Bragg, via Lynchburg and Knoxville. Johnson's 25,000 from Jackson, and Buckner's 5,000 from Knoxville, could have met them. With these accessions, Rosecrans might have been defeated, and an advance made into Ky., threatening Louisville and Cincinnati. If anything could have caused Grant's recall from Vicksburg, it would have been this. Surely the chances of success were greater, and of disaster less, than those involved in our crossing the bridgeless Potomac, into the heart of the enemy's country, where ammunition and supplies must come by wagons from Staunton, nearly 200 miles, over roads exposed to raids of the enemy from either east or west. In this position, a drawn battle, or even a victory, would still leave us compelled soon to find our way back across the Potomac. The trouble was the lack of railroad transportation. Whenever, therefore, we crossed the Potomac going northward, we were certain to have to recross it southward, in a few weeks, as a stone thrown upward is certain to come down. At that time Davis was sanguine of foreign intervention, and the Emperor Napoleon was permitting a French firm to build some formidable ironclads for the Confederate navy. These might have accomplished some results, had not the issue of the Gettysburg campaign induced the Emperor to withdraw his consent to their delivery.[10]

Many historians, including Sanger and Freeman, perceive Longstreet as a defensive fighter, overly critical of Lee's aggressive battles and tactics, but they fail to understand what he was telling them in his writings, how he thought the war should be conducted to advance the objectives of the South. Fighting battles on the defensive the South could conserve manpower by not exposing its troops to the more accurate long-range rifled musket and artillery. Actually, Colonel Walter Taylor stated this policy best:

> From the very necessities of the case, the general theory upon which the war was conducted on the part of the South was one of defense. The great superiority of the North in men and material made it indispensable for the South to husband its resources as much as possible, inasmuch as the hope of ultimate success which the latter entertained rested rather upon the dissatisfaction and pecuniary distress which a prolonged war would entail upon the former-making the people weary of the struggle-than upon any expectation of attaining peace by actually subduing so powerful an adversary.[11]

Longstreet embraced this concept as shown in his conduct in battle, the advice he gave, and his publications. Longstreet asserted:

> One mistake of the Confederacy was in pitting force against force. The only hope we had was to outgeneral the Federals. We were all hopeful and the army was in good condition, but the war had advanced far enough for us to see that a mere victory without decided fruits was a luxury we could not afford. Our numbers were less than the Federal forces, and our resources were limited while theirs were not. The time had come when it was imperative that the skill of generals and the strategy and tactics of war should take the place of muscle against muscle. Our purpose should have been to impair the morale of the Federal army and shake Northern confidence in the Federal leaders. We talked on that line from day to day, and General Lee, accepting it as a good military view, adopted it as the key-note of the campaign.[12]

When conditions warranted it, Longstreet did advocate offensive strategy and tactics but always used the terrain and ground cover to shield his troops to strike or turn the enemy's flanks or rear tactically while using interior lines to bring overwhelming concentration upon an isolated enemy's army strategically.

With the death of "Stonewall" Jackson, Lee made a recommendation to President Davis on May 20, 1863, that he had been contemplating for some time of reorganizing the army into three corps under Longstreet, Ewell, and A. P. Hill, as he considered the current arrangement too unwieldy.

Longstreet agreed with Lee's assessment of Ewell. However, on the other hand, he was of the opinion other generals had merited selection over A. P. Hill, such as Generals D. H. Hill or Lafayette McLaws, who were superior in rank, skill, judgment, and distinguished services but were not from Virginia. Longstreet and Jackson had been assigned by General Johnston.

Virginia-ism was viewed by many in the army as gross favoritism, before Chancellorsville McLaws wrote to Ewell on this subject concerning Longstreet:

> Do you know there is a strong feeling growing among the Southern troops against Virginia, caused by the jealousy of her own people for those from every other state? No matter who it is may perform a glorious act, Virginia papers give but a grudging praise unless the actor is a Virginian. No matter how trifling the deed may be which a Virginian performs is heralded at once as the most glorious of modern times. Longstreet has no superior as a soldier in the Southern Confederacy, yet the press never gave him proper credit, simply because he was not a Virginian.[13]

CHAPTER 4

Harrison the Spy

Advance to Gettysburg

On June 3, the Army of Northern Virginia was on the move. Lafayette McLaws's division of the First Corps led the way to Culpeper Court House from Fredericksburg, followed by Richard S. Ewell's corps (the divisions of Jubal Early, Robert E. Rodes and Edward Johnson) on June 4 and 5. June 4 had John Bell Hood's division starting from Orange Court House to Culpeper, and Jeb Stuart's cavalry formed a defensive screen north and east of the point of concentration at Culpeper. George Pickett's division was put in motion on June 5 and followed Hood's route. The first leg of the campaign was underway and by June 8, the First and Second Corps were encamped with Stuart's cavalry at Culpeper as Lee watched what Hooker's next play on the chessboard would be. A. P. Hill's Third Corps (divisions of Richard Anderson, Henry Heth, and William Pender) of about 20,000 was left in observation at Fredericksburg, facing off against Hooker's army of 80,000 on Stafford Heights.

Using the Bureau

Wisely, Hooker had instituted the Bureau of Military Information headed by Colonel George H. Sharpe to gather and assess military information, an entirely new approach in filtering useful intelligence from the myriad of data pouring in. Two balloons were set aloft, to spy on the Confederates, and had spotted some movement. Hooker had an inkling something was afoot and needed closer reconnaissance to determine its exact nature. Hooker wanted to test the waters and on the morning of June 6 had Sedgwick throw Howe's division of his corps across the Rappahannock at Franklin's Crossing, but Hill put on such a display of force as to mask the departure of the other corps; Hooker could not ascertain if Lee's whole army was still present at Fredericksburg. For over two weeks prior, Stuart's cavalry was concentrating and preparing at Culpeper, indicating some hostile intent; knowledge of this reached Hooker. Hooker wanted to neutralize this threat before Stuart did some damage, in a perceived cavalry raid reported as "the most important expedition ever attempted in this country." On the very day Howe's division crossed to the south side of the Rappahannock on two bridges, Hooker assembled a cavalry force to confront Stuart; on June 6 Hooker sent this dispatch to General Henry Halleck: "As the accumulation of the heavy Rebel force of cavalry about Culpeper may mean mischief, I am determined, if practicable, to break it up in its incipiency. I shall send all my cavalry against them, stiffened by about three thousand infantry."[1]

Stuart decided to put on a pageant on June 5 at nearby Brandy Station made up of five of his brigades, except those troopers on outpost duty in a grand review culminating in mock charges on the guns of the horse artillery firing blank rounds. Assured by Hill that he could hold at Fredericksburg, General Lee followed, arriving on June 7 at Culpeper. Stuart asked Lee if he could restage the event for him and some of his friends the next day, to which Lee agreed. Stuart assembled almost all his troopers on an open plain between Culpeper and Brandy Station while Lee sat motionless on his horse wearing a broad-brimmed hat on a hillock next to a pole flying a large Confederate flag. "Here I am," said the general in chief to Stuart, pointing with his finger to the bivouacs of the First Corps. "Here I am with my friends according to your invitation." It was agreed that on the following day Lee and his "friends"—that is to say, all of Longstreet's soldiers—should witness the cavalry review.[2] Lee wrote home that his chief of cavalry "was in all his glory."

A New Chief

On June 8 the Union cavalry under its new chief, 39-year-old Major General Alfred Pleasonton, replacing Stoneman, started upriver from Falmouth, grouped in three divisions commanded by Brigadier Generals John Buford (37), David Gregg (30), and Judson Kilpatrick (27). They converged on Brandy Station, attacking Stuart's corps, precipitating the largest cavalry engagement of the war. Longstreet was relieved Lee did not go over to the attack, as it confirmed a commitment to the defensive:

> The failure of General Lee to follow up his advantage by pouring the heavy force concentrated at Culpeper Court-House upon this detachment of the Federals, confirmed my convictions that he had determined to make a defensive battle, and would not allow any casual advantage to precipitate a general engagement. If he had any idea of abandoning the original plan of a tactical defensive, then, in my judgment, was the time to have done so.[3]

It as been asserted by Longstreet's critics and some historians that Longstreet thought Lee promised to fight a defensive battle during the Gettysburg campaign, while the above statement indicates Longstreet presumed there was a mutual understanding of tactics during the campaign.

Certain instructions found in Stuart's baggage and reports by contrabands previously attached to Lee's army were obtained by Pleasonton's cavalry, indicating a large portion of Lee's army at Culpeper. Lee had but two strategic options around Hooker's right: either striking at the Orange and Alexandria Railroad and get between the Army of the Potomac and Washington, as he had done to Pope, or push forward by the Shenandoah Valley toward Pennsylvania. Hooker had been aware of this likelihood and wanted to proceed directly against Richmond on Lee's weakened right, Swinton stated:

> It is an interesting fact that precisely this method of action was suggested by General Hooker a short time before he became aware of Lee's actual movement, and authority for its execution was asked in case the Confederate force should move northward. To this most judicious suggestion two replies, or rather two forms of the same reply-for the opinion was Halleck's-were returned. The one was from the President, disapproving the project, and couched in that quaint imagery Mr. Lincoln was wont to employ in the expression of his thoughts on the gravest subjects. "If Lee," said he, "should leave a rear force at Fredericksburg, tempting you to fall upon it, he would fight you in intrenchments, and have you at disadvantage; and so, man for man, worst you at that point, while his main force would in some way be getting an advantage of you northward. In a word, I would not take any risk of being entangled upon the river, like an ox jumped half over a fence, and liable to be torn by dogs front and rear, without a fair chance to gore one way or kick the other." The other reply was from General Halleck, and it expressed, in solemn military jargon, the same opinion so pungently conveyed by the President.[4]

Swapping Queens?

Rumor was that Lee would swap queens, Richmond for Washington, if Hooker went for the Confederate capital to which the historian the Comte de Paris, Louis-Phillippe II, a claimant to the French throne, who wrote *History of the Civil War*, considered a standard reference work, had this observation:

> Why not march directly upon the capital of the enemy? It was an almost infallible means of cutting short Lee's projects of invasion; and if the latter, to use a comparison which it is said he had just employed in talking with his generals, should attempt to play 'queen for queen,' if he should sacrifice Richmond in order to march upon Washington, all the advantage would have rebounded in favor of the Federals. In war, as well as in chess, such play always benefits him who has the most resources. The game was not equal, for Washington with its immense fortifications, its formidable artillery, its garrison of thirty-six thousand men, which Schenck's troops, coming from Harper's Ferry and Baltimore, would have increased to fifty thousand, could have defied all Lee's efforts; whilst without an army to cover Richmond, President Davis could not have defended his capital for five minutes, completely disgarnished as it was at that time.[5]

The variation Longstreet presented to send his two divisions to Tennessee for a concentration there while the rest of Lee's army guarded the capital seemed more and more like the safest play. Military engineer and Longstreet's artillery commander, E. P. Alexander, recalled: "I remember talking a great deal with Hood about our chances in an invasion of the enemy's territory & the impression I gathered of Hood's view was that we were taking a lot of chances."[6]

General Lee wasted no time. On June 10, the day after the cavalry clash, he put Ewell's Second Corps on the road from Culpeper Court House into the

Shenandoah Valley with the crippled Ewell riding in a buggy. Even before getting to the Culpeper Court House, Longstreet had primed Ewell as to the gist of the campaign.

Ewell's forces converged on Winchester in the northern Shenandoah Valley, a crossroads and rail terminus manned by 6,900 Union troops whose commander, Major General Robert H. Milroy, was being urged to move his force to Harpers Ferry by Union General in Chief Henry W. Hallock and President Lincoln but Milroy would not budge. There was another 1,800 men at Berryville. Milroy pulled his men into three forts north and west of Winchester upon Ewell's approach. Ewell found a long-wooded ridge that dominated the West Fort and, undetected, moved Early's division with 20 guns on it. About 5:00pm the guns erupted at the fort followed within 45 minutes by Brigadier General Harry T. Hays's Louisiana Brigade overrunning the stronghold. Milroy had his men evacuate at 10:00pm to Harpers Ferry but was intercepted in a night engagement at Stephenson's Depot at a bridge spanning a deep railroad cut by Johnson's division sent there to ambush them, as Ewell had correctly predicted Milroy's course of action. The result was Milroy's command was scattered: Milroy escaped with a handful of men; Ewell bagged 700 sick and 3,358 able-bodied prisoners, along with 23 fine guns and 300 loaded wagons inflicting 443 casualties at a cost of only 269 casualties, which included 47 killed, 219 wounded, and three prisoners.

"The Animal Must Be Slim"

Ewell's Second Corps pushed through the Valley of the Shenandoah with Jenkins's brigade of cavalry in advance while Brigadier General John D. Imboden's brigade, covering the left along the Alleghenies, destroyed the tracks of the Baltimore and Ohio Railroad and the Chesapeake and Ohio Canal severing communications with the west. Lee's army now stretched over 100 miles. General in Chief Henry Hallock and Secretary of War Edwin M. Stanton advocated their favored plan for Hooker to cut Lee's column in half, Lincoln wrote: "If the head of Lee's army is at Martinsburg and the tail of it on the plank-road between Fredericksburg and Chancellorsville, the animal must be very slim somewhere. Could you not break him?" Hooker had to conform to Lee's movements and, being denied a direct march on Richmond, placed his forces at Fairfax and Manassas to safeguard the approaches to Washington, sending General Alfred Pleasonton to feel the Confederates arrayed at the Blue Ridge Mountains.

Learning that Hooker had abandoned Stafford Heights on the 14th, A. P. Hill was ordered to join Longstreet at Culpeper, then follow the route traced by General Ewell into the Valley. General Ewell crossed the Potomac near Shepherdstown between June 15 and 18. On the 15th, Longstreet's First Corps trailed Ewell and shifted to the eastern slopes of the Blue Ridge occupying Snicker's and Ashby's gaps, with the main body of cavalry under General Stuart situated on Longstreet's front and flank to shield the Confederate movements. A. P. Hill's Third Corps passed to the rear of Longstreet crossing the Potomac at Shepherdstown on June 24 and 25. The First Corps was to act as a lure to draw Hooker from his base at Washington City; Longstreet stated: "Our movements at the beginning of the campaign were necessarily slow in order that we might be sure of having the proper effect on Hooker." Between June 17 and 21, Stuart fought Pleasonton's troopers in a series of small, intense cavalry skirmishes at Aldie, Middleburg, and Upperville, costing over 500 in killed, wounded, and missing. But Stuart prevented the enemy from penetrating his screen.

In the meantime, Lee, sensing the over-anxiety of the Lincoln administration for the safety of Washington, wanted to bring General Pierre G. T. Beauregard up to form a column or even an "army in effigy", as Lee termed it at Culpeper, to threaten Washington pulling troops from Hooker but this idea was not fulfilled as Longstreet noted:

> General Beauregard was to be called from his post, in the South, with such brigades as could be pulled away temporarily from their Southern service, and thrown forward, with the two brigades of Pickett's division (Jenkins's and Corse's) and such others as could be got together, along the Orange and Alexandra Railroad in threatening attitude towards Washington City, and he was to suddenly forward Pickett's brigades through the Valley to the division, and at his pleasure march on, or back towards Richmond.
>
> As the season of fevers along the coast of the Carolinas was approaching, General Lee thought that active operations in the far South, especially along the seaboard, would be suspended, that his move northward might draw most of them towards him, and possibly troops operating in the Southwest, the latter being really a prominent part of the object of his northern march. He thought that Beauregard's appearance in Northern Virginia would increase the known anxiety of the Washington authorities and cause them to draw troops from the South, when in the progress of events other similar movements might follow on both sides until important results could be developed north of the Potomac.

General Lee wanted to create a diversion to threaten Washington City by bringing General Beauregard up to destabilize Hooker's plans and create panic among the Federal authorities. Longstreet continued:

> His early experience with the Richmond authorities taught him to deal cautiously with them in disclosing his views, and to leave for them the privilege and credit of approving, step by step, his apparently hesitant policy, so that his plans were disclosed little at a time; and finding them slow in approving them, still slower in advancing the brigades of Pickett's division, and utterly oblivious of the effect of a grand swing north on our interior lines, he did not mention the part left open for Beauregard until he had their approval of the march of the part of his command as he held it in hand.
>
> The part assigned for Beauregard became the subject for correspondence between the authorities and the officers who knew nothing of the general ideas and plans. The latter failed to see any benefit to accrue by taking troops from their commands, and naturally offered objections to their going. The authorities, not comprehending the vast strength to be gathered by utilizing our interior lines, failed to bring about their execution, and the great possibility was not fully tested.[7]

Vain and Empty-Headed?

Criticism of the Brandy Station battle was getting loud, as many felt that Stuart and his generals had not been watchful and had allowed the enemy to surprise them which was due to "vain and empty-headed officers" offered the *Richmond Examiner* while the *Richmond Sentinel* proclaimed:

"Vigilance, vigilance, more vigilance, is the lesson taught us by the Brandy surprise. Let all learn it, from the Major General down to the picket."

This public criticism would induce Stuart "to do something to retrieve his reputation" assayed Major General Daniel Butterfield, Hooker's chief of staff.[8] Indeed, Stuart was urging Lee to allow his cavalry to get into the rear of the Union army to harass and damage, slowing it down, to which Lee gave permission on June 22, 1863. Longstreet wanted Stuart to accompany the First Corps as it moved from the Blue Ridge to cross the Potomac but had to leave without him since General Lee had allowed General Stuart discretionary powers.

But the exact point the cavalry force was to cross the Potomac was not determined, with two options open: either at Point of Rocks between the Blue Ridge and the Union army or east of Hooker's army between it and Washington at Hopewell Gap; Longstreet was left with making that decision. Longstreet did not want Stuart to leave but with Lee giving permission he had to accept the situation, so he enclosed a covering note with Lee's letter in acquiescence outlining the military parameters under which Stuart could leave and what route would be optimal if he did. Longstreet wanted Stuart to leave General Hampton in charge of the cavalry, accompanying his troops, and for Stuart to leave by Hopewell Gap, passing by the rear of the enemy.

Major John S. Mosby, "the boldest and most responsible of the partisan rangers," was advising Stuart that the Federal infantry was stationary encamped so wide apart that he could slip between two of the enemy's corps; this information was forwarded to General Lee. With this new eventuality, Lee sent Stuart a second set of instructions, asking Stuart to leave two brigades behind to watch Hooker's army guarding the flank and rear of Lee's army. Lee advised Stuart to take three brigades with him and cross the Potomac River at Shepherdstown into Maryland, moving to the right of Ewell's troops while gathering information and provisions.

Eight Days

Stuart took off on an eight-day jaunt that isolated him from Lee as if he were in another continent. What he happened upon was a dynamic Union army not in a state of inertia; he could not locate Mosby to clarify the Federal activity, and the other partisan scout, Stringfellow, assigned by Stuart to operate within the enemy's line, was captured. However, instead of reconsidering such a bold ride around, he pressed on. Longstreet believed Stuart did not comply with his requests:

In the body of my note were orders that he should report to me of affairs along the cavalry line before leaving; that he should assign General Hampton to command of the cavalry to be left with us, with orders to report at my head-quarters. These orders, emanating properly from the commander of the rear column of the army, should not have been questioned, but they were treated with contumely. He assigned General Robertson to command the cavalry that was left on the mountain, without orders to report at my head-quarters; and though left there to guard passes of the Blue Ridge, he rode on a raid, so that when the cavalry was most needed it was far away from the army. The raid and the absence of the cavalry at the critical moment were severely criticized through the army and the country. If General Stuart could have claimed authority of my orders for this action, he could not have failed to do so in his official account. He offered no such excuse, but claimed to act under the orders of his chief, and reported that General Lee gave consent to his application for leave to make the march. So our plans, adopted after deep study, were suddenly given over to gratify the youthful cavalryman's wish for a nomadic ride.[9]

General Longstreet asserted: The absence of Stuart's cavalry from the main body of the army, during the march, is claimed to have been a fatal error, as General Lee says: "No report had been received (on the 27th) that the enemy had crossed the Potomac, and the absence of the cavalry rendered it impossible to obtain accurate information." The army, therefore, moved forward, as a man might walk over strange ground with his eyes shut.[10]

Harrison

Although they lacked enough cavalry with the absence of Stuart to gather ample information about the Federals, it was obtained from another source. Longstreet wrote:

Before we left Fredericksburg for the campaign into Maryland and Pennsylvania, I called up my scout, Harrison, and, giving him all the gold he thought he would need, told him to go to Washington City and remain there until he was in possession of information which he knew would be of value to us, and directed that he should make his way back to me and report. As he was leaving, he asked where he would find me. That was information I did not care to impart to a man who was going directly to the Federal capital. I answered that my command was large enough to be found without difficulty. We had reached Chambersburg on the 27th of June and were remaining there to give the troops a rest, when my scout straggled into the lines on the night of June 28th. He told me he had been to Washington and had spent his gold freely, drinking in the saloons and getting upon confidential terms with army officers. In that way he had formed a pretty good idea of the general movements of the Federal army and the preparation to give us battle. The moment he heard Hooker had started across the Potomac he set out to find me. He fell in with the Federal army before reaching Frederick-his plan being to walk at night and stop during the day in the neighborhood of the troops. He said there were three corps near Frederick when he passed there, one to the right and one to the left, but he did not succeed in getting the position of the other. This information proved more accurate than we could have expected if we had been relying upon our cavalry. I sent the scout to report to General Lee, who was near, and suggested in my note that it might be well for us to begin to look to the east of the Blue Ridge. Meade was then in command of the Federal army, Hooker having been relieved.[11]

Longstreet's adjutant, Lieutenant Colonel Moxley Sorrel, declared: "It was on this, the report of a single scout, in the absence of cavalry, that the army moved."[12]

Lieutenant Colonel Sorrel made these remarks about the scout, Henry Thomas Harrison:

> While Longstreet was holding this brief independent command [Suffolk], a scout, more properly a spy, was placed at his service by the War Department. He was a man of about thirty years, calling himself a Mississippian, and was altogether an extraordinary character. He was paid in United States greenbacks. I approved requisition on the quarter-master every month for $150 for him. His time seemed to pass about equally within our lines and the enemy's. Harrison (such was his name) always brought us true information. There was invariable confirmation of his reports afterwards.
>
> While always suspicious that such secret instruments give away as much as they bring and may be in the pay of both sides, it was difficult to be sure of this in Harrison's case. He went everywhere, even through Stanton's War Office at Washington itself, and brought in much. We could never discover that he sold anything against us; besides, we had means and did verify his account of himself as coming from Mississippi. When Longstreet gave him up in September, he was sorry afterwards and missed the man. He made me try to get him back for our command, but I failed.[13]

Harrison brought useful information that the enemy was planning a move west into the Cumberland Valley into Lee's rear. Indeed, on June 26, Hooker thought of uniting the 11,000-man garrison under General William H. French on Maryland Heights protecting Harpers Ferry with General Henry W. Slocum's Twelfth Corps, executing this very action—to strike westward at Lee's line of communication with Virginia. General in Chief Hallock flatly refused, allowing Maryland Heights to be abandoned: "Maryland Heights have always been regarded as an important point to be held by us, and much expense and labor incurred in fortifying them."

Deprived of this freedom of action, Hooker, aware he had lost the support of the government, became incensed and asked to be relieved of command on June 27. Hallock, immediately dispatched Colonel James A. Hardie, his assistant adjutant general of the War Office staff, on a special train to place command of the army with Major General George Gordon Meade, Fifth Corps commander, deposing Hooker.

Longstreet thought Hooker's design a good one:

> If General Hooker had been granted the authority for which he applied, he would have struck our trains, exposed from Chambersburg to the Potomac without a cavalryman to ride and report the trouble. General Stuart was riding around Hooker's army, General Robertson was in Virginia, General Imboden at Hancock, and Jenkin's cavalry was at our front with General Ewell.[14]

With his communications threatened, Lee had to relieve this pressure by moving east of the mountains, forcing the enemy to counter this menace (Longstreet sent this suggestion with Harrison to Lee's headquarters); Lee's assistant adjutant, General Colonel Charles Marshall, gave this analysis:

> I had just returned to my tent, when I was sent for by the commanding general. I found him sitting in his tent with a man in citizen's dress, whom I did not know to be a soldier, but who, General Lee informed me was a scout of General Longstreet's, who had just been brought to meet him.

He told me that this scout had left the neighborhood of Frederickstown that morning, and had brought information that the Federal army had crossed the Potomac, and that its advance had reached Frederickstown, and was moving thence westward towards the mountains. The scout informed General Lee that General Meade was then in command of the army, and gave him the first information that he had received since he left Virginia of the movements of the enemy. He inferred from the fact that the enemy had turned westward from Frederickstown that his purpose was to enter the Cumberland Valley south of our army, and obstruct our communications through Hagerstown with Virginia. General Lee said that, while he did not consider that he had complete communication with Virginia, he had all the communication that he needed, as long as the enemy had no considerable force in the Cumberland Valley. His principal need for communication with Virginia was to procure ammunition, and he thought that he could always do that with an escort, if the valley was free from a Federal force, but should the enemy have a considerable force in the valley this would be impossible. He considered it of great importance that the enemy's army should be kept east of the mountains, and consequently he determined to move his own army to the east side of the Blue Ridge, so as to threaten Washington and Baltimore, and detain the Federal forces on that side of the mountains to protect those cities. He directed me to countermand the orders to General Ewell and General Hill, and to order the latter to move eastward on the road through Cashtown or Gettysburg as circumstances might direct. He ordered General Longstreet to prepare to move the next morning, following Hill.[15]

Foreign observers had been acquired by the Confederate army on this campaign: Captain Justis Scheibert of the Prussian Royal Engineers, Captain Fitzgerald Ross ("very Scotch as to name but Austrian to the core," wrote Sorrel) serving in the Austrian Hussars, *London Times* correspondent Francis Lawley, and a "delightful" addition to Longstreet's headquarters was Lieutenant Colonel Arthur Fremantle of the Coldstream Guards. All gave an insight into the workings of the Confederate command, particularly Fremantle's diary. Fremantle spent a good deal of time at the First Corps headquarters, and Longstreet enjoyed his company.

Shoes for Barefoot Men

General Heth's division part of A. P. Hill's corps reached Cashtown on June 29 and camped there; Heth received word there were shoes at Gettysburg for his barefooted men. Heth decided to send a foraging party to Gettysburg: "On the morning of June 30, I ordered Brigadier General Pettigrew to take his brigade to Gettysburg, search the town for army supplies (shoes especially), and return the same day."[16] Brigadier-General James J. Pettigrew's aide, Lieutenant Louis G. Young, heard the conversation and recollected: "The orders to him were peremptory, not to precipitate a fight."[17]

Lee did not want an engagement until all his troops were up. Pettigrew set off to Gettysburg with three regiments and a wagon train but after going only a short distance a scout sympathetic to the Confederate cause warned of Yankee cavalry approaching the town. Pettigrew rode ahead to reconnoiter and spotted enemy cavalry through his field glasses as he stood on a ridge, a report came to him of drumming indicating infantry. Though not a professional soldier, prudently,

Pettigrew obeyed his orders not to fight and withdrew to Cashtown. As Pettigrew was making his report of the day's events to Heth, A. P. Hill rode up and joined the conversation.

Pettigrew repeated his experiences to Hill at Heth's insistence; Hill was not buying it: "The only force at Gettysburg is cavalry, probably a detachment of observation. I am just from General Lee, and the information he has from his scouts corroborates that I have received from mine-that is, the enemy is still at Middleburg [Maryland, 20 miles south] and have not yet struck their tents." Heth spoke up: "If there is no objection, I will take my Division tomorrow and go to Gettysburg and get those shoes." Hill replied: "None in the world."[18]

In his official report, Hill asserted he wanted to probe at Gettysburg: "A courier was then dispatched with this information to the general commanding, and with orders to start Anderson early; also to General Ewell, informing him, and that I intended to advance the next morning and discover what was in my front."[19]

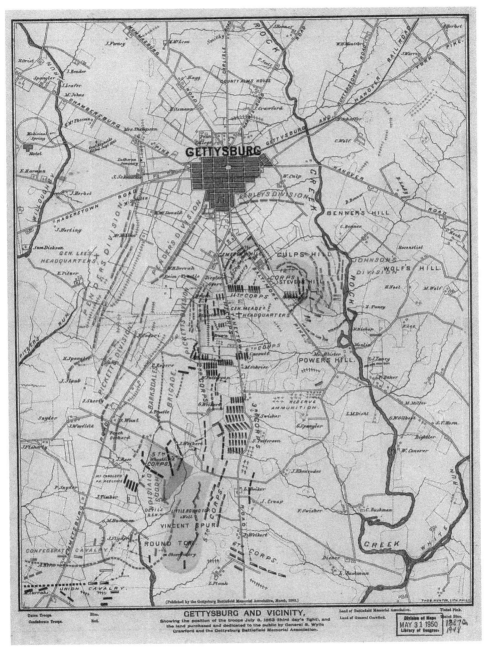

Battle of Gettysburg

CHAPTER 5

"Here's the Old Bulldog"

Gettysburg, Day One

Lee was not unsettled by Hill's message because Meade's army was reported far away. "Thus Hill's movement to Gettysburg was made of his own motion," commented Alexander, "and with knowledge that he would find the enemy's cavalry in possession. Ewell was informed of it. Lee's orders were to avoid bringing on an action. Like Stuart's raid, Hill's venture is another illustration of an important event allowed to happen without supervision. Lee's first intimation of danger of collision was his hearing Hill's guns at Gettysburg. He was much disturbed by it, not wishing to fight without the presence of his cavalry to gather fruit in case of victory."[1]

What were in front of Hill consisted of two brigades of John Buford's cavalry division that had been sent to reconnoiter Gettysburg in one of Joseph Hooker's last acts. But moving up behind Buford was Meade's left wing under John Reynolds; Meade's order was for Reynolds's First Corps to march to Gettysburg, followed closely by Howard's Eleventh Corps and Sickles's Third in near proximity for support.

Henry Heth encountered resistance from John Buford's vedette posts as he approached Gettysburg but as he later stated in his official report:

It may not be improper to remark that at this time-9 o'clock on the morning of July 1-I was ignorant what force was at or near Gettysburg, and supposed it consisted of cavalry, most probably supported by a brigade or two of infantry.[2]

The inexperienced Heth should have broken off the action and reported back to Hill but instead became enmeshed ever deeper in a battle he knew General Lee did not want at this time. John Buford wanted to hold up Heth until John Reynolds's infantry rolled into Gettysburg: "By daylight on July 1, I had gained positive information of the enemy's position and movements, and my arrangements were made for entertaining him until General Reynolds could reach the scene."

Every Fourth Man

Entertain him he did, with his troopers fighting dismounted, every fourth man designated as horse holder, firing their rapid-fire single-shot breech-loading carbines, allowing them to fire up to 14 shots per minute, while the Rebels would be lucky to fire three in the same time; Buford delayed Heth's division long enough until the blue coats of Reynolds's command came up and arrested Heth's forward motion, inflicting severe losses. General Reynolds's decision to aid Buford at Gettysburg opened the battle, he sent General Meade, commander of the Army of the Potomac, a dispatch that he would try to prevent the enemy from taking the heights (Cemetery Hill) near the town which he and Buford, "two men equally noted for quickness of perception, promptness of decision, and gallantry on the battlefield," saw as the key to the battlefield; Reynolds was killed early in the fighting. Meade had considered that Lee might concentrate his forces against portions of his army piecemeal and wanted to find a position where the army could fall back and make a stand to fight a defensive battle on ground of his own choosing. The staff of his chief engineer, Brigadier General Gouverneur K. Warren, chose the high ground behind Big Pipe Creek, a small tributary of the Monocacy River, named Parr's Ridge, a 20-mile chain of hills in Maryland just south of Meade's headquarters at Taneytown, positioned to cover his supply line to Washington and the approaches to Baltimore. Meade ordered a copy of the Pipe Creek circular be sent to his corps commanders, specifying conditions under which any one of them could initiate a pull back by the entire army to the Pipe Creek Line. However, due to delay by his chief of staff, Major General Daniel Butterfield, Reynolds never received a copy. Porter Alexander made this observation:

> Although Meade had selected his proposed line of battle behind Pipe Creek, and now announced his intentions to rest his troops, he still, on the 1st, ordered a further advance of each of his seven corps, as follows: The 5th corps was ordered to Hanover; the 6th corps to Manchester; the 12th corps to Two Taverns; the 3rd corps to Emmitsburg, and the 1st and 11th corps to Gettysburg. These advances were not intended to bring on a battle, but to cover the position selected, allowing space in front to delay the enemy's approach and give time for preparation. The instructions to Reynolds, who was in command on the left, were not to bring on a general engagement.
>
> But, though both Meade and Lee had cautioned their lieutenants to this effect, it was precipitated by Hill's initiative and Reynold's willing concurrence.[3]

Longstreet had established his headquarters near an abandoned sawmill at Greenwood, at the western entrance to the Cashtown Gap and, as was his custom, General Lee set up his headquarters a short distance away. Lieutenant Colonel Fremantle had joined the party prior and conversed with Longstreet, whom he considered a particularly taciturn man. They talked about Texas where Longstreet had been quartered quite a while.

General Lee was introduced by Longstreet to Fremantle who was very impressed with General Lee and the close relationship that had developed between Lee and Longstreet:

> The relations between him and Longstreet are quite touching-they are almost always together. Longstreet's corps complain of this sometimes, as they say that they seldom get a chance of

detached service, which falls to the lot of Ewell. It is impossible to please Longstreet more than by praising Lee. I believe these two generals to be as little ambitious and as thoroughly unselfish as any men in the world. Both long for a successful termination of the war, in order that they may retire into obscurity.[4]

The Confederate army started to move for a concentration at Cashtown or Gettysburg; Longstreet rode with Lee as they were accustomed to do so often:

> He [Lee] was in his usual cheerful spirits on the morning of the 1st, and called me to ride with him. My column was not well stretched on the road before it encountered the division of E. Johnson (Second Corps) cutting in on our front, with all of Ewell's reserve and supply trains. He ordered the First Corps halted, and directed that Johnson's division and train should pass on to its corps, the First to wait. During the wait I dismounted to give Hero (Longstreet's favorite horse), a little respite.
>
> After a little time General Lee proposed that we should ride on, and soon we heard reports of cannon. The fire seemed to be beyond Cashtown, and as it increased he left me and rode faster for the front.[5]

Fremantle accompanied Longstreet and recorded in his diary the regard and esteem the soldiers displayed toward the general:

> The first troops, alongside of whom we rode, belonged to Johnson's division of Ewell's corps. Among them I saw, for the first time, the celebrated 'Stonewall' Brigade, formerly commanded by Jackson.
>
> As they have nearly always been on detached duty, few of them knew General Longstreet, except by reputation. Numbers of them asked me whether the general in front was Longstreet; and when I answered in the affirmative, many would run on a hundred yards in order to take a good look at him. This I take to be an immense compliment from any soldier on a long march.
>
> After passing Johnson's division, we came up to a Florida brigade, which is now in Hill's corps; but as it had formerly served under Longstreet, the men knew him well. Some of them (after the General had passed) called out to their comrades, "Look out for work now, boys, for here's the old bulldog again."[6]

Longstreet was mindful that Gettysburg, with its many converging roads, was somewhat of strategic importance to General Lee: "From Gettysburg roads diverge to the passes of the mountains, the borders of the Potomac and Susquehanna, and the cities of Baltimore and Washington; so that it was something of a strategic point."[7]

Disadvantage Gray

The Confederates were at a disadvantage in logistics. Longstreet commented:

> It should be borne in mind that the field of contention was south and east of Gettysburg, so that the Union troops were from two to four miles nearer their formation for battle than were the Confederates, who had to march from two to four miles beyond the town.
>
> Referring to the map, it may be seen that the Confederate corps had two routes by which to march for concentration,-viz., from Heidlersburg to Cashtown, part of the Second Corps; on the road from Chambersburg, the First, Third and part of the Second Corps (with all the trains of the latter), with but a singletrack, the Chambersburg-Gettysburg turnpike. Some

of their distances were greater than any of the columns of the enemy, while the Army of the Potomac had almost as many routes of march as commands, and was marching from day to day anticipating a general engagement, which they were especially cautioned on the 30th was imminent.[8]

The Cashtown Gap soon became a bottleneck for the Confederate forces.

Longstreet accompanied by Colonel Fremantle found Lee on Seminary Ridge, Fremantle recorded in his diary:

> At 4:30 P. M. we came in sight of Gettysburg, and joined General Lee and General Hill, who were on the top of one of the ridges which form the peculiar feature of the country around Gettysburg. We could see the enemy retreating up one of the opposite ridges, pursued by the Confederates with loud yells. The position into which the enemy had been driven was evidently a strong one. His right appeared to rest on a cemetery, on top of a high ridge to the right of Gettysburg, as we looked at it.
>
> General Hill now came up and told me he had been very unwell all day, and in fact he looks very delicate. He said he had had two of his divisions engaged, and had driven the enemy four miles into his present position, capturing a great many prisoners, some cannon, and some colors.[9]

Hill's and Ewell's corps had broken the First and Eleventh Corps of the Union and had chased them through Gettysburg to the hills and ridges south of the town.

In a conversation with Brigadier General Isaac Trimble, a 61-year-old West Pointer, Lee discussed his plan for destruction of the Union army:

> Our army is in good spirits, not overfatigued, and can be concentrated in twenty-four hours or less. When they hear where we are, they will make forced marches to interpose between us and Baltimore and Philadelphia. They will come up, probably through Frederick, broken down with hunger and hard marching, strung out on a long line and much demoralized. When they come into Pennsylvania, I shall throw an overwhelming force on their advance, crush it, follow up the success, drive one corps back on another, and by successive repulses and surprises, before they can concentrate, create a panic and virtually destroy the army.[10]

At this point, Lee thought he had the offing of his plan within his grasp.

Longstreet arrived to find Lee and surveyed the Union stronghold on top of Cemetery Hill, which to Longstreet had no more significance than any other piece of real estate in the area and was certainly not important enough to waste soldiers' lives to try and acquire it:

> After a long wait I left orders for the troops to follow the trains of the Second Corps, and rode to find General Lee. His head-quarters were on Seminary Ridge at the crossing of the Cashtown road. Anderson's division was then filed off along the ridge, resting. Johnson's had marched to report to the corps commander. Dismounting and passing the usual salutation, I drew my glasses and made a studied view of the position upon which the enemy was rallying his forces, and of the lay of the land surrounding. General Lee was engaged at the moment. He had announced beforehand that he would not make aggressive battle in the enemy's country. After the survey and in consideration of his plans, noting movements of detachments of the enemy on the Emmitsburg road, the relative positions for manoeuvre, the lofty perch of the enemy, the rocky slopes from it, all marking the position clearly defensive,-I said, "We could not call the enemy to position better suited to our plans. All that we have to do is to file

around his left and secure good ground between him and his capital." This, when said, was thought to the opinion of my commander as much as my own. I was not a little surprised, therefore, at his impatience, as, striking the air with his closed hand, he said, "If he is there to-morrow I will attack him."[11]

Longstreet's strategy was to maneuver the Federal army out of its stronghold on Cemetery Ridge and compel them to attack the Confederate army in a strong defensive position by threatening their capital. With the advent of the new, more accurate long-range rifled musket, the advantage lay with the defenders in intrench-ments where they could inflict heavy casualties on the exposed attackers while their losses would be minimal since they were under cover. Longstreet did not want to squander the lives of his soldiers by putting them in harm's way in risky offensive operations that would produce barren results at best or, at worse, defeat. He realized the South's most important asset was its manpower, which had to be conserved. Longstreet continued:

> When I overtook General Lee, at five o'clock that afternoon, he said, to my surprise, that he thought of attacking General Meade upon the heights the next day. I suggested that this course seemed to be at variance with the plan of the campaign that had been agreed upon before leaving Fredericksburg. He said: "If the enemy is there to-morrow, we must attack him." I replied: "If he is there, it will be because he is anxious that we should attack him —a good reason, in my judgment, for not doing so." I urged that we should move around by our right to the left of Meade, and put our army between him and Washington, threatening his left and rear, and thus force him to attack us in such position as we might select. I said that it seemed to me that if, during our council at Fredericksburg, we had described the position in which we desired to get the two armies, we could not have expected to get the enemy in a better position for us than that he then occupied; that he was in strong position and would be awaiting us, which was evidence that he desired that we should attack him. I said, further, that his weak point seemed to be his left, that we might threaten it if we intended to maneuvre, or attack it if we determined upon a battle. I called his attention to the fact that the country was admirably adapted for a defensive battle, and that we would surely repulse Meade with crushing loss if we would take position so as to force him to attack us, and suggested that, even if we carried the heights in front of us, and drove Meade out, we should be so badly crippled that we could not reap the fruits of victory; and that the heights of Gettysburg were, in themselves, of no more importance to us than the ground we then occupied, and that the mere possession of the ground was not worth a hundred men to us. That Meade's army, not its position, was our objective. General Lee was impressed with the idea that, by attacking the Federals, he could whip them in detail. I reminded him that if the Federals were there in the morning, it would be proof that they had their forces well in hand, and with Pickett in Chambersburg, and Stuart out of reach, we should be somewhat in detail. He, however, did not seem to abandon the idea of attack on the next day. He seemed under a subdued excitement, which occasionally took possession of him when "the hunt was up," and threatened his superb equipoise. The sharp battle fought by Hill and Ewell on that day had given him a taste of victory.[12]

Longstreet wanted to move the army south and occupy a strong defensive position— perhaps, the Pipe Creek Line Meade had proposed for a defensive battle against Lee's army or he could attack Meade's left if the opportunity offered. Rather than discuss it further, Longstreet thought it better to let Lee reflect on battleplans.

Longstreet's discussion with General Lee is verified by Lee's military secretary, A. L. Long:

> Near the close of the action General Lee reached the field. Anderson's division came up soon afterward, and about the same time Longstreet arrived in advance of his corps, which was a few miles behind.
>
> This subject occupied Lee's attention upon perceiving the situation of affairs and the victory gained by his advance forces, and he entered into a conversation with Longstreet, in the presence of the writer, concerning the relative positions of the two armies and the movements it was advisable to make. Longstreet gave it as his opinion that the best plan would be to turn Meade's left flank and force him back to the neighborhood of Pipeclay Creek. To this General Lee objected, and pronounced it impracticable under the circumstances.

Elated by his initial victory, General Lee rejected General Longstreet's wise advice to move around Meade's left flank and interpose between Meade's army and Washington City. This would have compelled Meade to attack Lee's army in a strong defensive position. The Federal troops would be exposed to a withering fire from the new, highly accurate long-range rifled muskets and cannon, while the Confederates would be protected by intrenchments. It would have given Lee's army the decided advantage and possibly a crucial victory, forcing General Grant to terminate his siege of Vicksburg.

> At the conclusion of the conversation Colonel Long was directed to make a reconnaissance of the Federal position on Cemetery Ridge, to which strong line the retreating troops had retired. This he did, and found that the ridge was occupied in considerable force. On this fact being reported to General Lee, he decided to make no farther advance that evening, but to wait till morning before attempting to follow up his advantage. This decision the worn-out condition of his men and the strength of the position held by the enemy rendered advisable. He turned to Longstreet and Hill, who were present, and said, 'Gentlemen, we will attack the enemy in the morning as early as practicable.' In the conversation that succeeded he directed them to make the necessary preparations and be ready for prompt action the next day. Longstreet's corps was at the time near Cashtown, but bivouacked for the night on Willoughby's Creek, about four miles from the battlefield.[13]

All Longstreet knew at this time was that Lee was going on the offensive; he did not know when or where, but no order was issued to anyone then.

CHAPTER 6

"Up the Emmitsburg Road"

Gettysburg, Day Two

In his official report, Lee gave the following reasons for fighting an offensive battle on this ground:

> It had not been intended to deliver a general battle so far from our base unless attacked, but coming unexpectedly upon the whole Federal Army, to withdraw through the mountains with our extensive trains would have been difficult and dangerous. At the same time we were unable to await an attack, as the country was unfavorable for collecting supplies in the presence of the enemy, who could restrain our foraging parties by holding the mountain passes with local and other troops. A battle had, therefore, become in a measure unavoidable, and the success already gained gave hope of a favorable issue.[1]

Lee must have felt the hostility of the population in Pennsylvania, whereas in Tennessee, where Longstreet wanted to launch an offensive, there would have been many helping hands.

Before going to Seminary Ridge on July 1, Lee had an interview with General Anderson at Cashtown in which he expressed anxiety over Stuart's absence and what forces he was confronting at Gettysburg:

> About twelve o'clock I received a message notifying me that General Lee desired to see me. I found General Lee intently listening to the fire of the guns, and very much disturbed and depressed. At length he said more to himself than to me, "I cannot think what has become of Stuart. I ought to have heard from him long before now. He may have met with disaster, but I hope not. In the absence of reports from him, I am in ignorance as to what we have in front of us here. It may be the whole Federal Army, or it may be only a detachment. If it is the whole Federal force, we must fight a battle here. If we do not gain a victory, those defiles and gorges which we passed this morning will shelter us from disaster."[2]

None of these arguments were plausible, the Confederate army had about a week's food supply. Stuart's cavalry would arrive within 24 hours which Lee was well aware of after meeting with Andrew R. Venable, Stuart's assistant adjutant and inspector general, around 1:30pm on July 1. Stuart's cavalry would have provided cover for foraging, much needed intelligence, and protection for the trains, along with the entire Army of Northern Virginia in case of pull-back. The veteran troops could easily push aside the militia. In point of fact, Lee could hold tight and wait for his other troops to arrive, then gather intelligence and wait out Meade or maneuver around him at his leisure.

As Colonel E. P. Alexander pointed out:

> Now when it is remembered that we stayed for three days longer on that very ground, two of them days of desperate battle, ending in the discouragement of a bloody repulse, & then successfully withdrew all our trains & most of the wounded through the mountains; and finding the Potomac too high to ford, protected them all & foraged successfully for over a week in a very restricted territory along the river, until we could build a bridge, it does not seem improbable that we could have faced Meade safely on the 2nd at Gettysburg without assaulting him in his wonderfully strong position. We had the prestige of victory with us, having chased him off the field & through the town. We had a fine defensive position on Seminary Ridge ready at our hand to occupy. It was not such a really wonderful position as the enemy happened to fall into, but it was no bad one, & it could never have been successfully assaulted. The onus of attack was upon Meade anyhow. We could even have fallen back to Cashtown & held the mountain passes with all the prestige of victory, & popular sentiment would have forced Meade to take the aggressive.[3]

The Comte de Paris thought Lee had four possible choices and did not buy into Lee's reasoning that he had to fight an offensive battle because of the wagon trains:

> He [Lee] has four alternatives to chose from: he has the choice to retire into the gaps of South Mountain in order to compel Meade to come after him; or to wait steadily in his present positions for the attack of the Federals; or again, to manoeuvre in order to dislodge them from those they occupy by menacing their communications by the right or the left; or, finally, to storm these positions in front, in the hope of carrying them by main force. The best plan would undoubtedly have been the first, because by preserving the strategic offensive Lee would thus secure all the advantages of the tactical defensive. Once master of the mountain-passes, he may cover his retreat upon Hagerstown or Hancock on the one side, while still menacing the very heart of Pennsylvania on the other. Meade, being hard pressed by public opinion, will be compelled to attack him in as formidable positions as those of Cramton's and Turner's Gaps, where the preceding year a handful of men so long resisted McClellan's assaults. Lee, by way of excuse for not having adopted this plan, has alleged the impossibility of bringing to the rear in time the supply-trains which were crowding on the road from Chambersburg to Gettysburg: this excuse does not seem to us to be admissible, for the same trains were able to retrograde, without obstruction, during the night of the 4th and 5th, and such a movement would have been less dangerous after the victory of the 1st than after defeat of the 3rd.[4]

On July 1, Lee turned his attention to his left flank under Ewell to bear down on the Union army; he sent his adjutant General, Walter Taylor, to ask General Ewell to finish the job, as Taylor recounted:

> General Lee witnessed the flight of the Federals through Gettysburg and up the hills beyond. He then directed me to go to General Ewell and to say to him that, from the position he then occupied, he could see the enemy retreating over those hills, without organization and great confusion; that it was only necessary to press "those people" in order to secure possession of the heights, and that, if possible, he wished him to do this. In obedience to these instructions,

I proceeded immediately to General Ewell and delivered the order of General Lee; and after receiving from him some message in regard to the prisoners captured and the embarrassment of looking after them, I returned to General Lee and reported that his order had been delivered. General Ewell did not express any objection, or indicate the existence of any impediment, to the execution of the order conveyed to him, but left the impression upon my mind that it would be executed. In the exercise of that discretion, which General Lee was accustomed to accord to his lieutenants, and probably because of an undue regard for his admonition previously given, not to precipitate a general engagement, General Ewell deemed it unwise to make the pursuit. The troops were not moved forward, and the enemy proceeded to fortify the position which it was designed that General Ewell should seize.[5]

Cemetery Hill

General Ewell was confused by the contradiction in Lee's order that Taylor had delivered, "to carry the hill occupied by the enemy, if he found it practicable, but to avoid a general engagement until the arrival of the other divisions of the army ..."[6] Lee wanted Longstreet and his First Corps on hand before fighting a major battle. Ewell conferred with his two division commanders, Robert Rodes and Jubal Early, and sent his aide, Captain James Power Smith, to General Lee with a message: "They desired General Lee to be informed that they could go forward and take Cemetery Hill if they were supported on their right; that to the south of the Cemetery there was in sight a position commanding it which should be taken at once." Smith found Lee and Longstreet in discussion on Seminary Ridge and delivered Ewell's message. Lee inquired of Longstreet how near his closest division was. Longstreet answered six miles away; Smith observed that Longstreet "was indefinite and noncommittal." Lee sent a reply with Captain Smith to Ewell that "he regretted that his people were not up to support him on the right, but he wished him to take Cemetery Hill if it were possible; and that he would ride over and see him very soon."

Meanwhile, General Ewell began to conceive of a method to comply with Lee's orders, gain Cemetery Hill without bringing on a major battle. Lying 800 yards from Cemetery Hill, to the north was Culp's Hill that seemed to be overlooked by the Federals. He sent two staff officers, Lieutenants Thomas Turner and Robert Early, to reconnoiter Culp's Hill; they did not find any Yankees and detailed how Culp's Hill commanded Cemetery Hill and rendered it untenable. Ewell had one unengaged division under General Edward "Allegheny" Johnson marching toward Gettysburg. Allegheny Johnson was up. However, his division, after marching some 25 miles that day, was snarled in a traffic jam with a wagon train a mile away, which required another hour to unravel, making its arrival at sunset or later. Ewell pondered on this new wrinkle and thought of an alternative by using Hay's Louisiana and Avery's North Carolina brigades of Early's division already close by to take hold of Culp's Hill. Early balked at the task, saying his division "had been doing all the hard marching and fighting and was not in condition to make the move." Johnson did not like the implication of this remark with its disparaging comparison to his command and some hot words were exchanged between the two generals that Ewell broke off. Early's refusal and Ewell's acquiescence by not ordering the hill to be taken was a great disservice to Lee and the Confederate cause. Culp's Hill could have been easily seized; the Federals had only the exhausted and thinned-out Iron Brigade to defend Culp's. Ewell decided to assign Johnson's division the task of acquiring the hill. This dereliction ultimately cost the Confederates the battle; Early, who after the war accused Longstreet of losing the battle, was, in reality, the one who brought Lee's army to defeat.

Robert E. Lee rode over to his left to meet General Ewell at Second Corps headquarters at the Blocher House in an arbor near Carlisle Road. Also present at the meeting were Generals Rodes and Early. Lee wanted to know the overall state of the Second Corps and whether it was feasible to take Cemetery Hill the next day: "Can't you, with your corps, attack on this flank at daylight tomorrow," Lee inquired, according to Early having the only record of the conversation.

Early had examined the area on June 26 when passing through and objected: "ground over which we would have to advance on our flank was very rugged and steep," and that any assault must be made to "go on the left of the town right up against Cemetery Hill, and the rugged hills on the left of it, it would inevitably be at very great loss."

Early motioned to the high ground south of Cemetery Hill and pointed out it "must evidently command the enemy's position and render it untenable," Ewell and Rodes concurred with this assessment.

Lee asked: "Then perhaps I had better draw you around toward my right, as the line will be very long and thin if you remain here, and the enemy may come down and break through it?"

Again, Early differed: "We could repulse any force he could send against us," and it would demoralize the troops after winning such a dramatic victory to give up the ground they won besides our wounded and captured material could not be moved on such short notice.

A Parley

Once more, Ewell and Rodes sustained Early. Alexander gave this perspective of the parley of Lee and Ewell:

> Later in the afternoon Lee rode forward to arrange a renewal of the attack upon Cemetery Hill from the town the next morning. He held a long conference with Ewell, Early and Rodes, who urged, instead, that Longstreet should attack the enemy's left flank. No one of those present had more than a vague idea of the character and features of the enemy's line, and it is therefore not surprising that this advice, though very plausible in view of the success of former flank movements, was here the worst possible.

Alexander gave the following description of the topography of the Union position:

The enemy's line, though taken hurriedly upon the natural ridges overlooking the open country, which nearly surrounded it, was unique in both character and strength. In plan it nearly resembled a fish-hook, with its convexity toward us, forcing upon our line a similar shape with the concavity toward them. Their lines were interior and shorter, being scarcely three miles in length, giving ability to reenforce at any point by short cuts across the interior lines. Our exterior lines were about five miles in length, and to move from point to point required long, roundabout marches, often exposed to the enemy's view. Their force would allow 25,000 infantry and 100 guns for each mile of line. Ours would allow but 13,000 infantry and 50 guns per mile. Their flanks were at once unassailable and unturnable. Their left, which was the top of the fish-hook shank, rested on Big and Little Round Top mountains, and their right, which was the 'point' of the 'fish-hook' was on Culp's Hill over Rock Creek. Both flanks presented precipitous and rocky fronts, screened from artillery fire by forest growth, and the convexity of the line was such that the two flanks approached and each was able to reenforce the other. The shank of the fish-hook ran north, nearly straight, for about two miles from Little Round Top to Cemetery Hill, where the bend began. The bend was not uniform and regular, but presented a sharp salient at the north, and on the east a deep reentrant around which the line swept to reach Culp's Hill, and pass around nearly in an S.

Alexander always believed an attack on Cemetery Hill presented the best chance of success to break the Federal defenses. He felt Cemetery Hill on the Federal right flank was the most vulnerable portion of the Federal stronghold.

This salient upon Cemetery Hill offered the only hopeful point of attack upon the enemy's entire line, as will more fully appear in the accounts of the different efforts made at various places during the battle. It would be too much to say that an attack here on the morning of July 2 would have succeeded. But it is not at all too much to say that no other attack was possible at that time which would have had near as good chance of success, yet it was deliberately discarded, and Lee's conference closed with the understanding among all those present that Longstreet should attack in the morning upon the enemy's left. It was this which gave rise to the mistaken charges made after Lee's death that Longstreet had disobeyed orders in not attacking early on the 2d.

No orders whatever were given Longstreet that night. Before sunset, he had ridden back from his interview with Lee to meet his troops, who, about 4 P.M., marched from near Greenwood with orders to come to Gettysburg, 17 miles. About midnight they bivouacked four miles from the field. Marching again at dawn on the 2d, they arrived near the field between 6 and 8 A.M. His reserve artillery (the Washington artillery and Alexander's battalion), which was ordered to follow the infantry from Greenwood at midnight, was much detained upon the road by passing trains, and did not reach the field until 9 A.M.[7]

After the war, Early, with others, concocted a tale of a mysterious order for a sunrise attack General Lee supposedly gave Longstreet.

Porter Alexander discredited the notion of a "sunrise attack" order:

Sometime during the day, already, Longstreet's two divisions, Hood's & McLaws's, had been ordered forward. They bivouaced during the night about four miles off. It has been asserted by some that Longstreet was ordered to assault at sunrise but I do not find this assertion credible. Had Gen. Lee desired this, the one way to accomplish it would have been to have himself provided guides & ordered Longstreet's troops put in position during the night. It takes a little time to hunt out & reconnoiter a position which has to be attacked & the enemy's position here was never thoroughly developed until morning.[8]

General Lee was not satisfied with the arrangements for the Second Corps, as he believed nothing would be done where it was. He sent a note with his staff officer, Colonel Charles Marshall, to General Ewell requesting the Second Corps be moved to the right to augment the attack unless something could be accomplished as it was situated. This motivated General Ewell to ride back with Marshall to Lee's headquarters at 10:30pm; Ewell tabulated the series of events in his report:

> I received orders soon after dark to draw my corps to the right, in case it could not be used to advantage where it was; that the commanding general thought from the nature of the ground that the position for attack was a good one on that side. I represented to the commanding general that the hill above referred to was unoccupied by the enemy, as reported by Lieutenants Turner and Early, who had gone upon it, and that it commanded their position and made it untenable, so far as I could judge.

Johnson orders a reconnaissance of Culp's Hill:

> He decided to let me remain, and on my return to my headquarters, after 12 o'clock at night, I sent orders to Johnson by Lieut. T. T. Turner, aide-de-camp, to take possession of this hill, if he had not already done so. General Johnson stated in his reply to this order, that after forming his line of battle this side of the wooded hill in question, he had sent a reconnoitering party to the hill, with orders to report as to the position of the enemy in reference to it. This party, on nearing the summit, was met by a superior force of the enemy, which succeeded in capturing a portion of the reconnoitering party, the rest of it making its escape. During this conversation with General Johnson, one man arrived, bringing a dispatch, dated at 12 midnight, and taken from a Federal courier making his way from General Sykes to General Slocum, in which the former stated that his corps was then halted 4 miles from Gettysburg, and he would resume his march at 4 A. M. Lieutenant Turner brought this dispatch to my headquarters, and at the same time stated that General Johnson would refrain from attacking the position until I had received notice of the fact that the enemy were in possession of the hill, and had sent him further orders. Day was now breaking, and it was too late for any change of place.

General Ewell was ordered to coordinate his attack with Longstreet's:

> Meantime orders had come from the general commanding for me to delay my attack until I heard General Longstreet's guns open on the right. Lieutenant Turner at once returned to General Johnson, and delivered these instructions, directing him to be ready to attack, Early being already in line on the left and Rodes on the right of the main street of the town, Rodes' line extending out on the Fairfield Road.
>
> Early in the morning, I received a communication from the commanding general, the tenor of which was that he intended the main attack to be made by the First Corps, on our right, and wished me, as soon as the guns opened, to make a diversion in their favor, to be converted into a real attack if an opportunity offered.[9]

A Most Unfortunate Decision

Again Robert E. Lee was persuaded by Ewell's arguments and reversed his decision but, as Alexander indicated, it hampered the effectiveness of his army:

It was a most unfortunate decision, as will presently appear, for it fatally extended Lee's left flank. About midnight, Johnson's division was moved around the base of Culp's Hill and a reconnoitring party ascended, but found the enemy in possession. No one ordered the division to be carried back to the right, where it could have been of much service in subsequent operations, and where Lee had intended it to be. It was far too weak to attack the strong position of the enemy on Culp's Hill, and its communication with the rest of the army was long, roundabout, and exposed to the enemy's view. But the division was allowed to remain until the end of the battle, and, as long as it remained absent, the task before the remainder of the army was beyond its strength.[10]

Longstreet was not so assured of the outcome as his staff or many members of the army. In a letter he sent to Longstreet, Dr. Dorsey Cullen, the First Corps' medical director, recalled Old Pete's reaction:

> You had been at the front with General Lee, and were returning to your camp, a mile or two back. I spoke very exultingly of the victory we were thought to have obtained that day, but was surprised to find that you did not take the same cheerful view of it that I did; and presently you remarked, that it would have been better had we not fought than to have left undone what we did. You said that the enemy were left occupying a position that it would take the whole army to drive them from, and then at a great sacrifice.[11]

Longstreet was proactive in concentrating his corps for the coming engagement by issuing orders to Pickett's division at Chambersburg and Evander Law's brigade of Hood's division to move toward Gettysburg.

Longstreet rose between 3:00 and 3:30am, leaving his staff at breakfast to ride ahead to meet General Lee on Seminary Ridge. In his book *From Manassas to Appomattox* he wrote:

> The stars were shining brightly on the morning of the 2d when I reported at General Lee's headquarters and asked for orders. After a time Generals McLaws and Hood, with their staffs, rode up, and at sunrise their commands filed off the road to the right and rested. The Washington Artillery was with them, and about nine o'clock, after an all-night march, Alexander's batteries were up as far as Willoughby's Run, where he parked and fed, and rode to head-quarters to report.[12]

Sunrise at Gettysburg

Sunrise at Gettysburg on that date was at 4:35am In his book *General Lee 1861–1865,* Colonel Taylor repudiated the above statement by Longstreet; yet there are witnesses proving Longstreet's assertion. Colonel Fremantle scribbled in his diary:

> 2d July (Thursday)-We all got up at 3:30 A. M., and breakfasted a little before daylight.
> Colonel Sorrel, the Austrian, and I arrived at 5 A.M. at the same commanding position we were on yesterday, and I climbed up a tree in company with Captain Schreibert of the Prussian Army. Just below us were seated Generals Lee, Hill, Longstreet, and Hood, in consultation-the two latter assisting their deliberations by the truly American custom of whittling sticks. General Heth was also present; he was wounded in the head yesterday, and although not allowed to command his brigade, he insists upon coming to the field.[13]

Once more, Longstreet tried to persuade Lee to accept his strategy. Longstreet strongly adhered to the conviction that the object of the battle was Meade's army, not the position it held:

> On the morning of the 2d I joined General Lee and again proposed the move to Meade's left and rear. He was still unwilling to consider the proposition, but soon left me and rode off to see General Ewell and to examine the ground on our left with a view to making the attack at that point.[14]

General Lee hadn't totally rejected Longstreet's proposal. For some time, between late on the night of July 1 and early on July 2, Major G. Campbell Brown, Ewell's stepson, recorded in a memoir, inked not long after the war, his meeting on Ewell's behalf with General Lee. Lee cautioned him "to tell Gen. E. to be sure not to become too entangled with the enemy as to be unable readily to extricate his troops; for I have not decided to fight here, and may probably draw off by my right flank-so as to get between the enemy & Washington & Baltimore-& force them to attack us in position."[15]

Any consideration of a sunrise attack was out of the question, for at sunrise at 4:37am, General Lee was weighing his options, sending staff officer Colonel Charles Venable to General Ewell. In Longstreet's words: "About sunrise General Lee sent Colonel Venable, of his staff, to General Ewell's headquarters, ordering him to make a reconnaissance of the ground in his front, with a view of making the main attack on his left."[16]

Colonel Venable sent Longstreet a letter discussing his mission on the left, refuting any concept of a sunrise attack:

> University of Virginia, May 11th, 1875
> General James Longstreet
>
> Dear General-Your letter of the 25th ultimo, with regard to General Lee's battle order on the 1st and 2nd of July at Gettysburg, was duly received. I did not know of any order for an attack on the enemy at sunrise on the 2nd, nor can I believe any such order was issued by General Lee. About sunrise on the 2nd of July I was sent by General Lee to General Ewell to ask him what he thought of the advantages of an attack on the enemy from his position. (Colonel Marshall had been sent with a similar order on the night of the 1st.) General Ewell made me ride with him from point to point of his lines, so as to see with him the exact position of things. Before he got though the examination of the enemy's position, General Lee came himself to General Ewell's lines. In sending the message to General Ewell, General Lee was explicit in saying that the question was whether he should move all the troops around on the right, and attack on that side. I do not think that the errand on which I was sent by the commanding general is consistent with the idea of an attack at sunrise by any portion of the army.
>
> Yours, very truly,
> Chas. S. Venable.[17]

The other thing that General Lee did at sunrise was send a staff engineer, Captain Samuel R. Johnston, and Colonel Smith, to conduct a reconnaissance on the right, as Lee "wanted me to consider any contingency which might arise." Johnston was attended by Major John J. Clarke assigned by Longstreet to go with him; Clarke was a civil engineer from Petersburg, Virginia, having joined Longstreet's staff in May. They departed with a few other unidentified individuals. Artillery in chief, Brigadier General William Pendleton, announced he was scouting Seminary Ridge for suitable artillery placements; Lee had Armistead L. Long follow him "to examine and verify the position of the Confederate artillery." Soon Generals Lee and Longstreet were joined by Generals Powell Hill, Henry Heth, and John Hood with their staff. Hill was pale, languid, and weak from illness; his immune system had been compromised by a sexually transmitted disease in his youth.

When John Bell Hood rode up to Lee's headquarters, ahead of his division, Lee declared to him, "The enemy is here and if we do not whip him, he will whip us." Taking Hood aside, Longstreet explained, "The General is a little nervous this morning, he wishes me to attack; I do not wish to do so without Pickett. I never like to go into battle with one boot off."[18]

Returning at 8:00am, engineer Captain Samuel R. Johnston found General Lee sitting on a log with Generals Longstreet and Hill. "General Lee saw me and called me to him," recalled Johnson (only his account is on record), "the three Generals were holding up a map. I stood behind General Lee and traced on the map the route over which I had made the reconnaissance."

Johnston's fingers charted a journey proceeding west on Fairfield Road, crossing Willoughby Run, then heading along the creek's western bank until they moved up the slope of Warfield Ridge, a southern extension of Seminary Ridge, coming out opposite the Sherify Farm peach orchard along the Emmitsburg Road, then making his way to the two promontories at the left of the Union line he pointed to the smaller, northern eminence, Little Round Top, and told of his ascent part way up this hill.

"When I got to the extreme right of our reconnaissance on the Little Round Top, General Lee turned and looking at me, said, 'Did you get there?' I assured him that I did." Johnston wrote that Lee "was surprised at my getting so far, but showed clearly that I had given him valuable information."

Johnston's account played an integral part in Lee's battle stratagem; yet it was flawed. Had Johnston traveled where he told Lee his party had been, he would have encountered two Union infantry corps.

The Corps' encampments were north and west of Little Round Top and the Second Corps was passing behind the Round Tops, all making a considerable noise. In addition to two brigades of John Buford's cavalry with vedettes, Little Round Top was occupied by two regiments of Geary's Twelfth Corps division until well after daylight. However, according to Johnston, he spotted only a few cavalry in his entire three-hour journey: "Again got in sight of the Emmitsburg road, I saw three or four troopers moving slowly and very cautiously in the direction of Gettysburg."

The only plausible explanation of this discrepancy is that he bypassed the peach orchard to the south and unwittingly climbed the heavily wooded Round Top instead; he would not have seen or heard the infantry and cavalry close by or he never went as far as he claimed. Johnston's report left Lee with the impression that the Yankee left flank was "in the air" and susceptible to being rolled up toward Gettysburg.

When Johnston and Lee finished their discussion, Lee told Johnston to join Longstreet for a new assignment, which Johnston interpreted to mean "to aid him in any way that I could."

Major General Lafayette McLaws of Longstreet's corps appeared at 8:30am and reported to Longstreet and Lee, having ridden up to Lee's headquarters in advance of his division. Based on Johnston's information, Lee framed out a tactical scheme on his right. Lee spread out the map he was holding in front of McLaws and pointed to a line he had marked perpendicular to the Emmitsburg Road, near Sherify's peach orchard, and remarked to McLaws: "General, I wish you to place your division across this road, and I wish you to get there if possible without being seen by the enemy. Can you get there?"

"I know of nothing to prevent me," responded McLaws, "but I will take a party of skirmishers and go in advance and reconnoitre." Lee mentioned to McLaws that Johnston had already surveyed the area: "Captain Johnston of my staff has been ordered to reconnoitre the ground, and I expect he is about ready." What Lee meant was Johnston was prepared to lead McLaws's division to the jump-off point, but McLaws misunderstood. Thinking Johnston was about to leave for the reconnaissance, he asked to accompany him: "I will go with him."

Longstreet, pacing back and forth within earshot, knowing his corps had been adequately represented by Clarke, jumped in and exclaimed without an explanation: "No, sir, I do not wish you to leave your division."

Tracing a line parallel to the Emmitsburg Road with his finger, Longstreet said to McLaws: "I wish your division placed so."

"No, General," interdicted Lee. "I wish it placed just opposite." McLaws repeated his request to examine the ground with Johnston and "General Longstreet again forbade it," stated McLaws. "General Longstreet appeared as if he was irritated and annoyed but the cause I did not ask," wrote McLaws.

Longstreet's displeasure is best attested to by Sorrel:

> The story has been in part told by Longstreet. We can discover that he did not want to fight on the ground or on the plan adopted by the General-in-Chief. As Longstreet was not to be made willing and Lee refused to change or could not change, the former failed to conceal some anger. There was apparent apathy in his movements. They lacked the fire and point of his usual bearing on the battlefield. His plans may have been better than Lee's, but it was too late to alter them with the troops ready to open fire on each other.[19]

General Longstreet felt that an assault on the Union position would result in massive casualties due to the new weaponry. He did not see the necessity to fight at Gettysburg and preferred the tactical defense which would preserve the South's manpower and resources. His strategic plan was to out General Meade and force him to take the tactical offense.

A Great Sacrifice of Life?

It was nearly 9:00am when General Lee went for another trip to the Second Corps headquarters, Charles Venable had still not reported. When General Lee reached Ewell's headquarters, he learned that Richard Ewell was on a tour of inspection with Colonel Venable. However, Isaac Trimble was present in the capacity of aide and advisor to Ewell. Trimble conducted Lee to the cupola of an almshouse, affording a good view.

Observing the defenses on Culp's and Cemetery Hills, Lee declared: "The enemy have the advantage of us in a short and inside line, and we are too much extended. We did not or could not pursue our advantage of yesterday, and now the enemy are in a good position." At last Ewell and Venable returned from the tour, ever more of the opinion that conditions did not warrant an offensive on this end of the line. Once more Lee broached the possibility of moving the Second Corps to the right to enhance the offensive there, as before Ewell persuaded Lee to leave his corps near Gettysburg to create a diversion to tie down enemy units from being shifted against Longstreet, with the hope that it might be turned into a full-scale assault on Culp's Hill and Cemetery Hill if the opportunity presented itself; Jed Hotchkiss, one of Ewell's staff officers, noted: "General Lee was at our quarters in the am and there planned the movement, though not, in my opinion, very sanguine of its success. He feared we would only take it at a great sacrifice of life."

About 9am Colonel Long, having finished his assignments, joined Lee at Ewell's headquarters:

> After giving General Ewell instructions as to his part in the coming engagement, he proceeded to reconnoitre Cemetery Ridge in person. He at once saw the importance of an immediate commencement of the assault, as it was evident that the enemy was gradually strengthening his position by fresh arrival of troops, and the advantage in numbers and readiness which the Confederate army possessed was rapidly disappearing.
>
> Lee's impatience increased after this reconnaissance, and he proceeded in search of Longstreet, remarking, in a tone of uneasiness, "What can detain Longstreet? He ought to be in position now." This was about 10 A.M.[20]

Lee was becoming uneasy, for he saw for himself the build-up of the enemy, and time was going against him. By now he had concluded to attack on his right and was anxious for First Corps to assemble in full to begin the operation. Lee went to look for Longstreet, and on his way back to his headquarters on Seminary Ridge, he encountered Albert Jenkins, a brigadier general of cavalry. Lee's aide had been sent to bring in Jenkins while Lee was with Ewell. Ewell had complained that he

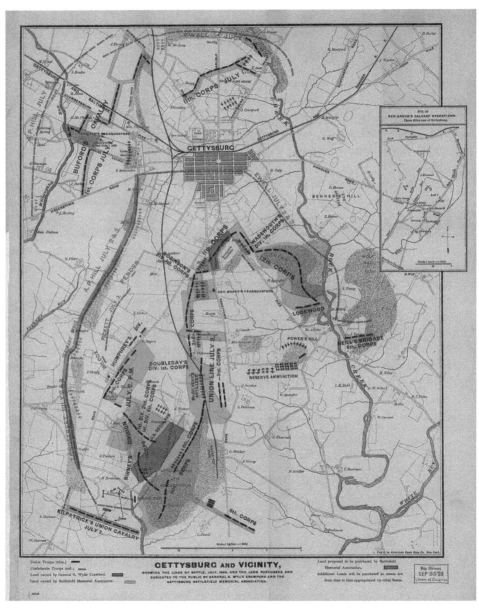

Gettysburg and Vicinity

had three infantry brigades occupied in guarding the left flank of the army. Lee had Jenkins's cavalry relieve them.

Next, Lee came upon an artillery unit he thought belonged to Longstreet's corps but it was actually part of A. P. Hill's. Lee asked, "Do you know where Longstreet is?" Hill's artillery chief, Colonel R. Lindsay Walker, said he knew where he was and would take Lee to him. Walker recalled: "As we rode together, General Lee manifested more impatience than I ever saw him exhibit upon any other occasion."

Just after 11am Lee found Longstreet and gave him orders:

> General Lee informed me that it would not do to have Ewell open the attack. He, finally, determined that I should make the attack on the extreme right. It was fully eleven o'clock when General Lee arrived at this conclusion and ordered the movement. In the meantime, by General Lee's authority, Law's Brigade, which had been put upon picket duty, was ordered to rejoin my command, and, upon my suggestion that it would be better to await its arrival, General Lee assented. We waited about forty minutes for these troops, and then moved forward.[21]
>
> Law had received his orders at three in the morning," recounted Longstreet, "and had marched twenty-three miles. The battle-ground was still five miles off by the route of march, but Law completed his march of twenty-eight miles in eleven hours,-the best marching done in either army to reach the field of Gettysburg."[22]

Alexander was designated to command Longstreet's artillery and sent ahead to the right with the artillery:

> About 11:00 A. M., his (Lee's) orders were issued. Anderson's division of Hill's corps was directed to extend Hill's line upon Seminary Ridge to the right, while Longstreet with Hood's and McLaws's divisions should make a flank march to the right and pass beyond the enemy's flank, which seemed to extend along the Emmitsburg road. Forming at right angles to this road, the attack was to sweep down the enemy's line from their left, being taken up successively by the brigades of Anderson's division as they were reached. Ewell's corps, holding the extreme left, was to attack the enemy's right on hearing Longstreet's guns. Longstreet was directed, in his march, to avoid exposing it to the view of a Federal signal station on Little Round Top Mountain.
>
> Meanwhile, on the arrival of Longstreet's reserve artillery in the vicinity of the field, I had been placed in charge of all the artillery of his corps, and directed to reconnoitre the enemy's left and to move some of the battalions to that part of the field. This had been done by noon, when three battalions, -my own, Cabell's and Henry's-were located in the valley of Willoughby Run awaiting the arrival of the infantry. Riding back presently to learn the cause of their non-arrival, the head of the infantry column was found halted, where its road became exposed to the Federal view, while messages were sent to Longstreet, and the guide sought a new route. The exposed point had been easily avoided by our artillery, by turning out through a meadow, but after some delay there came orders to the infantry to countermarch and take a road via "Black Horse Tavern." This incident delayed the opening of the battle nearly two hours.[23]

Delays

Actually, Longstreet's progress to the right was slowed by a series of interruptions, lags, and countermarching. What should have been a three-mile jaunt turned into a six-mile journey, taking roundabout routes to stay hidden from view. The six miles redoubled again, for the marchers, in some cases, had to retrace their footsteps back to the starting point and begin again; this made Longstreet quite indignant:

> A delay of several hours occurred in the march of the troops. The cause of the delay was that we had been ordered by General Lee to proceed cautiously upon the forward movement, so as to avoid being seen by the enemy. General Lee ordered Colonel Johnston, of his engineer corps, to lead and conduct the head of the column. My troops, therefore, moved forward under guidance of a special officer of General Lee, and with instructions to follow his directions. I left General Lee only after the line had stretched out on the march, and rode along with Hood's Division, which was in the rear. The march was necessarily slow, the conductor frequently encountering points that exposed the troops to the view of the signal station on Round Top. At length the column halted. After waiting some time, supposing that it would soon move forward, I sent to the front to inquire the occasion of the delay. It was reported that the column was awaiting the movements of Colonel Johnston, who was trying to lead it by some route by which it could pursue its march without falling under view of the Federal signal station. Looking up toward Round Top I saw the signal station was in full view, and, as we could plainly see the station, it was apparent that our heavy columns was seen from their position, and further efforts to conceal ourselves would be a waste of time.
>
> I became very impatient at this delay, and determined to take upon myself the responsibility of hurrying the troops forward. I did not order General McLaws forward, because, as the head of the column, he had direct orders from General Lee to follow the conduct of Colonel Johnston. Therefore, I sent orders to Hood, who was in the rear and not encumbered by these instructions, to push his division forward by the most direct route, so as to take position on my right. He did so, and thus broke up the delay. The troops were rapidly thrown into position, and preparations were made for the attack.[24]

Colonel Johnston lacked the competence for the assignments General Lee bestowed upon him and later protested that he "had no idea that I had the confidence of the great General Lee to such an extent that he would entrust me with the conduct of an army corps moving within two miles of the enemy line."[25]

"Much valuable time was lost by this trial," commented Sorrel, "which with better knowledge of the ground by General Lee's engineers would not have been attempted."[26]

Conditions on the right were not as expected from Johnston's intelligence when McLaws and Hood reached their assigned positions around 3:00pm McLaws dismounted at the edge of the woods and surveyed his front: "The view presented astonished me as the enemy was massed in my front, and extended to my right and left as far as the eye could see."

Union General Daniel E. Sickles was to position his Third Corps to the left of Second Corps southward along Cemetery Ridge, with Little Round Top as the anchor for his left flank by Meade's orders. Sickles wanted to post his corps 1,500 yards west of the bordering Emmitsburg Road on a ridge comparatively higher than the lower portion of Cemetery Ridge he was to hold.

Meade's artillery chief, Henry Hunt, who was to help situate Third Corps' guns, suggested Sickles reconnoiter Pitzer's Woods beyond Emmitsburg Road before doing anything, and Hunt would discuss the advance with Meade. Sickles sent the Third

Maine Regiment and Berdan's 1st U.S. Sharpshooters, an elite outfit armed mostly with Sharps rifles, to feel out the enemy. They encountered the Tenth and Eleventh Alabama Regiments of Wilcox's brigade part of Anderson's division and were driven back with severe losses.

Sickles did not want the Peach Orchard ridge taken by the enemy, so he advanced the entire Third Corps to that line at 2:00pm It is interesting to note that R. H. Anderson's division of Hill's corps, the base upon which the First Corps would make its deployment, was not in position until one o'clock, Longstreet's attack could not have launched until after this time at best.

Everything was ready, Longstreet's aide, Major Osmun Latrobe, was sent to McLaws with a directive: "proceed at once to the assault." McLaws informed Latrobe there was more than "a small force of the enemy in front," to which Latrobe made this rejoinder: "There is no one in your front but a regiment of infantry and a battery of artillery."

McLaws asked that Longstreet come forward and take a look. Latrobe rode back to Longstreet only to return with this instruction: "General Lee was with Longstreet and was impatient that the charge was delayed."

As this command was peremptory, McLaws replied he would go forward in five minutes. But shortly, another courier dashed up with new orders from Longstreet that Hood's division would charge first; Lee had altered the sequence of the attack.

Misgivings

General Hood had his own misgivings about the coming attack:

> This movement was accomplished by throwing out an advanced force to tear down fences and clear the way. The instructions I received were to place my division across the Emmitsburg road, form a line of battle, and attack. Before reaching this road, however, I had sent forward some of my picked Texas scouts to ascertain the position of the enemy's extreme left flank. They soon reported to me that it rested upon Round Top Mountain; that the country was open, and that I could march through an open woodland pasture around Round Top, and assault the enemy in flank and rear; that their wagon-trains were parked in rear of their line and were badly exposed to our attack in that direction. As soon as I arrived upon the Emmitsburg road, I placed one or two batteries in position and opened fire. A reply from the enemy's guns soon developed his lines. His left rested on or near Round Top, with line bending back and again forward, forming as it were a concave line, as approached by the Emmitsburg road. A considerable body of troops was posted in front of their main line between the Emmitsburg road and Round Top Mountain. This force was in line of battle upon an eminence near a peach orchard.
>
> Based on information from his scouts, General Hood wanted to turn Round Top and take the enemy in the flank and rear. Hood appealed to Longstreet for a change of plan. Hood continued:
>
> I was in possession of these important facts so shortly after reaching the Emmitsburg road that I considered it my duty to report to you (Longstreet) at once my opinion that it was unwise to attack up the Emmitsburg road as ordered, and to urge that you allow me to turn Round Top and attack the enemy in flank and rear. Accordingly, I dispatched a staff-officer bearing to you my request to be allowed to make the proposed movement on

account of the above-stated reasons. Your reply was quickly received: 'General Lee's orders are to attack up the Emmitsburg road.' I sent another officer to say that I feared nothing could be accomplished by such an attack, and renewed my request to turn Round Top. Again your answer was: 'General Lee's orders are to attack up the Emmitsburg road.' During this interim I had continued the use of the batteries upon the enemy, and had become more and more convinced that the Federal line extended to Round Top, and that I could not reasonably hope to accomplish much by the attack as ordered. In fact, it seemed to me the enemy occupied a position by nature so strong-I may say impregnable-that, independently of their flank fire, they could easily repel our attacks by merely throwing and rolling stones down the mountain-side as we approached.

A third time I despatched one of my staff to explain fully in regard to the situation, and suggested that you had better come and look for yourself. I selected in this instance my adjutant general, Colonel Harry Sellers, whom you know to be not only an officer of great courage, but also of marked ability. Colonel Sellers returned with the same message, "General Lee's orders are to attack up the Emmitsburg road." Almost simultaneously Colonel Fairfax of your staff rode up and repeated the above orders.

After this urgent protest against entering the battle at Gettysburg, according to instructions-which protest is the first and only one I ever made during my entire military career-I ordered my line to advance and make the assault.[27]

By now Lee and Longstreet separated, with Lee returning to his headquarters. However, he had given Longstreet no liberty to exercise discretion as to tactics. In fact, he had hamstrung him to the point of constriction, Longstreet explained the situation:

General Hood was ordered to send his select scouts in advance, to go through the woodlands and act as vedettes, in the absence of cavalry, and give information of the enemy, if there. The double line marched up the slope and deployed, -McLaws on the right of Anderson, Hood's division on his right, McLaws near the crest of the plateau in front of the Peach Orchard, Hood spreading and enveloping Sickle's left. The former was readily adjusted to ground from which to advance or defend. Hood's front was very rugged, with no field for artillery, and very rough for advance of infantry. As soon as he passed the Emmitsburg road, he sent to report of the great advantage of moving on by his right around to the enemy's rear. His scouting parties had reported that there was nothing between them and the enemy's trains. He was told that the move to the right had been proposed the day before and rejected; that General Lee's orders were to guide my left by the Emmitsburg road.

As McLaws's division came up on line, Barksdale's brigade was in front of a battery about six hundred yards off. He appealed for permission to charge and capture it, but was told to wait. On his right was Kershaw's brigade, the brigades of Semmes and Wofford on the second line. Hood's division was in two lines, -Law's and Robertson's brigades in front, G. T. Anderson's and Benning's in the second line. The batteries were with the divisions, -four to the division. One of G. T. Anderson's regiments was put on picket down the Emmitsburg road.

General Hood appealed again and again for the move to the right, but, to give more confidence to his attack, he was reminded that the move to the right had been carefully considered by our chief and rejected in favor of his present orders.

Longstreet clearly assessed the situation, concluding that the initiative had passed to the Confederates. A turning movement around the Union left would have compelled Meade to react and give battle on grounds favorable to Lee's army:

The opportunity for our right was in the air. General Halleck saw it from Washington. General Meade saw and was apprehensive of it. Even General Pendleton refers to it in favorable mention in his official report. Failing to adopt it, General Lee should have gone with us to his right. He had seen and carefully examined the left of his line, and only gave us a guide to show the way to the right, leaving the battle to be adjusted to formidable and difficult grounds without his assistance. If he had been with us, General Hood's messengers could have been referred to general-headquarters, but to delay and send messengers five miles in favor of a move that he had rejected would have been contumacious. The opportunity was with the Confederates from the assembling on Cemetery Hill. It was inviting of their preconceived plans. It was the object of and excuse for the invasion as a substitute for more direct efforts for the relief of Vicksburg. Confederate writers and talkers claim that General Meade could have escaped without making aggressive battle, but that is equivalent to confession of inertia that failed to grasp the opportunity.

Beaten in the battle of the 1st, dislodged of position, and outgeneraled, the Union army would have felt the want of spirit and confidence important to aggressive battle; but the call was in the hands of the Confederates, and these circumstances would have made their work more facile, while the Union commander would have felt the call to save his capital most imperative. Even as events passed it was thought helpful to the Union side to give out the report that General McClellan was at hand and would command the army.

Four of the brigades of Anderson's division were ordered to advance en echelon in support on my left.

At three o'clock the artillery was ordered to open practice. General Meade was then with General Sickles discussing the feasibility of withdrawing his corps to the position to which it was originally assigned, but the opening admonished him that it was too late. He had just sent a cipher telegram to inform General Hallock, commander-in-chief, that in the event of his having no opportunity to attack, and should he find the Confederates moving to interpose between him and Washington, he would fall back on his supplies at Westminster. (Report of Committee, vol. 1, p. 488) But my right division was then nearer to Westminster, and our scouting parties of infantry were within rifle range of the road leading to that point and to Washington. So it would have been convenient, after holding our threatening attitude till night, to march across his line at dark, in time to draw other troops in close connection before the next morning.[28]

General George Gordon Meade, commander of the Union army at Gettysburg, is quoted as saying: "Longstreet's advice was sound military sense; it was a step I most feared Lee would take."

Departing from Lee, Longstreet rode off to McLaws position and when he viewed the situation "was very much disconcerted and annoyed" according to McLaws; being opposed to an offensive battle, Longstreet was testy. He asked McLaws why he had not posted a battery on the road crossing the ridge he had tracked. McLaws replied it would draw counterfire, injuring the infantry nearby. Longstreet ordered the guns brought up, and sure enough they received the attention of the Federal gunners. It was a hard day on McLaws also and his frayed nerves were not helped by Longstreet's attitude; five days later he wrote of Longstreet to his wife: "During the engagement he was really excited giving constantly orders to everyone, and was exceedingly overbearing. I consider him a humbug, a man of small capacity, very obstinate, not at all chivalrous, exceedingly conceited, and totally selfish."

Obeying Lee

After visiting McLaws, Longstreet paid a call on General Hood, near 4 o'clock, who was making last-minute adjustments. Upon seeing the corps commander, Hood asked, for the last time, to strike the enemy flank and rear, to which Longstreet answered: "We must obey the orders of General Lee." Hood was disappointed but had great regard for Longstreet: "Of all the men living, not excepting our incomparable Lee himself, I would rather follow James Longstreet in a forlorn hope or desperate encounter against heavy odds. He was our hardest hitter."

The attack was to launch en echelon by divisions and even brigades within the divisions as instructed by General Lee, starting with Hood on the right, followed by McLaws to his left, and then Anderson; this type of attack wasted valuable time and allowed the enemy to concentrate their fire upon each charging unit.

Alexander opened a barrage against Sickle's exposed line at the Peach Orchard:

> I had hoped, with my 54 guns & close range, to make it short, sharp, & decisive. At close ranges there was less inequality in our guns, & especially in our ammunition, & I thought that if ever I could overwhelm & crush them I would do it now. But they really surprised me, both with the number of guns they developed, & the way they stuck to them. I don't think there was ever in our war a hotter, harder, sharper artillery afternoon than this.[29]

> Thus, about 3:45 P. M., Alexander continues, 36 guns were in action against the Peach Orchard, and the enemy's adjacent lines and 10 guns against the enemy's left. The ranges were generally between 500 and 700 yards. After this cannonade had continued for perhaps 30 minutes, Hood received the order to advance.

> Following the initiative prescribed by Lee, Longstreet, Hood, and McLaws all made progressive attacks. Hood at first advanced only his front line. McLaws was about to advance upon Hood's left very soon after, when Longstreet halted him. He was held back for about an hour, during which Hood's second line was sent in, and both lines suffered severely. Then McLaws advanced both lines of his right wing, Kershaw and Semmes, and, after a further interval of at least 20 minutes (long enough to cause severe loss to Kershaw's exposed left), Barksdale and Wofford followed. There were thus four partial attacks of two brigades each, requiring at least an hour and a half to be gotten into action; where one advance by eight brigades would have won a quicker victory with far less loss.[30]

After Hood's advance Longstreet went over to McLaws's division to coordinate its launch time in sequence:

> I rode to McLaws, found him ready for his opportunity, and Barksdale chafing at his wait for the order to seize the battery in his front. Kershaw's brigade of his right first advanced and struck near the angle of the enemy's line where his forces were gathering strength. After additional caution to hold his ranks closed, McLaws ordered Barksdale in. With glorious bearing he sprang to his work, overriding obstacles and dangers. Without a pause to deliver a shot, he had the battery. Kershaw, joined by Semmes's brigade, responded, and Hood's men, feeling the impulsion of relief, resumed their bold fight, and presently the enemy's line was broken through its length.[31]

General Lee's plan for this action was as follows:

It was determined to make the principal attack upon the enemy's left, and endeavor to gain a position from which it was thought that our artillery could be brought to bear with effect. Longstreet was directed to place the divisions of McLaws and Hood on the right of Hill, partially enveloping the enemy's left, which he was to drive in.

General Hill was ordered to threaten the enemy's center, to prevent re-enforcements being drawn to either wing, and to cooperate with his right division in Longstreet's attack.

General Ewell was instructed to make simultaneous demonstrations upon the enemy's right, to be converted into a real attack should opportunity offer.[32]

However, there was a lack of cooperation and coordination of action by Hill and Ewell in supporting Longstreet's assault; the responsibility for this rests squarely on Lee's shoulders.

Lee did not intervene at all according to Colonel Fremantle:

> As soon as the firing began, General Lee joined Hill just below our tree, looking through his field glass-sometimes talking to Hill and sometimes to Colonel Long of his staff. But generally he sat quite alone on the stump of a tree. What I remarked especially was, that during the whole time the firing continued, he only sent one message and only received one report. It is evidently his system to arrange the plan thoroughly with the three corps commanders, and then leave to them the duty of modifying and carrying it out to the best of their abilities.[33]

The Peach Orchard

The advance of the Federal Third Corps to the Peach Orchard was fortuitous for the Confederates according to Alexander:

> It exchanged strong ground for weak, and gave the Confederates an opportunity not otherwise possible. They would be quite sure to crush the isolated 3d corps. If their attack was properly organized and conducted, it might become possible to rush and carry the Federal main line in the pursuit of the fugitives.[34]

The Best Three Hours' Fighting

This is precisely what happened to the Union position; Longstreet gave this account:

> My corps occupied our right, with Hood on the extreme right, and McLaws next. Hill's Corps was next to mine, in front of the Federal centre, and Ewell was on our extreme left. My corps, with Pickett's Division absent, numbered hardly thirteen thousand men. I realized that the fight was to be a fearful one; but being assured that my flank would be protected by the brigades of Wilcox, Perry, Wright, Posey, and Mahone, moving en echelon, and that Ewell was to co-operate by a direct attack on the enemy's right, and Hill to threaten his centre, and attack if opportunity offered, and thus prevent reinforcements from being launched either against myself or Ewell, it seemed possible that we might possibly dislodge the great army in front of us. At half-past three o'clock the order was given General Hood to advance upon the enemy, and, hurrying to the head of McLaws' Division, I moved with his

line. Then was fairly commenced what I do not hesitate to pronounce the best three hours' fighting ever done by any troops on any battle-field. Directly in front of us, occupying the peach orchard, on a piece of elevated ground that General Lee desired me to take and hold for his artillery, was the Third Corps of the Federals, commanded by General Sickles. My men charged with great spirit and dislodged the Federals from the peach orchard with but little delay, though they fought stubbornly. We were then on the crest of Seminary Ridge. The artillery was brought forward and put into position at the peach orchard. The infantry swept down the slope and soon reached the marshy ground that lay between Seminary and Cemetery Ridges, fighting their way over every foot of ground and against overwhelming odds. At every step we found that reinforcements were pouring into the Federals from every side. Nothing could stop my men, however, and they commenced their heroic charge up the side of Cemetery Ridge. Our attack was to progress in the general direction of the Emmitsburg road, but the Federal troops, as they were forced from point to point, availing themselves of the stone fences and boulders near the mountain as rallying points, so annoyed our right flank that General Hood's Division was obliged to make a partial change of front so as to relieve itself of this galling flank fire. This drew General McLaws a little further to the right than General Lee had anticipated, so that the defensive advantages of the ground enabled the Federals to delay our purposes until they could occupy Little Round Top, which they just then discovered was the key to their position. The force thrown upon this point was so strong as to seize our right, as it were, in a vice.

Longstreet noted the progress of his soldiers:

Still the battle on our main line continued to progress. The situation was a critical one. My corps had been fighting over an hour, having encountered and driven back line after line of the enemy. In front of them was a high and rugged ridge, on its crest the bulk of the Army of the Potomac, numbering six to one, and securely resting behind strong positions. My brave fellows never hesitated, however. Their duty was in front of them and they met it. They charged up the hill in splendid style, sweeping everything before them, dislodging the enemy in the face of a withering fire. When they had fairly started up the second ridge, I discovered that they were suffering terribly from a fire that swept over their right and left flanks. I also found that my left flank was not protected by the brigades that were to move en echelon with it. McLaws' line was consequently spread out to the left to protect its flank, and Hood's line was extended to the right to protect its flank from the sweeping fire of the large bodies of troops that were posted on Round Top. These two movements of extension so drew my forces out, that I found myself attacking Cemetery Hill with a single line of battle against no less than fifty thousand troops.

My two divisions at that time were cut down to eight or nine thousand men, four thousand having been killed or wounded. We felt at every step the heavy stroke of fresh troops-the sturdy regular blow that tells a soldier instantly that he has encountered reserves or reinforcements. We received no support at all, and there was no evidence of co-operation on any side. To urge my men forward under these circumstances would have been madness, and I withdrew them in good order to the peach orchard that we had taken from the Federals early in the afternoon. I may be mentioned here, as illustrative of the dauntless spirit of these men, that when General Humphreys (of Mississippi) was ordered to withdraw his troops from the charge, he thought there was some mistake, and retired to a captured battery, near the swale between the two ridges, where he halted, and, when ordered to retire to the new line a second time, he did so under protest. Our men had no thought of retreat. They broke every line they encountered. When the order to withdraw was given, a courier was sent to General Lee, informing him of the result of the day's work.[35]

When the Federal Third Corps line shattered and stampeded after the salient at Sherify's peach orchard was breached, Colonels Holder and Griffin of the Seventeenth and Eighteenth Regiments urged Brigadier General William Barksdale to reform the ragged line of his brigade. Barksdale retorted: "No. Crowd them–we have them on the run. Move your regiments."[36]

Barksdale was mortally wounded trying to rally his men in the middle of a Union counterattack and died during the night in a Union hospital. Barksdale begged to get into the fray and had pleaded with General Longstreet. When they did go in, Barksdale's 1,400 Mississippians performed one of the grandest charges of the war, breaking up one blue formation after another until he was brought down.

At the opening of his attack, General Hood exhorted his men with a brief speech which ended, "Fix bayonets, my brave Texans, forward and take those heights!" Hood moved to a peach orchard on the grounds of the Bushman farm near the center of his division where he could observe and direct. As fortune would have it, a Yankee shell exploded 20 feet over his head, showering him with spherical case shot, severely wounding him in his left arm—he would lose the use of this arm. The commander of the 1st Texas witnessed the incident: "I saw him sway to and fro in the saddle and then start to fall from his horse, when he was caught by one of his aides." Gone with Hood was the tactical plan he had devised. When Major Harry Sellers told Hood that his final plea for a sweep around the Federal flank and rear was rejected by Longstreet, Hood disclosed to Sellers: "Very well, when we get under fire I will have a digression."[37] What he wanted to do was for the first wave to swing around the enemy's flank and the second wave to move inside. Brigadier Evander Law took command of the division but knew nothing of Hood's design, and the guidance necessary for the "digression" to be implemented was lost by default.

Talking to the Austrian military observer, Longstreet disclosed: "We have not been so successful as we wished," and attributed this to the fact that both of Hood and Barksdale had been put out of action."[38]

Success is a relative term, and in this case the ultimate success would have been to drive Meade's army from the heights. Lee should have added more punch to this assault and been present to react to changing conditions, Alexander made this incisive remark:

> Had Johnson's division been brought back from its isolated position, and had Lee been present to hear the report brought by Hood's scouts, the whole subsequent history of the battle might have been changed.[39]
>
> In allowing Ewell to remain where he was Lee lost the use of one-third of his army; the opportunity to take Culp's Hill had come and gone. Johnson's Division was demolished in repeated assaults against the formidable Union breastworks on Culp's Hill. Had it been with Longstreet it could have been used to take Little Round Top which was the key to the southern end of the Federal position as Culp's Hill was to the northern.

The Comte of Paris made this comment:

> Lee's first error was in giving too excessive a development to his line. He justly abandons the idea of making his principal attack on the left, because Cemetery Hill is too much exposed and too well fortified, while Culp's Hill, too rocky, is inaccessible to artillery; but he should from that moment have confined his efforts on that side to a simple feint, and, instead of extending that wing to the valley of Rock Creek, have rested it on Gettysburg, in order to be able to place the most potent means of action in the hands of Longstreet.[40]

Conspicuously Bad

There was no concert of action along the Confederate line, and Lee and his staff took no action, while Meade was very proactive directing operations.

> There was not during the war, wrote Alexander, a finer example of efficient command than that displayed by Meade on this occasion. He immediately began to bring to the scene reinforcements, both infantry and artillery, from every corps and from every part of the line. As will be seen in the account of the fighting, he had engaged, or in hand on the field, fully 40,000 men by the time that Longstreet's assault was repulsed.
>
> On the other hand, it must be said that the management of the battle on the Confederate side during this afternoon was conspicuously bad. The fighting was superb. But there appears to have been little supervision, and there was entire failure everywhere to conform to the original plan of the battle, as it had been indicated by Lee. Offensive battles are always more difficult to control than defensive, and there were two special difficulties on this occasion. First was the great extent of the Confederate lines–about five miles–and their awkward shape, making inter-communication slow and difficult. Second, was the type or character of the attack ordered; which may be called the echelon, or progressive type, as distinguished from the simultaneous. The latter should be the type for any battle in the afternoon. Battles begun by one command and to be taken up successively by others, are always much prolonged.[41]

Longstreet received no assistance from the other two corps in carrying the heights, allowing Meade to shift his forces to meet Longstreet's two divisions; Longstreet delineated:

> While Meade's lines were growing my men were dropping; we had no others to call to their aid, and the weight against us was too heavy to carry. The extreme left of our lines was only about a mile from us across the enemy's concentric position, which brought us within hearing of that battle, if engaged, and near enough to feel its swell, but nothing was heard or felt but the clear ring of the enemy's fresh metal as he came against us. No other part of our army had engaged! My seventeen thousand against the Army of the Potomac! The sun was down, and with it went down the severe battle. I ordered recall of the troops to the line of Plum Run and Devil's Den, leaving picket lines near the foot of the Round Tops. My loss was about six thousand, Meade's between twelve and fourteen thousand; but his loss in general and field officers was frightful.[42]

A decade later Longstreet wrote a letter to McLaws on the events on July 2: "It was my intention not to press this attack if it was likely to prove the enemy position too strong for my two divisions." However, he did not stop the charge, as his officers and men performed brilliantly in smashing each Yankee line.

What did Generals A. P. Hill and Ewell do to assist Longstreet? Alexander touched upon this:

> Both Hill and Ewell have orders to cooperate with Longstreet's battle, but they were limiting their cooperation to ineffective cannonading of the enemy's intrenchments in their front, while the enemy is stripping these of infantry and marching fresh divisions to concentrate upon Hood and McLaws, and the three brigades of Wilcox, Perry, and Wright, which had supported them.[43]

General Ambrose P. Hill was a bystander in all of the affairs on July 2. Hill left General Anderson to his own devices, only instructing him to keep the brigades of Carnot Posey and William Mahone as a reserve. Posey was eventually committed in a haphazard manner. Ambrose Wright and Posey asked for support but none came. When Cadmus Wilcox sent his adjutant, Captain Walter E. Winn, to find Anderson to get relief, he found Anderson and his staff at his headquarters, several hundred yards "back in the woods", lying about on the ground as though nothing was going on and with Anderson's horse tied to a tree.

After the war an angry Cadmus Wilcox wrote Lee:

> I am quite certain that Gen'l A. never saw a foot of the ground on which his three brigades fought on the 2nd of July. I may be wrong about Gen'l A., but I always believed that he was indifferent to his duties at Gettysburg. Could the division commander have seen with his own eyes, he would have without being asked sent other brigades forward." Even one of the privates in Anderson's division noticed the advance "lacked concert of movement" resulting in "a large sacrifice of life."[44]
>
> After the battle a Georgia reporter inferred that Mahone and Posey did not do their duty to which General Anderson replied in a note that they "were acting under instructions from himself" and "were in strict conformity with his orders" from his "own immediate commander [Hill]." The reporter concluded: "We are permitted to infer from the tenor of Gen. Anderson's card, [the movements were] arrested on orders from their military superiors."[45]

Alexander reiterated this story:

> Soon after this battle a newspaper correspondent, "P. W. A" described Wilcox's charge and his sending in vain to Anderson for reinforcements, and stated that Anderson had Posey's and Mahone's brigades idle, and that the battle was lost for lack of support. Anderson replied, admitting the facts, but stating that he was under orders from Hill to hold two brigades in reserve, and that when Wilcox's call for help was received he was unable to find Hill and refer the matter to him.[46]

Anderson was not at the front to supervise; Hill did even less. Hill was with Lee at Lee's headquarters, so, ultimately, the blame lies with Lee for not ordering Hill to oversee that his corps take a more active role. Longstreet always believed Anderson did not adequately protect his left, letting his brigades go astray. In fact, Wilcox's brigade reached the foot and Wright's brigade gained the crest of Cemetery Ridge driving the enemy down the opposite side but had become detached from McLaws and had gone beyond the supporting brigades and had to retire after being attacked in front and on both flanks.

On Lee's left flank the assaults were not coordinated to assist in a timely manner, Alexander relates:

> It is now time to see how Lee's orders were being interpreted and carried out upon the left. The official reports are a painful record of insufficient comprehension of orders and inefficient attempts at execution, by officers each able to shift the blame of failure upon other shoulders than his own. Between the lines the apparent absence of supervision excites constant wonder. But everywhere that the troops fought their conduct was admirable.
>
> Ewell, as before told, was ordered to attack with Johnson's division when he heard the sound of Longstreet's guns. Ewell says that later his instructions were modified into 'making a diversion,' but Lee's report does not recognize such modification. Ewell interpreted his orders as calling only for a cannonade. It must be admitted that any serious attack by Johnson would have been suicidal. The enemy's lines were of exceptional strength, which is noted in the Federal reports.

Single Position

Ewell's and Hill's artillery were poorly placed, and their cannonade accomplished little. Alexander continues:

> Added to these difficulties was the fact that there was but a single position where the Confederates could plant guns to fire upon this line, and that an inferior one, giving little shelter and exposed to enfilade fire. It was so contracted that with difficulty 14 guns were crowded upon it, within about 1000 yards of the enemy. It might have been foreseen that this battery, exposed to the fire of double its number of guns, would soon be put out of action. That was what happened: its commander, an especially gallant 'Boy Major,' Latimer (under 21 years), being killed. Besides these guns Ewell's diversion embraced six rifles, in rear of Latimer at a range of 2000 yards; and 12 more, on Seminary Ridge to the left of Hill's artillery at a range of over a mile. Hill's artillery comprised 55 guns on Seminary Ridge. So the whole assistance given to Longstreet's attack between 4 P.M. and darkness by the other two corps was confined to an artillery duel by 32 guns of Ewell and 55 of Hill, mostly at extreme ranges. But the value of this duel as assistance to Longstreet was absolutely nothing, for it did not prevent the enemy from withdrawing troops from every corps in his line to repel our assault.
>
> This cannonading was maintained for about two hours, after which it gradually diminished until dark. Meanwhile, about six o'clock, Ewell had sent orders to each of his division commanders to attack the enemy's lines in his front. This involved for Johnson an attack upon Culp's Hill. The division had not been pushed close to the hill in preparation for an assault, although one had been contemplated all day. It now had a full mile to advance and Rock Creek had to be crossed. This could only be done at few places and involved much delay. Only three of Johnson's four brigades moved to attack.
>
> The whole of the 12th corps had been withdrawn from the lines except Greene's brigade {Union}. This brigade was being extended when its advance was met by Steuart, who, got possession only of empty trenches. Johnson's other brigades found the trenches in front of their approach held by Greene's thin line, but in the darkness of the woods, the steep and rocky ground, and the abattis and obstructions in front, Johnson's line was halted at irregular distances, and the attack resolved itself into a random and ineffective musketry fire. Nothing more was possible. And even had they found more trenches vacant and occupied them, Meade could at will concentrate ample force to drive them out. The more one studies the situation, the more strange it seems that Lee abandoned his first purpose to withdraw Johnson from his false position.

Early's Attack

Alexander pointed out Ewell's failure to adequately support Longstreet's assault in a timely manner; Hill did even less:

> Early's attack is next to be described. It, too, was isolated, inadequate, and unsupported. It necessarily failed. Both attacks were in progress at the same time, but Longstreet's, which they were intended to support, had already ceased. Like Johnson's division, Early was also short one brigade, Smith's having been sent to guard the rear from the direction of York. Gordon also was not engaged, as Early soon realized that the attack was an isolated one and would be quickly repulsed.

E. Porter Alexander gave this detailed account of missed opportunities the Confederates overlooked and the sequence of battle which lacked organized and coordinated support for Longstreet's attack on the second day:

> It only remains to show why Rodes failed to cooperate with Early and Johnson as Ewell had ordered. The fault was with Ewell himself. We have already seen that he had allowed Johnson's division to remain all day so far from the position which he was to attack that, when ordered to advance, darkness fell upon him before he could reach it. Similarly, Ewell had allowed both of his other divisions to locate themselves far out of reach of the places where they were likely to be needed. Of his own motion, however, Early had advanced half of his division at dawn to the Federal skirmish line, and these two brigades were ready to advance when ordered.
>
> Rodes had remained about the northwestern edge of the town, near where the fighting of the first day had ended, and was still there when orders came to attack. He was already preparing to advance, having seen both infantry and artillery withdrawn by the enemy from his front to resist Longstreet's pressure upon their left. But his location was so unfortunate that, in spite of this warning, both Johnson's and Early's attacks were begun and finished before Rodes had reached the enemy's skirmish line.

Rodes's Report

Finding then his opportunity gone, Rodes wisely desisted. But as Lee and his staff during the morning had visited Ewell's lines, it is strange that such faulty locations escaped notice and correction. Rodes's report not only shows the badness of his original position, but tells of an excellent one for the attack which, so far, had entirely escaped recognition of any Confederate reconnoitering officer. His report says:

> Orders given during the afternoon, and after the engagement had opened on the right, required me to co-operate with the attacking force as soon as any opportunity of doing so with good effect was ordered. Seeing the stir alluded to, I thought that opportunity had come, and immediately sought General Early, with a view of making an attack in concert with him. He agreed with me as to the propriety of attacking, and made preparations accordingly. I hastened to inform the officer commanding the troops on my right (part of Pender's division) that, in accordance with our plan, I would attack just at dark, and proceeded to make my arrangements; but having to draw my troops out of town by the flank, change the direction of the line of battle, and then to traverse a distance of 1,200 or 1,400 yards, while General Early had to move only half that distance without change of front, the result was that, before I drove the enemy skirmishers in, General Early had attacked and had been compelled to withdraw.

After driving in the enemy's skirmishers, the advance line was halted by General Ramseur, who commanded the right brigade, to enable him to report to me certain important facts (for statement of which I refer to his report) he had discovered as to the nature of the ground and of the defenses. These facts, together with Early's withdrawal, of which I had been officially informed, and the increased darkness, convinced me that it would be a useless sacrifice of life to go on, and a recall was ordered. But instead of falling back to the original line, I caused the front line to assume a strong position in the plain to the right of the town, along the hollow of an old roadbed. This position was much nearer the enemy, was clear of the town, and was one from which I could readily attack without confusion.

E. Porter Alexander was convinced that the weakest point in the Federal defensive arrangement was the portion of Cemetery Hill on the Federal right flank and offered the best chance for a successful onslaught:

Rodes's description of his new position is of special interest. Taken in connection with his statement of the distance to be traversed by Early's charge, it shows the existence of far more favorable ground for an attack upon Cemetery Hill than is to be found elsewhere upon the Federal line of battle from Culp's Hill to Little Round Top. It was open to our occupation from the afternoon of the first day, when Ewell stopped the pursuit, and it must ever remain a grave reflection upon the Confederate conduct of the battle that the weakest part of the Federal position was the only portion which was not attacked.[47]

Longstreet was bewildered that no help was forthcoming:

It may be imagined that I was astonished at the fact, that we received no support after we had driven the Federals from the peach orchard and one thousand yards beyond. If General Ewell had engaged the army in his front at that time (say four o'clock) he would have prevented their massing their whole army in my front, and while he and I kept the two wings engaged, Hill would have found their centre weak, and should have threatened it while I broke through their left and dislodged them. Having failed to move at four o'clock, while the enemy was in his front, it was still more surprising that he did not advance at five o'clock with vigor and promptness, when the trenches in front of him were vacated, or rather held by a single brigade (as General Meade's testimony before the Committee on the Conduct of the War states). Had he taken these trenches and scattered the brigade that held them, he would have found himself in the Federal's flank and rear. His attack in the rear must have dislodged the Federals, as it would have been totally unexpected-it being believed that he was in front with me. Hill, charging upon the centre at the same time, would have increased their disorder and we would have won the field. But Ewell did not advance until I had withdrawn my troops, and the First Corps, after winning position after position, was forced to withdraw from the field with two corps of their comrades within sight and resting upon their arms. Ewell did not move until about dusk (according to his own report). He then occupied the trenches that the enemy had vacated (see General Meade's report). The real cause of Ewell's non-compliance with General Lee's orders was that he had broken his line of battle by sending two brigades off on some duty up the York Road. General Early says that my failure to attack at sunrise was the cause of Ewell's line being broken at the time I did attack. This is not only absurd, but impossible. After sunrise that morning, Colonel Venable and General Lee were at Ewell's headquarters discussing the policy of opening the attack with Ewell's Corps. They left Ewell with this definite order: that he was to hold himself in readiness to support my attack when it was made. It is silly to say that he was ready at sunrise, when he was not ready at four o'clock when the attack was really made. His orders were to hold himself in readiness to co-operate with my attack when it was made. In breaking his line of battle he rendered himself unable to support me when he would have been potential.[48]

In contrast to Hill and Ewell, Longstreet was very involved at the front. Fremantle jotted in his diary:

At 5:45 all became comparatively quiet on our left and in the cemetery; but volleys of musketry on the right told us that Longstreet's infantry were advancing, and the onward progress of the smoke showed he was progressing favorably. About 6:30 there seemed to be a check, and even a slight retrograde movement. Soon after 7, General Lee got a report by signal from Longstreet to say 'We are doing well.'

A little before dark the firing dropped off in every direction, and soon ceased altogether. We then received intelligence that Longstreet had carried everything before him for some time, capturing several batteries, and driving the enemy from his positions; but when Hill's Florida brigade and some other troops gave way, he was forced to abandon a small portion of the ground he had won, together with all the captured guns, except three. His troops, however, bivouacked during the night on ground occupied by the enemy this morning.[49]

The fighting of July 2 was over. Of the three corps commanders, only A. P. Hill reported in person to Lee's headquarters; Longstreet and Ewell sent staff officers with their reports. Hearing the voice of A. P. Hill, Lee emerged from his tent, made his way through a group of officers, walked over to Hill, grasped him by the hand and said: "It is all well, General. Everything is well." But was everything really "all well"? General Lee told the Prussian observer, Major Justus Scheibert of the Prussian Royal Engineers, he made his plans as perfect as possible and brought his troops to the battlefield: "The rest must be done by my generals and their troops, trusting to Providence for the victory."[50]

God Helps Those

There is a saying: "God helps those who help themselves." Lee and his staff did nothing that summer day of July 2 to help themselves to bring about that victory. In an astonishing statement, Colonel Taylor of Lee's staff said: "The whole affair was disjointed. There was an utter absence of accord in the movements of the several commands, and no decisive results attended the operations of the second day."[51]

This from a man whose chief responsibility it was to see that the affair was synchronized; had this been done, Meade might have been pushed off Cemetery Hill. Ultimately, the responsibility rests with Lee.

Once Lee had determined that his main attack was on the right by Longstreet, he should have shifted as many troops to Longstreet as possible to provide the power to gain victory; he should have pulled in his left and made only a demonstration there. Longstreet should have had authority over all attacking troops; Hill should not have influenced Anderson as to what units would be attacking. There is no question the attack was underpowered and much blood was spilled, with no chance of a victorious result.

Though Longstreet believed that had the attack been delayed longer, it might have been beneficial to the Confederates:

> The Virginia writers have been so eager in their search for a flaw in the conduct of the battle of the First Corps that they overlook the only point into which they could have thrust their pens.
>
> At the opening of the fight, General Meade was with General Sickles discussing the feasibility of moving the Third Corps back to the line originally assigned for it, but the discussion was cut short by the opening of the Confederate battle. If that opening had been delayed thirty or forty minutes the corps would have been drawn back to the general line, and my first deployment would have enveloped Little Round Top and carried it before it could have been strongly manned, and General Meade would have drawn off to his line selected behind Pipe Creek. The point should have been that the battle was opened too soon.[52]

On July 2, 1863, a couple of new factors came into play for the Confederate forces. Pickett's division was up after being relieved of guard duty at Chambersburg by cavalry, and Stuart's cavalry was finally reunited with the army. Lee raised his arm and, with irritation, exchanged these few words when Stuart reached him: "General Stuart, where have you been? For three days not one word from you!"

Rumors were flying as to what would be the plan for the next day:

> "During the evening I found my way to Gen. Longstreet's bivouac, a little ways in the rear," Alexander asserted, "to ask the news from other quarters & orders for the morning. From elsewhere the news was indefinite, but I was told that we would renew the attack early in the morning. That Pickett's division would arrive and would assault the enemy's line. My impression is the exact point for it was not designated, but I was told it would be to our left of the Peach Orchard. And I was told too to select a place for the Washington Artillery which would come to me at dawn."[53]

Lee instructed that General Stuart's command be placed "on the left wing of the Army of Northern Virginia." According to Stuart's adjutant general, Major Henry B. McClellan:

> Stuart's object was to gain position where he could protect the left of Ewell's corps, and would also be able to observe the enemy's rear and attack it in case the Confederate assault on the Federal lines [was] successful. He proposed, if the opportunity offered, to make a diversion which might aid the Confederate infantry to carry the heights held by the Federal army.[54]

CHAPTER 7

"We Gained Nothing But Glory"

Gettysburg, Day Three

In his report, General Lee made an assessment of the day's fighting and his plan for July 3:

> The result of this day's operations induced the belief that, with proper concert of action, and with increased support that the positions gained on the right would enable the artillery to render the assaulting columns, we would ultimately succeed, and it was accordingly determined to continue the attack. The general plan was unchanged. Longstreet, re-enforced by Pickett's three brigades, which arrived near the battlefield during the afternoon of the 2d, was ordered to attack the next morning, and General Ewell was directed to assail the enemy's right at the same time. The latter, during the night, re-enforced General Johnson with two brigades from Rodes' and one from Early's division.[1]

Lee came to his decision without consulting a single one of his corps commanders, while Meade held a conference with his generals where it was decided to stay and await Lee's attack. One incident influenced Meade's decision to stay at Gettysburg: "In this connection," Alexander narrates,

> I pause in my narrative a moment to refer to a story which occasionally crops up in print. It is that during the night of July 2nd Gen. Meade was determined to retreat. This is said to have been testified by his chief of staff, Gen. Butterfield, before the Committee on [the] Conduct of the War. There is also evidence of the existence of a report in the Federal army that a force under Beauregard was approaching to re-inforce Gen. Lee. And it is a fact that some weeks before Gen. Lee had written three letters to Prest. Davis, begging that Gen. Beauregard should be sent up in person to Culpeper, with even any few old troops which might be scared up out of jails or hospitals just as a source to start rumors from, for he appreciated the absurd insanity of fear felt for the safety of Washington City. Now Mr. Davis does not seem to have realized the value of this suggestion, for it was surely worth, at least, having Beauregard give a few days to it. And Mr. Davis wrote at last a letter to Gen. Lee saying that it was impracticable to get any force under Beauregard. And in his office the immense blunder was made of sending that letter by a courier & not putting it in cipher. The courier was captured on July 2, in Greencastle, by Capt. Ulric Dahlgren, who appreciated the importance of this letter, & hurried to Gettysburg with it, reaching there toward midnight & delivering the letter to Meade.
>
> Of all that there is no doubt. And Dahlgren was soon after jumped three ranks to the rank of a colonel, & he is said to have told his friends that his promotion was for capturing a letter & delivering it to Gen. Meade in time to prevent him from retreating from Gettysburg.

However this may be it is instructive to note how careless it is to send valuable information around without putting it in cipher.[2]

Longstreet's command was busy during the night trying to find a key to unlock the Federal position:

As his [Lee's] head-quarters were about four miles from the command, I did not ride over, but sent, to report the work of the second day. In the absence of orders, I had scouting parties out during the night in search of a way by which we might strike the enemy's left, and push it down towards his centre. I found a way that gave some promise of results, and was about to move the command, when he rode over after sunrise and gave his orders. His plan was to assault the enemy's left centre by a column to be composed of McLaws's and Hood's divisions reinforced by Pickett's brigades. I thought that it would not do; that the point had been fully tested the day before, by more men, when all were fresh; that the enemy was there looking for us, as we heard him during the night putting up his defences; that the divisions of McLaws and Hood were holding a mile along the right of my line against twenty thousand men, who would follow their withdrawal, strike the flank of the assaulting column, crush it, and get on our rear towards the Potomac River; that thirty thousand men was the minimum of force necessary for the work; that even such force would need close co-operation on other parts of the line; that the column as he proposed to organize it would have only about thirteen thousand men (the divisions having lost a third of their number the day before); that the column would have to march a mile under concentrating battery fire, and a thousand yards under long-range musketry; that the conditions were different from those in the days of Napoleon when field batteries had a range of six hundred yards and musketry about sixty yards.

He said the distance was not more than fourteen hundred yards. General Meade's estimate was a mile or a mile and a half (Captain Long, the guide of the field of Gettysburg in 1888, stated that it was a trifle over a mile). He then concluded that the divisions of McLaws and Hood could remain on the defensive line; that he would reinforce by the divisions of the Third Corps and Pickett's brigades, and stated the point to which the march should be directed. I asked the strength of the column. He stated fifteen thousand.[3]

He replied, pointing his fist at Cemetery Hill: "The enemy is there, and I am going to strike him." I felt then that it was my duty to express my convictions; I said: "General, I have been a soldier all of my life. I have been with soldiers engaged in fights by couples, by squads, companies, regiments, divisions and armies, and should know, as well as any one, what soldiers can do. It is my opinion that no fifteen thousand men ever arrayed for battle can take that position," pointing to Cemetery Hill. General Lee, in reply to this, ordered me to prepare Pickett's Division for the attack. I should not have been so urgent had I not foreseen the hopelessness of the proposed assault. I felt that I must say a word against the sacrifice of my men; and then I felt that my record was such that General Lee would or could not misconstrue my motives. I said no more, however, but turned away. The most of the morning was consumed in waiting for Pickett's men, and getting into position. The plan of the assault was as follows: Our artillery was to be massed in a wood from which Pickett was to charge, and it was to pour a continuous fire upon the cemetery. Under cover of this fire, and supported by it, Pickett was to charge.[4]

Longstreet's testimony is affirmed by Lee's official report:

General Longstreet's dispositions were not completed as early as expected, but before notice could be sent to General Ewell, General Johnson had already become engaged, and it was too late to recall him. The enemy attempted to recover the works taken the previous evening, but was repulsed, and General Johnson attacked in turn.

After a gallant and prolonged struggle, in which the enemy was forced to abandon part of his intrenchments, General Johnson found himself unable to carry the strongly fortified crest of the hill. The projected attack on the enemy's left not having been made, he was enabled to hold his right with a force largely superior to that of General Johnson, and finally to threaten his flank and rear, rendering it necessary for him to retire to his original position about 1 p.m.

General Longstreet was delayed by a force occupying the high, rocky hills on the enemy's extreme left, from which his troops could be attacked in reverse as they advanced. His operations had been embarrassed the day previous by the same cause, and he now deemed it necessary to defend his flank and rear with the divisions of Hood and McLaws. He was, therefore, re-enforced by Heth's division and two brigades of Pender's to the command of which Major-General Trimble was assigned. General Hill was directed to hold his line with the rest of his command, afford General Longstreet further assistance, if required, and avail himself of any success that might be gained.

A careful examination was made of the ground, secured by Longstreet, and his batteries placed in positions, which, it was believed, would enable them to silence those of the enemy. Hill's artillery and part of Ewell's was ordered to open simultaneously, and the assaulting column to advance under cover of the combined fire of the three. The batteries were directed to be pushed forward as the infantry progressed, protect their flanks, and support their attacks closely.[5]

What Lee was thinking in ordering a column to strike at Cemetery Ridge, moving across a mile-wide field without any soft cover whatsoever is a matter of conjecture; this type of warfare suggested, to Longstreet, battles reminiscent of Napoleon which could no longer be fought in this fashion with the advent of the rifled musket and cannon, with their greater range and accuracy. In fact, the new weaponry greatly enhanced the defensive, causing the attackers to suffer greater casualties which is why Longstreet strove to force Meade to attack. By 1863 the great bulk of the Army of the Potomac was armed exclusively with rifled muskets, as was most of the Army of Northern Virginia. Alexander stated: "The Confederate infantry by this time were about nine-tenths armed with the rifled musket, muzzle loading, mostly of caliber .58, but some of caliber .54."[6] In appointing Porter Alexander to head the artillery arm of the First Corps, Longstreet made a wise choice: "Our artillery was in charge of General E. P. Alexander, a brave and gifted officer. Colonel Walton was my chief of artillery; but Alexander, being at the head of the column, and being first in position, and being, beside, an officer of unusual promptness, sagacity, and intelligence, was given charge of the artillery."[7] Longstreet made this observation: "The artillery appointments were so superior that our officers sometimes felt humiliated when posted to unequal combat with their better metal and munitions. In small arms also the Union troops had the most improved styles."[8]

Some historians claim that Longstreet received orders during the night of July 2 that he was to attack with Pickett's division early in the morning of July 3; Colonel Taylor, Lee's adjutant general, claims Longstreet was ordered to attack with the divisions of Hood and McLaws in support of Pickett. Longstreet vehemently denied these allegations; Alexander, who surely would have heard of these orders as head of the First Corps artillery, wrote in his memoirs, disputing the first allegation: "He

[Johnson] had been ordered by Ewell to attack at daylight, under the impression that Longstreet would attack at the same hour. In fact, however, Longstreet received no orders during the night, and the troops required for his attack could not be gotten into their positions before noon."[9]

All this is corroborated and clarified by Colonel Armistead L. Long's synopsis of events on the morning of July 3:

> The dawn of the 3d of July found the two armies in the position in which the battle of the preceding day had ended. Though Cemetery Ridge remained intact in the hands of the Federals, yet the engagement had resulted at every point on an advantage to the Confederates. Longstreet had cleared his front of the enemy, and occupied the ground from which they had been driven. Ewell's left held the breastworks on Culp's Hill on the extreme right of the Federal line. Meade's army was known to have sustained heavy losses. There was, in consequence, good reason to believe that a renewed assault might prove successful. Ewell's position of advantage, if held, would enable him to take the Federal line in reverse, while an advance in force from Longstreet's position offered excellent promise of success. General Lee therefore determined to renew the assault.
>
> Longstreet, in accordance with this decision, was reinforced, and ordered to assail the heights in front on the morning of the 3d, while Ewell was directed to make a simultaneous assault on the enemy's right. Longstreet's dispositions, however, were not completed as early as those of Ewell, and the battle opened on the left before the columns on the right were ready to move. Johnson, whose men had held the captured breastworks, had been considerably reinforced during the night, and was on the point of resuming the attack when the Federals opened on him at four o'clock with a heavy fire of artillery which had been placed in position under cover of darkness. An infantry assault in force followed, and, though Ewell's men held their ground with their usual stubbornness, and maintained their position for four hours, they were finally forced to yield the captured breastworks and retire before the superior force of the enemy.
>
> This change in the condition of affairs rendered necessary a reconsideration of the military problem, and induced General Lee, after making a reconnaissance of the enemy's position, to change his plan of assault. Cemetery Ridge, from Round Top to Culp's Hill, was at every point strongly occupied by Federal infantry and artillery, and was evidently a very formidable position. There was, however, a weak point upon which an attack could be made with a reasonable prospect of success. This was where the ridge, sloping westward formed the depression through which the Emmettsburg road passes. Perceiving that by forcing the Federal lines at that point and turning toward Cemetery Hill the right would be taken in flank and the remainder would be neutralized, as its fire would be as destructive to friend as foe, and considering that the losses of the Federal army in the two preceding days must weaken its cohesion and consequently diminish its power of resistance. General Lee determined to attack at that point, and the execution of it was assigned to Longstreet, while instructions were given to Hill and Ewell to support him, and a hundred and forty-five guns were massed to cover the advance of the attacking column.
>
> The decision here indicated was reached at a conference held during the morning on the field in front of and within cannon-range of Round Top, there being present Generals Lee, Longstreet, A. P. Hill and H. Heth, Colonel A. P. Long, and Major C. S. Venable. The plan of attack was discussed, and it was decided that General Pickett should lead the assaulting column, to be supported by the divisions of McLaws and Hood and such other forces as A. P. Hill could spare from his command. The only objection offered was by General Longstreet, who remarked that the guns on Round Top might be brought to bear on his right. This objection was answered by Colonel Long, who had said that the guns on Round Top could be suppressed

by our batteries. This point being settled, the attack was ordered, and General Longstreet was directed to carry it out.

Pickett's division was fresh, having taken no part in the previous day's fight, and to these veterans was given the post of honor in the coming affray, which promised to be a desperate and terrible one.[10]

Longstreet had this interpretation of events on the morning of July 3, in his report:

On the following morning our arrangements were made for renewing the attack by my right, with a view to pass around the hill occupied by the enemy on his left, and gain it by flank and reverse attack. This would have been a slow process, probably, but not very difficult. A few moments after my orders for the execution of this plan were given, the commanding general joined me, and ordered a column of attack to be formed of Pickett's, Heth's and part of Pender's divisions, the assault to be made directly at the enemy's main position, the Cemetery Hill. The distance to be passed over under the fire of the enemy's batteries, and in plain view, seemed too great to insure great results, particularly as two-thirds of the troops to be engaged had been in a severe battle two days previous, Pickett's division alone being fresh.[11]

Long's account substantiates that, indeed, Longstreet did receive his orders for Pickett's charge on the morning of the July 3. If there was an order on Thursday night, he never received it; apparently Ewell did receive his the night of July 2. For his part, Pickett arrived late in the afternoon of July 2 within three miles of the battlefield, sent Major Walter Harrison to report to General Lee and went personally to report to General Longstreet where the two spent some time watching the fighting; Longstreet told him to bivouac his troops. Major Harrison came from General Lee, delivering this message to Pickett in Longstreet's presence: "Tell General Pickett I shall not want him this evening, to let his men rest, and I will send him word when I want him." This is the only message sent to him by Lee and if Lee had wanted him to attack early in the morning, surely he would have sent another, as Pickett's division was the only available reinforcements for Longstreet. Initially it was Lee's intention to use Hood's and McLaws's divisions with Pickett but he changed his mind–as indicated in his official report quoted above–when Longstreet demurred, pointing out that the enemy on the Round Tops would crush his assault in flank and rear and cut off Lee's line of retreat. Lee agreed and changed the composition of the assaulting column to include Hill's men and left Hood and McLaws in place. It is possible Colonel Taylor only heard or was told only a portion of the conversation between Lee and Longstreet; certainly, Colonel Long did not hear the whole conversation, because he was unaware that Longstreet objected to using Hood and McLaws in the assault; apparently the aides were not privy to the entire discussion and their recollections were fragmentary and incomplete.

It is interesting to ascertain the great reliance General Lee and Colonel Long placed on the artillery arm of the army to incapacitate the enemy's guns. Alexander was confounded by this:

It seems remarkable that the assumption of Col. Long so easily passed unchallenged that Confederate guns in open and inferior positions could "suppress" Federal artillery fortified upon commanding ridges. Our artillery equipment was usually admitted to be inferior to the enemy's in numbers, calibres, and quality of ammunition.[12]

Long's account of events on July 3 is corroborated by Alexander:

Early in the morning General Lee came around, and I was told that we were to assault Cemetery Hill, which lay rather to our left. This necessitated a good many changes of our positions, which the enemy did not altogether approve of, and they took occasional shots at us, though we shifted about, inoffensively as possible, and carefully avoided getting into bunches. But we stood it all meekly, and by 10 o'clock, Dearing having come up, we had seventy-five guns in what was virtually one battery, so disposed as to fire on Cemetery Hill and the batteries south of it, which would have a fire on our advancing infantry. Pickett's division had arrived, and his men were resting and eating.[13]

Once Longstreet received his orders, he studied the field and briefed Gen. Pickett as to what was expected of his division:

Pickett was put in position and received directions for the line of his advance as indicated by General Lee. The divisions of the Third Corps were arranged along his left with orders to take up the line of march, as Pickett passed before them, in short echelon. We were to open with our batteries, and Pickett was to move out as soon as we silenced the Federal batteries. The artillery combat was to begin with the rapid discharge of two field-pieces as our signal. As soon as the orders were communicated along the line, I sent Colonel E. P. Alexander (who was commanding a battalion of artillery and who had been an engineer officer) to select carefully a point from which he could observe the effect of our batteries. When he could discover the enemy's batteries silenced or crippled, he should give notice to General Pickett, who was ordered, upon receipt of that notice, to move forward to the attack. When I took Pickett to the crest of Seminary Ridge and explained where his troops should be sheltered, and pointed out the direction General Lee wished to take and the point of the Federal line where the assault was to be made, he seemed to appreciate the severity of the contest upon which he was about to enter, but was quite hopeful of success. Upon receipt of notice, he was to march over the crest of the hill down the gentle slope and up the rise opposite the Federal stronghold. The distance was about fourteen hundred yards, and for most of the way the Federal batteries would have a raking fire from Round Top, while the sharpshooters, artillery, and infantry would subject the assaulting column to a terrible and destructive fire. With my knowledge of the situation, I could see the desperate and hopeless nature of the charge and the cruel slaughter it would cause. My heart was heavy when I left Pickett. I rode once or twice along the ground between Pickett and the Federals, examining the positions and studying the matter over in all its phases as far as we could anticipate.[14]

General Longstreet did what he could to maximize the chance of success: "Division commanders were asked to go to the crest of the ridge and take a careful view of the field, and to have their officers there to tell their men of it, and to prepare them for the sight that was to burst upon them as they mounted the crest."[15]

There is no question that General Lee knew and approved the composition of the attacking column, as he inspected every portion of it with General Longstreet:

After our troops were all arranged for assault, General Lee rode with me twice over the lines to see that everything was arranged according to his wishes. He was told that we had been more particular in giving the orders than ever before; that the commanders had been sent for, and the point of attack had been carefully designated, and that the commanders had been directed to communicate to their subordinates, and through them to every soldier in the command, the work that was before them, so that they should nerve themselves for the attack, and fully understand it. After leaving me, he again rode over the field once, if not twice, so that there was really no room for misconstruction or misunderstanding of his wishes.[16]

Alexander positioned the artillery of the First Corps and notified Longstreet around 11:00am that it was completed:

The Reserve Artillery of Longstreet's corps, in the Gettysburg campaign, consisted of the Washington Artillery of New Orleans, then under Major Eshleman, nine guns, and my own battalion of twenty-six guns. Besides these, the artillery of the corps comprised Cabell's, Henert's and Dearing's battalions of eighteen guns each. The latter battalions were usually attached, on the march, respectively to McLaws's, Hood's, and Pickett's divisions of infantry."[17]

Preparations were complete and Longstreet was informed by William Owen of the Washington Artillery what the signal was:

The signal agreed upon was two guns fired in quick succession by the Washington Artillery, at the peach-orchard. The commanders of all the batteries and battalions of artillery in position were notified, and information of the fact communicated by me to Gen. Longstreet, who was standing with Gen. Pickett in front of the latter's division, which was lying down concealed by the woods from the enemy's view. Gen. Longstreet said, "All right, tell Col. Walton I will send him word when to begin."

Returning to the position of the Washington Artillery we all quietly awaited the order to open the ball. At 1:30 P.M. a courier dashed up in great haste, holding a little slip of paper, torn evidently from a memorandum-book, on which, written in pencil and addressed to Colonel Walton, as we were sitting on our horses in a grove of oaks on the Emmitsburg pike, opposite the peach-orchard, was the following:

"Headquarters, July 3d, 1863. Colonel: Let the batteries open. Order great care and precision in firing. If the batteries at the Peach Orchard cannot be used against the point we intend attacking, let them open on the enemy on the rocky hill.

Most respectfully,

J. Longstreet, Lieutenant-General Commanding."

The order to fire the signal-gun was immediately communicated to Major Eshleman, commanding the Washington Artillery, and the report of the first gun rang out upon the still summer air. There was a moment's delay with the second gun, a friction-primer having failed to explode. It was but a little space of time, but a hundred thousand men were listening. Finally, a puff of smoke was seen at the Peach Orchard, then came a roar and a flash, and 138 pieces of Confederate artillery opened upon the enemy's position, who replied with 80 guns more and the deadly work began with the noise of the heaviest thunder.[18]

With everything in readiness "Old Pete" sent the above note to commence the cannonade: "When satisfied that the work of preparation was all that it could be with the means at hand, I wrote Colonel Walton. At the same time a note to Alexander directed that Pickett should not be called until the artillery practice indicated fair opportunity. Then I rode to a woodland hard by, to lie down and study for some new thoughts that might aid the assaulting column."[19]

The note alarmed Alexander:

> Meanwhile, some half-hour or more before the cannonade began, I was startled by the receipt of a note from Longstreet as follows:-"Colonel: If the artillery fire does not have the effect to drive off the enemy or greatly demoralize him, so as to make our effort pretty certain, I would prefer that you should not advise Pickett to make the charge. I shall rely a great deal upon your judgment to determine the matter, and shall expect you to let Gen. Pickett know when the moment offers."
>
> Until that moment, though I fully recognized the strength of the enemy's position, I had not doubted that we could carry it, in my confidence that Lee was ordering it. But here was a proposition that I should decide the question. Overwhelming reasons against the assault at once seemed to stare me in the face. Gen. Wright of Anderson's division was standing with me. I showed him the letter and expressed my views. He advised me to write them to Longstreet, which I did as follows:
>
> "General: I will only be able to judge of the effect of our fire on the enemy by his return fire, as his infantry is little exposed to view and the smoke will obscure the field. If, as I infer from your note, there is any alternative to this attack, it should be carefully considered before opening our fire, for it will take all the artillery ammunition we have left to test this one, and if the result is unfavorable we will have none left for another effort. And even if this is entirely successful, it can only be so at a very bloody cost."
>
> To this note, Longstreet soon replied as follows:
>
> "Colonel: The intention is to advance the infantry if the artillery has the desired effect of driving the enemy's off, or having other effect such as to warrant us in making the attack. When that moment arrives advise Gen. Pickett and of course advance such artillery as you can use in aiding the attack."[20]
>
> Gen. Wright read this & said, "He has put the responsibility back upon you."
>
> Now, I had already decided in my own mind that I could see nothing during the cannonade upon which any safe opinion could be founded; & that the question, whether or not that attack was to be made, must be decided before the cannonade opened. I had tried to avoid the responsibility of the decision, but in vain. Gen. Lee had originally planned it, & half the day had been spent in preparation. I determined to cause no loss of time by any indecision on my part. As to the question of supports, that I supposed would be the one to which Gen, Lee himself would have given his own special attention-far more than to any particular features of the ground. And I heard a sort of camp rumor, that morning, that Gen. Lee had said he intended to march every man he had upon that cemetery hill that day.
>
> But before deciding absolutely, I rode back for a little interview with Pickett himself. I did not tell him my object, but just felt his pulse, as it were, about the assault. He was in excellent spirits & sanguine of success. Then I determined to let Gen. Longstreet know I intended to put Pickett in. I wrote him just these words: "General. When our artillery fire is at its best I shall order Gen. Pickett to charge."[21]

With the onus of approving the charge placed on his shoulders by General Longstreet, Alexander started to have doubts about the feasibility of launching such an enterprise.

He did not believe the barrage would be effective in suppressing the Federal guns and ammunition was in short supply. The advance would be three-fourths of a mile over open ground at the center of the Federal line, where the troops would be subjected to continuous fire from the jump-off point by the highly accurate long-range artillery and rifles, plus enfilade fire from the Round Tops. He now saw it as a pointless bloodbath, squandering the lives of the soldiers; one has to wonder what General Lee was thinking in ordering this charge.

Evidently the cannonade was to be allowed to begin. Then the responsibility would be upon me to decide whether or not Pickett should charge. If not, we must return to Va. to replenish ammunition, and the campaign would be a failure. I knew that our guns could not drive off the enemy, but I had a vague hope that with Ewell's and Hill's cooperation something might happen, though I knew little either of their positions, their opportunities, or their orders.

It must have been with bitter disappointment that Longstreet saw the failure of his hope to avert a useless slaughter, for he was fully convinced of its hopelessness. Yet even he could have scarcely realized, until the event showed, how entirely unprepared were Hill and Ewell to render aid to his assault and to take prompt advantage of even temporary success. None of their guns were posted with a view to cooperative fire, nor to follow the charge, and much of their ammunition had been prematurely wasted. [A little before noon there sprung up upon our left a violent cannonade which was prolonged for fully a half-hour, and has often been supposed to be a part of that ordered to precede Pickett's charge. It began between skirmishers in front of Hill's corps over the occupation of a house. Hill's artillery first took part in it, it was said, by his order. It was most unwise, as it consumed uselessly a large amount of his ammunition, the lack of which was much felt in the subsequent fighting. Not a single gun of our corps fired a shot, nor did the enemy in our front.] And although Pickett's assault, when made, actually carried the enemy's guns, nowhere was there the slightest preparation to come to his assistance. The burden of the whole task fell upon the 10 brigades employed. The other 27 brigades and 56 fresh guns were but widely scattered spectators.

It was just 1 P.M. by my watch when the signal guns were fired and the cannonade opened. The enemy replied rather slowly at first, though soon with increasing rapidity. Having determined that Pickett should charge, I felt impatient to launch him as soon as I could see that our fire was accomplishing anything. I guessed that a half-hour would elapse between my sending him the order and his column reaching close quarters. I dared not presume on using more ammunition than one hour's firing would consume, for we were far from supplies and had already fought for two days. So I determined to send Pickett the order at the very first favorable sign and not later than after 30 minutes' firing.

At the end of 20 minutes no favorable development had occurred. More guns had been added to the Federal line than at the beginning, and its whole length, about two miles, was blazing like a volcano. It seemed madness to order a column in the middle of a hot July day to undertake an advance of three-fourths of a mile over open ground against the centre of that line.

But something had to be done. I wrote the following note and dispatched it to Pickett at 1:25:-'General: If you are to advance at all, you must come at once or we will not be able to support you as we ought. But the enemy's fire has not slackened materially and there are still 18 guns firing from the cemetery.'[22]

Pickett was with Longstreet when he received the above note and showed it to Longstreet.

Longstreet was reluctant to order the charge, believing the attack was doomed to failure. He felt his soldiers would be uselessly slaughtered in a senseless assault, with no chance of success and to no advantage, but he was compelled by Lee's orders:

> After I read the note, Pickett said to me: "General, shall I advance?" My feelings had so overcome me that I would not speak, for fear of betraying my want of confidence to him. I bowed affirmation, and turned to mount my horse. Pickett immediately said: "I shall lead my division forward, sir." I spurred my horse to the wood where Alexander was stationed with the artillery. When I reached him, he told me of the disappearance of the seven guns which were to have led the charge with Pickett, and his ammunition was so low that he could not properly support the charge. I at once ordered him to stop Pickett until the ammunition had been replenished. He informed me that he had no ammunition with which to replenish. I then saw that there was no help for it, and that Pickett must advance under his orders.[23]

After sending Pickett the previous note, Alexander spotted a change in the disposition of the enemy's guns:

> I had hardly dispatched this note, when I began to notice signs of some of the enemy's guns ceasing to fire. At first, I thought it only crippled guns; but soon, with my large glass, I discovered entire batteries limbering up & leaving their positions. Now it was a very ordinary thing with us to withdraw our guns from purely artillery duels, & save up every thing for their infantry. But the Federals had never done anything of that sort before, & I did not believe they were doing it now. Knowing what a large reserve force they always kept, I supposed that they were only relieving exhausted batteries with fresh ones, as I had relieved the Washington Arty. at Marye's Hill. But the fresh ones not promptly appearing, I said, "If they don't put fresh batteries there in five minutes this will be our fight." I spent the five minutes with my glass studying their lines every where. Some batteries still kept up their fire, but there was not a single fresh gun replacing any that had withdrawn. Of course, I knew that what were withdrawn was still there-just behind the hills-& that nothing but a desperate infantry fight could decide the day; but I felt encouraged to believe that they had felt very severe punishment, & that my fire had been generally well aimed & as effective as could be hoped. For surely here was a new departure in their conduct.
>
> So I wrote another note to Pickett & sent it at 1:35-ten minutes after the first note, "For God's sake come quick. The 18 guns are gone. Come quick or I can't support you." I sent two written & one verbal message to that effect, for I was afraid of losing time in little preliminaries, & I wanted to get them inspired to disregard everything but getting there.
>
> Some five or ten minutes after sending my last note Gen, Longstreet rode up all alone. I was expecting Pickett every moment, & was all impatience for him to come, for the fire of our own guns was also now much reduced, & I was not sure how much was due to exhaustion of ammunition, & how much might be only because the enemy had nearly ceased firing. I had given no orders to cease or slacken at all, whether the enemy did or not, & I wished the fire kept going to our utmost capacity until the crisis was past.
>
> So when Gen. Longstreet came I told him how the enemy had withdrawn their guns, & we would certainly get a favorable start; but I expressed impatience at Pickett's delay, & I told him of the Richardson guns being taken off, & said I feared the support I could give might not be all I wished, & had counted upon. By the way this was the first that Gen. Longstreet knew of my having these guns at all. I had been hoping to give him a little agreeable surprise with them when I ran them out into the field. Gen. L. spoke at once, & decidedly, "Go & halt Pickett right where he is, & replenish your ammunition." I said, "General, we can't do that. We nearly emptied the trains last night. Even if we had it, it would take an hour or two, & meanwhile

the enemy would recover from the pressure he is now under. Our only chance is to follow it up now-to strike while the iron is hot." He answered, "I don't want to make this attack-I believe it will fail-I do not see how it can succeed-I would not make it even now, but that Gen, Lee has ordered & expects it." He made these statements, with slight pauses in between, while he was looking at the enemy's position through his field glasses.[24]

Longstreet and Alexander were both dismounted as Longstreet slowly spoke these words with great emotion; he was vacillating as to whether to stop the charge. "I felt that he was inviting a word of acquiescence on my part," Porter Alexander remarked,

and that if given he would again order, "Stop Pickett where he is." But I was too conscious of my own youth and inexperience to express any opinion not directly asked. So I remained silent while Longstreet fought out his battle alone and obeyed his orders.[25]

After sending my last "hurry up" notes to Pickett at 1:35 p.m., I do not recall looking at my watch again that day. So I cannot be absolutely sure, but I think it was not earlier than 1:50, nor later than 2 p.m., when with great relief & delight, I saw Pickett's line approaching at a good fast gait.[26]

The grand exchange of artillery fire had taken a heavy toll on both armies; Longstreet stated: "The Confederates had the benefit of converging fire into the enemy's massed position, but the superior metal of the enemy neutralized the advantage of position. The brave and steady work progressed."[27]

Now was the time for Alexander to bring up his guns to support Pickett. General Pendleton had loaned Alexander nine short-range 12-pounder howitzers, under the command of Major Richardson, from Hill's chief of artillery, Colonel R. I. Walker; Alexander wanted them to move forward in advance of Pickett. Alexander placed the nine guns in a little hollow behind some woods and had his courier, Arthur C. Catlett, note the exact location of the guns. When he sent Catlett, "who was an excellent and reliable man," to bring up Major Richardson with his guns, they were missing. Later he found that General Pendleton had taken four or five of the guns and Major Richardson had moved the rest a short distance to get out of range of the enemy's shells thrown at A. P. Hill's guns in the artillery duel prior to the main barrage.

Alexander ordered up only those guns with enough long-range projectiles for 15 shots, more or less on the average of one or two out of every five guns–15 or 18 in all; the rest would wait for the storming column to advance and then fire over their heads. The ammunition chests were nearly empty but the caissons could not find the ordnance train; the reserve artillery trains had been moved back for safety by Pendleton but he left no one at their former location to tell where they were.

Quality of the Confederate ordnance came into play at this juncture. Some of the Confederate rifle shells had a tendency to "tumble"; moreover, the Bormann fuse, used commonly in the Confederate munitions, had a high failure rate and did not explode over their targets, and there were always shortages. This caused Alexander much concern:

> First it must be borne in mind that our Confederate artillery could only sparingly, & in great emergency, be allowed to fire over the heads of our infantry. We were always liable to premature explosions of shell & shrapnel, & our infantry knew it by sad experience, & I have known of their threatening to fire back at our guns if we opened over their heads. Of course, solid shot could be safely used, but that is the least effective ammunition, & the infantry would not know the difference & would be demoralized & angry all the same.[28]

The lack of training was an added factor Alexander had to contend with: "The great majority of the batteries took the field without having ever fired a round in practice [because of powder shortages], and passed through the war without aiming a gun at any target but the enemy."[29]

Deception

The slackening of the Federal fire was a deception contrived by the Eleventh Corps' artillery chief, Major Thomas Osborn. It appeared General Lee was planning an infantry assault on the center, and Osborn wanted to encourage this by having the artillery cease fire, so Lee would think his onslaught of shot and shell a success and send in his infantry to certain carnage. He pitched his idea to Henry Jackson Hunt, chief of artillery of the Army of the Potomac, who liked the plan, took responsibility for the decision to implement it, and went to the commander in chief, General Meade, for approval. Meade was thinking along the same lines, so it was an easy sell. Brevet Major General Henry J. Hunt believed his guns could stop the charge if his gunners saved their ammunition for the infantry:

> It was of first importance to subject the enemy's infantry, from the first moment of their advance, to such a cross-fire of our artillery as would break their formation, check their impulse, and drive them back, or at least bring them to our lines in such a condition as to make them an easy prey. There was neither time nor necessity for reporting this to General Meade, and beginning on the right, I instructed the chiefs of artillery and battery commanders to withhold their fire for fifteen or twenty minutes after the cannonade commenced, then to concentrate their fire with all possible accuracy on those batteries which were most destructive to us-but slowly, so that when the enemy's ammunition was exhausted, we should have sufficient left to meet the assault. I had just given these orders to the last battery on Little Round Top, when the signal-gun was fired, and the enemy opened with all their guns.[30]

Not all the battery commanders used restraint in the counterfire.

Pickett was to aim his division at a "little clump of trees" (Copse of Trees) and Ziegler's Grove. He had only three of his brigades (5,830 officers and men) with him as Jenkins's and Corse's brigades were detached. Pickett put Garnett and Kemper in the first line with Armistead in the second. The brigades of Wilcox (1,036) and Perry's Florida brigade (444) under Colonel David Lang of Anderson's division were to the right and rear of Pickett as a flank guard. To Pickett's left separated by Spangler's Woods was Heth's division in the first wave, Birkett Fry's brigade (824) at the center upon which the grand charge would guide; the brigades of Marshall (Pettigrew's old brigade) (1,205), Davis (1,605) and Brockenbrough (821) followed in order all under the command of Johnston Pettigrew in place of the wounded Harry Heth. In the second wave supporting Pettigrew were Colonel Lowrance's (Scale's) (951)and Lane's (1,355) brigades of Dorsey Pender's division, both were led by Major General Isaac Trimble. Anderson's brigades of Wright, Posey and Mahone to the left were to support Pettigrew and Trimble as Anderson reported: "I received orders to hold my division in readiness to move up in support, if it should be necessary." Combined these brigades brought the total for the assault to around 15,000 suggesting that James Longstreet's figure was on the mark.

Longstreet watched the assault:

> Confederate batteries put their fire over the heads of the men as they moved down the slope, and continued to draw the fire of the enemy until the smoke lifted and drifted to the rear, when every gun was turned upon the infantry columns. The batteries that had been drawn off were replaced by others that were fresh. Soldiers and officers began to fall, some to rise no more, others to find their way to the hospital tents. Single files were cut here and there, then the gaps increased, and an occasional shot tore wider openings, but, closing the gaps as quickly as made, the march moved on. The divisions of McLaws and Hood were ordered to move to closer lines for the enemy on their front, to spring to the charge as soon as the breach to the centre could be made. The enemy's right overreached my left and gave serious trouble. Brockenbrough's brigade went down and Davis's in impetuous charge. The general order required further assistance from the Third Corps if needed, but no support appeared. General Lee and the corps commander were there, but failed to order help.[31]

Longstreet was dismayed that Pickett's division was to be sacrificed to no purpose; that this style of attack was outmoded with the introduction of the rifled musket and cannon:

> That day at Gettysburg was one of the saddest of my life. Before them lay the ground over which they were to pass to the point of attack. Intervening were several fences, a field of corn, a little swale running through it, and then a rise from that point to the Federal stronghold. As soon as Pickett passed the crest of the hill, the Federals had a clear view and opened their batteries, and as he descended the eastern slope of the ridge his troops received a fearful fire from the batteries in front and from Round Top. The troops marched steadily, taking the fire with great coolness. As soon as they passed my batteries, I ordered my artillery to turn their fire against the batteries on our right then raking our lines. They did so, but did not force the Federals to change the direction of their fire and relieve our infantry. As the troops were about to cross the swale. I noticed a considerable force of Federal infantry moving down as though to flank the left of our line. I sent an officer to caution the division commanders to guard against that move, at the same time sending another staff-officer with similar orders so as to feel assured the order would be delivered. Both officers came back bringing their saddles, their horses having been shot under them. After crossing the swale, the troops kept the same steady step, but met a dreadful fire at the hands of the Federal sharp-shooters; and as soon as the field was open the Federal infantry poured down a terrific fire which was kept up during the entire assault. The slaughter was terrible, the enfilade fire of the batteries on Round Top being very destructive. At times one shell would knock down five or six men. I dismounted to relieve my horse and was sitting on a rail fence watching very closely the movements of the troops. Colonel Fremantle, who had taken a position behind the Third Corps where he would be out of reach of fire and

at the same time have a clear view of the field, became so interested that he left his position and came with speed to join me. Just as he came up behind me, Pickett had reached a point near the Federal lines. A pause was made to close ranks and mass for the final plunge. The troops on Pickett's left, although advancing, were evidently a little shaky. Colonel Fremantle, only observing the troops of Picket's command, said to me, "General, I would not have missed this for anything in the world." He believed it to be a complete success. I was watching the troops supporting Pickett and saw plainly they could not hold together ten minutes longer. I called his attention to the wavering condition of the two divisions of the Third Corps, and said they would not hold, that Pickett would strike and be crushed and the attack would be a failure. As Pickett's division concentrated in making the final assault, Kemper fell severely wounded. As the division threw itself against the Federal line Garnett fell and expired. The Confederate flag was planted in the Federal line, and immediately Armistead fell mortally wounded at the feet of the Federal soldiers. The wavering divisions then seemed appalled, broke their ranks, and retired. Immediately the Federals swarmed around Pickett, attacking on all sides, enveloped and broke up his command, having killed and wounded more than two thousand men in about thirty minutes. They then drove the fragments back upon our lines. As they came back I fully expected to see Meade ride to the front and lead his forces to a tremendous counter-charge. Sending my staff-officers to assist in collecting the fragments of my command, I rode to my line of batteries, knowing they were all I had in front of an of the impending attack, resolved to drive it back or sacrifice my last gun and man. The Federals were advancing a line of skirmishers which I thought was the advance of their charge. As soon as the line of skirmishers came within reach of our guns, the batteries opened again and their fire seemed to check at once the threatened advance. After keeping it up a few minutes the line of skirmishers disappeared, and my mind was relieved of the apprehension that Meade was going to follow us.

General Lee came up as our troops were falling back and encouraged them as well as he could; begged them to re-form their ranks and reorganize their forces, and assisted the staff-officers in bring them all together again. It was then he used the expression that has been mentioned so often: "It was all my fault; get together, and let us do the best we can toward saving that which is left us."[32]

Fremantle left this account of Pickett's futile charge over some very exposed terrain and Longstreet's resolve after the repulse:

The distance between the Confederate guns and the Yankee position-i.e., between the woods crowning the opposite ridges-was at least a mile-quite open, gently undulating, and exposed to artillery the whole distance. This was the ground which had to be crossed in today's attack. Pickett's division, which had just come up, was to bear the brunt in Longstreet's attack, together with Heth and Pettigrew in Hill's corps. Pickett's division was a weak one (under 5000), owing to the absence of two brigades.

We [Fremantle and an Austrian officer] the returned to the hill I was on yesterday. But finding that, to see the actual fighting, it was absolutely necessary to go into the thick of the thing, I determined to make my way to General Longstreet. It was then about 2:30. After passing General Lee and his staff, I rode on through the woods in the direction in which I had left Longstreet.

I soon began to meet many wounded men returning from the front. Many of them asked in piteous tones the way to a doctor or an ambulance. The further I got, the greater became the number of wounded. At last I came to a perfect stream of them flocking through the woods in numbers as great as the crowd in Oxford Street in the middle of the day. Some were walking alone on crutches composed of two rifles, others were supported by men less badly wounded than themselves, and others were carried on stretchers by the ambulance corps; but in no case did I see a sound man helping the wounded to the rear, unless he carried the red badge of the ambulance corps. They were still under a heavy fire; the shells were continually bringing down great limbs of trees, and carrying further destruction amongst this melancholy procession.

I saw all this in much less time than it takes to write it, and although astonished to meet such vast numbers of wounded, I had not seen enough to give me any idea of the real extent of the mischief.

For the first time I then had a view of the open space between the two positions, and saw it covered with Confederates slowly and sulkily returning towards us in small broken parties, under a heavy fire of artillery. But the fire where we were, was not as bad as further to the rear: for although the air seemed alive with shell, yet the greater number burst behind us.

General Longstreet earned the title "Bulldog":

The General told me that Pickett's division had succeeded in carrying the enemy's position and capturing his guns, but after remaining there twenty minutes, it had been forced to retire, on the retreat of Heth and Pettigrew on its left. No person could have been more calm or self-possessed than General Longstreet under these trying circumstances, aggravated as they now were by the movements of the enemy, who began to show a strong disposition to advance. I could now thoroughly appreciate the term bulldog, which I had heard applied to him by the soldiers. Difficulties seem to make no other impression upon him than to make him a little more savage.

Major Walton was the only officer with him when I came up-all the rest had been put into the charge. In a few minutes Major Latrobe arrived on foot, carrying his saddle, having just had his horse killed. Colonel Sorrel was also in the same predicament, and Captain Goree's horse was wounded in the mouth.

The General was making the best arrangements in his power to resist the threatened advance, by advancing some artillery, rallying the stragglers, &c. I remember seeing a General (Pettigrew, I think it was) [This officer was afterwards killed at the passage of the Potomac.] come up to him, and report that "he was unable to bring his men up again." Longstreet turned upon him and replied with some sarcasm: "Very well; never mind, then, General; just let them remain where they are: the enemy's going to advance, and will spare you the trouble."

He asked for something to drink. I gave him some rum out of my silver flask, which I begged he would keep in remembrance of the occasion; he smiled, and, to my great satisfaction, accepted the memorial. He then went off to give some orders to M'Laws's division. Soon afterwards I joined General Lee, who had in the meanwhile come to that part of the field on becoming aware of the disaster.

General Lee's magnificent conduct after the battle:

If Longstreet's conduct was admirable, that of General Lee was perfectly sublime. He was engaged in rallying and in encouraging the broken troops, and was riding about a little in front of the wood, quite alone-the whole of his staff being engaged in a similar manner further to the rear. His face, which is always placid and cheerful, did not show signs of the slightest disappointment, care, or annoyance; and he was addressing to every soldier he met a few words of encouragement, such as, "All this will come right in the end; we'll talk it over afterwards; but, in the meantime, all good men must rally. We want all good and true men just now," &c.

I saw General Wilcox (an officer who wears a short round jacket and a battered straw hat) come up to him, and explain, almost crying, the state of his brigade. General Lee immediately shook hands with him and said cheerfully, "Never mind, General, all this has been my fault-it is I that have lost this fight, and you must help me out of it in the best way you can."

It is difficult to exaggerate the critical state of affairs as they appeared about this time. If the enemy or their general had shown any enterprise, there is no saying what might have happened.

General Lee and his officers were evidently fully impressed with a sense of the situation; yet there was much less noise, fuss, or confusion of orders than at an ordinary field day. The men, as they were rallied in the wood, were brought up in detachments, and lay down quietly and coolly in the positions assigned to them.

We heard that Generals Garnett and Armistead were killed, and General Kemper mortally wounded; also, that Pickett's division had only one field officer unhurt. Nearly all this slaughter took place in an open space about one square mile, and within one hour.[33]

Pickett's Charge was crushed and repulsed but too late Wilcox's brigade came up passing Alexander's guns: As we watched, we saw them close in upon the enemy in smoke and dust, and we ceased firing and waited the result. It was soon manifest in a gradual diminution of the fire and in a stream of fugitives coming to the rear pursued by some fire but not as much, it seemed to me, as might have been expected.

After perhaps 20 minutes, during which the fire has about ceased, to my surprise there came forward from the rear Wilcox's fine Ala, brigade, which had been with us at Chancellorsville, and, just 60 days before, had won the affair at Salem Church. It had been sent to reenforce Pickett, but was not in the column. Now, when all was over, the single brigade was moving forward alone, and there was no one in authority to halt it. They were about 1,200 strong and on their left were about 250, the remnant of Perry's Fla. brigade. It was at once both absurd and tragic.

They advanced several hundred yards beyond our guns, under a sharp fire. Then they halted and opened fire from some undergrowth and brushwood along a small ravine. Federal infantry soon moved out to attack their left, when Perry fell back past our guns; Wilcox moved by his right flank and making a circuit regained our lines at the Peach Orchard. His loss in this charge was about 204 in killed and wounded. Perry's loss was about proportional, with some prisoners in addition.[34]

Pickett had sent his aide, Captain Robert A. Bright, calling on General Longstreet for support for the breakthrough. Just as Bright found Longstreet, sitting alone on a snake-rail fence by Spangler's Woods near the center of the line, Colonel Fremantle, the British observer, had just joined Longstreet and, believing the charge successful, interrupted: "I would not have missed it for the world." Longstreet responded, "I would, Colonel Fremantle, the charge is over." Longstreet directed Pickett's aide: "Captain Bright, ride to General Pickett and tell him what you have heard me say to Colonel Fremantle." Before Bright started to reverse course, Longstreet hailed him back, and, pointing toward Sherify Farm, called out, "Captain Bright! Tell General Pickett that Wilcox's Brigade is in the peach orchard, and he can order him to his assistance." Pickett called up Wilcox but, as Alexander remarked, "There was nothing for them to support."

Longstreet summed up the repulse this way:

As they started up the ridge, over one hundred cannon from the breastworks of the Federals hurled a rain of canister, grape, and shell down upon them; still they pressed on until halfway up the slope, when the crest of the hill was lit with a solid sheet of flame as the masses of infantry rose and fired. When the smoke cleared away, Pickett's Division was gone. Nearly two-thirds of his men lay dead on the field, and the survivors were sullenly retreating down the hill. Mortal man could not have stood that fire. In half an hour the contested field was cleared and the battle of Gettysburg was over.[35]

"We gained nothing but glory," asserted a Virginian, "and lost our bravest men."[36]

General Longstreet tried to console Pickett as he exclaimed: "General, I am ruined. My division is gone; it is destroyed."

After the threat of a counterattack had passed, during the afternoon, General Longstreet sent Sorrel with orders for Hood and McLaws to withdraw their divisions to the rear of the Emmitsburg Road, the line they had occupied prior to the assault on July 2nd. Longstreet had very few cavalry with him on the right and had posted G. T. Anderson's brigade with Bachman's and Reilly's batteries to check the Union cavalry. Just after the charge, and before Hood and McLaws pulled back, General Kilpatrick sent a brigade of cavalry under General Elon J. Farnsworth to attack the rear of Longstreet's right division. The ground, covered with rocks and stone fences, was not suited for cavalry and Farnsworth lost his life, along with a great number of sabers. Longstreet believed that better use could have been made of Farnsworth: "Kilpatrick's mistake was in not putting Farnsworth in on Merritt's left, where he would have had an open ride, and made more trouble than was ever made by a cavalry brigade."[37] Alexander was convinced that Kilpatrick could have gotten into the Confederate trains, which were practically unguarded; there were merely 100 cavalry videttes on picket duty who could have been easily brushed aside. The bulk of the Confederate cavalry was on the left, under Stuart; this cavalry advanced and became severely engaged with Gregg's division, resulting in a draw, pulling closed the final curtain on the battle of Gettysburg.

After the battle Fremantle made his way back behind the lines:

> At 7:30, all idea of a Yankee attack being over, I rode back to Moses's tent, and found that worthy commissary in very low spirits, all sorts of exaggerated rumors having reached him. On my way I met a great many wounded men, most anxious to inquire after Longstreet, who was reported killed; when I assured them he was quite well, they seemed to forget their own pain in the evident pleasure they felt in the safety of their chief. No words that I can use will adequately express the extraordinary patience and fortitude with which the wounded Confederates bore their sufferings.[38]

CHAPTER 8

"A Very Taciturn and Undemonstrative Man"

Gettysburg, Day Four

Longstreet Was a Prisoner

The two armies faced off on July 4. Lee pulled Ewell's corps back to Seminary Ridge from its positions near Culp's Hill and in the town of Gettysburg; A. P. Hill's corps remained in the center and the right flank retired behind Willoughby Run. During the day, Fremantle chronicled this amusing incident regarding Longstreet:

> Lawley, the Austrian, and I walked up to the front about eight o'clock, and on our way we met General Longstreet, who was in a high state of amusement and good humor. A flag of truce had just come over from the enemy, and its bearer announced among other things that "General Longstreet was wounded, and a prisoner, but would be taken care of." General Longstreet sent back word that he was extremely grateful, but that, being neither wounded nor a prisoner, he was quite able to take care of himself. The iron endurance of General Longstreet is most extraordinary. He seems to require neither food nor sleep. Most of his staff now fall fast asleep directly they get off their horses, they are so exhausted from the last three day's work. (Longstreet's supposed capture at Gettysburg was a case of mistaken identity. When his troops were forced back in their attack on July 2, among the wounded left behind was a Colonel Powell of the Texas 5th Regiment. Powell was a short, stocky man with a full beard and looked very much like Longstreet. The report quickly spread among the Union troops that the general himself had been taken, and it was some time before the mistake was cleared up.)[1]

General Lee had to retreat, for he was low on ammunition, with only "enough for one day's fight." "During the afternoon of the 3rd," Alexander asserted, "Lee determined upon immediate retreat to Va. Such an end to our invasion had, indeed, been inevitable from the beginning, but the difficulties were now greatly increased."[2] General Lee met with his generals to discuss the retreat at Hill's headquarters. Jed Hotchkiss remarked in his diary: "The Generals had a council at General A. P. Hill's headquarters on the Cashtown Road, about sun-down, and decided to fall back."[3]

Map Upon Their Knees

A. P. Hill's corps was to lead the retreat, and Lee spent until about 1:00am in the morning with Hill seated on campstools in Hill's wall-tent with a map spread upon their knees to explain what was expected. After leaving Hill, Lee met with General Imboden who had just come back with 2,100 sabers and McClanahan's six-gun battery of horse artillery from raids on the left of Lee's army. Imboden was assigned to bring the wounded in a train of wagons and ambulances constituting nearly all the transportation of General Lee's army back to Virginia by a different route than the main army; making his way westward through the Cashtown Gap in South Mountain on the Chambersburg road, southward to Greencastle, then via the Williamsport pike to Williamsport on the Potomac, some 42 miles, ford the river and make for Winchester. General Lee sent him, Major Eshleman of Longstreet's corps (considered one of the best artillery officers in the army) of the Washington Artillery of New Orleans, with eight Napoleon guns; Longstreet had picked this one, as it was his smallest artillery battalion–Captain William A. Tanner with a four-gun battery and a Whitworth rifle under Lieutenant William Pegram. The rear guard consisted of Hampton's cavalry brigade commanded by Colonel P. M. B. Young with a four-gun battery of Captain James F. Hart's horse artillery.

Around noon on July 4, William Owen approached Longstreet as he surveyed the lines:

> Batteries are in position, but with only a scant supply of ammunition, but the enemy apparently evinces no curiosity as to our condition. At about noon I rode over to a hill where Longstreet has taken up his position to overlook the whole field. He is looking well, and seems evidently determined to put on the best face possible. "What o'clock is it?" he asks.-"Eleven fifty-five" is my answer. "General," I added, "this is the 'glorious fourth,' we should have a salute from the other side at noon."
>
> Twelve o'clock came, but no salute. "Their artillery was too much crippled yesterday to think of salutes," said the General. "Meade is not in good spirits this morning."
>
> The General then went on to say that last evening, a little after dark, he rode along our skirmish line near the peach-orchard, where he came across a battery of artillery. He was surprised to find it so far in advance of our line of infantry, and inquired whose it was.
>
> A tall officer, quietly smoking a pipe, approached, and said, "I am the captain." It was "Buck" Miller, of the Third Company of Washington Artillery. When he recognized the General, he informed him he 'was out there to have a little skirmishing on his own account, if the "Yanks came out of their holes." The General laughed at the captain's idea of 'skirmishing' with 12-pounder Napoleons. Ever since the battle of Sharpsburg (Antietam), when the Third Company held the centre of our line, and Longstreet and staff worked with the guns, Miller has been a great favorite at head-quarters.[4]

In the afternoon Colonel Fremantle visited Longstreet's headquarters and they discussed the battle:

> At 2 P.M. we walked to General Longstreet's camp, which had been removed to a place three miles distant, on the Fairfield Road. General Longstreet talked to me for a long time about the battle. He said the mistake they had made was in not concentrating the army more, and in failing to make the attack yesterday with 30,000 men instead of 15,000.
>
> The advance had been in three lines, and the troops of Hill's corps who gave way were young soldiers, who had never been under fire before. He thought the enemy would have attacked

had the guns been withdrawn. Had they done so at that particular moment immediately after the repulse, it would have been awkward; but in that case he had given orders for the advance of Hood's division and M'Laws's on the right. I think, after all, that General Meade was right not to advance-his men would never have stood the tremendous fire of artillery they would have been exposed to.[5]

General Lee joined Longstreet's bivouac on the Fairfield Road where Fitzgerald Ross recorded that they were "engaged in earnest conversation." Another heard Lee say, "I thought my men were invincible."[6]

Thunder and Lightning

The retreat was marred by "thunder and lightning, torrents of rain" slowing the progress. "We took eight hours to go as many miles," Fremantle wrote down, and this had a harsh effect on the wounded in General Imboden's train:

> Shortly after noon on the 4th the very windows of heaven seemed to have opened. The rain fell in blinding sheets; the meadows soon overflowed and fences gave way before the raging streams. During the storm, wagons, ambulances and artillery carriages by hundreds-nay, by thousands-were assembling in the fields along the road from Gettysburg to Cashtown, in one confused and apparently inextricable mass. As the afternoon wore on there was no abatement in the storm. Canvas was no protection against its fury, and the wounded men lying upon the naked boards were drenched. Horses and mules were blinded and maddened by the wind and water, and became almost unmanageable. The deafening roar of the mingled sounds of heaven and earth all around us made it almost impossible to communicate orders, and equally difficult to execute them.[7]

The one benefit to the storm was that it delayed Meade's pursuit, allowing Lee to escape unscathed.

Imboden's column reached Williamsport but was attacked there early in the morning on the 6th by the cavalry divisions of Generals Buford and Kilpatrick; Imboden dismounted his cavalry, armed the wagoners with the guns of the wounded and posted his artillery replenished by two wagonloads of artillery ammunition rushed from Winchester on the hills about the town, his whole force not exceeding three thousand men and successfully saved Lee's transportation which could not be replaced in the Confederacy against 7,000 assailants, this action was called "the wagoners' fight." Fitzhugh Lee arrived with three thousand fresh horsemen and sustained Imboden; darkness ended the fighting with Williamsport secure. On the same day Stuart also drove back part of Kilpatrick's cavalry division at Hagerstown securing this important hub of a road network.

When Lee's army arrived at Williamsport, it found the river swollen and rising from the recent rains and could not ford it there. The ford was now under 13 feet of water; moreover, a pontoon bridge left at Falling Waters six miles downstream was weakly guarded and had been destroyed on July 4 by a party of Yankee cavalry sent by General French from his Harper's Ferry garrison. The only passage was a small cable ferry at Williamsport capable of carrying only two wagon loads.

Lee's army had its back to the raging Potomac, ammunition low, fresh provisions cut off, and Meade's army approaching where defeat would bring ruin. Early Tuesday on July 7, E. Porter Alexander joined the engineers to select and form a fortified line of battle to meet Meade's army: "There was no very well defined & naturally strong line, & we had to pick & choose, & string together in some places by make-shifts & some little work."[8] "A fairly good line was found with its right flank on the Potomac near Downsville, passing by St. James College and resting its left on the Conococheague. Longstreet's corps held its right, Hill the centre, and Ewell the left."[9] Downsville was a key point protecting the pontoon bridge and it was heavily defended by Longstreet's corps; St. James College's buildings were utilized to strengthen the defense in that sector. The line selected was occupied by Lee's army on July 11, as Meade's army was fast drawing near by July 10 and the infantry and artillery set to work making the fortifications stronger. Alexander noticed that Lee was visibly anxious over the approaching action, as he never saw him before or after; Lee personally overlooked the disposition of Longstreet's corps.

Mule Chases a Grizzly Bear

Meade was very slow in his pursuit. In Alexander's words: "Up to now, the enemy had pursued us as a mule goes on the chase of a grizzly bear-as if catching up with us was the last thing he wanted to do."[10] Meade had a reconnaissance done on July 12, after which he decided to have a demonstration by his army to probe for any weak points in Lee's line for conversion into a full-blown attack if one was found on July 13, but his leading officers were adverse to the proposal. However, President Lincoln sent positive orders on the evening of July 13 for General Meade to attack; on July 14 Meade moved upon the Confederate works, "but the mule had not yet caught up with the bear."[11]

Reconstructing a Bridge

General Lee put Jackson's former quartermaster, Major John A. Harman, in charge of reconstructing the pontoon bridge at Falling Waters; seven of the original pontoons were recovered and new ones constructed by taking down barns, dismantling warehouses, and disassembling wharves along the Chesapeake and Ohio Canal, commandeering the necessary sawmills and tools, thereby fashioning 15 pontoons caulked with tar and oakum in 68 hours, according to the Prussian observer, Captain Justus Scheibert, who helped with the work. They were floated down to Falling Waters and assembled into an 800-foot floating bridge using crossbeams and planking-"a crazy affair," as Sorrel described it. Further rains fell on the 7th and 8th.

Nevertheless, by the 13th the river was falling steadily and lowered to the critical level of four feet at the Williamsport ford, allowing infantry to the ford. General Lee ordered a crossing during the night of July 13. Longstreet was put in charge of the operation: "General Lee, worn by the strain of the past two weeks, asked me to remain at the bridge and look to the work of the night."[12] Longstreet's First Corps was to cross the pontoon bridge at dark followed by Hill's Third Corps, while Ewell's Second Corps crossed at the ford; the caissons pulled out of the line at 5:00pm. Large bonfires of fence rails and torches were kept up, to light the entrance upon the bridge, and on the Virginia shore to mark their target at the ford. Heth's division was the sole rear guard, defending a defensive line thrown up in three full days of work by the engineers on a ridgeline a mile and a half from the pontoon bridge, with Fitzhugh Lee's cavalry picketing in front of them; the cavalry crossed the river, leaving behind a squadron for duty who passed Heth's line without giving notice, so when Major Peter Weber with about 40 sabers of the 6th Michigan advanced on the Confederate works, they were thought to be friendly. They charged a portion of the Confederate line but were quickly repulsed, Major Weber and nine-tenths of his command shot down. During the melee, General Pettigrew received a mortal wound. He was unhorsed in the fight as his hand had been wounded on the third day of fighting at Gettysburg and he could not manage his horse when he rose. He was hit in the stomach by a pistol-shot and died three days later. By noon on the 14th, Lee's army was back on Virginia soil with the loss of two guns and about 500 stragglers; the Gettysburg campaign was over.

Colonel Fremantle made his leave of the Army of Northern Virginia and Longstreet: "Longstreet is generally a very taciturn and undemonstrative man, but he was quite affectionate in his farewell. His last words were a hearty hope for the speedy termination of the war."[13]

Casualties were equally heavy on both sides, with the Confederates suffering slightly more; the North could absorb such losses; the South could not. Historian Livermore gave a very accurate estimate of the losses in *Numbers and Losses in the Civil War*, with Confederate casualties at 3,903 killed, 18,735 wounded, and 5,425 missing, totaling 28,063, while Federal casualties ran 3,155 killed, 14,529 wounded, and 5,365 missing, 23,049 all told during the campaign. According to Adjutant General Walter H. Taylor of the Army of Northern Virginia, on May 31, 1863, the numbers were infantry, 59,457; cavalry, 10,292; artillery, 4,702; and total effective, 74,451. Effective strength of the Army of the Potomac was 115,256; infantry and artillery, 100,283; and cavalry, 14,973, as of June 30, 1863.

CHAPTER 9

Lee's Old War Horse

Gettysburg Reconsidered

There are many considerations and inquiries that are brought to mind in regard to the whole Gettysburg campaign.

In allowing Stuart to detach three brigades of cavalry, Lee compromised his entire campaign. Alexander expounded on this:

> About June 22, as Hill and Longstreet drew near the Potomac, ready to cross, Stuart made to Lee a very unwise proposition, which Lee more unwisely entertained. It was destined to have an unfortunate influence on the campaign.
>
> In view of the issues at stake, and the fact that already he had been deprived of two promised brigades (Corse's and Jenkins's), it was unwise even to contemplate sending three brigades of cavalry upon such distant service. When one compares the small beneficial results of raids, even when successful, with the risks here involved, it is hard to understand how Lee could have given his consent.[1]

Longstreet had this outlook on Stuart's action:

> As to the failure of Stuart to move with the army to the west side of the Blue Ridge, I can only call attention to the fact that General Lee gave him discretionary orders. He doubtless did as he thought best. Had no discretion been given to him, he would have known and fallen into his natural position —my right flank. But authority thus given to a subordinate general, implies an opinion on the part of the commander that something better than the drudgery of a march, along our flank might be open to him, and one of General Stuart's activity and gallantry should not be expected to fail to seek it.[2]

"General Stuart should not have been permitted to leave the general line of march, thus forcing us to march blindfolded into the enemy's country; to this may be attributed, in my opinion, the change of the policy of the campaign."[3]

The policy Longstreet refers to is the understanding agreed upon with Lee to wage an "offensive strategical but defensive tactical plan" for the campaign. "The long & the short of the matter seems to me as follows," stated Alexander, "Longstreet did not wish to take the offensive. His objection to it was not based at all upon the peculiar strength of the enemy's position for that was not yet recognized, but solely on general principles."[4] Longstreet wanted to conserve his soldier's lives and considered the tactical defensive to be more economical in resources, manpower, and material by not exposing the troops. Whereas the tactical offensive would expend the lives of the soldiers at a cost the South could not afford in view of the numerical disparity between the two opponents and the impact of the new weaponry.

The first day of fighting was a success for the Confederates but the enemy was not pursued and pushed off the heights, Cemetery Ridge and Culp's Hill, as should have been done. Longstreet believed General Lee, who was on the field, should have been decisive in his directives to General Ewell:

> General Lee explains his failure to send positive orders to Ewell to follow up the flying enemy as follows: "The attack was not pressed that afternoon, the enemy's force being unknown, and it being considered advisable to await the arrival of the rest of our troops. Orders were sent back to hasten their march, and, in the meantime, every effort was made to ascertain the numbers and positions of the enemy, and find the most favorable point to attack." Pursuit "pell-mell" is sometimes justified in a mere retreat. It is the accepted principle of action in a rout. General Early, in his report of this day's work, says "the enemy had been routed." He should, therefore, have been followed by everything that could have been thrown upon his heels, not so much to gain the heights, which were recognized as a rallying point, but to prevent his rallying at all in time to form lines for another battle. If the enemy had been routed, this could and should have been done. General Hays told me, ten years after the battle, that he "could have seized the heights without the loss of ten men."[5]

In an article published in the *Journal of the Military Service Institution*, June 1911, John Cabell Early, nephew of Major General Jubal Early, was present at a conference of generals around midnight after the action on July 1 and gives this insight into Lee's thinking:

> While I do not, after the lapse of so many years, recall all the details of this conference, yet the substance of it is distinctly fixed in my memory. The main subject of debate was as to whether General Lee should advance that night and occupy the hills which, when the fighting commenced next morning, were occupied by General Meade's army. The conference was divided into two parties, one advising immediate advance and occupation, and the other, including General Lee, cautious and doubting the wisdom of an advance. Whilst General Lee fully admitted the advantage of a strong defensive position, he said his men had made a fatiguing march and gone through a battle, whereas most of Meade's men were fresh. He said he did not know whether Meade was already occupying those hills or, if so, in what force, and consequently he could not tell what resistance he might have to encounter and even if he could take possession of those hills, he might be surrounded, and the escape of his army would be difficult in view of the fact that he was without the possibility of assistance, whereas his opponent would have almost unlimited reinforcements and resources at his command, that the loss of his [Lee's] army would mean the loss of the Southern cause, whereas in case of defeat, he could withdraw in comparative safety as long as he did not allow himself to be cooped up.[6]

As the enemy was not pursued and driven from the heights and was reported to be growing stronger, one has to wonder why Lee attacked the next day when there were so many options available and all his forces were not up. He had provisions enough to take a defensive stand on Seminary Ridge and await the rest of his army with the hope of Meade attacking. Alexander, the historian-soldier, had this reaction when he saw the battlefield: "Instinctively the idea arose, 'If we could only take position here and have them attack us through this open ground!' But I soon learned that we were in no such luck-the boot, in fact, being upon the other foot."[7] Lee knew that Pickett's division and Stuart's cavalry would be with him by July 2; he could have waited. Another option was to move onto South Mountain toward his trains. Finally, he could have moved his army between Meade and Washington as Longstreet wanted. Knowing the over-anxiety of the Yankees for the safety of Washington, Lee must have been aware that political pressure on Meade would have mounted for an assault upon Lee to open communications with the Capitol. Lee had even concocted a plan to feed those fears by having Beauregard come to Culpeper Court House, ostensibly to organize an army there, with the object of moving on Washington.

From telegraphs exchanged between Halleck and Meade, Longstreet was convinced the Army of the Potomac would have abandoned Cemetery Ridge if his advice was followed:

> While I was trying to persuade General Lee to turn the Federal left on the 1st of July, Hallock telegraphed Meade as follows:
>
> Washington, D.C., July 1st, 1863.
>
> "The movements of the enemy yesterday indicate his intentions to either turn your left, or to cover himself by the South Mountain and occupy Cumberland Valley. Do not let him draw you too far to the east."
>
> Again on the same day:
>
> "Your tactical arrangements for battle seem good, so far as I can judge from my knowledge of the character of the country; but in a strategic view, are you not too far east, and may not Lee attempt to turn your left and cut you off from Frederick? Please give your full attention to this suggestion."
>
> The next day, just thirty minutes before my assault, General Meade telegraphed General Halleck at 3 P. M.:
>
> "If I find it hazardous to do so (meaning to attack), or am satisfied that the enemy is endeavoring to move to my rear and interpose between me and Washington, I shall fall back to my supplies at Westminster."
>
> From this we know that the ground of the Gettysburg cemetery could have been occupied without the loss of a man, yet even at this late date, some of the Virginians, not satisfied with the sacrifice already made, wish that I, who would and could have saved every man lost at Gettysburg, should now be shot to death.
>
> If we had made the move around the Federal left, and taken a strong position, we should have dislodged Meade without a single blow; but even if we had been successful at Gettysburg, and had driven the Federals out of their stronghold, we would have won a fruitless victory, and returned to Virginia conquered victors. The ground they occupied would have been worth no more to us than the ground we were on. What we needed was a battle that would give us decided fruits, not ground that was of no value. I do not think there was any necessity for giving battle at Gettysburg. All of our cavalry was absent, and while that has been urged by some as a reason why the battle should have been made at once, to my mind it was one of the strongest reasons for delaying the battle until everything was well in hand. The cause of the battle was simply General Lee's determination to fight it out from the position in which he was at that time.[8]

Concentration Not Dispersion

July 2 was the decisive day of the battle. Lee was determined to attack and hold the initiative. He decided to assault the Federal left and sent Longstreet's two divisions (Hood's and McLaws's) on a meandering march led by his misguiding engineer, Johnston, losing much time. Lee had wanted to move Ewell's corps from its position near Culp's Hill to support this attack but Ewell convinced him to leave it where it was, which would not have been so bad had Longstreet's attack been made against the Federal right (Cemetery Hill); there was an excellent jump-off point near Gettysburg, making possible a successful assault which will be discussed latter. An attack near Gettysburg could have been launched early in the morning. What Lee needed was concentration not dispersion; this is what he ended up with by curving Ewell's corps around to Culp's Hill and sending Longstreet far to his right.

Alexander called attention to this aspect of the battle not generally well known:

> There was one other occurrence of this night which I have never seen a comment upon, by any writer, & yet it seems to me to involve one of the vital points of the battle. Ewell's troops were all placed beyond, or N. E. of Gettysburg, bent around toward the point of the fish hook of the enemy's position. It was an awkward place, far from our line of retreat in case of disaster & not convenient either for re-inforcing others or being reinforced. And as already been explained this part of the enemy's position was in itself the strongest & it was practically almost unassailable. On the night of the 1st Gen. Lee ordered him to withdraw & brought around to our right of the town. Gen. Ewell had seen some ground he thought he could take & asked permission to stay & take it. Gen. Lee consented, but it turned out early next morning that the position could not be taken. Yet the orders to come out from the awkward place he was in-where there was no reasonable probability of his accomplishing any good on the enemy's line in front & where his artillery was of no service-were never renewed & he stayed there till the last. The ground is there still for any military engineer to pronounce whether or not Ewell's corps & all his artillery was not practically paralysed & useless by its position during the last two days of the battle.[9]

Longstreet's attack hit hard but lacked the magnitude to accomplish its task. Had a couple of divisions or just Johnson's division been added on the right, Longstreet would have had the capacity to drive Meade off the heights. As it was, the Second and Third Corps did not move against the enemy in conjunction with Longstreet's attack:

> General Lee's orders had been that when my advance was made, the Second Corps (Ewell), on his left, should move and make a simultaneous attack; that the Third Corps (Hill) should watch closely and engage so as to prevent heavy massing in front of me. Ewell made no move at all until about eight o'clock at night, after the heat of the battle was over, his line having been broken by a call for one of his brigades to go elsewhere. Hill made no move whatever, save of the brigades of his right division that was covering our left.[10]

Longstreet continued:

> While the co-operation of Generals Ewell and Hill, on the 2d, by vigorous assault at the moment my battle was in progress, would, in all probability, have dislodged the Federals from their

position, it does not seem that such success would have yielded the fruits anticipated at the inception of the campaign. The battle, as it was fought, would, in any result, have so crippled us that the Federals would have been able to make good their retreat, and we should soon have been obliged to retire to Virginia with nothing but victory to cover our waning cause.[11]

Cul-de-Sac of Death

At this juncture, there was still the possibility of maneuvering the enemy out of his strong position, and Longstreet was exploring this option, but Lee wanted to continue attacking. The attack Lee proposed on July 3 was totally hopeless and Longstreet foresaw the outcome. However, Lee was adamant; Alexander recognized the defects of the ground selected:

> But the technical problems of all battlefields are of deep interest to me, &, particularly so, are those of this great field. And, as a student of such technical questions, I think that all military engineers, who will study that field, will agree that the point selected for Pickett's attack was very badly chosen-almost as badly chosen as it was possible to be. I have no idea by whom it was done-whether by a general or staff officer, or a consultation of officers. There was a rumor, in our corps, that Ewell & Hill each reported against assault in his front, & so, by a process of exhaustion, it came to Longstreet's.
>
> Briefly described, the point we attacked is upon the long shank of the fishhook of the enemy's position, & our advance was exposed to the fire of the whole length of that shank some two miles. Not only that, that shank is not perfectly straight, but it bends forward at the Round Top end, so that rifled guns there, in secure position, could & did enfilade the assaulting lines. Now add that the advance must be over 1,400 yards of open ground, none of it sheltered from fire, & very little from view, & without a single position for artillery where a battery could get its horses & caissons under cover.
>
> I think any military engineer would, instead, select for attack the bend of the fishhook just west of Gettysburg. There, at least, the assaulting lines cannot be enfiladed, and, on the other hand the places selected for assault may be enfiladed, & upon shorter ranges than any other parts of the Federal lines. Again there the assaulting column will only be exposed to the fire of the front less than half, even if over one fourth, of the firing front upon the shank. These considerations are alone enough to determine the question, even if the exposed approach should be 1,400 yards wide & destitute of cover. But I believe it is certainly much more favorable.[12]

Pickett's men were sent into a huge amphitheater with hills on three sides, bristling with cannon-a "cul-de-sac of death" James Kemper called it.

This most favorable point of attack was never appreciated by the Confederates, nor did they utilize their artillery opportunely. Alexander made this clear: "Moreover, here, the point selected and the method of attack would certainly have been chosen for us by the enemy had they had the choice. Comparatively the weakest portion of their line was Cemetery Hill, and the point of greatest interest in connection with this battle is the story of our entire failure to recognize this fact."

Lee's army was approaching Gettysburg from the west. The Confederates could have concentrated against Cemetery Hill on the Federal right flank rather than dispersed in a wide arc around the Union defenses. They could have delivered a heavy blow to dislodge the enemy, aided by a concentrated artillery barrage of enfilading shell fire. In all probability they would have routed the Federals.

One Advantage of Exterior Lines

Alexander continued:

> There was one single advantage conferred by our exterior lines, and but one, in exchange for many disadvantages. They gave us the opportunity to select positions for our guns which could enfilade the opposing lines of the enemy. Enfilading fire is so effective that no troops can submit to it long. Illustrations of this fact were not wanting in the events of the day. What has been called the shank of the Federal fish-hook, extending south from the bend at Cemetery Hill toward Little Round Top, was subject to enfilade fire from the town and its flanks and suburbs. That liability should have caused special examination by our staff and artillery officers, to discover other conditions which might favor an assault. There were and are others still easily recognizable on the ground. The salient angle is acute and weak, and within about 500 yards of its west face is the sheltered position occupied by Rodes the night of July 2d, which has already been mentioned.
>
> From nowhere else was there so short and unobstructed an approach to the Federal line, and one so free from flank fire. On the northeast, at but little greater distance, was the position whence Early's two brigades the evening before had successfully carried the east face of the same salient. Within the edge of the town between these two positions was abundant opportunity to accumulate troops and to establish guns at close ranges.
>
> As long as Gettysburg stands and the contour of its hills remains unchanged, students of the battlefield must decide that Lee's most promising attack from first to last was upon Cemetery Hill, by concentrated artillery fire from the north and assaults from the nearest sheltered ground between west and northeast.
>
> That this was not realized at the time is doubtless partly due to the scarcity of trained staff and reconnoitering officers, and partly to the fact that Ewell had discontinued and withdrawn the pursuit on the afternoon of the 1st, when it was about to undertake this position. Hence the enemy's pickets were not driven closely into their lines, and the vicinity was not carefully examined. Not a single gun was established within a thousand yards, nor was a position selected which enfiladed the lines in question.
>
> Quite by accident, during the cannonade preceding Pickett's charge, Nelson's battalion of Ewell's corps fired a few rounds from a position which did enfilade with great effect part of the 11th corps upon Cemetery Hill, but the fire ceased on being sharply replied to. Briefly the one weak spot of the enemy's line and the one advantage possessed by ours were never apprehended.[13]

Ewell's Failure to Utilize His Artillery

Porter Alexander was critical that Ewell's corps put into action only 33 guns for the bombardment:

> The great criticism which I have to make on the artillery operations of the day is upon the inaction of the artillery of Ewell's corps. Our position on the exterior line, as I have explained, placed us under many & serious disadvantages. But it gave us one single advantage. It enabled us to enfilade any of the enemy's positions, near the centre of their line, with our artillery fire. Now, a battery established where it can enfilade others need not trouble itself about aim. It

has only to fire in the right direction & the shot finds something to hurt wherever it falls. No troops, infantry or artillery, can long submit to an enfilade fire. But, both infantry & artillery lines which we were to attack could have been enfiladed from somewhere in our lines near Gettysburg. There is where the use of a chief of artillery for the army comes in. He visits & views the entire field & should recognize & know how to utilize his opportunities. The chief of each corps only sees his own ground. I never had an idea of the possibility of this being done at the time, for I had but the vaguest notion of where Ewell's corps was. And Ewell's chief doubtless had as vague ideas of my situation & necessities. But Gen. Lee's chief should have known, & given every possible energy to improve the rare & great chance to the very uttermost. Only one of Ewell's five fine battalions, & he had some of the very best in the army, & under officers second to none in either army, participated in our bombardment at all. It only fired a few dozen shots, for, apparently, it could not see what it was doing. But every shot was smashing up something, &, had it been increased & kept up, it is hard to say what might have resulted.

Let it be remembered, too, that enfilading guns need not be close, & need not to be on hill tops, nor even able to see where their shots are going. They may fire from a ravine, where they cannot themselves be seen, & they only need the direction & the approximate distance. Signals from other points can tell them when they are about right, & then, safe themselves, they can do the most effective artillery work in the world. That neglect was a serious loss. Every map of the field cries out about it.[14]

General Pendleton

Brigadier General Pendleton did not have the competence and capacity for the position he held and failed miserably in effectively utilizing the long arm of the army in fighting this battle and contributed heavily to the loss. Yet, he was the first to shift the blame to Longstreet but his hands were dirty. After Sharpsburg an artilleryman expressed this opinion of him: "By the way Pendleton is Lee's weakness, P. is like the elephant, we have him & we don't know what on earth to do with him, and it costs a devil of a sight to feed him."[15] Pendleton was referred to as "Old Mother Pendleton" by the subordinate artillery officers who worked around him. Had Pendleton done his job properly and made Lee aware of the ammunition-supply shortage, "the charge would not have been made," as General McLaws noted.

In his official report of the Gettysburg battle, General Lee faulted Pendleton:

> His batteries reopened as soon as they appeared. Our own having nearly exhausted their ammunition in the protracted cannonade that preceded the advance of the infantry, were unable to reply, or render the necessary support to the attacking party. Owing to this fact, which was unknown to me when the assault took place, the enemy was enabled to throw a strong force of infantry against our left, already wavering under a concentrated fire of artillery from the ridge in front, and from Cemetery Hill, on the left.[16]

The Confederates were deficient in proficient staff officers and engineers, as perceived by General Edward Porter Alexander:

> Finally, I again connect our failure in this battle with a deficiency of well trained staff officers, which I have often before noted. Not only did we greatly lack expert military engineers, but the general weakness of staff force had, I think, the effect of having many things done by verbal

instructions which should be put in writing. For in written orders there is apt to be more attention to small details, such as may be overlooked in verbal.

Scarcely any of our generals had half of what they needed to keep a constant & close supervision on the execution of important orders. And that ought always to be done. An army is like a great machine, and in putting it into battle it is not enough for its commander to merely issue the necessary orders. He should have a staff ample to supervise the execution of each step, & to promptly report any difficulty or misunderstanding.[17]

Many opportunities were missed and poor choices were made with undue delays and no harmony of action due to these deficiencies.

One has to wonder at General Lee's relentless compulsion to stay on the offense and ignore Longstreet's sound advice after the initial contact. "On the first day we had taken the aggressive," expounded Alexander:

Although a casual reading of Gen. Lee's report suggests that the aggressive on the second day seemed forced upon him, yet the statement is very much qualified by the expression "in a measure," & also by the reference to the hopes inspired by our partial success. I think it must be frankly admitted that there was no real difficulty, whatever, in our taking the defensive the next day; & in our so manouvring afterward as to have finally forced Meade to attack us.

I think it a reasonable estimate to say that 60 per cent of our chances for a great victory were lost by our continuing the aggressive. And we may easily imagine the boon it was to Gen. Meade (who was neither a man of any high degree of decision, or if aggression; & who was now entirely new to his great responsibility, & evidently oppressed by it) to be relieved from the burden of making any difficult decision, such as he would have had to do if Lee had been satisfied with his victory of the first day; & then taken a strong position & stood on the defensive. Now the gods had flung to Meade more than impudence itself could have dared to pray for-a position unique among all the battlefields of the war, certainly adding fifty per cent to his already superior force, and an adversary stimulated by success to an utter disregard of all physical disadvantages & ready to face for nearly three quarters of a mile the very worst that all his artillery & infantry could do. For I am impressed by the fact that the strength of the enemy's position seems to have cut no figure in the consideration of the question of the aggressive; nor does it seem to have been systematically examined or inquired into-nor does the night seem to have been utilized in any preparation for the morning. Verily that night it was pie for Meade![18]

Bloodiest Road

"Never was I so depressed as upon that day [July 3]," lamented Longstreet. "I felt that my men were to be sacrificed, and that I should have to order them to make a hopeless charge."[19] Years after the war Longstreet wrote his book *From Manassas to Appomattox,* and the memories of the useless slaughter of his men must have made him feel bitter when he wrote the words: "That he [General Lee] was excited and off his balance was evident on the afternoon of the 1st, and he labored under that oppression until enough blood was shed to appease him."[20] Yet there were others who had similar feelings about the battle. The soldier-historian Edward Porter Alexander expressed identical sentiments: "Then perhaps in taking the aggressive at all at Gettysburg in 1863 & certainly in the place & dispositions for the assault on the 3rd day, I think, it will undoubtedly be held that he [General Lee] unnecessarily took the most desperate chances & the bloodiest road."[21]

My Old War Horse

The warmhearted affiliation between Generals Lee and Longstreet after the battle is validated by John D. Imboden, Brigadier General of Cavalry, C. S. A. during an interview with General Lee as pontoons were constructed to cross the Potomac after the retreat from Gettysburg:

> As we were talking General Longstreet came into the tent, wet and muddy, and was cordially greeted by General Lee in this wise: 'Well, my old war-horse, what news do you bring us from the front?' That cordial greeting between chief and lieutenant is a sufficient answer, in my mind, to the statements of alleged ill feeling between the two men growing out of affairs at Gettysburg. It has been said that if "Stonewall" Jackson had been in command at Gettysburg, Longstreet would have been shot. This is a monstrous imputation upon General Lee, no less than upon Longstreet, and utterly without foundation, in my opinion. They were surely cordial on the 9th of July, 1863.[22] In point of fact, General Lee admitted to Colonel T. J. Goree, of Texas, General Longstreet had been right: "I was present, however, just after Pickett's repulse, when General Lee so magnanimously took all the blame of the disaster upon himself. Another important circumstance, which I distinctly remember, was in the winter of 1864, when you (General Longstreet) sent me from East Tennessee to Orange Court-House with some dispatches to General Lee. Upon my arrival there, General Lee asked me into his tent, where he was alone, with two or three Northern papers on the table. He remarked that he had just been reading the Northern reports of the battle of Gettysburg, that he had become satisfied from reading those reports that if he had permitted you to carry out your plans on the 3d day, instead of making the attack on Cemetery Hill, he would have been successful. He said that the enemy seemed to have anticipated the attack on their centre, in consequence of which they had withdrawn the larger part of their force from their left flank, and from Round Top Mountain, and that if you had made your flank movement early on the morning of the 3d day as you desired that you would have met with but little opposition. To this conversation I am willing, if necessary, to make affidavit.
>
> On the 2d and 3d days of the battle before the fighting commenced, I know that Genl. Lee was constantly with you, and that any movement that you made, as well as all delays, was with his advice and concurrence."[23]
>
> Captain Erasmus Taylor, a member of Longstreet's staff, also claimed to have witnessed a letter General Lee sent to Longstreet in Tennessee: "In East Tennessee, during the winter of 1863-64, you called me into your quarters, and asked me to read a letter just received from General Lee in which he used the following words: 'Oh, general, had I but followed your advice, instead of pursuing the course that I did, how different all would have been!' You wished me to bear this language in mind as your correspondence might be lost."
>
> "Erasmus Taylor"
> "Orange County, Va."[24]

By Longstreet's account, the subject of Gettysburg was only brought up only once with General Lee: "General Lee and myself never had any deliberate conversation about Gettysburg. The subject was never broached by either of us to the other. On one occasion it came up casually, and he said to me (alluding to the charge of Pickett, on the 3d), 'General, why didn't you stop all that thing that day?' I replied that I could not, under the circumstances, assume such a responsibility, as no discretion had been left me."[25]

Longstreet did an interview for the *Washington Post* in 1893, in which he gave an insight into Gettysburg and the difference in styles of generalship between Lee and himself:

> Gen. Lee displayed his greatest weakness as a tactical commander at Gettysburg, although, for the reasons named, Antietam might well have been to us far more disastrous had the Federal army there been commanded by such a man as Grant. The tactics at Gettysburg were weak and fatal to success. Gen. Lee's attack was made in detail and not in one co-ordinate, overwhelming rush, as it should have been. The first collision was an unforeseen accident. We did not invade Pennsylvania to merely fight a battle. We could have gotten a battle anywhere in Virginia, and a very much better one than that offered us at Gettysburg. We invaded Pennsylvania not only as a diversion to demoralize and dishearten the North, but if possible to draw the Federals into battle on our own terms. We were so to manoeuver as to outgeneral the Union commander, as we had done in the second Manassas campaign; in other words, to make opportunities for ourselves, and take prompt advantage of the most favorable one that presented itself. I had confidence that this was the purpose of Gen. Lee, and that he could accomplish it. We were not hunting for any fight that was offered.

Longstreet felt there was no necessity to fight at Gettysburg. General Lee was overly belligerent and unwisely played against long odds to try winning a battle he could have easily avoided. Longstreet was content to analyze the situation, weigh the odds of success or failure, and react accordingly, even refusing battle if conditions were unfavorable.

> When in the immediate presence of the enemy Gen. Lee reversed this offensive-defensive policy-the true and natural one for us-by precipitating his army against a stronghold from which I doubt if the Federals could have been driven by less than 100,000 fresh infantry. That is all there is of Gettysburg; we did the best we could; we failed simply because we had undertaken too great a contract and went about it the wrong way. Like Pope at Manassas, Lee at Gettysburg outgeneraled himself.

Highly Educated, Theoretical Soldiers

"It was at Gettysburg," resumed General Longstreet:

> where Gen. Lee's pugnacity got the better of his strategy and judgment and came near being fatal to his army and cause. On the third day, when I said to him no fifteen thousand soldiers this world had ever produced could make the march of a mile under that tremendous artillery and musketry fire and break the Federal line along Cemetery Ridge, he determinedly replied that the enemy was there and he must be attacked. His blood was up. All the vast interests at stake and the improbability of success would not deter him. In the immediate presence of the enemy Gen. Lee's mind, at all other times calm and clear, became excited. The same may be

said of McClellan, Gustavus Smith, and most other highly educated, theoretical soldiers. Now, while I was popularly called a fighting general, it was entirely different with me. When the enemy was in sight I was content to wait for the most favorable moment to strike-to estimate the chances, and even decline battle if I thought them against me. There was no element in the situation that compelled Gen. Lee to fight the odds at Gettysburg.

General Lee was a large-minded man, of great and profound learning in the science of war. In all strategical movements he handled a great army with comprehensive ability and signal success. His campaigns against McClellan and Pope fully illustrate his capacity. On the defensive Gen. Lee was absolutely perfect. Reconciled to the single purpose of defense, he was invincible. This is demonstrated by his Fredericksburg battle, and again in the Wilderness area of Spotsylvania, at Cold Harbor, and before Petersburg.

Longstreet believed General Lee displayed superior skill on the defensive but threw caution to the wind when committed to an offensive operation.

The Science and Art of War

But of the art of war, more particularly that of giving offensive battle, I do not think Gen. Lee was a master. In science and military learning he was greatly the superior of Gen. Grant or any other commander on either side. But in the art of war I have no doubt that Grant and several other officers were his equals. In this field his characteristic fault was headlong combativeness; when a blow was struck he wished to return it on the spot. He chafed at inaction; always desired to beat up the enemy at once and have it out. He was too pugnacious. His impatience to strike, once in the presence of the enemy, whatever the disparity of forces or relative conditions, I consider the one weakness of Gen. Lee's military character.

"This trait of aggressiveness," continued General Longstreet, after a pause, "led him to take too many chances-into dangerous situations. At Chancellorsville, against every military principle, he divided his army in the presence of an enemy numerically double his own. Harper's Ferry and Antietam were even worse."[26]

The newspapers were very critical of General Lee, the government, and the Gettysburg campaign.

The *Charleston Mercury* labeled the Gettysburg campaign as the "ill-timed Northern campaign," consuming resources better applied to the straitened western theater. "It is impossible for an invasion to have been more foolish and disastrous."[27] "The expression of discontent in the public journals at the result of the expedition," as Lee termed it, grew to a point where General Lee offered his resignation to President Davis, who refused it.

A few days later Senator Louis Wigfall of Texas wrote to a fellow congressman concerning Lee's performance and Davis's support of him: "His blunder at Gettysburg, his wretched handling of his troops, & his utter want of generalship have only increased Davis's admiration for him. I was in Richmond soon after his defeat & was told that Davis was almost frantic with rage if the slightest doubt was expressed." Regarding General Lee's "capacity & conduct. He was at the same time denouncing Johnston in the most violent ... manner & attributing the fall of Vicksburg to him & him alone."[28]

General Longstreet had this reflection on Lee's offer of resignation:

> General Lee suffered during the campaign from his old trouble, sciatica, and as soon as he found rest for his army applied to the authorities for a change of commanders. The President refused, pleading that he had no one to take his place. At the time he had two generals of his own choosing who were not in authority adequate to their rank, -Joseph E, Johnston, the foremost soldier of the South, who had commanded the army from its organization until he was wounded at Seven Pines, and G. T. Beauregard, the hero of Sumter and the first Bull Run, well equipped and qualified for high command. But the President was jealous of Johnston, and nourished prejudice against Beauregard.[29]

Longstreet would have been a good candidate but was not in the running. He was in disfavor with the president for a comment he made in February 1862 after the surrender of Fort Donelson about the strategy of Albert Sidney Johnston commanding in the western theater and who was admired by Davis. Hood was "present on the occasion of the first broach between Gen. Longstreet and Mr. Davis," as he described:

> After the fall of Fort Donelson, where Gen. Albert Sidney Johnston lost such a chance as but few men ever have given them in a lifetime, I was in Richmond and was present at a reception given by Mr. Davis. We had just been talking of Fort Donelson—I mean a few of us—and wondering how upon earth, with three full divisions of infantry holding one of the strongest positions in the Confederacy, Gen Johnston had not done better, when Mr. Davis joined us. He had not heard what we said, and observed he had just written Gen. Johnston to tell him he thought that he had done very well, that he had not been on the ground, and all that. Of course there was a profound silence. We could not contradict the Chief Magistrate, and we did not at all agree with him. Mr. Davis noted the silence very quickly, and his eyes began to gleam with anger. Just then Gen. Longstreet was announced. He came in, made his respects to Mrs. Davis, and then, seeing the president crossed the room to speak to him.
>
> "I say, Longstreet," Mr. Davis began, "I have just been telling these gentlemen what I wrote Gen. Albert Sidney Johnston this afternoon, and I infer that they don't agree with me. Now, what do you think of his action in regard to Fort Donelson?"
>
> "There was a stillness. Longstreet looked at each of us, but we could say nothing. Now, no man in the army had a sharper tongue than 'Old Pete,' as you know Longstreet was called, and, from his manner, I knew something was coming. And it did come."
>
> "I suppose I never had much discretion," said Longstreet to me afterward, "but I simply couldn't help it."
>
> "What do I think, Mr. President?" he drawled. "Well, I'll tell you. Gen. Johnston reminds me very much of a young doctor I once heard of. He had just left the schools and put out his shingle when he was called to attend an accouchement. Several days after some one asked him how he had got on. 'Oh! Very well,' he jauntily replied. 'Did you safely deliver your patient,' the questioner continued. 'Well-er-no,' he said 'the lady unfortunately died.' 'But I suppose the baby was all right wasn't it?' the friend went on. 'No, sorry to say the baby died too.' 'Well, what do you mean by telling me you did very well, when both mother and child died?' insisted the questioner. 'Oh! I succeeded in saving the old man,' the young medico concluded."
>
> "We did not dare laugh," said Gen. Hood, "and Longstreet did not move a muscle of his face. Mr. Davis actually became livid with passion. He was one of the few men I have ever known who had no idea of a joke, and always took one made in his presence as an affront aimed at

himself. Finally he said, "Ah, you are pleased to be witty at my expense I presume. Permit me to bid you good evening, Sir," and Mr. Davis left us feeling anything but comfortable, I assure you.

"Why, what's the matter?" said Longstreet, in some surprise. "Have I done anything wrong?" Then we told him what had been said before he came in. "By Jove!' he ejaculated, 'I've done it, sure enough!"

"Mr. Davis never forgave me," said Gen. Longstreet to me as we were going to Bragg's relief at Chickamauga.

"To show how he felt, after I had been a corps commander, and was at home wounded," said Gen. Longstreet to the writer, "Mr. Davis actually sent to me to know if I would take command of Hood's Division, when that officer was sent to relieve Gen. Joseph E. Johnston. I replied, that as soon as I was able to command anything I should go back to my own corps. That, as you may imagine, ended the correspondence, and I went back and resumed the command of the First Corps as soon as I could ride."

This was the feeling between Longstreet and Mr. Davis when the war closed.[30]

Longstreet would not have known that President Davis had a hand in the loss of Fort Donelson by dispersing Johnston's forces so he could not concentrate an effective force to counter General Grant.

CHAPTER 10

Precursor to Chickamauga

Western Concentration

With the fortunes of the South waning, Longstreet again looked to the western theater to reverse the course:

> I do not think the general effect of the battle was demoralizing, but by a singular coincidence our army at Vicksburg surrendered to Grant on the 4th, while the armies of Lee and Meade were lying in front of each other, each waiting a movement on the part of the other, neither victor nor vanquished. This surrender, taken in connection with the Gettysburg defeat, was, of course, very discouraging to our superior officers, though I do not know that it was felt as keenly by the rank and file. For myself, I felt that our last hope was gone, and that it was now only a question of time with us. When, however, I found that Rosecrans was moving down toward Georgia against General Bragg, I thought it possible we might recover some of our lost prospects by concentrating against Rosecrans, destroying his army, and advancing through Kentucky.[1]

Longstreet knew Bragg did not have the logistical support to bring the fight to Rosecrans over the barren Cumberland Mountains but with Rosecrans being prodded by Washington to move against the Army of Tennessee, the strategic picture changed dramatically. He appreciated and took interest in the strategic importance of the western theater and his plan was very sound. Again, Longstreet pushed for concentration in Tennessee, using the railroad to quickly shunt troops, taking advantage of the Confederacy's interior lines.

Alexander made this observation about the strategic situation the Confederacy faced:

> The prospects of the Confederacy had been sadly altered by our failures at Gettysburg and Vicksburg. Grant would now be able to bring against us in Ga. Rosecrans reenforced by the army which had taken Vicksburg. To remain idle was to give the enemy time to do this. Once more the necessity was upon us to devise some offensive which might bring on a battle with approximately equal chances. Lee, accordingly, urged forward the building up of his own army with the design of an early aggressive movement against Meade. It must be admitted that the opportunity for such was slight. The enemy's fortified lines about Alexandria were too near; as was proven later, when in Nov. an advance was actually attempted.[2]

General Lee was called to Richmond on August 24 for conferences with President Davis, for the Confederacy was now in a state of crisis due to the recent severe reverses at Gettysburg and Vicksburg. Charleston, South Carolina, was under siege and Wilmington, North Carolina (the main port for fast British merchantmen to bring in munitions), was under threat by Federal land operations. Longstreet was left in command of the army while Lee was away; Lee was again thinking of taking the offensive against Meade in Virginia and asked Longstreet to prepare the army for offensive operations.

Western Concentration

As he had in January, and in May 1863. Longstreet advocated a western concentration in Tennessee; he did not see the strategic situation in Virginia as promising:

> Headquarters,
> September 2, 1863
> General R. E. Lee,
> Commanding, &c.:
>
> General: Your letter of the 31st is received. I have expressed to Generals Ewell and Hill your wishes, and am doing all that can be done to be well prepared with my own command. Our greatest difficulty will be in preparing our animals. I do not know that we can reasonably hope to accomplish much here by offensive operations, unless you are strong enough to cross the Potomac. If we advance to meet the enemy on this side, he will, in all probability, go into one of his many fortified positions; these we cannot afford to attack.
>
> I know but little of the condition of our affairs in the west, but am inclined to the opinion that our best opportunity for great results is in Tennessee. If we could hold the defensive here with two corps, and send the other to operate in Tennessee with that army, I think we could accomplish more than by an advance from here.
>
> The enemy seems to have settled down upon the plan of holding certain points by fortifying and defending, while he concentrates upon others. It seems to me that this must succeed, unless we can concentrate ourselves, and, at the same time, make occasional show of active operations at all points. I know of no other means of acting upon that principle at present, excepting to depend upon our fortifications in Virginia, and concentrate with one corps of this army, and such as may be drawn from others, in Tennessee, and destroy Rosecrans' army. I feel assured that this is practicable, and that greater advantage will be gained than by any operations from here.
>
> I remain, general, very respectfully, your most obedient servant,
>
> James Longstreet,
> Lieutenant-General.[3]

In mid-August Longstreet had written to the Secretary of War, upon previous invitation to give his strategic views, regarding a concentration in the western theater:

> While the army was lying idle on the south bank of the Rapidan my mind reverted to affairs in the West, and especially to the progressive work of the Union army in Tennessee towards the northern borders of Georgia. Other armies of the South were, apparently, spectators, viewing those tremendous threatenings without thought of turning minds or forces to arrest the march of Rosecrans.
>
> To me the emergency seemed so grave that I decided to write the Honorable Secretary of War (excusing the informality under the privilege given in his request in May) expressing my

opinion of affairs in that military zone. I said that the successful march of General Rosecrans's army through Georgia would virtually be the finishing stroke of the war; that in the fall of Vicksburg and the free flow of the Mississippi River the lungs of the Confederacy were lost; that the impending march would cut through the heart of the South, and leave but little time for the dissolution; that to my mind the remedy was to order the Army of Northern Virginia to defensive work, and send detachments to reinforce the army in Tennessee; to call detachments of other commands to the same service, and strike a crushing blow against General Rosecrans before he could receive reinforcing help; that our interior lines gave the opportunity, and it was only by the skillful use of them that we could reasonably hope to equalize our power to that of the better-equipped adversary; that the subject had not been mentioned to my commander, because like all others he was opposed to having important detachments of his army so far beyond his reach; that all must realize that our affairs were languishing, and that the only hope of reviving the waning cause was through the advantage of interior lines.[4]

This is substantiated by Alexander:

> It was not until Aug. 15, two weeks after the army was safe behind the Rapidan, that Longstreet again called the attention of Sec'y Seddon to the tremendous threatenings of the situation, and pointed out the one hope of escape which he could suggest. There seems to have been no reply. A few days later, in conversation with Lee, Longstreet again expressed his views. Lee was unwilling to consider going west in person, but approved the sending of Longstreet, and even spoke of his being given independent command there, if the War Department could be brought to approve.[5]

Save the Country

Longstreet wrote his friend and political patron Senator Wigfall to assist in a transfer to the west. He felt his advice was not heeded and, given the weight it deserved by General Lee, perhaps he felt a greater compatibility in tactics and strategy with General Joseph Johnston and a chance to obtain his own command where he could express his ideas:

> August 18th 1863
> My Dear General:
>
> I have just sent a private letter to Mr. Seddon asking him to send me to the west. If you can give the time and inclination to it, I would like to ask you to go to Richmond to urge this. That is if you think it wise. My only desire in the matter is to save the country. If I remain here I fear that we shall go, little at a time, till all will be lost. I hope that I may get west in time to save what there is left of us. I dislike to ask for anything, and only do it under the impression that if I do not our days will be numbered. I have no personal motives in this for with either Bragg's or Pemberton's Army I shall be second to Johnston and therefore in the same relative position as I am at present. I am not essential here, on the contrary, I am satisfied that it is a great mistake to keep me here.
>
> I remain with great respect
>
> J. Longstreet
> Hon. L. T. Wigfall
> Chancellorsville[6]

After writing the Secretary of War, the matter was broached in conversation between Longstreet and Lee:

> A few days after the letter was dispatched the subject happened up while discussing affairs with General Lee, when I felt warranted in expressing my views and relieving my mind of the serious apprehensions that haunted me. He inquired if I was willing to go west and take charge there. To that I consented, provided the change could be so arranged as to give me an opportunity, by careful handling of the troops before accepting battle, to gain their confidence, providing, at the same time, that means could be arranged for further aggressive march in case of success.

Davis had wanted General Lee to assume command in the Tennessee area but Lee expressed the opinion that officers already there could perform the duty. Colonel John W. Fairfax, one of Longstreet's staff officers, inferred years after the war that there was speculation Longstreet was to replace Bragg.[7]

"Old Pete," in a reply to a letter from Lee, expressed his willingness to trade places with Bragg, not for personal gain but to enhance the cause and because he felt he could make a difference:

> Headquarters,
> September 5, 1863.
> General R. E. Lee,
> Commanding, &c.:
>
> General: Your letter of the 4th is received.
>
> I do not know enough of our facilities for transporting troops, &c., west, to say what time would be consumed in moving my corps to Tennessee and back.
>
> Your information will enable you to determine this much better than I. I believe, though, that the enemy intends to confine his great operations to the west, and that it is time that we were shaping our movements to meet him.
>
> If this army is ready to assume offensive operations, I think that it would be better for us to remain on the defensive here, and to re-enforce the west, and take the offensive there. We can hold here with a smaller force than we would require for offensive operations; and if it should become necessary to retire as far as Richmond temporarily, I think that we could afford to do so than we can to give up any more of our western country. I will say more; I think that it is time that we had begun to do something in the west, and I fear if it is put off any longer we shall be too late.
>
> If my corps cannot go west, I think that we might accomplish something by giving me Jenkins', Wise's, and Cooke's brigades, and putting me in General Bragg's place, and giving him my corps. A good artillery battalion should go with these brigades. We would surely make no great risk in such a change and we might gain a great deal.
>
> I feel that I am influenced by no personal motive in this suggestion, and will most cheerfully give up, when we have a fair prospect of holding our western country,
>
> I doubt if General Bragg has confidence of his troops or himself either. He is not likely to do a great deal for us.
>
> I remain, most respectfully, your obedient servant,
>
> James Longstreet,
> Lieutenant General.[8]

Lieutenant General James Longstreet (C.S.A.), commanded the First Corps of the Army of Northern Virginia, brilliant tactician, and strategist. He was severely wounded by his own troops during the battle of the Wilderness. (Library of Congress)

Lieutenant General Ambrose Powell Hill (C.S.A.), commanded the Third Corps of the Army of Northern Virginia. Longstreet believed Major Generals Daniel Harvey Hill or Lafayette McLaws would have been more qualified to lead the corps. (Library of Congress)

Lieutenant General Ulysses S. Grant (Union), commander of all Union forces in 1864. Considered by Longstreet as the best Union general. (Library of Congress)

Lieutenant General Richard S. Ewell (C.S.A.), commanded the Second Corps of the Army of Northern Virginia. Longstreet felt Ewell was qualified for the command. (Library of Congress)

Major General George G. Meade (Union), commanded the Army of the Potomac at the battle of Gettysburg and the battle of the Wilderness. (Library of Congress)

General Braxton Bragg (C.S.A), commanded the Army of Tennessee at the battle of Chickamauga. He was considered the worst general in the Confederate army. However, Bragg was a favorite of President Davis who made him his military advisor after Bragg's resignation following his defeat at Missionary Ridge. (Library of Congress)

Major General William S. Rosecrans (Union), commanded the Union army at Chickamauga and was soundly defeated and pushed back to Chattanooga. Rosecrans was considered a good strategist. (Library of Congress)

Lieutenant General Leonida Polk (C.S.A.) was a trained soldier and a bishop in the Episcopal Church. He commanded the right wing at the battle of Chickamauga but was scapegoated by General Bragg for not following orders. (Library of Congress)

General Robert E. Lee (C.S.A.), commander of the Army of Northern Virginia. Lee and Longstreet had a close professional and personal relationship. (Library of Congress)

Major General Ambrose Burnside (Union), commanded the Army of the Potomac at the battle of Fredericksburg and also confronted Longstreet at Knoxville. (Library of Congress)

General Joseph E. Johnston (C.S.A.), Longstreet considered him to be the best general in the Confederacy. (Library of Congress)

Major General Joseph Hooker (Union), commanded the Army of the Potomac in the battle of Chancellorsville. (Library of Congress)

Major General George E. Pickett (C.S.A.), commanded a division in Longstreet's First Corps and led an assault on Meade's lines on the third day of fighting July 3 at Gettysburg. (Library of Congress)

Major General James Ewell Brown "Jeb" Stuart (C.S.A.), commanded Lee's cavalry. Longstreet described him as "endowed by nature with the gifts that go to make a perfect cavalryman." (Library of Congress)

Major General Lafayette McLaws (C.S.A.), senior division commander in Longstreet's First Corps. He had been a childhood friend of Longstreet and fellow classmate at West Point. (Library of Congress)

Major General John Bell Hood (C.S.A.), commanded a division in Longstreet's First Corps. He was wounded at Gettysburg on the second day July 2 and disabled for the rest of the battle. (Library of Congress)

Little Round Top is the smaller of two hills, the other being Big Round Top near Gettysburg. It was unsuccessfully assaulted by Confederate troops in an attack on the Union left flank on July 2, 1863. (Library of Congress)

Culp's Hill anchored the Union right flank during the battle of Gettysburg. It was assaulted by the third division, commanded by Major General Edward "Allegheny" Johnson of Ewell's corps on July 2, 1863, but the attack failed to carry the hill. (Library of Congress)

Rifled cannon was a vast improvement over the smoothbore cannon. The rifling gave the cannon longer range and better accuracy. (Library of Congress)

The Whitworth gun was a breech-loader, firing an elongated 12-pound shell. It was imported from England and used primarily by the Confederate forces. It was highly accurate and could fire solid shot beyond 2,800 yards. (Library of Congress)

President Jefferson Davis of the Confederacy. He considered himself a military genius but lacked the necessary knowledge of the profession of arms. (Library of Congress)

Lieutenant General Thomas J. "Stonewall" Jackson (C.S.A.) commanded the Second Corps of the Army of Northern Virginia. Colonel Armistead Long of Lee's staff compared Longstreet and Jackson in his memoirs. He believed Longstreet had "superior intelligence," while Jackson had an "iron mind." (Library of Congress)

General Pierre Gustave Toutant Beauregard (C.S.A.), commanded Confederate forces at First Manassas. He was under the displeasure of President Jefferson Davis throughout the war. (Library of Congress)

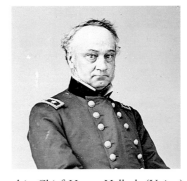

General-in-Chief Henry Halleck (Union) was promoted to that command on July 23, 1862 and got the nickname "Old Brains." He was responsible for training, equipping, and deploying Union soldiers in the war. (Library of Congress)

Brigadier General Louis Trezevant Wigfall (C.S.A.), who resigned his commission in February, 1862 to become a Confederate States senator from Texas from 1862 to 1865. He split with President Jefferson Davis as the Civil War progressed. He was a close friend and advocate for Longstreet and Joseph E. Johnston. (Library of Congress)

Brigadier General Micah Jenkins (C.S.A.), Longstreet thought Jenkins was one of the finest officers in the army. Jenkins was killed in the battle of the Wilderness on May 6, 1864. (Library of Congress)

Brigadier General William Barksdale (C.S.A.), commanded a brigade in McLaws's division of Longstreet's corps at Gettysburg and was wounded and died on July 3, 1863. (Library of Congress)

Major Osmun Latrobe (C.S.A.), was on Longstreet's staff as assistant adjutant and inspector general. (Library of Congress)

Adjutant General of the Army of Northern Virginia Walter Taylor (C. S. A.), was on General Robert E. Lee's staff as aide-de-camp. He is on Lee's left in the photo. He wrote a book, *General Lee His Campaigns in Virginia 1861–1865 with Personal Reminiscences*. (Library of Congress)

Lieutenant General Jubal Early (C.S.A.), commanded a division in Ewell's Second Corps in the battle of Gettysburg. Early was relieved of command by Lee on March 30, 1864; he was the only corps commander Lee dismissed. After the war, Jubal Early concocted a story implying Longstreet lost the battle of Gettysburg. (Library of Congress)

Pickett's Charge, showing the desperate attack and fighting on the third day in the battle of Gettysburg which was a useless sacrifice of life, with no benefit. (Library of Congress)

Brigadier General Winfield Scott Hancock (Union), commanded the Second Corps of the Army of the Potomac at the battle of Gettysburg and repulsed Pickett's Charge on the third day of fighting. He was also in the battle of the Wilderness where his corps was flanked and routed by Longstreet. (Library of Congress)

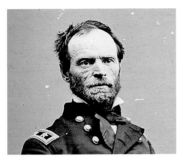

Major General William Tecumseh Sherman (Union), commanded three armies—the Army of the Cumberland, the Army of the Tennessee, and the Army of the Ohio—in confronting CSA General Joseph E. Johnston's Army of Tennessee in the Atlanta campaign. (Library of Congress)

Lieutenant General John Pemberton (C.S.A.), commanded the Army of Mississippi and, due to conflicting orders from President Jefferson Davis and General Joseph E. Johnston, became entrapped in the fortress city of Vicksburg by General Ulysses S. Grant. After a long siege, he surrendered on July 4, 1863. (Library of Congress)

C.S.A. Vice President Alexander Stephens, in 1862 he expressed opposition to the Davis administration on conscription, impressment, financial and taxation policies, and Davis's military strategy. He was arrested for treason on May 11, 1865, and imprisoned until October 1865. (Library of Congress)

Little Round Top, showing Confederate dead from the assault on the Union left flank on July 2, 1863. (Library of Congress)

Brigadier General William Nelson Pendleton (C.S.A.), led the artillery branch of the Army of Northern Virginia. When General Robert E. Lee took command, he wanted to remove him, but Pendleton was a personal friend of President Jefferson Davis. General Lee had Pendleton assigned to administrative tasks for the last two years of the war, to which he was more suited. (Library of Congress)

Chickamauga, showing the hard fighting between Confederate forces under Bragg opposed by Union forces under Rosecrans. Bragg was on the offensive and suffered proportionately more casualties. (Library of Congress)

Knoxville, showing the Confederate assault on Fort Sanders, which failed. (Library of Congress)

Wilderness, showing the dense vegetation of the area which made cavalry and artillery useless and gave advantage to Lee's smaller army. (Library of Congress)

Lieutenant General Joseph Wheeler (C.S.A.), commanded the cavalry of the Army of Tennessee and guarded the left flank in the battle of Chickamauga. Wheeler and his troopers accompanied Longstreet in his pursuit of Burnside as the Union forces pulled back to Knoxville. (Library of Congress)

Lieutenant General Simon Bolivar Buckner (C.S.A.), Buckner's corps fought under General Longstreet on the left flank during the battle of Chickamauga. (Library of Congress)

Major General Henry Heth (C.S.A.), Heth's division inadvertently started the battle of Gettysburg when he went to Gettysburg looking for shoes for his troops. Heth's division of A. P. Hill's corps fought in the battle of the Wilderness in 1864. (Library of Congress)

Major General John Cabell Breckinridge (C.S.A.), saw service in the western and eastern theater of the Confederacy during the war. (Library of Congress)

Major General Cadmus Marcellus Wilcox (C.S.A.), his brigade covered the right flank of Pickett's Charge on July 3. Union artillery on Cemetery Ridge broke up Wilcox's assault and he had to retreat. (Library of Congress)

Major General William Dorsey Pender (C.S.A.), he was severely wounded in the thigh in the battle of Gettysburg and died on July 18, 1863. His division was in support of Longstreet's assault on the right on July 2. (Library of Congress)

Brigadier General G. Moxley Sorrel (C.S.A.), Longstreet's chief of staff for three years of the war. (Wikipedia)

Lieutenant Thomas Jewett Goree (C.S.A.), a Texan who traveled to Richmond with Longstreet in the spring of 1861 and became one of Longstreet's most capable staff officers. (Wikipedia)

Colonel Edward Porter Alexander (C.S.A.), Chief of Artillery Longstreet's First Corps. from the fall of 1862 until Appomat Alexander was promoted to brigadier general in 1864. (Wikipe

The same day Longstreet wrote the above letter, Richmond consented to Longstreet heading west with two infantry divisions—McLaws's and Hood's—followed by Alexander's Battalion of Artillery of 26 guns.

This was none too soon as Alexander alluded:

> The Confederacy still held unimpaired the advantage of the "Interior Lines," already spoken of as open to them in May, and then urged by Longstreet both upon Secretary Seddon and Lee. These still offered the sole opportunity ever presented the South for a great strategic victory. Already, however, movements of the enemy were on foot which, in a few weeks, would enable them to close the shorter route from Richmond to Chattanooga via Knoxville, and leave us only the much longer and less favorable line via Weldon, Wilmington, and Augusta. Unfortunately, no one but Longstreet seems to have appreciated this.[9]

Prompt and Vigorous Execution

Longstreet's plan to quickly join Bragg was upended by a series of events:

> The success of the plan was thought from the first to depend upon its prompt and vigorous execution, and it was under these conditions that General Lee agreed to re-inforce the army in Tennessee, together with the assurance that vigorous pursuit, even to the Ohio River, should follow success. The onward march was repeatedly urged, not only in return for the use of part of the army, but to relieve General Lee of apprehension from the army in front of him; but it was not until the 9th of September that the first train came to Orange Court-House to start with its load of troops. Meanwhile, General Buckner had left his post in East Tennessee and marched south to draw nearer the army under General Bragg about Chattanooga, leaving nothing of his command in East Tennessee except two thousand men at Cumberland Gap, under General Frazer, partially fortified. General Burnside had crossed the mountains, and was not only in East Tennessee, but on that General Frazer surrendered to him his command at Cumberland Gap without a fight.
>
> These facts were known to the Richmond authorities at the time of our movements, but not to General Lee or myself until the move was so far advanced as to prevent recall.[10]

If General Lee had been made aware of Burnside's thrust into East Tennessee, he indicated he would have preferred Longstreet be sent to that area to oppose Burnside instead of to Bragg. The same day John W. Frazer surrendered—September 9—Bragg evacuated Chattanooga and fell back to the Chickamauga River; that very day the first train arrived at Louisa Court House to transport Longstreet's troops. What should have been a trip of 540 miles by the direct route turned into a difficult excursion of 775 miles.

Longstreet conveyed annoyance that he or some other worthy officer was not designated to supplant Bragg as commander of the Army of Tennessee in a letter to Wigfall:

> Richmond, Va.
> Sept. 12th 63
> Dear General
>
> Your letter of the 8th is received. I am on my way to join Bragg but have some hope that I may not visit your friends at Camp Chase. If I should get that far into the enemy's country however

I hope that I may be able to bring your friends to see you. I have met with some sympathy all along my route thus far which is of course very gratifying. But I am also somewhat gratified to find myself in better spirits under adverse circumstances than my friends are. I have learned after much experience that one must after expressing views, fight for them if he hopes to have them adopted. So I shall hereafter contend with more pertinacity for what I know to be right. Yet I yield it in the very outset.

I don't think that I should be under Bragg. And would fight against it if I saw any hope of getting anyone in the responsible position except myself. If I should make any decided opposition the world might say that I was desirous of a position which would give me fame. So I conclude that I may be pardoned if I yield my principle under the particular circumstances.

Hood's Division are in route and the most of my command are rapidly moving on to Bragg. I hope that we may be with him in Tuesday's move.

Do not forget me because I have gone so far away from you.

I would write more, but if I should start to go further into matters I should write more than I have time to write and send than you would be inclined to read. I will reserve it for a general talk. Most sincerely yours

Hon. L. T. Wigfall J. Longstreet[11]

Longstreet had complete confidence in his ability to take Bragg's place but did not want to press for intervention, otherwise others would say he was too ambitious and promoting himself. However, he was willing to serve with Joseph E. Johnston at the helm, indicating his motives were more complex and not solely for self aggrandizement but to win the war. Some historians felt Longstreet hungered for Bragg's command but this was not the case. Longstreet felt the enterprise needed someone other than Bragg, of whom he must have surely received reports and stories from Bragg's subordinates of his lack of competence and ability to command. Longstreet would certainly have been a better choice than Bragg, as there were many officers who questioned Bragg's fitness to command. Unfortunately for Longstreet, and the Confederacy, Jefferson Davis gave his unswerving loyalty to this incompetent general.

As things stood now Longstreet was to reinforce Bragg, defeat Rosecrans, and return quickly to Virginia to stave off Meade. There was much concern that Richmond might fall in his absence; Meade outnumbered Lee by half with Longstreet's corps, and if Meade came at him with Longstreet gone, he did not know if he could hold Richmond:

Camp Near Orange Court-House,
September 11, 1863
His Excellency Jefferson Davis,
President Confederate States, Richmond, Va.:

Mr. President: I replied by telegraph to your dispatch of the 10th instant. I think if Pickett's division is retained it had better be kept entire. Its brigades are small. Should, if possible, be recruited, and it will be more efficient united. It will require some days for it to march to Richmond, and in the meantime Wise can be made ready. Longstreet should have reached Richmond last evening, and can make all necessary arrangements.

The defenses around Richmond should now be completed as soon as possible. I did not see any connection or communication between the redoubts for the defense of Drewry's Bluff from a land attack, and the defensive line around Manchester. This is important, and also that there should be obstructions in the river connecting this intermediate line (as it is termed) on both sides of the river. Should the enemy's land forces drive us from Drewry's Bluff, they would remove the obstructions at that point, and although we might be able to hold the intermediate line, his gunboats could ascend the river and destroy Richmond. I think, too, Colonel Gorgas should commence at once to enlarge his manufacturing arsenals, &c., in the interior, so that if Richmond should fall we would not be destitute. These are only recommended as prudential measures, and such as, should the necessity for them ever arise, we will then wish had been taken.

Scouts on the Potomac report 4 large schooners crowded with troops, passing up the river on the 8th instant. I think they must have come south of James River. Scouts should be sent to Suffolk and elsewhere to ascertain what points have been evacuated.

If I was a little stronger, I think I could drive Meade's army under cover of the fortifications of Washington before he gathers more re-enforcements. When he gets all his re-enforcements I may be forced back to Richmond. The blow at Rosecrans should be made promptly, and Longstreet returned.

I am, with great respect, your obedient servant,

R. E. Lee,
General.[12]

On the day "Old Pete" sent Wigfall a letter, he sent one to General Lee expressing the same concerns General Lee articulated to President Davis over Richmond and for his quick return:

Extract of Letter From General Longstreet.
Headquarters,
Richmond, September 12, 1863.
General R. E. Lee,
Commanding:

General: Anderson's brigade was so far on its way toward Charleston when your telegram got here that it could not be diverted, and fearing that if I sent Jenkins on to take his place that General Beauregard would keep both, I concluded that the wisest and safest plan would be to put Jenkins' brigade in Anderson's place in Hood's division. It has been so arranged. I intended to have suggested before leaving you, that our defenses around Richmond be so arranged that we might (in the event we should be forced to give up Richmond) hold Drewry's and Chaffin's Bluffs, with a garrison of 15,000 or 20,000 men, until we could collect enough here to retake Richmond. I suppose we might hold our vessels here, under the protection of these fortifications, until we could recover the city. But if we should give up the river to the enemy, there would be but little prospect of our getting back the capital during the war. As I have never seen the positions of these bluffs, I do not know whether this arrangement is a practicable one.

I hope to start west on Monday morning. If I can do anything there, it shall be done promptly. If I cannot, I shall advise you to recall me. If I did not think our move a necessary one, my regrets at leaving you would be distressing to me, as it seems to be with the officers and men of my command. Believing it to be necessary, I hope to accept it and my other personal inconveniences cheerfully and hopefully. All that we have to be proud of has been accomplished under your eye and under your orders. Our affections for you are stronger, if it is possible for them to be stronger, than our admiration for you.

I remain, general, most respectfully and affectionately, your obedient servant,

James Longstreet,
Lieutenant-General.[13]

While Longstreet was in preparation to move to Tennessee, the government requested two of his brigades be sent to Charleston, South Carolina, which had been under attack for almost two months. Anderson's brigade was sent as Longstreet explained to General Lee along with Henry A. Wise's brigade; Longstreet retained Micah Jenkins's brigade, whose commander he considered one of his best fighting officers as well as General Goode Bryan's Georgia brigade.

Beat Those People Out in the West

After Longstreet made his final preparations for the trip, he went to see General Lee at his tent before parting:

As I left General Lee's tent, after bidding him goodby, he walked out with me to my horse. As my foot was in the stirrup he said again, "Now, general, you must beat those people out in the West." Withdrawing my foot to respectful position I promised, "If I live; but I would not give a single man of my command for a fruitless victory." He promised again that it should be so; said the arrangements had been made that any success that we had would be followed; that orders to that effect had been given; that transportation was also ordered to be prepared, and the orders would be repeated.[14]

As Longstreet's troops embarked on the trains for their journey west, Walter H. Taylor of Lee's staff reflected:

We all disliked very much to see this splendid section of our army leave us. No better troops could be found anywhere than those under General Longstreet, and he was so strong in defense,-our "Old War Horse," as he was familiarly called. There was never any doubt about the security of a position that was held by him. Although he realized the necessity for his going, and indeed was anxious to go, and even suggested that he be placed in command of the army in Tennessee, still he felt a certain kind of regret at leaving.[15]

Westward Ho

The operation was labeled "Westward Ho" and the inadequate Confederate railroad system was greatly taxed by the undertaking: "There were two routes between Richmond and Augusta, one via Wilmington, the other through Charlotte, North Carolina, but only a single track from Augusta to Chattanooga," Longstreet asserted. "The gauges of the roads were not uniform, nor did the roads connect at the cities (except by drays and other such conveyances). The roads had not been heavily worked before the war, so that the rolling stock was light and limited."[16] Porter Alexander found the railroad system did a satisfactory job despite its condition:

> It could scarcely be considered rapid transit, yet under the circumstances it was really a very creditable feat for our railroad service under the attendant circumstances. We found ourselves restricted to the use of one long roundabout line of single-track road of light construction, much of it of the "stringer track" of those days, a 16-pound rail on stringers, with very moderate equipment and of different gauges, for the entire service at the time of a great battle of the principal armies of the Confederacy. The task would have taxed a double-tracked road with modern equipment.[17]

Longstreet's chief of staff, Moxley Sorrel said:

> The movement was to be wholly by train, and to any one familiar with the railroad service at the South in the last part of 1863 little need to be said of the difficulties facing the Quartermaster-General {Brigadier-General A. R. Lawton}.
>
> He was to pick up their camps near Gordonsville and the Rapidan, nine strong divisions of infantry and six batteries of artillery, and land them without serious accident and no delay with their ambulances and light vehicles near Chattanooga or Lookout Mountain. This feat was accomplished without stint of honor or praise, be it said, to the Quartermaster-General's department. Never before were so many troops moved over such worn-out railways, none first-class from the beginning. Never before were such crazy cars-passenger, baggage, mail, coal, box, platform, all and every sort wabbling on the jumping strap-iron-used for hauling good soldiers. But we got there nevertheless.[18]

As the troops assembled to board the trains, General Hood went to the train station to say farewell. Some of his brigade and regimental officers appealed to him to assume command of the division despite his arm being disabled at Gettysburg. General Hood courageously acquiesced. On Monday, September 14, Longstreet boarded a train from Richmond where he had set up temporary headquarters at the Spotswood Hotel to coordinate troop departures.

Lieutenant Colonel Sorrel arrived in Georgia with General Longstreet and Lieutenant Colonel Manning:

> It was about three o'clock in the afternoon of September 19 that our rickety train pulled up, with jerks and bangs, at the little railway landing, called Catoosa Platform. Longstreet and some of his personal staff, Colonels Sorrel and Manning, were in this train and immediately took horse. The remainder of the staff, with most of the horses, were on a train two or three hours later. The Lieutenant-General and part of his at once started to find General Bragg.
>
> That General should surely have had guides to meet and conduct us to the conference on which so much depended. A sharp action had taken place during the day and it would appear that if Bragg wanted to see any body, Longstreet was the man. But we were left to shift for ourselves, and wandered by various roads and across small streams through the growing darkness of the Georgia forest in the direction of the Confederate General's bivouac. At one point in our hunt for him we narrowly escaped capture, being almost in the very center of a strong picket of the enemy before our danger was discovered. A sharp right-about gallop, unhurt by the pickets' hasty and surprised fire, soon put us in safety, and another road was taken for Bragg, about whom by this time some hard words were passing.

But all things have an end, even a friendly hunt for an army commander, and between 10 and 11 o'clock that night we rode into the camp of Gen. Braxton Bragg. He was asleep in his ambulance, and when aroused immediately entered into private conference with Longstreet. It lasted about an hour, and in that time the plan of battle for the next day was definitely settled, and than we all took to the leafy ground under the tall oaks and hickories for some sleep against the work before us.[19]

General Braxton Bragg

The man Longstreet conferred with, General Braxton Bragg, the commander of the Army of Tennessee, had an eccentric and curious personality with poor interpersonal skills which soured his relations with his officers and men. Lieutenant Colonel Fremantle of the Coldstream Guards from England gave a description of Bragg:

This officer is in appearance the least prepossessing of the Confederate generals. He is very thin. He stoops, and has a sickly, cadaverous, haggard appearance, rather plain features, bushy black eyebrows which unite in a tuft on the top of his nose, and a stubby iron-gray beard; but his eyes are bright and piercing. He has the reputation of being a rigid disciplinarian, and of shooting freely for insubordination. I understand he is rather unpopular on this account, and also by reason of his occasional acerbity of manner.[20]

Dr. D. W. Yandell, medical director for the Department of the West, made this evaluation of General Bragg: "General Bragg is either stark mad or utterly incompetent. He's ignorant of both the fundamental principles and details of his noble profession, and has lost the confidence of both his men and his officers."[21]

General Bragg made his plan of battle for September 20 as described by D. H. Hill:

Longstreet arrived at 11 P.M. on the 19th. Soon after, General Bragg called together some of his officers and ventured upon that hazardous experiment, a change of organization in face of the enemy. He divided his army into two wings; he gave to Polk the right wing, consisting of the corps of Hill and Walker, and the division of Cheatham,-comprising in all 18,794 infantry and artillery, with 3500 cavalry under Forrest; to Longstreet he gave the left wing, consisting of the corps of Buckner and Hood, and the division of Hindman,-22,849 infantry and artillery, with 4000 cavalry under Wheeler. That night Bragg announced his purpose of adhering to his plan of the 19th for the 20th, viz., successive attacks from right to left, and he gave his wing commanders orders to begin at daylight.[22]

The army Longstreet was to fight with, as well as its commander, had some deficiencies: "Neither in armament, equipment, or organization was the Western army in even nearly as good shape as the Army of Northern Virginia," wrote Alexander.

About one-third of the infantry was still armed only with the smooth-bore musket, caliber .69. Only a few batteries of the artillery were formed into battalions, and their ammunition was all of inferior quality. Rosecrans had the superiority of his small-arms and rifled artillery over the inferior equipment of the Confederates. It is well recognized that the defensive role is the least hazardous, and, on this campaign, Rosecrans, although on the strategic offensive, gladly seized the tactical defensive when Bragg incautiously gave him the privilege.

Bragg's daily experience in the handling of his army should have warmed him that it was not a military machine which could be relied upon to execute orders strictly, or to be alert to seize passing opportunities, and it is safe to say that its power for offence was scarcely 50 per cent of what the same force would have developed upon the defensive.[23]

Independent Scouts

"The want of information at General Bragg's headquarters was in striking contrast with the minute knowledge General Lee always had of every operation in his front," D. H. Hill noted, "and I was most painfully impressed with the feeling that it was to be a hap-hazard campaign on our part."

He seems to have had no well-organized system of independent scouts, such as Lee had, and such as proved of inestimable service to the Germans in the Franco-Prussian war. For information in regard to the enemy, apparently, he trusted alone to his very efficient cavalry. But the Federal cavalry moved with infantry supports, which could not be brushed aside by our cavalry. So General Bragg only learned that he was encircled by foes, without knowing who they were, what was their strength, and what were their plans. His enemy had a great advantage over him in this respect.

The nightmare upon Bragg for the next three days was due, doubtless, to his uncertainty about the movements of his enemy, and to the certainty that there was not that mutual confidence between him and some of his subordinates that there ought to be between a chief and his officers to insure victory. Bragg's want of definite and precise information had led him more than once to issue "impossible" orders, and therefore those intrusted with their execution got in the way of disregarding them. Another more serious trouble with him was the disposition to find a scapegoat for every failure and disaster. This made his officers cautious about striking a blow when an opportunity presented itself, unless they were protected by a positive order.[24]

CHAPTER 11

Bull of the Woods

Chickamauga

Bragg's army had been engaged with the enemy on September 18 and 19 in severe skirmishes in an attempt to turn the Federal left. Bragg did not readjust his battle plan for the 20th. The attack was to be opened on the extreme right in echelon, with each brigade commander attacking after the one to his right, driving the Federal forces south on the La Fayette and Dry Valley roads, cutting off Rosecrans from Chattanooga; Rosecrans had read Bragg's intent and had planned accordingly. Bragg had given only verbal orders for a daylight attack to General Leonidas Polk, his right-wing commander; General John C. Breckinridge's division of D. H. Hill's corps was to open the battle at daylight but no one had communicated this to him or Hill, though Breckinridge had slept the night at Polk's campfire. Colonel Archer Anderson, Lieutenant J. A. Reid, and Major A. C. Avery of Hill's staff had a chance meeting with Polk about midnight but Polk never mentioned the attack was to begin at daylight and, instead, chose to return to his headquarters at Thedford's Ford and composed the order selecting as courier, John Fisher, not a staff member but an enlisted man in the Orleans Light Horse Troop, Polk's escort, to bear the copy to Hill. Fisher searched for four hours and not only failed to find Hill but never reported it.

Polk rose about daylight and learned that the order was never delivered to Hill. He sent another order: "Move upon and attack the enemy as soon as you are in position." Hill concluded his men were not in position and wrote Polk, telling him his men were not aligned properly. Breckinridge's division was just coming up having been delayed by Polk at his headquarters and his wagons got lost during the night; Some of the men had not eaten for 24 hours. The Yankees had felled trees all night, building rude works about breast high using logs and rails, creating a major obstacle too strong to be taken by main assault. Also, Hill was unsure if cavalry covered his flank; he decided to let the men draw breakfast rations and let Polk deal with these issues.

General Polk rode up and, according to Hill, assented to the delay and let the men distribute rations. Just after General Polk left Hill, General Bragg arrived on horseback and inquired why the attack was not made at daylight. Hill answered this was the first he had heard of a daylight attack. Bragg ordered Hill to attack as quickly as possible but Polk, and certainly Bragg, should have been at the front to make preparations. Hill called on Forrest for cavalry on his right. Forrest sent the division of Brigadier General Frank Armstrong; dismounted beyond its right was Forrest's other cavalry division under Pegram. The alignment of rest of Hill's corps got sorted out by the intervention of Hill, Polk, and Bragg. Hill shifted two of Breckinridge's three brigades—those of Generals Dan Adams and Marcellus Stovall—slightly more to the right so they overlapped the Federal entrenchments; nonetheless, Breckinridge had no reserve, and not enough power was placed on the right in support. Reconnaissance by the light of day revealed the road on the Union left was "open, unguarded nor under close observation," which invited a flank movement, interposing on the Union line of communications and forcing the Union army out of his works to attack. In spite of this, Bragg, not particularly adaptable in his tactical or strategic thinking, ordered a direct assault on the works as originally planned.

Bragg had his back to the Chickamauga River—"Chickamauga" loosely translated from the Cherokee meant "River of Death." The West Chickamauga River rises from the mountains to the south and courses northeast to converge with the Tennessee River; Mission Ridge runs parallel to the river which lies in a valley between the ridge and Pidgeon Mountain. Its precipitous banks are steep, bluff-like, and rocky or low and swampy on either side; the land is flat, covered by an unbroken forest of scrub oak, cedar, and pine, with stands of hickory and oak occasionally broken by small farms; visibility was limited to 100 feet or less. The river is sluggish, not clear, and shallow, never exceeding 10 feet in depth during rainstorms, a Rebel thought it was "too large for the appellation of creek and yet does not rise to the dignity of a river." Five bridges and nine fords were the crossing points that the large bodies of infantry, cavalry, and all wagons would have to employ. Rosecrans's army backed on Mission Ridge.

At 9:30am the battle began. Breckinridge's third brigade commanded by General Ben Hardin Helm, President Abraham Lincoln's brother-in-law, smashed against the Federal log breastworks and was broken up into fragments, losing a third of the brigade; Helm gave up his life in the try. Adams and Stovall had more success flanking the Federal fortifications but no help was given to them and they were pushed back with heavy losses.

General Thomas, whose command was holding the salient of breastworks on the Federal left, became overly concerned by the unremitting Rebel attacks and sent aides to Rosecrans, making repeated calls for heavy reinforcements. Rosecrans lost his poise and started pulling supports from his right, thus unduly weakening that sector.

At sunrise—5:45am—General James Longstreet was up and becoming acquainted with his forces on the left wing. He was totally unfamiliar with the ground and had been given only a crude map by Bragg. His first order of business was to make contact with Polk's troops to his right. He found his former academy classmate, Major General Alexander P. Stewart, whose division of Buckner's corps was on the right of Longstreet's wing and had him march to connect with Polk's left. Stewart found he was a quarter of a mile in front of Patrick Cleburne's division and had to bend back his right flank to make room for Cleburne. Longstreet had at his disposal 19 batteries but, to his chagrin, "No chief of artillery for the command reported, and a brief search failed to find one. The field, as far as it could be surveyed, however, was not a field, proper, but a heavy woodland, not adapted to the practice of artillery."[1]

To gather information about the topography, Longstreet, before retiring on the night of the 19th, inquired about residents from the vicinity serving in the Confederate army and hit upon and consulted with young Tom Brotherton, who had enlisted in the Confederate army, leaving his family farm which was just behind the Union lines and in whose woods the enemy was situated. Longstreet learned from his front-line commanders that Union forces opposite his wing had been posted adjoining to and on this farm. Deciding that the Brotherton farm of 700 acres was the crucial point to concentrate his attack, he formed an assault column of 11,000 men in just under 70 acres of forest, poised like a spear to pierce the Union lines. Longstreet was convinced that no troops without intrenchments could stand such an attack by this column. Bushrod Johnson's division held the narrow front line just over 500 yards wide as the cutting edge of the spear. Behind Johnson was Hood's division commanded by Brigadier General Evander Law, and the third line consisted of Kershaw's and Humphrey's brigades of Lafayette McLaws's division, which had just arrived and brought up before the advance, making eight brigades in all. The entire column was led by the ferociously aggressive Major General John Bell Hood. Longstreet ordered the divisions configured "to form with two brigades in the front line, and one supporting where there were three brigades, and two supporting where there were more than three," the distance between the lines was "thirty or forty yards," according to Perry, who commanded Law's brigade.[2]

To the left of Longstreet's column was Thomas Hindman's division, then William Preston's, each with two brigades up and one in reserve. Preston completed Longstreet's wing and was the pivot for a wheel to the left which Bragg desired when Longstreet's wing advanced. As Bragg wanted to assault the Union lines, Longstreet had no choice, though he felt the "main column of attack" would give his attack greater depth and penetrating power but his preference would have been for a flank or rear movement. Longstreet was not intimate with Bragg as with Lee; nor did he have any knowledge of the terrain or battle conditions. since he arrived late at night so he went along with the program. The thickly wooded field at Chickamauga provided cover for the advancing troops, whereas at Gettysburg the field was open and the troops exposed. Longstreet's dispositions in this battle are studied as models by European staffs, such were his contributions to the art of war.

General Hood had arrived on September 18 and had been engaged in combat for two days but found the mood of the Army of Tennessee to be extremely negative:

> In the evening, according to my custom in Virginia under General Lee, I rode back to Army headquarters to report to the Commander-in-Chief the result of the day upon my part of the line. I there met for the first time several of the principal officers of the Army of Tennessee, and, to my surprise, not one spoke in a sanguine tone regarding the result of the battle in which we were then engaged.[3]

When Longstreet inspected the lines on the morning of the 20th, he met Hood and acted as a tonic to revive Hood's spirits:

> During that night, after a hard day's fight by his old and trusty troops, General Longstreet joined the Army. He reported to General Bragg after I had left Army headquarters, and, the next morning, when I had arranged my columns for the attack and was awaiting the signal on the right to advance, he rode up, and joined me. He inquired concerning the formation of my lines, the spirit of our troops, and the effect produced upon the enemy by our assault. I informed him that the feeling of officers and men was never better, that we had driven the enemy fully one mile the day before, and that we would rout him before sunset. The distinguished general instantly responded with that confidence which had so often contributed to his extraordinary success, that we would of course whip and drive him from the field. I could but exclaim that I rejoiced to hear him so express himself, as he was the first general I had met since my arrival who talked of victory.[4]

Longstreet exuded confidence and positive feelings to his officers and troops as they looked upon him calmly puffing his meerschaum pipe—the picture of composure.

The delay on the right proved beneficial to Longstreet in that he had the time to survey the battlefield, prepare his command for action, and pinpoint the locality to drive in his column. Longstreet grew impatient and sent a messenger to Bragg:

> As the grand wheel to the left did not progress, I sent, at eleven o'clock, to say to General Bragg that my column of attack could probably break the enemy's line if he cared to have it go in. Before answer came, General Stewart, commanding my right division, received a message from General Bragg to go in and attack by his division, and reported that the Confederate commander had sent similar orders to all division commanders. He advanced, and by severe battle caused the Union reserve division under General Brannan to be drawn to the support of that front, and this attack, with that of the divisions of our right against those of Baird, Johnson, Palmer, and Reynolds, so disturbed General Thomas that other reinforcements were called to support the defence.
>
> General Stewart was in hot engagement before word reached me that the battle had been put in the hands of division commanders; but my orders reached General Hood in time to hold him and commanders on his left before he received notice from the commanding general, and the brigades of Kershaw and Humphreys were ordered nearer the rear of his column. The divisions of B. R. Johnson and Hindman were ordered to follow in close echelon on Hood' left. Buckner's pivoting division under Preston was left to the position to which the Confederate chief had assigned it.[5]

Major Pollock Lee had ordered Stewart forward at Bragg's bidding and was moving down the left wing to give the same message to each division commander without informing Longstreet. When Longstreet learned of this, he sent his staff officers to restrain Hood and Johnson before Lee arrived.

About 11:30am Longstreet launched his assault in a planned effort—not the disjointed fighting on the right by Polk. By sheer chance, Bushrod Johnson discovered a quarter-mile gap had opened in the Union lines in the Brotherton fields just as the column swept across the La Fayette road. The gap was created when General Rosecrans sent an urgent message to General Thomas J. Wood: "The general commanding directs that you close up on Reynolds as fast as possible, and support him." Captain Sanford Kellogg, one of Thomas's staff officers, had returned to Rosecrans's headquarters, reporting a gap in the line which he believed was created by a division being pulled out to help Thomas. Wood knew the division of General John Milton Brannan was between his division and Reynolds' but it had drawn back into a thick forest apparently not visible to Kellogg. Nevertheless, General Wood decided to regard the order as peremptory and pulled out his division, although he knew the Rebels were in close contact. Wood had been upbraided twice for not obeying Rosecrans's commands promptly: the first, a written admonishment by telegraph for a failed reconnaissance of Lookout Mountain. Then, in front of his staff, for not moving his men from a reserve position, Rosecrans had scolded him: "What is the meaning of this, sir? You have disobeyed my specific orders! By your damnable negligence you are endangering the safety of the entire army, and, by God, I will not tolerate it! Move your division at once, as I have instructed, or the consequences will not be pleasant for yourself!"[6] As he waved the order before his staff, Wood uttered these words: "Gentlemen, I hold the fatal order of the day in my hand and would not part with it for five thousand dollars," and he "was glad the order was in writing, as it was a good thing to have for future reference."[7] Then he placed it securely in his pocket notebook. To fill the vacancy in the line, McCook ordered Davis to bring Martin's undersized brigade from a reserve position to the south to take Wood's place just as Longstreet struck. At the same time Sheridan was moving two of his brigades to assist Thomas in a sidelong motion behind where Wood had been.

Porter Alexander depicted the results of the breakthrough:

> On receipt of the order, Wood, leaving his skirmishers in front, started his division at a double-quick to the left, passing in rear of Brannan's division to reach the right of Reynolds. He had advanced but little more than a brigade length when Johnson's Confederate division, supported by Hood and Hindman, burst through the forest in front and fell upon the movement. Had this movement of Wood's division been foreseen by the Confederates and prepared for, it could not have happened more opportunely for them. Longstreet has been given great credit for it, which, however, he never claimed. It was entirely accidental and unforeseen, but in a very brief period it threw the entire left flank of the enemy in a panic.
>
> Longstreet's advance cut off the rear of Buell's brigade of Wood's division, and two brigades of Sheridan's advancing to fill the gap being opened behind Wood [actually Sheridan was going to help Thomas to the north]. These brigades did not make enough resistance to check the Confederates, whose triple lines could be seen advancing and who now followed the fugitives. Hindman's brigade, diverging to the left, routed the division of Davis and captured 27 guns

and over 1000 prisoners. Rosecrans, McCook and Crittenden were all caught and involved in the confusion of a retreat which soon became a panic. It was not, however pursued and might have halted and been re-formed within a mile of the field without seeing the enemy. The retreat, however, was continued to Chattanooga. A severe check was sustained by Manigault, who attacked Wilder's brigade. This brigade had two regiments armed with Spencer repeating rifles, and the 29th Ill. serving with it on this occasion, carried the same arm. They occupied a very favorable position on a steep ridge and their fire at close quarters was very severe and drove back the first advance. Then, finding themselves isolated, they presently withdrew from the field.[8]

So heavy was the fire from Wilder's Spencers that Longstreet, hearing the clatter from nearly a half mile off, thought for a moment that a fresh Federal corps had come crashing down on his left.[9]

Bragg's plan was for Longstreet to swing left but Longstreet, the eminent tactician he was, quickly perceived a swivel to the right would be more effective, as the Union defenders were moving to their left, he could bag Rosecrans's army in a sweeping envelopment; the Union Twentieth and Twenty-first Corps were smashed to pieces by the flank attack, collapsed, and retreated. Just at this juncture General Hood "was fearfully wounded, supposed to be fatally."[10] Hood related the incident: "I was pierced with a Minie ball in the upper third of the right leg; I turned from my horse upon the side of the crushed limb and fell-strange to say, since I was commanding five divisions-into the arms of some of the troops of my old brigade, which I had directed so long a period, and upon so many fields of battle."[11] General Hood was borne to a hospital of his old division in the rear where his leg was amputated by Dr. T. G. Richardson of New Orleans; he was Chief Medical Officer of the Army of Tennessee at the time and from 1878 to 1879 the president of the Medical Association of the United States.

Longstreet's composure during the fight was commented on by Lieutenant James Fraser of the Fifteenth Alabama in the brigade of Brigadier General Zachariah Deas: "Longstreet is the boldest and bravest looking man I ever saw. I don't think he would dodge if a shell burst under his chin."[12] William Miller Owen of the Washington Artillery recalled Longstreet's calm demeanor in a crisis:

> During the heat of this battle Gen. Benning, of Georgia, one of the bravest men that ever lived, came charging up to Gen. Longstreet in great agitation. He was riding an artillery horse, and was using a rope trace for a whip. His hat was gone, and he was much disordered. "General," he said, "my brigade is utterly destroyed and scattered." Gen. Longstreet approached him, and said quietly, "Don't you think you can find one man, General?"- "One man?" he said, with astonishment. "I suppose I could. What do you want to do with him?"- "Go and get him," Longstreet said very quietly, laying his hand upon his arm, "and bring him here; then you and I and he will charge together. This is the sacred soil of Georgia, General, and we may as well die here as anywhere." He looked at Gen. Longstreet curiously a moment, then laughed, and, with an oath, lashed his horse with his rope trace, and was off like a flash.
>
> In a few moments he swept by at the head of a command he had gathered together somehow or other, and he was in the fight again.
>
> Gen. Longstreet does not think it necessary to swear at the men, to whoop 'em up as it were; he always adopts the demeanor of quiet assurance and confidence, which is always better than strong oaths.[13]

As the fighting raged, Colonel Thomas Claiborne, temporarily serving on Buckner's staff, rode along the line, searching for Longstreet, to deliver a message from Buckner that William Preston's division was being held in reserve. When Claiborne found Longstreet, he "had sort of a toothpick in his mouth, and thoughtfully gazed at me." Just as Claiborne was relaying the message, an artillery shell whizzed past and the staff officer ducked. "I see you salute them," joked Longstreet.

"Yes, every time," responded Claiborne.

"If there is a shell or bullet over there destined for us," Longstreet drawled, "it will find us."

Longstreet then directed Claiborne to tell Buckner that "if I send again, to send a Brigade."[14]

Longstreet was elated with the progress and was directing the fighting around Dyer farm where Brigadier General Benjamin Humphreys met him. Humphreys had succeeded to command the brigade of William Barksdale after his death at Gettysburg. Humphreys saluted and looked at Longstreet's face: "I never saw him wear so bright and jubilant a countenance," remembered Humphreys. Longstreet returned the salute and jokingly said: "Drive them, General, these western men can't stand it any better than the Yankees we left in Virginia."[15]

Rosecrans left the field to rally the retreating troops for a defensive stand at Chattanooga; left to his own defenses, Major General George Thomas, commander of the Fourteenth Corps, though Virginia-born had remained loyal to the Union despite family objections, made a skillful and stubborn resistance on the Union left and was given the sobriquet "Rock of Chickamauga."

Remnants of the Federal right were rallying on Snodgrass Hill and Horseshoe Ridge to make a stand against the Confederate onslaught. Horseshoe Ridge is described by Glenn Tucker in his book of the battle:

> It is in no manner shaped like a horseshoe, nor is it possible while the trees are in foliage-as they were on September 20-to gain a very clear conception of the outlines of the elevation, which would more closely resemble an octopus with shortened tentacles, or an irregularly shaped starfish, than a horseshoe. It is high ground with a number of ridges or "hogbacks" extending from the center toward south and east, and consequently with a number of ravines, most of them relatively shallow, running up the center of the hump. Colonel Archer Anderson called the ridges "bastion-like spurs," and so they proved to be.[16]

Horseshoe Ridge consisted of three hills (simply named Hills One, Two, and Three), heavily wooded and covered in underbrush. The Union left flank held behind log fortifications at Kelly Field, while the center and right bent back at right angles to the left.

"Calls were repeated for the cavalry to ride in pursuit of the retreating forces, and guard the gaps of the ridge behind the enemy standing in front of our right wing," Longstreet admonished but the cavalry never came.[17]

Chickamauga Battlefield

Snodgrass Hill

General Bushrod Johnson focused his next effort on a spur of Horseshoe Ridge—Snodgrass Hill; Longstreet had his men reorganize and refresh. Lieutenant James Fraser of the 50th Alabama, Deas' brigade, wrote: "We pursued the flying enemy for more than a mile and a half, and when at last we were ordered to halt by our generals, we were tired, scattered and exhausted."[18]

Longstreet touched upon occurrences after the breakthrough:

> General Johnson thought he had the key of the battle near Snodgrass Hill. It was a key, but a rough one. He was ordered to reorganize his own brigades and those of Hindman's division for renewed work; to advance a line of skirmishers, and give time to the troops for refreshment, while I rode along the line to observe the enemy and find relations with our right wing.
>
> It was after one o'clock, and the hot and dry and dusty day made work fatiguing. My lunch was called up and ordered spread at some convenient point while I rode with General Buckner and the staffs to view the changed conditions of the battle. I could see but little of the enemy's line, and only knew of it by the occasional exchange of fire between the lines of skirmishers, until we approached the angle of the lines. I passed the right of our skirmishers, and, thinking I had passed the enemy's, rode forward to be accurately assured, when I suddenly found myself under near fire of his sharpshooters concealed behind the trees and under the brush. I saw enough, however, to mark the ground line of his field-works as they were spread along the front of the right wing, and found I was very fortunate in having the forest to cover the ride back until out of reach of their fire. In the absence of a chief of artillery, General Buckner was asked to establish a twelve-gun battery on my right to enfilade the enemy's works and line standing before our right wing, and then I rode away to enjoy my spread of Nassau bacon and Georgia sweet potatoes. We were not accustomed to potatoes of any kind in Virginia, and thought we had a luxury, but it was very dry, as the river was a mile and more from us, and other liquids were over the border.[19]

Some historians wonder why Longstreet did not detect a half-mile gap in the Federal lines as he rode with Buckner east from the Vittetoe house toward the blacksmith shop. Obviously, the dense forest had a lot to do with it along with the sharpshooters; it was not the job of the commanding general to make such a reconnaissance but rather to the division commanders to send scouts to probe the Federal lines for openings and report back to Longstreet. Scouting was not a strong suit in the Army of Tennessee.

At 2:45pm the men were halted to regroup and rest.

During lunch, Longstreet received a message by courier—Bragg wished to see him:

> He was some little distance in rear of our position. [Bragg's temporary headquarters was at Jay's Mill.] The change of the order of battle was explained, and the necessity under which it came to be made. We had taken some thirty or more field-pieces and a large number of small-arms, and thought that we had cut off and put to disorder the Twentieth and Twenty-first Corps that had retreated through the pass of the Ridge by the Dry Valley Road. He was informed of orders given General Johnson for my left, and General Buckner for a battery on the right. I then offered as suggestion of the way to finish our work that he abandon the plan of battle by our right wing, or hold it to defence, draw off a force from that front that had rested since the left wing took up battle, join them with the left wing, move swiftly down the Dry Valley road,

pursue the retreating forces, occupy the gaps of the Ridge behind the enemy standing before our right, and call that force to its own relief.

He was disturbed by the failure of his plan and the severe repulse of his right wing, and was little prepared to hear suggestions from subordinates for other moves or progressive work. His words, as I recall them, were: 'There is not a man in the right wing who has any fight in him.' From accounts of his former operations I was prepared for halting work, but this, when the battle was at its tide and in partial success, was a little surprising. His humor, however, was such that his subordinate was at a loss for a reopening of the discussion. He did not wait, nor did he express approval or disapproval of the operations of the left wing, but rode for his head-quarters at Reed's Bridge.

There was nothing for the left wing to do but work along as best it could. The right wing ceased its active battle as the left forced the enemy's right centre, and the account of the commanding general was such as to give little hope of his active use of it in supporting us.[20]

In July 1884 General Longstreet wrote to General D. H. Hill about his meeting with Bragg:

It is my opinion that Bragg thought at 3 P.M. that the battle was lost, though he did not say so positively. I asked him at that time to reenforce me with a few troops that had not been so severely engaged as mine, and to allow me to go down the Dry Valley Road, so as to interpose behind Thomas and cut off his retreat to Chattanooga, at the same time pursuing the troops that I had beaten back from my front. His reply, as well as I can remember, was that he had no troops except my own that had any fight left in them, and that I should remain in the position in which I then was. After telling me this, he left me, saying, "General, if anything happens, communicate with me at Reed's Bridge."

"Bragg seems not to have known that Cheatham's division and part of Liddell's had not been in action that day," was D. H. Hill's assessment. Rosecrans was carried away by the rout of his right wing, while Bragg took himself completely out of the battle, the unusual circumstances which were addressed by D. H. Hill: "It probably never happened before for a great battle to be fought to its bloody conclusion with the commanders of each side away from the field of conflict. But the Federals were in the hands of the indomitable Thomas, and the Confederates were under their two heroic wing commanders Longstreet and Polk."[21]

After a short rest, Longstreet launched a series of hammer-like blows against Thomas's right and center, starting at 1:00pm, with Kershaw pursuing Colonel Charles G. Harker to Snodgrass Hill. The Federal right was in such shambles that it was thought one knock by a Confederate division would completely unhinge the whole flank. Kershaw struck with his own brigade on the left and Humphreys's brigade on the right. But on the knoll, he encountered Harker, William B, Hazen, and William Stoughton, whose troops had rallied and were able to repulse Kershaw's repeated attempts.

In the second phase Longstreet sent in Bushrod Johnson's and Hindman's divisions consisting of the brigades of Deas, Manigault, Gregg, Patton, Anderson, and McNair, assailing Thomas's bastion front and rear:

After his lunch, General Johnson was ordered to make ready his own and Hindman's brigades, to see that those of Hood's were in just connection with his right, and await the opening of our battery. Preston's division was pulled away from its mooring on the river bank to reinforce our worn battle. The battery not opening as promptly as expected, General Johnson was finally ordered into strong, steady battle. He pushed through part of the woodland, drove back an array of artillery and the supporting infantry, and gained other elevated ground. The sound of the battle in his rear, its fire drawing nearer, had attracted the attention of General Granger of the reserve corps, and warned him that it was the opportunity for his command. He marched, without orders, towards the noise, and passed the front of Forrest's cavalry and the front of our right wing, but no report of his march was sent to us. Day was on the wane. Night was advancing. The sun dipped to the palisades of Lookout Mountain, when Lieutenant-Colonel Claiborne reported that the cavalry was not riding in response to my calls. He was asked to repeat the order in writing to General Wheeler, and despatched at 5:09 P. M.

Then our foot-scouts reported that there was nothing on the road taken by the enemy's retreating columns but squads of footmen. Another written order for the cavalry was despatched at 5:30.[22]

Bushrod Johnson attacked Horseshoe Ridge in front as Hindman worked Deas's brigade around Brannan's right to flank it and open an oblique fire on his rear. Just when it looked like the Federal right would be annihilated, Gordon Granger arrived and sent Walter C. Whitaker's and John Mitchell's brigades under James Steedman to dislodge the Rebels, preventing a catastrophe; Steedman suffered heavy losses in dislodging Hindman. Not only this, Granger brought with him 95,000 extra rounds of ammunition, as the cartridge boxes of Thomas's troops were almost empty, his soldiers checking the dead and wounded for ammunition. The fighting all along the line was intense according to D. H. Hill: "It began at 3:30 p.m. A terrific contest ensued. The bayonet was used, and men were killed and wounded with clubbed muskets."[23]

At 4:00pm General Longstreet, believing the time had come for a decisive blow, keeping up pressure at each end of the line, launched the third and final phase of his assault upon the heights at the Snodgrass house, using Preston's division, his last reserve:

> It was evident that with this position gained I should complete master of the field. I therefore ordered General Buckner to move Preston forward. Before this, however, General Buckner had established a battery of 12 guns, raking down the enemy's line which opposed our Right Wing, and at the same time having fine play upon any force that might attempt to re-enforce the hill that he was about to attack. General Stewart, of his corps, was also ordered to move against any such force in flank. The combination was well-timed and arranged. Preston dashed gallantly at the hill. Stewart flanked a re-enforcing column and captured a large portion of it. At the same time the fire of the battery struck such terror into a heavy force close under it that we took there also a large number of prisoners. Preston's assault, though not a complete success at the onset, taken in connection with the other operations, crippled the enemy so badly that his ranks were badly broken, and by flank movement and another advance the heights were gained.[24]

John Dyer was with General Preston as a courier and familiarized him with the terrain of Horseshoe Ridge; Dyer's farm, the largest on the battlefield, belonged to his father.

William Preston (1816–1887) was a native of Kentucky; he graduated from Harvard University with a law degree in 1838 and took up the practice of law. He was related to Joseph E. Johnston. During the Mexican War he served as lieutenant colonel with the 3rd Kentucky. He was elected to both houses of the state legislature after the Mexican War and to Congress in 1853 and became minister to Spain in 1858. He returned to the United States when the Civil War broke out and was staff officer to Albert Sidney Johnston, his brother-in-law, until his death at Shiloh. On April 14, 1862 he was appointed brigadier general. He led a division at Chickamauga in Longstreet's Wing. "This was my first meeting with the genial, gallant, lovable William Preston," Longstreet referred to him at Chickamauga, meeting him for the first time.[25] Preston's division was Longstreet's largest and most formidable, numbering 4,078 officers and men, in three brigades: 2003 in Archibald Gracie's, Robert C. Trigg's brigade had 1,199, and 876 troops in John Kelly's.

General Alexander Peter Stewart, who was called "Old Straight" by his men, took a little cajoling from Sorrel to get him to pitch into the Federal column moving across his front:

> An incident of the day of battle will indicate some differences between the Eastern and Western armies in the reception of orders. While Thomas was heavily reinforcing his right, a column of fours was seen marching across Gen. A. P. Stewart's front. If attacked, its destruction was certain. I pointed out the opportunity to General Stewart, his position being admirable for the purpose. His answer was that he was there by orders and could not move until he got other orders. I explained that I was chief of staff to Longstreet and felt myself competent to give such an order as coming from my chief, and that this was customary in our Virginia service. General Stewart, however, courteously insisted that he could not accept them unless assured the orders came direct from Longstreet. Valuable time was being lost, but I determined to have a whack at those quick-moving blue masses. Asking General Stewart to get ready, that I hoped soon to find Longstreet, I was off, and luckily did find him after an eager chase. Longstreet's thunderous tones need not be described when, in the first words of explanation, he sent me back with orders to Stewart to fall on the reinforcing column with all his power. Stewart was ready and pushed forward handsomely. In a few minutes, with little or no loss to himself, he had broken up Thomas's men and taken many prisoners. This was quite late in the afternoon, twilight coming on.[26]

The battery of Major Samuel Williams, placed by Buckner at the Poe House, opened a barrage after some delay. This was made more terrible by the addition of two batteries of Major Felix Robertson from the army's reserve artillery, making 20 guns in total. Simultaneously, the right wing, now under D. H. Hill's oversight, which had been idle while Longstreet's attacks crashed into the Federals on Horseshoe Ridge, went into action as Preston charged; the batteries of James Postell Douglas, John H. Calvert, Henry C. Semple and John Scogin softened up the Yankee breastworks prior to the right wing going in. Daniel H. Hill noted:

Longstreet was determined to send Preston with his division of three brigades under Gracie, Trigg, and Kelly, aided by Robertson's brigade of Hood's division, to carry the heights-the main point of defense. His troops were of the best material and had been in reserve all day; but brave, fresh, and strong as they were, it was with them alternate advance and retreat, until success was assured by a renewal of the fight on the right. At 3:30 P. M. General Polk sent an order to me to assume command of the attacking forces on the right and renew the assault. Owing to a delay in the adjustment of our lines, the advance did not begin until 4 o'clock. The men sprang to their arms with the utmost alacrity, though they had not heard of Longstreet's success, and they showed by their cheerfulness that there was plenty of 'fight in them.' Cleburne ran forward his batteries, some by hand, to within three hundred yards of the enemy's breastworks, pushed forward his infantry, and carried them. General J. K. Jackson, of Cheatham's division, has a bloody struggle with the fortifications in his front, but had entered them when Cheatham with two more of his brigades, Maney's and Wright's, came up. Breckinridge and Walker met with but little opposition until the Chattanooga Road was passed, when their right was unable to overcome the forces covering the enemy's retreat. As we passed into the woods west of the road, it was reported to me that a line was advancing at right angles to ours. I rode to the left to ascertain whether they were foes or friends, and soon recognized General Buckner. The cheers that went up when the two wings met were such as I had never heard before, and shall never hear again.

Preston gained the heights a half hour later, capturing 1000 prisoners and 4500 stand of arms. But neither right nor left is entitled to the laurels of a complete triumph. It was the combined attack, which, by weakening the enthusiasm of the brave warriors who had stood on the defense so long and so obstinately, won the day.

Thomas had received orders after Granger's arrival to retreat to Rossville, but, stout soldier as he was, he resolved to hold his ground until nightfall. An hour more of daylight would have ensured his capture. Thomas had under him all the Federal army, except the six brigades which had been driven off by the left wing.[27]

The victory was the first and only won by the armies in the western Confederacy. The Army of Tennessee captured over 8,000 prisoners, 51 guns, as well as 2,381 rounds of artillery ammunition, and 23,281 small arms together with 135,000 rifle cartridges. The price in blood was staggering: Bragg's army lost 2,673 killed, 16,274 wounded, and 2,003 missing, totaling 20,950 casualties. Alone, Longstreet suffered 1,856 killed, 6,506 wounded, and 270 missing, a total of 8,632. Being on the defensive, the figures for Rosecrans were less: 1,656 killed, 9,749 wounded, and 4,774 missing, a total of 16,179 casualties.

Bull of the Woods

The soldiers of the Army of Tennessee gave Lee's War Horse the nickname "Bull of the Woods." Longstreet had brought the army to victory against remarkable odds; he was given command of a wing of the army at the last minute on unknown ground against an unfamiliar enemy, commanding troops he was not accustomed to. On the field of battle General Breckinridge was cheered as he rode along his line and replied to the troops: "Longstreet is the man my boys, Longstreet is the man."[28]

Longstreet sent a cryptic note to Bragg at 6:15pm saying, "We have been entirely successful in my command today" and that he hoped "to be ready to renew the conflict at an early hour tomorrow." It was written about one hour before Preston gained Snodgrass Hill and the Union army's final retreat, leaving Bragg in the dark as to what transpired.[29] Surely Bragg should have been aware of the results from staff members or other officers, but most of all as commander in chief he should have been near the battlefield; Longstreet wrote to D. H. Hill in July 1884: "It did not occur to me on the night of the 20th to send Bragg word of our complete success. I thought that the loud huzzas that spread over the field just at dark were a sufficient assurance and notice to any one within five miles of us."[30] Even if Longstreet had sent such a message of victory, it is doubtful Bragg would have given much credence to it. General Leonidas Polk rode over to Bragg's headquarters at 1:00am together with Lieutenant Colonel Spence and Polk's son-in-law, Colonel William Gale, where Polk told Bragg the Federals were "routed and flying precipitately from the field" and suggested immediate pursuit to recapture Chattanooga. General St. John Liddell recalled Polk simply could not persuade Bragg. "Bragg could not be induced to look at it in that light, and refused to believe that we had won a victory," wrote Gale.[31] Bragg would not even believe an eyewitness account of the headlong flight of the Federals affirmed by a Confederate private captured the previous day but who escaped amid the confusion of the retreat. When Bragg's generals had the man brought to Bragg, he asked the private sternly, "Do you know what a retreat looks like?" The private stared back at Bragg and replied, "I ought to, General, I've been with you during your whole campaign."[32]

Longstreet had his troops recoup during the night: "The enemy had fought every man that he had, and every one had been in turn beaten. As it was almost dark I ordered my line to remain as it was, ammunition boxes to be refilled, stragglers to be collected, and everything in readiness for the pursuit in the morning."[33]

CHAPTER 12

"Longstreet Is the Man"

Chickamauga's Aftermath

By morning, even a man as obtuse as Bragg finally perceived that the Federals had left the field and asked Longstreet for advice on strategy:

> Early on the 21st, the commanding general stopped at my bivouac and asked my views as to our future movements. I suggested crossing the river above Chattanooga, so as to make ourselves sufficiently felt on the enemy's rear as to force his evacuation of Chattanooga, and, indeed, force him back upon Nashville, and if we should find our transportation inadequate for a continuance of this movement, to follow up the railroad to Knoxville, destroy Burnside, and from there threaten the enemy's railroad communication in rear of Nashville. This I supposed to be the only practicable flank movement, owing to the scarcity of our transportation, and it seemed to keep us very nearly as close to the railroad as we were at the time. At parting I understood the commanding general to agree that such was probably our best move, and that he was about to give the necessary orders for its execution.[1]

Longstreet was not the only one to perceive the opportunity afforded to Confederate arms by this great victory; General Forrest was in his saddle before dawn, leading his troopers to ascertain the condition of the demoralized Federals. He captured some signal officers who told him Rosecrans was going to abandon Chattanooga. He scratched a note to Polk at 9:00am:

> On the Road
> September 21, 1863
> Genl
>
> We are in a mile of Rossville. Have been to the point of Missionary Ridge. Can see Chattanooga and everything around. The enemy's trains are leaving, going around the point of Lookout Mountain.
> The prisoners captured report two pontoons thrown across for the purpose of retreating.
> I think they are evacuating as hard as they can go. They are cutting timber down to obstruct our passage.
> I think we ought to press forward as rapidly as possible.
>
> Respectfully,
> N. B. Forrest
> Please forward to Gen. Bragg

No answer came, so he sent a second message directly to General Bragg, telling him, "Every hour is worth a thousand men." Still nothing was heard of. Forrest went in person to confront General Bragg on the night of September 21; Bragg told him supplies were short. Forrest retorted, "We can get all the supplies our army needs in Chattanooga." Bragg was adamant. Forrest snarled to his officers, "What does he fight battles for?"[2]

Longstreet confronted Bragg as to the implications of the pull-back:

> When asked if he had abandoned the course upon which his march was ordered, he said the people would be greatly gratified to know that his army was marching through the streets of Chattanooga with bands of music and salutations of the soldiers. I thought, and did not fail to say, that it would give them greater pleasure to know that he has passed the Tennessee River, turned the enemy out of Chattanooga in eager flight, to save his rearward lines, whilst we marched hammering against the broken flanks of his columns. But the cavalry had reported that the enemy was in hurried and confused retreat, his trains crossing the river and passing over the nose of Lookout Mountain in disorder.[3]

Perhaps Forrest's message influenced Bragg to change his mind, although his report states other reasons:

> The suggestion of a movement by our right immediately after the battle to the north of the Tennessee and thence upon Nashville requires notice only because it will find a place on the files of the department. Such a movement was utterly impossible for want of transportation. Nearly half of our army consisted of re-enforcements just before the battle without a wagon or an artillery horse, and nearly, if not quite, a third of the artillery horses on the field had been lost. The railroad bridges, too, had been destroyed to a point south of Ringgold, and on all the road from Cleveland to Knoxville. To these insurmountable difficulties were added the entire absence of means to cross the river except by fording at a few precarious points too deep for artillery and the well known danger of sudden rises, by which all communication would be cut, a contingency which did actually happen a few days after the visionary scheme was proposed. But the most serious objection to the proposition was its entire want of military propriety. It abandoned to the enemy our entire line of communication and laid open to him our depot of supplies, while it placed us with a greatly inferior force beyond a difficult and at times impassible river, in a country affording no subsistence to men or animals. It also left open to the enemy, at a distance of only 10 miles, our battle-field, with thousands of our wounded and his own, and all the trophies and supplies we had won. All this was to be risked and given up for what? To gain the enemy's rear and cut him off from his depot of supplies by the route over the mountains when the very movement abandoned to his unmolested use the better and more practical route, of half the length, on the south side of the river. It is hardly necessary to say the proposition was not even entertained, whatever may have been the inferences drawn from subsequent movements.[4]

Bragg ignored Longstreet's sound advice to threaten Rosecrans's communications and force him out of Chattanooga and Middle Tennessee, and settled down for a siege: "When General Bragg found the enemy had changed his mind," Longstreet expanded,

> and was not inclined to continue his rearward march, he stretched his army in a semicircle of six miles along the southeast front of Chattanooga, from the base of Lookout Mountain on

his left, to his right resting on the Tennessee River, and ordered Alexander's batteries to the top of the mountain, my command, McLaws's, Hood's and Walker's divisions, occupying the left of his line of investment. His plan was to shell the enemy from his works by field batteries, but the works grew stronger from day to day on all sides of the city. Our infantry was posted along the line, as supports for the batteries, with orders not to assault unless especially ordered.[5]

General Bragg should have listened to Longstreet; Longstreet wanted to leave a small force to watch Rosecrans and flank him to cut off his supplies. Rosecrans was crushed by the defeat; only 35,000 answered muster and only 10 days' rations remained. Rosecrans thought the Confederates had a much larger force than his own. The slightest nudge would have pushed him back. Besides, time was against the Confederates, as the Federal War Department was trying frantically to move troops from Grant's and Burnside's armies as well as the Army of the Potomac.

The field fortifications built upon the former Rebel defenses at Chattanooga were getting stronger daily and after a week's practice by the artillery, this method was found ineffective. On September 30 Bragg decided to break up the Federal line of supply by a grand cavalry raid. He ordered General Wheeler to organize a force. Supplies had been sent by rail from Nashville to Rosecrans's army at Chattanooga. But now, the supplies could only be taken as far as Bridgeport, Alabama, 27 miles west of Chattanooga, as the Confederates had burned the railroad bridge across the Tennessee River at that juncture and its artillery prevented travel by the direct route. Subsequently, wagons had to take a roundabout route of 60 miles northeast up the valley of the Sequatchie River to Anderson's Crossroads, then southeast over a windy, steep, rocky road over Walden's Ridge to the banks of the Tennessee where they crossed into the town on a pontoon bridge.

Cavalry Raid

On October 1, Wheeler launched the cavalry raid with 5,000 troopers under Brigadier Generals William Martin and John Wharton. They crossed the Tennessee River and attacked a Federal caravan of 800 wagons at Anderson's Crossroads in the Sequatchie Valley, burning 300 and shooting or sabering more than a thousand mules and also destroying some railroad bridges. The raid caused some loss of supplies but did not convince Rosecrans to abandon Chattanooga, while Wheeler suffered heavy losses totaling about 700 killed or wounded. Disappointed, Bragg came up with another plan involving Longstreet's sector:

At that time the shortest line of the enemy's haul of provisions from the depot at Stevenson was along the road on the north bank of the river. The Confederate chief conceived, as our cavalry ride had failed of effect, that a line of sharp-shooters along the river on our side could break up that line of travel, and ordered, on the 8th of October, a detail from my command for that purpose. As the line was over the mountain about seven miles beyond support, by a rugged road not practicable for artillery, I ordered a brigade of infantry detailed to go over and protect the sharp-shooters from surprise or capture. The detail fell upon Law's brigade. The line for this practice extended from the east side of Lookout Creek some ten miles down the river. The effect of the fire was about like that of the cavalry raid. It simply put the enemy on shorter rations until he could open another route for his trains.[6]

So Bragg stood by maintaining his siege while precious time went by to the advantage of the Federals; the head of the Bureau of War for the Confederate government made this disclosure in his diary on October 4, 1863:

> Our intelligence from every quarter is that the enemy are bending every energy in every direction for the relief of Rosecrans. Two corps of Grant's army are on the way, one by way of Corinth, the other by the road north of the Tennessee from Memphis. Troops have been sent from the East also, besides all which were in East Tennessee, Bragg holds all the railroads, on the east at Cleveland [Tenn.], on the west from Lookout Mountain. Rosecrans gets his supplies by wagons from Stevenson [Alabama], and doubtless from the Sequatchie Valley. Johnston sent Major General Stephen D. Lee with 2000 cavalry several days ago in the direction of Murfreesboro. There is great danger that the great reinforcements which are moving to his [Rosecrans's] assistance will reach him before he is compelled to evacuate Chattanooga, or if not, [they will] soon after put him in a position to resume the offensive with a superior force. A victory to yield fruits must either be more decisive on the field or be pressed to better results. I greatly fear it will prove rather a barren one.[7]

Quarrel With His Generals

The diarist Mary Chesnut lamented about Bragg and his siege:

> Bragg-thanks to Longstreet and Hood, he won Chickamauga. So we looked [for] results that would pay for our losses in battles, at least. Certainly they would capture Rosecrans. No! There sits Bragg-a good dog howling on his hind legs before Chattanooga, a fortified town-and some Yankee Holdfast grinning at him from his impregnable heights. Waste of time.
> "How?"
> "He always stops to quarrel with his generals."[8]

After Chickamauga it seemed Bragg had a greater desire to wage war upon his own officers than on Rosecrans and his army cooped up at Chattanooga. Hardly had the smoke cleared when he targeted Hindman for the debacle at McLemore's Cove earlier in the campaign (on September 11) and Polk for not attacking at daylight on September 20 at Chickamauga. On September 22 Bragg sent Polk an official demand for a report explaining his failure to attack at daylight as ordered; when no report was forthcoming, another demand was issued on September 25. Polk replied on September 28, citing his inability to locate D. H. Hill as the reason for the delay; this did not satisfy Bragg and on the following day he suspended Major General Hindman and Lieutenant General Polk from their commands, banishing them to Atlanta.

Bragg had lost the respect of his soldiers and the confidence of his generals; atop Missionary Ridge, General Preston wrote his nephew on October 3: "We are still here, another victory and the result nothing. All are disheartened." General William

Mackall, Bragg's own chief of staff, remarked that he knew of not one contented general in the army.[9] In a letter to his wife, Captain Charles Blackford sized up Bragg's relationship with his troops:

> Bragg ought to be relieved or disaster is sure to result. The men have no faith. The difference between this army and Lee's is very striking. When the men move in the Army of Northern Virginia, they think they are doing the proper thing, whether it be backward or forward, and if all the success anticipated is not secured, at all events it is not Lee's fault. Down here the men seem to feel the wrong thing is being done whatever it be and when success is secured they attribute it to anybody else than Bragg. Thus they give the whole credit of Chickamauga to Longstreet.[10]

The senior officers of the army—Polk, Longstreet, D. H. Hill, and Buckner—met secretly on September 26 to oust Bragg; all believed Bragg incompetent to lead the army in battle and that he had squandered the fruits of victory by not pressing Rosecrans. Polk and Longstreet, being the most influential in Richmond, were designated to initiate a letter-writing campaign.

Nothing but the Hand of God

Longstreet was delegated to contact the Secretary of War and did so on September 26:

> Headquarters,
> Near Chattanooga, September 26, 1863.
> Hon. J. A. Seddon,
> Secretary of War:
>
> Sir: May I take the liberty to advise you of our conditions and our wants? On the 20th instant, after a very severe battle, we gained a complete and glorious victory-the most complete victory of the war, except, perhaps, the first Manassas. On the morning of the 21st General Bragg asked my opinion as to our best course. I suggested at once to strike at Burnside, and if he made his escape to march upon Rosecrans' communication in the rear of Nashville. He seemed to adopt the suggestion, and gave the order to march at 4 o'clock in the afternoon. The Right Wing of the army marched some 8 or 10 miles, my command following the next day at daylight. I was halted at the crossing of the Chickamauga, and on the night of the 22d the army was ordered to march for Chattanooga, thus giving the enemy two days and a half to strengthen the fortifications here already prepared for him by ourselves. Here we have remained under instructions that the enemy shall not be assaulted. To express my convictions in a few words, our chief has done but one thing that he ought to have done since I joined his army. That was to order the attack upon the 20th. All other things that he has done he ought not to have done. I am convinced that nothing but the hand of God can save or help us as long as we have our present commander.
>
> Now to our wants. Can't you send us General Lee? The army in Virginia can operate defensively, while our operations here should be offensive-until we have recovered Tennessee, at all events. We need some such great mind as General Lee's (nothing more) to accomplish this. You will be surprised to learn that this army has neither organization nor mobility, and I have doubts if its commander can give it them. In an ordinary war I could serve without complaint under any one whom the Government might place in authority, but we have too

much at stake in this to remain quiet under such distressing circumstances. Our most precious blood is now flowing in streams from the Atlantic to the Rocky Mountains, and may yet be exhausted before we have succeeded. Then goes honor, treasure, and independence. When I came here I hoped to find our commander willing and anxious to do all things that would aid us in our great cause, and ready to receive what aid he could get from his subordinates. It seems that I was greatly mistaken. It seems he cannot adopt and adhere to any plan or course, whether of his own or of some one else. I desire to impress upon your mind that there is no exaggeration in these statements. On the contrary, I have failed to express my convictions to the fullest extent. All that I can add without making this letter exceedingly long is to pray you to help us, and speedily.

I remain, with the greatest respect, your obedient servant,

J. Longstreet,
Lieutenant-General.[11]

This letter caused a sensation in the Confederate capital; the head of the Bureau of War made this notation in his diary:

Oct. 8. General Longstreet has written to the Secretary of War a letter which has filled me with concern. He says Bragg has done but one thing he ought to have done since he (General Longstreet) has been out there and that was the order to attack on September 18. After the battle he lost two days by contradictory orders, which Rosecrans used to strengthen his position; and he (Longstreet) expressed the opinion that nothing will be effected under Bragg's command. He says the army is equal to any achievement and urges in conclusion that General Lee be sent there to command, the army in Virginia being left to act wholly on the defensive. [In margin, written Oct. 1865:] This letter made Bragg a bitter enemy of Longstreet and strange to say President Davis sided with Bragg, and subsequently to the end of the war showed strong personal dislike of Longstreet. Longstreet's letter seems to me to be written without feeling and purely from a sense of duty.[12]

Longstreet sent three letters: one on the same day he wrote to Seddon, also on October 6 and 11. Longstreet asked Lee to take command of the Army of Tennessee. Lee replied on October 26 after moving upon Meade to prevent the detachment of reinforcements for Rosecrans:

I rejoice in your victory deeply. It seemed to me to have been complete. I wish it could have been followed up by the destruction of the Federal army. As regards your proposition as to myself, I wish I could feel that it was prompted by other reasons than kind feelings to myself. I think you could do better than I could. It was with that view I urged your going. The President, being on the ground, I hope will do all that can be done. He has to take a broad view of the whole ground, and must order as he deems best. I will cheerfully do anything in my power. In addition to other infirmities, I have been suffering so much from rheumatism in my back that I can scarcely get about. The first two days of our march I had to be hauled in a wagon, and subsequently every motion of my horse, and indeed of my body, gave much pain. I am rather better now, though still suffering.

Lee felt too disabled by his ill health to make such a harsh journey west but finished with these kind words for Longstreet: "I missed you dreadfully and your brave corps. Your cheerful face and strong arm would have been invaluable. I hope you will return to me."[13]

On October 4 the corps commanders held a secret meeting to draft a petition to President Davis for Bragg's removal, probably instigated by Polk before he left for Atlanta. The document was carefully worded to avoid any mention of Bragg's military failings, which might be interpreted as mutinous, but rather that "the condition of his health unfits him for the command of an army in the field." General Longstreet claims that D. H. Hill told him after the war he wrote it. Evidence indicates General Buckner made some revisions to the form. The petition was left at Hill's headquarters for the most part, as his was in the central part of the line. In all, 12 general officers signed the document, ten from Hill's and Buckner's corps and only two from Longstreet's, the position of the signatures indicating it reached him last. Bragg got wind of the petition and, in Mackall's words, it "caused him much distress and mortification."[14] On October 5 Bragg appealed by telegraph to President Davis to intercede. Davis had already sent Colonel James Chesnut, husband of famed diarist Mary Chesnut, to assess conditions in the Army of Tennessee after Bragg had refused to rescind the suspensions of Polk and Hindman. Chesnut talked with Polk in Atlanta on October 3, then had a discussion with Longstreet near Chattanooga. What he heard and observed caused him to wire Davis on October 5: "Your immediate presence in this army is urgently demanded."[15] Davis left by train on the morning of October 6 and was in Atlanta on October 8 to confer with Polk.

Davis tried to persuade Polk to return to the Army of Tennessee, with all charges dismissed, but Polk said he would rather resign than serve under Bragg. However, he said he would accept a transfer to another department.

Davis's lack of tact in the handling of the insurrection in the Army of Tennessee against Bragg shows he was completely out of touch with affairs in the western theater. Davis arrived at Bragg's headquarters by train on October 9 and brought with him as Polk's replacement Lieutenant General John C. Pemberton who had just surrendered Vicksburg. Surely, Davis should have known the low esteem the troops had of him; Hardee warned Davis in August that he [Pemberton] was too unpopular to serve with the Mississippi army and Governor John Pettus of Mississippi forwarded a report that the parolees from Vicksburg and Port Hudson would not serve under Pemberton. Davis equated Lee's unpopularity after the defeat at Gettysburg with Pemberton's after the fall of Vicksburg and deemed them both unwarranted. Nevertheless, the troops would not have Pemberton; John B. Jones made this entry in his diary: "October 12th. -Hon. G. A. Henry, Senator from Tennessee writes to the Secretary [Seddon] that it is rumored that Gen. Pemberton is to command Gen. Polk's corps in Tennessee. He says if this be true, it will be disastrous; that the Tennessee troops will not serve under him, but will mutiny and desert."[16] General Mackall related to General Joe Johnston how he broke the news to Pemberton:

> Pemberton consulted me about staying here in command of a corps. I told him that there was not a division in this army that would be willing to receive him; that I was sorry to be obliged to tell him this unpleasant truth, but so it was. He told me Bragg wanted him to stay. I told

him Bragg ought to understand the temper of his army better than I did, but that we did not always agree upon the point. He goes away, however.[17]

The Generals Cast a Vote of No Confidence in Bragg

Davis met with Bragg in private on the afternoon of October 9; Bragg asked to be relieved of command, which Davis refused to accept and, instead, called a meeting of the corps commanders at Bragg's headquarters, ostensibly to discuss future military operations. However, Davis did not stick to the topic but asked a poignant question of Longstreet, Hill, Buckner, and Cheatham:

> The President came to us on the 9th of October and called the commanders of the army to meet him at General Bragg's office. After some talk, in the presence of General Bragg, he made known the object of the call, and asked the generals, in turn, their opinion of their commanding officer, beginning with myself [Longstreet]. It seemed rather a stretch of authority, even with a President, and I gave an evasive answer, and made an effort to turn the channel of thought, but he would not be satisfied, and got back to his question. The condition of the army was briefly referred to, and the failure to make an effort to get the fruits of our success, when the opinion was given, in substance, that our commander could be of greater service, elsewhere than at the head of the Army of Tennessee. Major-General Buckner was called, and gave opinion somewhat similar. So did Major-General Cheatham, who was then commanding the corps recently commanded by Lieutenant-General Polk, and General D. H. Hill, who was called last, agreed with emphasis to the views expressed by others.[18]

Longstreet made some biting remarks that Bragg "was incompetent to manage an army or put men into a fight," adding he "knew nothing of the business."[19] Mackall informed Joseph E. Johnston that Longstreet's words carried a lot of weight with the army: "I think Longstreet has done more injury to the general than all the others put together. You may understand how much influence with his troops a remark from a man of his standing would have to the effect that Bragg was not on the field and Lee would have been."[20] Sorrel set the stage of the meeting:

> Mr. Davis made his celebrated visit to the camp to see and hear for himself. It is difficult, even now, to recall and realize that unprecedented scene. The President, with the commander-in-chief, and the great officers of the army, assembled to hear the opinion of the General's fitness for command. In the presence of Bragg and his corps commander he asked of each his opinion, and his reasons if adverse. This was eye to eye with the President, the commander-in-chief and the generals. There was no lack of candor in answer to such challenge with men like Longstreet, Cheatham, Hill, Cleburne, and Stewart. Some very plain language was used in answer, but it seems that one and all were quite agreed as to Bragg's unfitness for command of that army. These opinions were received by the President and his general without comment, and Mr. Davis got more than he came for.[21]

Porter Alexander made this assessment of Bragg:

> I don't think Gen. Bragg inspired any enthusiasm in his men-certainly nothing to be compared with what I was accustomed to see in Virginia. And, to go a step further, he certainly never impressed me as a man of intellectual power-as a cool & clear thinker, at all. And to be entirely

frank there were some who did not hesitate openly to say that he was simply muddle headed & especially that he never could understand a map, & that it was a spectacle to see him wrestle with one, with one finger painfully holding down his own position.[22]

Longstreet Meets with President Davis

On the next day, October 10, Davis and Longstreet had an all-day huddle:

The next morning the President called me to private conference, and had an all day talk. He thought to assign me command, but the time had passed for handling that army as an independent force. Regarding this question, as considered in Virginia, it was understood that the assignment would be made at once, and in time for opportunity to handle the army sufficiently to gain the confidence of the officers and soldiers before offering or accepting battle. The action was not taken, a battle had been made and won, the army was then seriously entangled in a quasi siege, the officers and soldiers were disappointed, and disaffected in morale. General Grant was moving his army to reinforce against us, and an important part of the Union army of Virginia was moving to the same purpose.

In my judgment our last opportunity was lost when we failed to follow the success at Chickamauga, and capture or disperse the Union army, and it could not be just to the service or myself to call me to a position of such responsibility. The army was part of General Joseph E. Johnston's department, and could only be used in strong organization by him in combining its operations with his other forces in Alabama and Mississippi. I said that under him I could cheerfully work in any position. The suggestion of that name only served to increase his displeasure, and his severe rebuke.

I recognized the authority of his high position, but called to his mind that neither his words nor his manner were so impressive as the dissolving scenes that foreshadowed the dreadful end. He referred to his worry and troubles with politicians and non-combatants. In that connection, I suggested that all that the people asked for was success; with that the talk of politicians would be as spiders' webs before him. And when restored to his usual gracious calm I asked to have my resignation accepted, to make place for some one who could better meet his ideas of the important service. He objected that my troops would not be satisfied with the change. I suggested a leave of absence, as winter was near, when I would go to the Trans-Mississippi Department, and after the troops were accustomed to their new commander, send in my written resignation, from Texas, but he was not minded to accept that solution of the premises.

The interview was exciting, at times warm, but continued until Lookout Mountain lifted above the sun to excuse my taking leave. The President walked as far as the gate, gave his hand in his usual warm grasp, and dismissed me with his gracious smile; but a bitter look lurking about its margin, and the ground-swell, admonished me that clouds were gathering about head-quarters of the First Corps even faster than those that told the doom of the Southern cause.[23]

It is interesting to note that Lieutenant General Hardee also declined the command. Longstreet asked the president to designate a replacement for General Hood who had been severely crippled and not expected to return to active duty. As the president made no recommendation, Longstreet suggested the senior Brigadier General Micah Jenkins, a "bright, gallant and efficient officer of more than two years' experience in active warfare, loved by his troops." The president spoke of the services of the next in rank, General Evander Law, who had commanded the division both at Gettysburg and Chickamauga after Hood was wounded but Davis failed to name a successor. After the interview with Longstreet, Davis conferred with Buckner who again reiterated Bragg's shortcomings as commander.

The lack of confidence in Bragg expressed at these meetings should have convinced Davis to find a replacement for the good of the Army of Tennessee and the Southern cause. Remarkable as it may seem, Davis kept him on; not because he believed in Bragg's capabilities but because Bragg was one of his favorites as the soldier-historian Porter Alexander pointed out:

> As it was now beginning to become apparent that our victory at Chickamauga would be a fruitless one, there began to spring up all over the South many evidences of great dissatisfaction with Gen, Bragg as the commander of the army; and, although our generals in the field kept their own counsel, I am sure that very few, if any of them, were sanguine of any success under his leadership.
>
> But Gen. Bragg had one strong hold. He had the thorough confidence of President Davis, than whom no man was ever a more persistent friend, through evil report or good.
>
> And, now, when the feeling against Gen. Bragg was rising & spreading on every hand, Mr. Davis paid a visit to the army & exercised his best influence to allay it there, &, after his return, he made some public addresses, calculated to have similar effect upon the press throughout the country.
>
> As will soon appear, however, he only succeeded in postponing Gen. Bragg's removal for a few weeks. For before the end of November the general received at Missionary Ridge the most complete, thorough, & disgraceful defeat which ever befell a Confederate army, & after that it was only possible (to) let him down easy, with a few weeks' command in winter quarters, & then Gen. Jos. E. Johnston replaced him.
>
> But, even then, Mr. Davis found a soft place for him, & took him into the War Department as a sort of general advisor, & kept him there until the close of the war.[24]

Thus, the road to the devastating defeat of the Army of Tennessee on Missionary Ridge at the hands of General Grant was paved by Davis's decision to maintain Bragg. Longstreet criticized President Davis in an interview in the *Washington Post* on June 11, 1893: "at one time or another he had exasperated and alienated most of (his) generals" while holding "to his mediocre favorites with surprising tenacity."[25]

Within two days of the meeting, Bragg, upheld by Davis, retaliated on his detractors. The first victim was D. H. Hill, who was now being blamed for the failures on the morning of September 20. On October 11 Bragg asked Davis to relieve Hill from duty, stating: "Possessing some high qualifications as a commander, he still fails to such an extent in others more essential that he weakens the morale and military tone of his command. A want of prompt conformity to orders of great importance is the immediate cause of this application." Davis authorized Hill's removal and on October 15 Hill was surprised to find he had been discharged. The next day Hill, along with his aide, Colonel Archer Anderson, arrived at Bragg's headquarters demanding an explanation but Bragg was evasive, citing it was only done for the good of the army's efficiency and harmony. Indeed, after the war, Bragg told Major E. T. Sykes, one of his few remaining friends, he had dismissed Hill for engaging in "mutinous assemblage."[26] Hill entreated Davis who not only refused to consider his appeal but withheld his nomination of Hill to the Confederate Senate for the rank of lieutenant general, a position Hill was appointed to three months earlier when Davis asked him to go to Bragg's army in July. Polk was assigned to Joseph E. Johnston in Mississippi, taking Hardee's corps, while Hardee replaced Polk as corps commander under Bragg. The Department of East Tennessee which had been directed by Simon Buckner was dissolved and Buckner lost his corps, being reduced to a division commander. Bragg had always desired to break up the powerful Tennessee and Kentucky cliques in his army; he proceeded to disperse and reassign them. William Mackall, who resigned as Bragg's chief of staff on October 16, asserted: "I do not know a single contented general in this army; a very sad fact in the presence of the enemy."[27] William Preston summed it up: "I have a dull future before me with Bragg. No approval or praise if I win, ruin and censure if I lose. I intend to get away if I can."[28]

Change of Base

Before Davis left, he called a war council, probably on October 11, to formulate a plan. Longstreet made his contribution based on the changing conditions:

> A day or two after this interview the President called the commanders to meet him again at General Bragg's head-quarters. He expressed desire to have the army pulled away from the lines around Chattanooga and put to active work in the field, and called for suggestions and plans by which that could be done, directing his appeal, apparently, to me as first to reply.
>
> I suggested a change of base to Rome, Georgia, a march of the army to the railway bridge of the Tennessee River at Bridgeport, and the crossing of the river as an easy move,-one that would cut the enemy's rearward line, interrupt his supply train, put us between his army at Chattanooga and the reinforcements moving to join him, and force him to precipitate battle or retreat.
>
> General Bragg proposed that we march up and cross the river and swing around towards the enemy's rear and force him out by that means. No other plans were offered, nor did other officers express preference for either of the plans that were submitted.
>
> Maps were called for and demonstrations given of the two plans, when the President ordered the move to be made by the change of base to Rome, and in a day or two took leave of us.[29]

Wisely, Longstreet wanted to pull back the army for security to Rome, Georgia— already a war industry center, providing an excellent logistical base—then operate against the Federal supply depot at Bridgeport, Alabama, and seize this important railroad terminus needed to transport those supplies, additionally, cutting off reinforcements from Virginia and Mississippi and thus rendering Rosecrans's position untenable. Bragg had received his instructions from the president but refused to fall back, citing inclement weather; his army remained stationary in a siege, while the Federals were building up.

Longstreet had his command posted on Lookout Mountain, facing east, while the bulk of the army with Bragg was on Missionary Ridge:

> In his official account, General Bragg said that the road on the south side was left under my command, which is misleading. My command-three divisions-was on his line of investment, east of the city and of the mountain; the road was west of the mountain from six to twenty miles from the command. We were in support of his batteries, to be ready for action at the moment his artillery practice called for it. We held nearly as much of his line as the other eight divisions. None of the commanders had authority to move a man from the lines until the 8th of October, when he gave orders for posting the sharp-shooters west of the mountain. The exposure of this detachment was so serious that I took the liberty to send a brigade as a rallying force for it, and the exposure of these led me to inquire as to the assistance they could have from our cavalry force operating on the line from the mountain to Bridgeport, some eight or ten miles behind them. The cavalry was not found as watchful as the eyes of the army should be, and I reported them to the general, but he thought otherwise, assured me that his reports were regular, daily and sometimes oftener.
>
> Nevertheless, prudence suggested more careful guard, and I ordered Captain Manning, who brought from Virginia part of my signal force, to establish a station in observation of Bridgeport and open its communication with my head-quarters. General Bragg denied all reports sent him of the enemy from my signal party, treated them with contempt, then reported that the road was under my command.[30]

Meanwhile, General Grant had arrived on October 23 to take charge at Chattanooga, and General George H. Thomas replaced Rosecrans three days later. Conditions in Chattanooga were becoming critical due to the shortage of provisions, as the supply route was long and treacherous. A plan was formulated to break the siege by the chief engineer of the Army of the Cumberland, Brigadier General William F. "Baldy" Smith. Smith had carefully studied the topography between the army at Chattanooga and its supply base at Bridgeport and found a way to shorten the route, making it easier. The Tennessee River flowed west past Chattanooga; proceeding south, it abruptly turned northwest two and a half miles from Chattanooga, forming a U around a tongue of land called Moccasin Point—named so because it resembled the shape of an Indian shoe. Two miles upstream from the foot of Lookout Mountain was Brown's Ferry on the western bank of the Tennessee, affording an excellent place to cross and connect to a road traversing Moccasin Point—two miles to the pontoon bridge already in use north of Chattanooga. From Brown's Ferry the river continued northwestward to Walden's Ridge, then turned abruptly south for seven miles creating a long peninsula on which lay the northwestern spur of Raccoon Mountain to Kelley's Ferry, which could be reached by steamboat from Bridgeport. What's more important, a road through Raccoon Mountain at Cummings Gap linked Kelley's Ferry to Brown's Ferry but the Rebels controlled this road with guns on Raccoon Mountain and pickets posted along the river at Brown's Ferry; if the Federals could seize this road, the overland haul would be eight miles all out of range of the Rebel guns on Lookout Mountain.

Brown's Ferry

Smith devised a three-pronged attack on Brown's Ferry—the crucial point for success. Smith had devised a sawmill, using, as Grant said, "an old engine found in the neighborhood," actually from a nearby cotton gin, building and caulking 50 pontoon-transport boats and two flatboats to carry a picked force of 1,500 under Brigadier General William B. Hazen to float downstream with the current from Chattanooga in the early-morning mist at 3:00am on October 27. A second force of two brigades of infantry, a battalion of engineers, and three batteries of artillery—about 3,500—commanded by Brigadier General William B. Turchin, marched across Moccasin Point to the far bank from Brown's Ferry, accompanied by Smith. The third prong was General Joseph Hooker with a force of the XI and XII Corps from the Army of the Potomac, coming from Bridgeport through Lookout Valley to support the attacks on Brown's Ferry and clear the area from there to Kelley's Ferry by opening Cummings Gap and dislodging the Rebel guns on Raccoon Mountain. The operation went off flawlessly; Hazen's 1,500 troops lying flat and motionless in their boats as they drifted down the river and reached Brown's Ferry in two hours at 5:00am, half an hour before dawn, surprising and brushing aside the Rebel pickets while the oarsmen in the vacated pontoon boats ferried Turchin's men across from the opposite bank where they had waited in hiding under cover of brush and darkness. One thing remained to be done to hold the bridgehead: a steep ridge commanding the ferry landing had to be taken. On top of the hill were six Confederate companies under Colonel William C. Oates, a most promising young officer in Longstreet's command. But instead of waiting for the Yankees to come to him, he obliged the Yankees by going for them; Oates recalled telling his officers "to deploy their men at one pace apart and instruct them to walk right up to the foe, and for every man to place the muzzle of his rifle against the body of a Yankee when he fired." The results were predictable: the outnumbered and outflanked Confederates were thrown into retreat toward Lookout Mountain, carrying the wounded Oates with them he was felled by a bullet in the right hip. The bridgehead was now secure, protected by light breastworks in a defensive perimeter covered by artillery on the other side. Planking was placed on the pontoon-transports, creating a serviceable bridge allowing Grant and Thomas to send whatever reinforcements were needed. Total Federal casualties were 38 with only six fatalities; as an added bonus, Raccoon Mountain and Cummings Gap were abandoned by the Confederates and fell into Federal hands. Hooker crossed over to Bridgeport and advanced as scheduled, arriving on October 28. Major General Oliver O. Howard was in the lead with two XI Corps divisions under Adolph von Steinwehr and Carl Schurz, followed by Brigadier General John W. Geary's division of Slocum's XII Corps; General Slocum and one of his divisions were left behind near Bridgeport to guard the Nashville and Chattanooga Railroad as instructed.

Longstreet was not surprised by the outcome:

> The sharp-shooters had been posted for the sole purpose of breaking up the haul along the other bank, and not with a view of defending the line, nor was it defensible, while the enemy had every convenience for making a forced crossing and lodgement.
>
> The Confederate commander [Bragg] did not think well enough of his line when he had it to prepare to hold it, but when he found that the enemy proposed to use it, he thought to order his infantry down to recover the ground just demonstrated as indefensible, and ordered me to meet him on the mountain next morning to learn his plans and receive his instructions for the work.
>
> That afternoon the signal party reported the enemy advancing from Bridgeport in force, -artillery and infantry. This dispatch was forwarded to head-quarters, but was discredited. It was repeated about dark, and again forwarded and denied.
>
> On the morning of the 28th I reported as ordered. The general complained of my party sending up false alarms. The only answer that I could make was that they had been about two years in that service, and had not made such mistakes before.
>
> While laying his plans, sitting on the point of Lookout rock, the enemy threw some shells at us, and succeeded in bursting about two hundred feet below us. That angered the general a little, and he ordered Alexander to drops some of his shells about their heads. As this little practice went on, a dispatch messenger came bursting through the brushwood, asking for General Longstreet, and reported the enemy marching from Bridgeport along the base of the mountain, -artillery and infantry. General Bragg denied the report, and rebuked the soldier for sensational alarms, but the soldier said, "General, if you will ride to a point on the west side of the mountain I will show them to you." We rode and saw the Eleventh and Twelfth Corps under General Hooker, from the Army of the Potomac, marching quietly along the valley towards Brown's ferry. The general was surprised. So was I. But my surprise was that he did not march along the mountain top, instead the valley. It could have been occupied with as little loss as he afterwards had and less danger, he had marched by our line of cavalry without their knowing, and General Bragg had but a brigade of infantry to meet him if he had chosen to march down along the top of the mountain, and that was posted twenty miles from support.
>
> My estimate of the force was five thousand. General Bragg thought it not so strong, and appearance from the elevation seemed to justify his estimate. Presently the rear-guard came in sight and made his bivouac immediately in front of the point upon which we stood. The latter force was estimated at fifteen hundred, and halted about three miles in rear on the main body.[31]

Soldier-historian Edward Porter Alexander's journal indicated Bragg had designed to attack Hazen at Brown's Ferry until Hooker arrived:

> Before Bragg could concentrate enough to attack them, Hooker appeared, coming from Bridgeport, with the 11th and 12th corps of the Army of the Potomac. These had been hurried out to reinforce Rosecrans, when the Federals realized that Longstreet had reinforced Bragg.
>
> This, of course, put an end to the contemplated attack, but, with very questionable judgment, Bragg ordered a night attack upon a portion of Geary's division of the 12th corps (about 1500 strong with four guns), which had encamped at a point called Wauhatchie. This was about three miles from Brown's Ferry, where Hooker, with the remainder of his force, had united with the force under Hazen.
>
> Night attacks are specially valuable against troops who have been defeated and are retreating. They are of little value under any other circumstances. The war, too, had now reached a stage where men had become impossible to replace in the Confederate ranks. Nothing could be

more injudicious than to sacrifice them, even for a success, which would have no effect upon the campaign.

That was the case in this instance. Near at hand, the Federals had double or treble the force of the Confederates, and the camp to be attacked was two miles within the Federal lines.[32]

The attack at Wauhatchie in Lookout Valley was a complete blunder, with the Confederates lucky to come out of it with minimal losses.

As October came to an end, suppositions were circulating in the camps that Longstreet was to be sent on a mission into East Tennessee to subdue Burnside's army:

> About the 1st of November it was rumored about camp that I was to be ordered into East Tennessee against General Burnside's army. At the moment it seemed impossible that our commander, after rejecting a proposition for a similar move made just after his battle, when flushed with victory and the enemy discomfited, could now think of sending an important detachment so far, when he knew that, in addition to the reinforcements that had joined the Union army, another strong column was marching from Memphis under General Sherman, and must reach Chattanooga in fifteen or twenty days. But on second thoughts it occurred to me that it might, after all, be in keeping with his peculiarities, and then it occurred to me that there are many ways to compass a measure when the spirit leads. So I set to work to try to help his plans in case the report proved true.
>
> After a little reflection it seemed feasible that by withdrawing his army from its lines about Chattanooga to strong concentration behind the Chickamauga River, and recalling his detachment in East Tennessee (the latter to give the impression of a westward move), and at the moment of concentration sending a strong force for swift march against General Burnside.-strong enough to crush him,-and returning to Chattanooga before the army under General Sherman could reach there (or, if he thought better, let the detachment strike into Kentucky against the enemy's communications), something worth while could be affected.[33]

Bragg Sends Longstreet to Attack Burnside's Army

Bragg called a council of war on November 3 with his corps commanders, Longstreet, Lieutenant General Hardee, and Major General Breckenridge, where Bragg stated his plan to send Longstreet into East Tennessee to destroy Ambrose Burnside's Army of the Ohio. Longstreet energetically asserted the move could be made against Burnside with a force great enough to crush him, but the detachment of so large a force would leave Bragg's army vulnerably spread along a semicircle of eight miles, with the enemy concentrated at the center. He wanted Bragg's entire army to retire behind the Chickamauga, then turn against Grant after Burnside was quickly defeated and he returned. The council did not listen to his sound advice; Longstreet was to advance on Burnside with his two divisions of Major General Lafayette McLaws and Brigadier General Micah Jenkins's 10,000 infantrymen and Alexander and Leyden's artillery and Major General Joseph Wheeler's 5,000 cavalrymen. Again, Longstreet remonstrated:

> I repeated the warning that the move as ordered was not such as to give assurances of rapid work, saying that my march and campaign against the enemy's well-guarded positions must be

made with care, and that would consume so much time that General Grant's army would be up, when he would organize attack that must break through the line before I could return to him. His sardonic smile seemed to say that I knew little of his army or of himself in assuming such a possibility. So confident was he of his position that I ventured to ask that my column should be increased to twenty thousand infantry and artillery, but he intimated that further talk was out of order.[34]

The Comte de Paris made this observation of Bragg's decision:

It was decided that Bragg should remain in front of Chattanooga with the greater part of his army, and that meanwhile Longstreet should attack Burnside in the upper Tennessee Valley. It was expected that the commander of the First corps, acting with accustomed vigor, without be trammeled by any superior authority, might strike at Knoxville a telling blow, and then retrace his steps quick enough again to head off Sherman on the slopes of Missionary Ridge. The calculation was fallacious and this division of the army was imprudent, especially in the presence of an enemy engaged in concentrating his forces. In a word, the advantages to be derived from the campaign, even if it were successful, were smaller than the positive risks it entailed. For the defeat, and even the capture, of the Army of the Ohio, isolated in the Alleghanies, was a misfortune which the Federals could repair, because it would not cause them to lose any of their most important conquests, whereas the absence of Longstreet would expose Bragg's army to an irredeemable disaster, since he would surrender to Grant the heart of the Confederacy.[35]

On Saturday October 3, 1863 Robert Kean, Head of the Confederate Bureau of War, made an entry in his diary of reports on Bragg:

Accounts from Bragg's army are worse and worse. Colonel St. John [Isaac M., Supt. of the Nitre and Mining Bureau] showed me a letter from Captain Clark of the engineers, expressing in the strongest manner the same state of hopeless distrust and disorganization in that army stated by so many others, foreboding nothing but evil from Bragg's command of it. Yet the President seems fatally bent on retaining him now that the enemy have resumed the offensive just below Lookout Mountain, having crossed over three corps. I expect the next intelligence will be that our army has fallen back as it did before the battle of Chickamauga. All that bloodshed has been in vain. Clark mentions that on the day of the after the battle, perhaps on the field itself, Breckinridge rode down his line and was vehemently cheered. His reply was "Longstreet is the man my boys, Longstreet is the man." I think there is an evident disposition on the part of the friends of the latter to make him the man to supplant Bragg. The inability of Bragg to be further useful there is manifest to nearly all.[36]

CHAPTER 13

"They Had Few Equals and ... No Superiors"

Knoxville

For Longstreet the Chickamauga campaign had ended and he was embarked on a new campaign toward Knoxville: "On Nov. 3 he (Bragg) issued orders for Longstreet's corps, with Wheeler's cavalry, to attack Burnside's corps at Knoxville," wrote Edward Alexander,

> which was to be assailed at the same time by a force of perhaps 4,000 men under Ransom, coming from southwest Virginia. With the remainder of his army, Bragg proposed to hold his present lines, in front of Chattanooga, during the absence of Longstreet's division. As these lines occupied a concave front of fully eight miles against an enemy concentrated in four, they were necessarily weak and unable to quickly reenforce threatened points. Longstreet pointed out their disadvantages and urged a withdrawal of the remainder of the army to a strong defensive position behind the Chickamauga River, and that his own force for the attack on Burnside at Knoxville should be increased to 20,000 men, to insure quick and easy work, and save any dependence upon the hypothetical force from southwest Virginia. Bragg, however, overruled all suggestions, and Longstreet was put in motion on Nov. 4 for Knoxville, with Wheeler's two divisions (four brigades) of cavalry.[1]

On November 4 Longstreet moved his troops—McLaws's and Jenkins's divisions of infantry, the battalions of artillery of Alexander (23 guns) and Leyden (12 guns), and five brigades of Wheeler's cavalry with 12 guns—numbering 5,000 cavalry and 10,000 infantry and artillery to Tyner's Station and Tunnel Station to proceed by rail to Sweetwater, Tennessee, within 40 miles of Knoxville. But the trains failed to arrive, as Bragg had sent them ahead to bring back Stevenson with all his troops from Sweetwater where they had been posted to guard against Burnside. Longstreet became impatient with the delay, which had been caused by Bragg's quartermaster who was responsible for transportation; he had his battery and officers' horses and wagons move by the wagon road and his officers and troops march along the railroad until cars could be found to carry them.

While waiting for the trains to move his troops, Longstreet wrote letters to his friends in the army, explaining he was so busy he was unable to say goodbye. He sent a note to General Simon Bolivar Buckner on Wednesday November 5, 1863, asking for maps of East Tennessee and reliable sources for information about the enemy. He was displeased with the timing of the move saying, "I came to the conclusion that it was to be the fate of our army to wait until all good opportunities had passed, and then, in desperation, seize upon the least favorable movement." Longstreet explained he wanted to concentrate the entire army in a strong position behind the Chickamauga River, even withdrawing from East Tennessee to deceive the enemy, then spring on Burnside with 20,000. After destroying him, he would move into the enemy's rear and his communications, dislodging them from Chattanooga while the remainder of the army would be safe and strongly posted. "Under present arrangements, however, the lines are to be held as they now are and the detachment is to be of twelve thousand," Longstreet continued. "We thus expose both to failure, and really take no chance to ourselves of great results. The only notice my plan received was a remark that General Hardee was pleased to make, 'I don't think that that is a bad idea of Longstreet's.'"[2] General Buckner endorsed the letter and returned it to Longstreet, feeling it would bear upon the debacle of Bragg's defeat on Missionary Ridge in November.

When the trains finally arrived, according to Sorrel:

> The cars and railway by which we helped the transportation were almost comical in their inefficiency. The railroad was of heavy grades and the engines light-powered. When a hill was reached the long train would be instantly emptied-platforms, roofs, doors, and windows-of our fellows, like ants out of a hill, who would ease things by trudging up the dirt road and catching on again at the top; and so it went on as far as the railroad would serve us.[3]

Longstreet reflected back on the campaign and how different things might have turned out had his strategy been implemented in May:

> At that time General Grant was marching to lay siege upon Vicksburg. The campaign in Virginia had been settled, for the time, by the battle of Chancellorsville. Our railways were open and free from Virginia through East Tennessee, Georgia, Alabama, to Central Mississippi. The armies of Rosecrans and Bragg were standing near Murfreesboro' and Shelbyville, Tennessee. The Richmond authorities were trying to collect a force at Jackson, Mississippi, to drive Grant's army from the siege. Two divisions of the First Corps of the Army of Northern Virginia were marching from Suffolk to join General Lee at Fredericksburg. Under these circumstances, positions, and conditions, I proposed to Secretary Seddon, and afterwards to General Lee, as the only means of relief for Vicksburg, that Johnston should be ordered with his troops to join Bragg's army; that the divisions marching for Fredericksburg should be ordered to meet Johnston's, the transit over converging lines would give speedy combination, and Johnston should be ordered to strike Rosecrans in overwhelming numbers and march on to the Ohio River.
>
> As the combination of September and the battle of Chickamauga drew General Grant's army from its work in Mississippi to protect the line through Tennessee and Kentucky, and two Federal corps from the Army of the Potomac, the inference is fair that the earlier, more powerful combination would have opened ways for grand results for the South, saved the eight thousand lost in defending the march for Vicksburg, the thirty-one thousand surrendered there, Port Hudson and its garrison of six thousand, and the splendid Army of Northern Virginia the twenty thousand lost at Gettysburg. And who can say that with these sixty-five thousand soldiers saved, and in the ranks, the Southern cause would not have been on a grand ascending

grade with its bayonets and batteries bristling on the banks of the Ohio River on the 4th day of July, 1863!

The elections of 1862 were not in support of the Emancipation Proclamation. With the Mississippi River still closed, and the Southern army along the banks of the Ohio, the elections of 1864 would have been still more pronounced against the Federal policy, and a new administration could have found a solution of the political imbroglio. "Blood is thicker than water."[4]

Edward Porter Alexander agreed with this assessment:

> The immense possibilities of the situation show the soundness of the strategy in sending troops from Virginia to help out pressure in Georgia. They show that it would, probably, have been best to have played that game in June instead of the Gettysburg campaign. They show that even after the Gettysburg campaign it would have been best to adopt it with at least two weeks' delay. And they show that in the next campaign of 1864 such a movement would have offered, probably, the very best chance of defeating Sherman.[5]

As Longstreet proposed the plan to concentrate in Tennessee, he should have been placed in charge of the campaign. Once again Longstreet had no qualms about serving with Joseph E. Johnston in command, whom he considered the best general in the Confederacy. Under no conditions should Bragg have been left in command. Unlike Johnston and Longstreet who understood the art of war and would use finesse to defeat the enemy, Bragg, who had very limited scope, preferred to fight his battles in a linear style, relying on costly frontal assaults while placing his headquarters too far from the field to react to changing conditions.

Longstreet did not know it but the Knoxville campaign was concocted by President Davis in communications with General Bragg; Longstreet was not privy of these discussions. Bragg wanted to be rid of Longstreet, as he was one of the generals who wanted him removed from command. He wrote to President Davis on October 31, 1863: "The Virginia troops will move in the direction indicated as soon as practicable. This will be great relief to me."[6] President Davis desired to bring Longstreet closer to the Virginia theater and General Lee, who was receiving increased pressure, stating to Bragg on October 29, 1863:

> In this connection it has occurred to me that if the operations on your left should be delayed, or not be of prime importance, that you might advantageously assign General Longstreet with his two divisions to the task of expelling Burnside, and thus place him in position, according to circumstances, to hasten or delay his return to the army of General Lee. In that quarter General Lee, with a very inferior force, has by great activity and boldness gained some recent successes over the enemy; but Meade's great and increasing numbers renders it very desirable that General Lee's troops should be returned to him at the earliest practicable day.[7]

When Longstreet, who had proceeded his men to Sweetwater, met General Stevenson, he was very disappointed to find that the abundance of rations there, which had been promised to him, were to be removed by Bragg's order when Stevenson's command retired to Bragg's army. This was very problematic. Bragg's instructions were for him to "capture or destroy Burnside's army," which had to be done at once before Sherman arrived and Grant took the offensive. The First Corps had come west from warm weather in Virginia, leaving their winter clothing and blankets behind, along with all their wagon transportation, moving into East Tennessee on short rations. Longstreet lost a few days foraging the countryside for livestock and wheat to mill into flour; Major Raphael Moses, Longstreet's chief of commissary, snagged a supply of fresh pork from Stevenson's commissary officer. Bragg could have insured a complete and speedy success by joining Stevenson's division to Longstreet and allowing Walker's division to remain as part of Longstreet's command; he would have had 32,000 infantry, over 5,000 cavalry, and additional artillery, plus enough provisions and transportation. To make matters worse, Longstreet's army had only those baggage-wagons taken from the field of battle and had to rely on Bragg's generosity. They ended up with only 113 wagons, 30 wagons shy of the 143 allowed by General Orders, No. 182, Army Headquarters. "The condition of what we had," wrote Captain Frank Potts, Longstreet's assistant quartermaster, "was beyond all question the worst I ever saw; wagons frequently breaking down, mules just able in a large proportion of cases to carry their harness, harness much worn, and many teams without collars and saddles."[8] Eventually Bragg sent 64 more wagons and teams of the same inferior quality. When Longstreet complained to Bragg about the want of transport, Bragg replied: "Transportation in abundance was on the road and subject to your orders." Longstreet retorted: "You are very much mistaken in supposing that any authority over transportation has ever been extended to me. I have several times made known to you our delays, and your dispatch just received is the first intimation that I could exercise any authority."[9]

Bragg was constantly prodding Longstreet to move rapidly. Longstreet shot back a letter on November 11, 1863:

> Please inform the commanding general that I am fully aware of the importance of activity in military operations. I have lost no time on any occasion during this war. The delay that occurs is one that might have been prevented, but not by myself. The troops are not yet here, the supply train is not here, nor have my troops any meat rations. I was assured by the commanding general that we should find a surplus of provisions in this country, and really we find none but breadstuffs. As soon as I find a probability of moving with almost certain starvation, I shall move, provided, the troops are up. If the troops that are opposed to me are in a demoralized condition, as your letter intimates, without being beaten in battle, what must be the condition of those of General Rosecrans'army? I think, however, that it is a bad principle in war to despise your enemy.[10]

Frustrated by Bragg's goading and his lack of help, Longstreet laid it on the line:

> Weary of the continual calls of General Bragg for hurried movements, it seemed well to make cause for him to assign another commander or to move him to discontinue his work at a paper record; so I wired to remind him that he assured me before sending me away that he was safe in his position, and that he was told before my leaving that the command was not strong enough to excuse any but a careful, proper campaign; that he had since been informed that all delays of our movements were due to his inefficient staff corps, and we were dependent upon

foraging for our daily rations for men and animals. It began to look more like a campaign against Longstreet than against Burnside.[11]

Longstreet asked for a quartermaster who knew the resources of East Tennessee, an engineer officer who had served with General Buckner when he commanded the Department of East Tennessee, and some maps and information about the region. The only thing he received were some inaccurate and incomplete maps, although the area had been occupied by the Confederates for more than two years; General Buckner plotted out a rough draft of the roads and streams between Loudon and Knoxville.

In his correspondence with the War Department. Bragg tried to put the onus of blame on Longstreet for any failures. Longstreet commented:

> Thus we found ourselves in a strange country, not as much as a day's rations on hand, with hardly enough land transportation for ordinary camp equipage, the enemy in front to be captured, and our friends in rear putting in their paper bullets. This sounds more like romance than war, but I appeal to the records for the facts, including reports of my chiefs of quartermaster and subsistence departments and General Alexander's account of the condition of some of the battery horses and ammunition.[12]

By November 12, 1863 Longstreet was ready for an advance on Burnside, as his troops were finally up and sufficient provisions had been obtained; it had taken eight days for Longstreet's men and equipment to cover the 60 miles to Sweetwater. The Washington authorities were very anxious for the safety of Burnside and plied Grant with dispatches for his relief. Burnside's dispatches exuded great confidence and, in fact, he suggested that he could help Grant by delaying Longstreet, drawing him further from Chattanooga and keeping him from getting back in time for the battle. Grant liked the idea and telegraphed Burnside on the 14th:

> Sherman's advance has reached Bridgeport. His whole force will be ready to move from there by Tuesday at furthest. If you can hold Longstreet in check until he gets up, or, by skirmishing and falling back, can avoid serious loss to yourself, and gain time, I will be able to force the enemy back from here, and place a force between Longstreet and Bragg that must inevitably make the former take to the mountain-passes by every available road, to get to his supplies. Sherman would have been here before this but for the high water in Elk River driving him some thirty miles up the river to cross.[13]

To counter Longstreet's 15,000, Burnside had the greater force of 28,786, consisting of the IX Corps (5,697) and the XXIII Corps (23,089), with 22 pieces of heavy artillery and 142 field guns; other troops guarded the Cumberland Gap and the Virginia frontier. When he heard Longstreet was on the move, Burnside left with 5,000, all of Edward Ferrero's division, and a portion of White's and Hartranft's, to detain Longstreet, leaving behind a strong force at Knoxville to construct extensive fieldworks under the direction of two distinguished officers of the engineer corps, Colonel Orville E. Babcock and Captain Orlando M. Poe.[14] Burnside had the

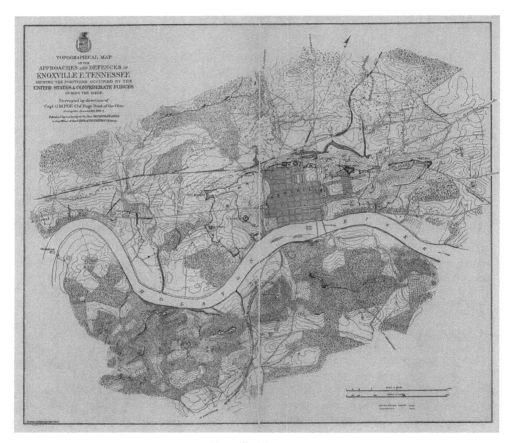

Knoxville, Tennessee

railroad bridge which crossed the Tennessee River at Loudon destroyed and took up his pontoon bridge.

"Orders were issued on the 12th for the general move of my cavalry by Marysville, the infantry and artillery along the railroad route. Pains were taken to have the bridge equipments carried by hand to the river, and skirmishing parties put in the boats and drifted to the opposite bank," Longstreet wrote. "The troops in rear were marched during the night to be in the vicinity of Loudon and held in readiness in case the enemy came to oppose our crossing. The bridge was laid under the supervision of General Alexander and Major Clark, our chief engineer, at Huff's Ferry, without serious resistance."[15]

"A bridge train had been prepared by the engineers, and it had been our intention to use it across the Little Tennessee, or Halston, above its confluence and through Marysville," Sorrel explained.

> But here again was disappointment; there were pontoons but no train for hauling.
>
> We were thus forced to throw our bridge across at Loudon, where, fortunately, the boats could be floated direct from cars, without need of wagons, and there that curious bridge was laid by our worthy engineers. It was a sight to remember. The current was strong, the anchorage insufficient, the boats and indeed entire outfit quite primitive, and when lashed finally to both banks it might be imagined a bridge; but a huge letter "S" in effect it was with its graceful reverse curves. But no man should abuse the bridge by which he safely crosses, and this one took us over, using care and caution. I shall always love the looks of that queer bridge.[16]
>
> A bridge-head was secured after some skirmishing and defences constructed on the 13th and 14th; on the 15th Jenkins' division and Alexander's artillery took the lead along the railroad route toward Lenoir's Station in pursuit of Burnside with McLaws' division and Leyden's artillery following. On the 13th, while the pontoon bridge was being constructed, three brigades of Longstreet's cavalry under Major General Joseph Wheeler were given the mission to occupy the commanding heights south of the Holston River opposite Knoxville. Wheeler dispersed an outpost of the Eleventh Kentucky Cavalry regiment at Marysville and drove towards the heights. Wheeler was delayed by two regiments of Burnside's cavalry commanded by Brigadier General William P. Sanders, an officer of much promise respected for his skill and energy; the remainder of the cavalry using picks and axes felled trees for abatis and threw up breastworks. When he reached the heights, they were heavily fortified, quite steep and unassailable, during Longstreet's siege of Knoxville Union forces built three extensive forts Dickerson, Higley and Stanley on the heights; Wheeler withdrew to rejoin Longstreet's main force.

Longstreet found the topography favored the retreating army: "All along the route of the railroad the valley between the mountain and the river is so narrow and rough that a few thousand men can find many points at which they can make successful stands against great odds. Our course was taken to turn all of those points by marching up the road on the west side of the mountain."[17]

> Jenkins pressed vigorously against Burnside's forces at Lenoir turning right at a fork two miles from the station to confront Burnside, advancing a strong line of skirmishers under charge of Lieutenant-Colonel Logan and Lieutenant-Colonel Wylie of the Fifth South Carolina Volunteers closely supported by Jenkins' brigade. Burnside finding the enemy pressing closely on his front and right flank decided to pull out. The weather was very bad and the roads worse with mud

knee deep in many places, to save his guns Burnside abandoned the wagons of White's division to add the teams to those of the artillery, some sixteen to twenty animals to a piece, to extract them from the mire. Burnside left behind nearly a hundred wagons loaded with food, camp equipage and over one hundred thousand rounds of musket ammunition and several hundred artillery shells additionally spades, picks and axes strewn upon the ground; the Confederates also found a permanent camp for winter quarters of log houses with plaster walls and glass windows. The Yankees had broken up the running-gear on the wagons temporarily disabling them.

Longstreet was hampered by a lack of knowledge of the terrain: "Not having a map of the topography of the country, I was of necessity dependent upon such information as I could get from the guides and from my own observation."[18] A guide promised to lead Longstreet's men to a spot where they could cut off Burnside's retreat from Lenoir's Station and was sent with a brigade but missed the route, and the enemy escaped during the night, heading for Campbell's Station.

On November 16 at 2:00am Longstreet learned from a Southern sympathizer that the Confederates could win the race to Campbell's Station by a shorter route to the crossroads unknown to the Federals by which they could intercept Burnside's retreat to Knoxville.[19] McLaws's division moved down this road, while Jenkins's division followed directly behind the rearguard, his skirmishers on double time.

Campbell's Station

Campbell's Station, a railway station, is situated about 10 miles from Lenoir and 15 southwest to Knoxville. Concord Road, from the south, intersected the Kingston Road to Knoxville at a crossroads about one mile from the station. Behind Campbell's Station was an isolated ridge commanding all the approaches. Longstreet quickly realized that by taking possession of it he could corner Burnside's army—with its back against a stream, it could not cross. Burnside became aware of the danger when McLaws brushed his flank. He ordered Brigadier General John F. Hartranft's division, leading the march, to cut across the woods on the run; they just reached the crossroads at noon a quarter of an hour before the Confederates. Longstreet was confident of a favorable outcome: "As the rear of the enemy was open and could be covered, success would have been a simple victory, and the enemy could have escaped to his trenches at Knoxville, leaving us crippled and delayed; whereas as he stood he was ours."[20] Jenkins stationed his division on the right as Alexander's batteries opened up but, due to defective ammunition, many of his shells exploded before they reached their target, sometimes as soon as they left the muzzles of his guns. General McLaws's division was placed on the left; Hart's cavalry brigade joined him there to observe the enemy.

Longstreet attempted to envelop Burnside's flank:

McLaws was ordered to use one of his brigades well out on his left as a diversion threatening the enemy's right, and to use Hart's cavalry for the same purpose, while General Jenkins was ordered to send two of his brigades through a well-covered way off our right to march out well past the enemy's left and strike down against that flank and rear. General Law, being his officer next in rank, was ordered in charge of his own and Anderson's brigades.[21]

What happened next became a controversy until well after the war; General Jenkins reported in his official account: "In a few minutes, greatly to my surprise, I received a message from General Law that in advancing his brigades he had obliqued so much to the left as to have gotten out of his line of attack. This careless and inexcusable movement lost us the few moments in which success from this point could be attained."[22] Burnside watched the movement from a nearby hill and took the necessary precautions to protect his rear. His army slipped away to Knoxville that night after his wagons were safely past; Burnside suffered 31 killed, 211 wounded, and 76 missing, while Longstreet had 22 killed and 152 wounded. The bulk of Burnside's army was now within the Knoxville defenses and Longstreet had to conduct a regular siege.

Longstreet and McLaws made their headquarters at "Bleak House," the home of Robert H. Armstrong, one of three brothers, all of whom had houses from Robert's brick house to Knoxville.

As Burnside made his way into the city; he deployed Brigadier General William Sanders' cavalry to cover his withdrawal. Sanders had his cavalry dismount and build a long, heavy line of fence rails over 3-feet high, and nearly as thick, on a low ridge in open grassland, engaging the brigade of Brigadier General Joseph Kershaw, McLaws's division, with their carbines. Alexander was ordered by Longstreet to knock about the rails with his guns, driving them out. He found a hidden route and brought his guns behind the second Armstrong house within 300 yards of the rail breastworks while he snuck two South Carolina regiments in a swale without the enemy knowing. The guns rolled out and fired solid shot while the infantry charged; it had the desired effect—Sanders' cavalrymen broke. Sanders received a mortal wound rallying his men; he was shot through the stomach, dying within a day or two in the bridal suite of Knoxville's Lamar House Hotel, used as a hospital. Fort Loudon was renamed Fort Sanders in his honor; nicknamed "Dock Sanders," he was a cadet friend of Alexander and a cousin to Jefferson Davis.

Fort Sanders

Longstreet examined the defenses and found Fort Sanders to be the most feasible point to assail. He outlined its structure:

Fort Loudon, afterwards called for the gallant Sanders, who fell defending it, was a bastion earthwork, built upon an irregular quadrilateral. The sides were south front, one hundred and fourteen yards; west front, ninety-five yards; north front, one hundred and twenty-five yards; east front, eighty-five yards. The eastern front was open, intended to be closed by a stockade. The south front was about half finished; the western front finished, except cutting the embrasures, and the north front nearly finished. The bastion attacked was the only one that was finished. The ditch was twelve feet wide, and generally seven to eight feet deep. From the fort the ground sloped in a heavy grade, from which the trees had been cut and used as abatis, and wire network was stretched between the stumps.[23]

By November 20, the Confederate line was finished and an attack could have been realized by the 21st or 22nd. Alexander had arranged 30 guns to enfilade the fort and had placed four howitzers of Fickling's battery on skids near the third Armstrong house to lob shells into the fort like mortars. A night attack was planned for November 22 by McLaws, but after consulting his officers, McLaws stated a daylight assault was preferred.

By now the Federals in Knoxville were on reduced rations of food, even though the besiegers had not encircled the city; forage was so scarce, draft animals were slain and thrown in the river. The Confederates had rigged up a ferry using an old flat boat and some telegraph wire and were able to retrieve the shoes of the dead horses or mules floating down; they were very hard up for horseshoes.

Major Fairfax of Longstreet's staff crossed this ferry and reconnoitered the other side, finding a high hill about 2,400 yards from Fort Sanders looking down upon and enfilading the enemy's line from the fort to the river. Longstreet postponed the attack and directed Parker's rifled battery be brought over, along with Law's and Robertson's brigades of infantry of Jenkins's division for support. The pontoon bridges at Lenoir's were hauled up by part of the supply train to connect this detachment to the main force; Alexander, who was in charge of the artillery, did not like the idea due to the great range and poor quality of the rifled ammunition. Thus, more time was lost. Work was started on Monday November 23 and all was ready to commence fire by sunrise on Wednesday, November 25.

General Leadbetter

Just then, Longstreet received a telegram from General Bushrod R. Johnson at Loudon on November 25. He was coming from Bragg's army with his own and Archibald Gracie's brigades, some 2,600 men, to reinforce Longstreet and would arrive that afternoon. Along with these troops came Brigadier General Danville Leadbetter, Bragg's chief engineer, and at 52, being the oldest military engineer in Confederate service, he was a graduate of the West Point class of 1836—the class ahead of Bragg's. He had supervised the construction of the defenses at Knoxville when it was in Confederate hands. Leadbetter was sent by Bragg at the request of General Hardee, his most dependable corps commander, "to explain to him [Longstreet] your views respecting the designs of the enemy" and that "if Burnside is strongly fortified and cannot be captured without a siege, my [Hardee's] conviction is that he ought to retire without delay." Leadbetter was informed that infantry and artillery from Virginia were within five- or six-days' march. The cavalry had already arrived, the investment would be complete, and Burnside would be forced to surrender in two weeks; he was already on half rations. Leadbetter knew a siege would be the best device but time was running out. Bragg wanted Longstreet to attack Burnside "very promptly."[24]

Already having postponed the attack to await the arrival of Johnson's and Gracie's brigades, Longstreet and Leadbetter made a reconnaissance encompassing the enemy's fortifications on Thursday, November 26. Leadbetter agreed with Longstreet that Fort Sanders was assailable but showed a preference to attack Mabry's Hill on the extreme right flank of the Union line. Porter Alexander believed Leadbetter was mistaken in the choice of ground: "In fact our own pickets had been advanced but little beyond Second Creek, and Leadbetter's opinion was based upon very imperfect and distant views."[25] Longstreet ordered Parker's battery back across the river; Captain Parker had to haul all his guns and ammunition back across in the little ferry boat. It took him part of that night and into the next day. Due to a lack of agreement between Longstreet and Leadbetter, another reconnaissance was scheduled for Friday, November 27.

Alexander recounted this reconnaissance:

> Early in the morning Longstreet & Leadbetter started with McLaws & Jenkins & Johnson & several of the brigade commanders & myself. And, near the left flank, we found Gen. Wheeler waiting for us with a brigade of cavalry. With this he drove in the enemy's pickets opposite our left, handling it very prettily, & enabled our party to make a thorough & complete examination of the whole ground. There never was a more complete fiasco than the attempt to find a favorable point for attack. Everywhere we saw near a mile of open level ground obstructed by a creek & artificial ponds, without cover anywhere, even for skirmishers, & all under fire of formidable breast works on commanding hills. It required no discussion, & even Leadbetter had not a word to say. When we had seen all there was to see, the party turned & came back to a point on our lines where we could get a good view of Fort Sanders. From where we stood, the parapet of one of the bastions was in relief against the sky. As we were looking we saw a soldier mount the parapet to come out across the ditch to the picket line. Longstreet exclaimed, & fixed his glasses on him, &, as he walked across the ditch, he said, "The ditch catches him to his waist." The ditch at that point afterwards proved to be five feet deep, & the man was probably using a plank crossing.[26]

Everyone agreed Fort Sanders was the place and Longstreet ordered the operation for November 28 at noon and had Parker's battery move again to the south side of the river. However, the weather was bad with fog and rain as to obscure the view of the artillery, so it was postponed to the 29th.

On November 28, upon hearing rumors of a major battle at Chattanooga against Bragg's forces by the enemy, Major General Lafayette McLaws wrote Longstreet a letter asking if the attack should be delayed until they had heard the results of the battle.

Longstreet replied to McLaws that the assault must go forward and asked for his cooperation.

Plan of Attack

Porter Alexander spelled out the plan for the attack:

> First, our howitzers rigged as mortars were to open & have a reasonable time to practice & get their ranges, before any other shots were fired by anything else. Then the other batteries were to begin, very slowly & carefully, getting the range, & enfilading the main lines next to the fort. Then a big cloud of skirmishers was to make a rush, & take & occupy the enemy's rifle pits from the north of the fort through the west to the south, that the fort should be the centre of a concentrated fire of sharpshooters located around an entire semi circumference. Then all the guns & mortars should unite & fire rapidly, but carefully for about 20 minutes. Then the storming column should advance.
>
> It seems to me that by such an attack we would have had that fort in our grip & have been able to keep down the little fire it was able to deliver at best, & that whatever obstacle the ditch might prove, it could then be deliberately examined, undertaken, & overcome, cutting little steps where needed. If our infantry once scaled the parapet the fort was ours. And the Federal lines became untenable when we held the fort.[27]

While on his way to consult with Longstreet at his headquarters at the Armstrong house in the afternoon of November 28, Brigadier General Micah Jenkins met Brigadier General Gracie, who told him the ditch in front of the fort was 4- or 5-feet deep with an ascent of 11 or 12 feet from the bottom of the ditch up slippery clay. This greatly concerned him but when Jenkins arrived at the Armstrong house, he found Longstreet had left but General McLaws—who also used the house as his headquarters—was there. Jenkins offered a wise suggestion to McLaws, "that the assailing party carry fascines [a long bundle of sticks bound together] to fill the ditch; but he said they knew nothing about such things, and they would trust to luck in getting around or over."[28]

Later that evening General Jenkins encountered Colonel Porter Alexander: "A little before sundown that evening I left Longstreet's headquarters to return to my camp, across Second Creek," expounded Alexander:

> I had crossed the creek & gotten about a half mile on my road when I met Gen. Jenkins. He said, "Alexander, I want you to go back with me to Longstreet's. McLaws's troops are to form the storming column tomorrow, & I don't think McLaws has provided any ladders. I am going to urge Longstreet to order him to do so, for we don't know what we are going to find, & we ought to be well prepared in advance. I want you to go back with me & add your influence to mine."
>
> Now there was a good deal of detail to be determined about the storming column, relating to its size, its tactical formation, its equipment, & its exact procedure, to all of which I had given but little thought, believing the infantry officers who would be in charge would be the most competent judges to decide them all. Now I at once realized that Jenkins's suggestion was a very important one, & that I ought to go back with him & help him urge it. But I was feeling unusually tired, the roads were reached, & I was anxious to get back home before dark. So I let sloth & fatigue prevail against the promptings of my conscience, & I said, "Jenkins, your influence will be enough. The matter is very simple & obvious. And if my opinion is of any weight you can tell the general that you met me & discussed it with me & that I asked you to say that I most heartily concur in your opinion."

Jenkins seemed disappointed, but went on, and my conscience began to reproach me at once. For in such matters as this every ounce of precaution possible to obtain should be had, even if it cost a ton of trouble. No one can ever tell what particular ounce will turn the scale. I consoled myself, however, thinking that in the morning there would still be time-even after the artillery began, to tear some stable to pieces if necessary & make ladders in an hour.

But I never dreamed that within a couple of hours Longstreet was going to change his mind, & completely alter the whole plan of attack. Had I gone on with Gen. Jenkins the chances are that some intimation of this new scheme would have been dropped & we might have shown its absurdities. For some of its features were crazy enough to have come out of Bedlam, & I will go to my grave believing that Leadbetter devised it & imposed it upon Longstreet, & he afterward preferred to accept the responsibility rather than plead that he had let himself be so taken in. I will give the orders, which we received about 8 o'clock that night, & every (one) can judge for himself if I speak of them fairly. They were short & simple. Instead of the attack by main force, & artillery, as planned for sunrise and after a good breakfast, an attempt would be made to surprise the fort a little before dawn. As a preliminary step, the enemy's rifle pits were to be attacked, captured & occupied at 11 P.M. Then the assaulting troops would be formed at once in the rear of these pits, & held there all night but without fires. At the appointed hour in the morning a few shots from one of my batteries would be the signal for the infantry to assault the fort.

It should be noted that the legitimate occasion for resorting to a night surprise is when material disadvantages attend an attack by main force, & daylight. Here the very reverse obtained. It would have (been) impossible, I think, to find on the continent another earth work so advantageously situated for attack. No military engineer could ask for an easier task. It was like a one move problem in chess.[29]

Jenkins wrote a letter that evening to Longstreet, recapping what General Gracie had told him about the ditches and his conversation with McLaws. Longstreet replied but from the letter, one can see he was misled by his observation of the man crossing the ditch: "The ditch is probably at some points not more than 3 feet deep and 5 to 6 feet wide; at least, we so judged it yesterday in looking at a man walk down the parapet and over the ditch. I thought that you saw the man, as you had been with us. I have no apprehension of the result of the attack if we go at it. We should avail ourselves of everything, however, that may aid us or relieve us."[30]

Fort Sanders's Defenses

The fort had thick earthen walls 8-feet high, surmounted by cotton bales covered with rawhide to prevent ignition by gunfire. It was built upon an irregular quadrilateral of which the sides were west front, 95 yards; north front, 125 yards; east front, 85 yards; and south front, 125 yards. It was not enclosed, with the eastern front intentionally left open to allow access. It had a ditch in front of the bastion faces, 12-feet wide and from 6- to 8-feet deep depending upon accidents of the ground; the escarps (the wall of the ditch surrounding a rampart) were vertical and the berm (a space of about a foot between the edge of the ditch and the foot of the parapet of the exterior slope) was cut away. The ground sloped in a steep gradient from all sides of the fort; the trees were all cut and used as abatis on the glacis (a bank of earth in front of the fortification). The fort was still unfinished in spots; the west side had no embrasures. A Mr. Hoxie, in charge of the railroad property at Knoxville, produced a lot of old telegraph wire which was stretched between tree stumps and stakes a few inches above the ground, creating a network entanglement as an obstruction. The fort was manned by a garrison of 220 men belonging to the 79th New York and 17th Michigan, the division commander General Ferrero was in the works; 12 pieces of artillery were mounted in the fort of Benjamin's and Buckley's batteries and a section of Roemer's (four 20-pounder Parrotts, six 12-pounder Napoleons, and two 3-inch rifled guns).

The fort had some unique features that made it favorable for the assault; apparently, Leadbetter did not make a complete and thorough examination of Fort Sanders before making his suggestion to Longstreet to rearrange the attack.

About 10:00pm, at moonrise, the Confederate infantry skirmishers advanced around Fort Sanders and captured the Union rifle pits by 11:00pm, taking 50 or 60 prisoners; the rest of the Union skirmishers retired into their lines. Naturally, this action put the fort on alert. The storming columns, consisting of two regiments of Humphrey's Mississippi brigade, three regiments of Bryan's Georgia brigade and four regiments of William Wofford's Georgia Brigade under Colonel Solon Ruff, and all of McLaws's division, with Anderson's Georgia brigade of Jenkins's division to support the storming column on the left east of the fort, formed in the rear of the pits behind sheltered ground; the temperature was freezing, with a fine mist falling and no fires allowed. The troops lay on their arms and suffered greatly. From time to time the fort discharged a gun, firing canister or shell.

Just around dawn, three guns—each from different batteries—fired successively, signaling the advance of the storming columns as the sharpshooters opened up upon the parapet; the signal also alerted the defenders. Alexander fired a dozen guns, bursting shells around and just behind the fort to arrest reinforcements from coming up; he watched the onslaught: "There was no special preparation of any part of the assaulting force as a storming column, with ladders, or guides, or special destination & instruction. The tactical formation was merely three brigades abreast in line of battle-just what it would have been in attacking a force in a wheat field!"[31] The units were supposed to begin within 150 to 200 yards of the fort but were started much farther back in error during the darkness of night. The troops ran into the telegraph wire tangle but they soon tore it away without great loss or delay. However, the columns converged into a mass where the units became indistinguishable by their officers. They reached the ditch and many leaped in, nearly filling it. A Union officer made this observation: "Having no scaling-ladders, a portion of the men, scrambling over the shoulders of their comrades, planted the battle-flags of the 13th and 17th Mississippi and the 16th Georgia upon the parapet, but every man who rallied to them was either killed or captured, and the flags were taken."[32] The ground was frozen and slippery from the previous day's rain and freezing weather;

the defenders had washed the slopes of the parapet with water which formed into ice in the cold night air. Axes, billets of wood, and stones were thrown over the parapets into the ditch. Cannon shells with three-second fuses were lit and tossed among the attackers in the ditch. Lieutenant Samiel L. Benjamin, the artillery commander in the fort, had instructed his men to prepare 50 of them: "It stilled them down," he said grimly.[33] "Longstreet, seeing the flash of their explosions, and thinking them to be our own shells falling short, ordered the cessation of the slight artillery fire which we had continued to throw on the flanks and beyond the fort," Alexander stated.[34] As daylight came, enfilade fire from both sides of the fort increased in intensity, multiplying the casualties. Those in the ditch found it equally difficult to advance or retreat. Some slipped away; about 200 surrendered.

Longstreet watched the action close up:

> The troops marched steadily and formed regularly along the outside of the works around the ditch. I rode after them with the brigades under General B. R. Johnson until within five hundred yards of the fort, whence we could see our advance through the gray of the morning. A few men were coming back wounded. Major Goggin, of General McLaws's staff, who had been at the fort, rode back, met me, and reported that it would be useless for us to go on; the enemy had so surrounded the fort with network of wire that it was impossible for the men to get in without axes, and that there was not an axe in the command. Without a second thought I ordered the recall, and ordered General Johnson to march his brigades back to their camps. He begged to be allowed to go on, but, giving full faith to the report, I forbade him. I had known Major Goggin many years. He was a class-mate at West Point, and had served with us in the field in practical experience, so that I had confidence in his judgment.
>
> Recall was promptly sent General Jenkins and his advance brigade under General Anderson, but the latter, seeing the delay at the fort, changed his direction outside the enemy's works and marched along their front to the ditch, and was there some little time before he received the order. In his march and countermarch in front of the enemy's line he lost four killed and thirty-three wounded.[35]

Jenkins had asked Longstreet to go in and Alexander was elated:

> Soon after the repulse I heard, with great delight, that Jenkins had asked and obtained permission to make a fresh attempt, for I felt the utmost confidence that a concentrated fire by daylight from our 34 guns and mortars, with 1000 sharp-shooters whom we could shelter within close range, could silence the fort entirely, enabling a storming column to plant ladders, fill the ditch with fascines, and cut footholds in the scarp, so that an overwhelming force might reach the interior. But before arrangements could be made Longstreet received official intelligence of Bragg's disaster and an order to abandon the siege of Knoxville and to move promptly to join Bragg. A renewal of the attack was, therefore, thought inexpedient, and orders were at once given to move all trains to the rear, in preparation for a retreat southward at night.[36]

Burnside offered a flag of truce for Longstreet to remove his dead and wounded, which was accepted by Longstreet.

"General Longstreet takes upon himself the failure of the assault," asserted Sorrel. "It seems conclusive to him that it was due to the order for recall. He had long known Goggin."[37]

Brigadier General Orlando M. Poe, an engineer in charge of the Union works, gave Longstreet and his men a great compliment: "No one is more ready and willing than the writer to admit the excellence of the troops that fought us at Knoxville. They had few equals, and I believe no superiors."[38]

Major Branch, of Major General Robert Ransom's staff, brought a telegram from President Davis about half an hour after the repulse at Fort Sanders, informing Longstreet to the effect, "Bragg has been forced back by numbers and that we were to co-operate with his army." Longstreet issued orders for preparations to march south after nightfall to join Bragg at Ringgold, but, before nightfall, messages by courier from Bragg indicated that he had fallen back as far as Dalton, and a large force under Sherman was marching to relieve Burnside, closing the route to Dalton.[39] The only communication to Bragg was through an impracticable mountainous route southwest through upper Georgia, some 200 miles—an area destitute of supplies. Longstreet, after consulting with his generals, determined to hold the lines at Knoxville until the enemy was within a day's march, to relieve the pressure on Bragg. The retreat began on December 4 during a heavy rainstorm. The roads were in bad condition, but Longstreet's troops made the18 miles to Blain's Cross Roads where they encamped. General Ransom's artillery and infantry joined them there on December 5, having been called up by Longstreet. The Knoxville campaign cost the Confederates a loss of 1,296, while the Union losses were 1,481.

CHAPTER 14

"Strategic Importance of the Field"

East Tennessee

The retreat continued for a total of 65 miles in four days to Rogersville: "There was good foraging in the country, and we halted at Rogersville on the 9th to accumulate supplies," professed Sorrel:

> Up to this date it had not been our General's intention to stay in the Tennessee Valley. He was looking eastward, but more hopefully toward some combinations and increase of force by which a powerful demonstration could be made into Kentucky through the Cumberland Gap. But at Rogersville the foraging officers brought in roseate reports of plenty in the land. It appeared to be overflowing with subsistence for an army; cattle, swine, corn, sorghum, and honey were abundant, and it was decided we should winter in these beautiful valleys, watered by the Holston, the French Broad, the mouth of the Chucky and Nolachucky. Truly was it a fertile and smiling land to be still showing all this abundance, ravaged and harried as it had been alternately by Union and Confederate forces, and with such a population! It could well be said that "Only man was vile."[1]

On December 10, President Davis gave Longstreet discretionary authority over all troops and activities in the department. Longstreet retained Martin's cavalry which Bragg had called for (the cavalry was now under Major General William T. Martin, as Major General Joseph Wheeler had been ordered back to Bragg).

Strategic and Political Importance

East Tennessee was an area of strategic and political importance. The region had a strong Union sentiment and the Washington authorities wanted it cleansed of any Confederate forces that might abuse the loyal population. But more important was its proximity to Kentucky and the Ohio River which, if invaded, would jeopardize President Lincoln's bid for re-election in 1864.

Grant urged Burnside to pursue Longstreet. Burnside ordered Major General John G. Parke, Burnside's chief of staff, to march against Longstreet with the Ninth and Twenty-third Corps under the orders of Generals Robert Potter and Mahlon Manson, attended by Brigadier General James Shackelford's cavalry division—a force of 8,000 infantry and 4,000 cavalry. Burnside requested to be relieved of command at Knoxville, and on December 12 Major General John G. Foster replaced him; Foster had arrived at Knoxville from the Cumberland Gap.

Parke pulled up as Stephen Rutledge and Shackelford went on to Bean's Station, a small mountain village along an old stagecoach line between Clinch Mountain and the Holston River, with his cavalry and a brigade of infantry. Longstreet saw an opportunity to net the force at Bean's Station, since the terrain was mountainous and inaccessible except by "very rough passes." All Longstreet's infantry, with Johnson's division in front, marched on Bean's Station on the afternoon of Monday, December 14. Jones's two brigades of cavalry were sent north around Clinch Mountain to occupy Bean's Station Gap on one flank, and Martin's four brigades of cavalry moving south of the Holston River, crossing at Kelley's Ferry on the other flank to get behind Shackelford. The infantry struck the Union position, in which a sharp fight ensued. General Gracie received a ball in his forearm, but Martin did not cross successfully and Jones arrived early at the Gap, capturing 68 wagon loads. Then he withdrew after nightfall to feast on the sugar, coffee, and bacon, leaving the Gap open for the main column of Federals to escape during the night. Johnson suffered 222 casualties; Shackelford reported 115. In the morning Longstreet's men found only "empty camp-kettles, mess-pans, tents, and a few abandoned guns and twelve prisoners." Longstreet sent his troops in pursuit on the 15th trying to catch the enemy before they reached the defenses of Knoxville. Parke fell back to Blain's Cross Roads where General Foster with the Fourth Corps reinforced him. Battle was offered, as his numbers had grown to 26,000 opposed by Longstreet's 20,000 but the winter weather grew heavy and the roads became too soft for artillery and trains, so both armies went into winter quarters. Longstreet commented: "I could have precipitated an affair of some moment, both at this point and at Bean's Station Gap, but my purpose was, when I fought, to fight for all that was on the field. The time was then for full and glorious victory; a fruitless one we did not want."[2]

The Confederate forces made their camps along the East Tennessee and Virginia railroad and commenced repair of the rails and bridges to open communications with Richmond, Virginia.

Provisions

Longstreet looked back in retrospect on that winter:

> The transfer of the army to the east bank of the river was executed by diligent work and the use of such flatboats and other means of crossing as we could collect and construct. We were over by the 20th, and before Christmas were in our camps along the railroad, near Morristown. Blankets and clothes were very scarce, shoes more so, but all knew how to enjoy the beautiful country in which we found ourselves. The French Broad River and the Holston are confluent at Knoxville. The country between and beyond them contains as fine farming lands and has as delightful a climate as can be found. Stock and grain were on all farms. Wheat and oats had been hidden away by our Union friends, but the fields were full of maize, still standing. The

country about the French Broad had hardly been touched by the hands of the foragers. Our wagons immediately on entering the fields were loaded to overflowing. Pumpkins were on the ground in places like apples on a tree. Cattle, sheep, and swine, poultry, vegetables, maple-sugar, honey, were all abundant for immediate wants of the troops.

When the enemy found we had moved to the east bank, his cavalry followed to that side. They were almost as much in want of the beautiful foraging lands as we, but we were in advance of them, and left little for them. With all the plentitude of provisions and many things which seemed at the time luxuries, we were not quite happy. Tattered blankets, garments, and shoes (the latter going-many gone) opened ways, on all sides, for piercing winter blasts. There were some hand-looms in the country from which we occasionally picked up a piece of cloth, and here and there we received other comforts, some from kind and some from unwilling hands, which nevertheless could spare them. For shoes we were obliged to resort to the raw hides of beef cattle as temporary protection from the frozen ground. Then we began to find soldiers who could tan the hides of our beeves, some who could make shoes, so who could make shoe-pegs, some who could make shoe-lasts, so that it came about that the hides passed rapidly from the beeves to the feet of the soldiers in the form of comfortable shoes. [They were able to produce 100 pairs of shoes per day.] Then came the opening of the railroad, and lo and behold! a shipment of three thousand shoes from General Lawton, quartermaster-general! Thus the urgent needs were supplied, and the soldier's life seemed passably pleasant, -that is in the infantry and artillery. Our cavalry were looking at the enemy all this while, and the enemy was looking at them, both frequently burning powder between their lines.

General Sturgis had been assigned to the cavalry of the other side to relieve General Shackelford, and he seemed to think that the dead of winter was the time for cavalry work; and General Martin's orders were to have the enemy under his eyes at all hours. Both were vigilant, active, and persevering.[3]

Longstreet had found some of his officers wanting in their conduct during the campaign and started proceedings against them in mid-December. Brigadier General Jerome B. Robertson had been complained about by General Hood before he was seriously wounded at Chickamauga. Also, Robertson had performed poorly in the night attack of October 28 near Lookout Mountain. Brigadier General Micah Jenkins laid out a charge of "conduct highly prejudicial to good order and military discipline" on December 18 in regard to Robertson's performance at Bean's Station.

On the day before Robertson was charged, Lieutenant Colonel Moxley Sorrel issued Special Orders to Major General Lafayette McLaws, relieving him of further duties.

Longstreet thought Brigadier General Evander McIver Law had shown bad attitude and poor conduct both at Lookout Mountain on October 29 and at Campbell's Station on November 16 and was going to press charges, However, General Law had the good sense to resign. So, it seemed he no longer wished to serve with Jenkins in command of his division. Sorrel explained:

General E. M. Law handed in his resignation and asked leave of absence on it-this about December 20th. It was cheerfully granted, and then General Law asked the privilege of taking the resignation himself to Richmond. It was unusual, but was allowed. From this afterwards grew serious complications, involving Law's arrest by Longstreet, his support by the Executive, and Longstreet's threat of resignation from the army, in which he was upheld by General Lee. And the Lieutenant-General had his way. Law was not again in Longstreet's command.[4]

On December 30, 1863 General Longstreet charged General Lafayette McLaws with three specifications regarding the assault on Fort Sanders at Knoxville.

Longstreet Resigns

Longstreet sensed that the failure of his subordinates reflected upon his ability as commander. On the same day Longstreet had pressed formal charges against McLaws, he sent a letter of resignation from his headquarters at Russellville, Tennessee, to General Samuel Cooper.

During the severe cold spell at the end of December 1863 into the new year, the thermometer approached zero. Longstreet took this time to reflect:

> The season seemed an appropriate one for making another effort to be relieved from service,-that service in which the authorities would not support my plans or labors,-for now during the lull in war they would have ample time to assign some one to whom they could give their confidence and aid. But this did not suit them, and the course of affairs prejudicial to order and discipline was continued. It was difficult under the circumstances to find apology for remaining in service.[5]

Word had reached Longstreet that the president had requested Congress to arrange for another general of full rank to command the Trans-Mississippi Department, a measure designed solely to raise the rank of Lieutenant General Kirby Smith, who had charge of that department for a year. Longstreet felt slighted, since he had been a major in the "old army" from July 19, 1858, while Smith was from January 31, 1861—though Longstreet was a paymaster and Smith in the line. However, both were appointed lieutenant general on the same date in the Confederate army; Smith's name was just below Longstreet's.[6]

On January 9, 1864, General Samuel Cooper, adjutant and inspector general, asked General Lee for advisement concerning Longstreet's resignation request.

On the following day, General Lee fielded Cooper's question:

> I have received your letter of the 9th instant in reference to request of General Longstreet to be relieved from his present command and of his corps. I do not know the reasons that have induced him to take this step, but hope that they are not such as to make it necessary. I do not know any one to take his place in either position. I do not think it advantageous that he and Lieutenant-General Ewell should exchange corps, believing that each corps would be more effective as at present organized. I cannot, therefore, recommend their exchange.[7]

It is interesting to note the high regard and esteem General Lee placed on Longstreet and his generalship—that he was irreplaceable and had no equal in the Confederate army.

Longstreet never had the issue of his resignation resolved. As late as February 6, 1864 he demurred to General Samuel Cooper, adjutant and inspector general: "I made application some time ago to be relieved from the responsibilities of a separate command, and have been constantly expecting that I would be advised whether I would be relieved or not, and have therefore preferred to wait to know what was to be my position before taking any steps toward a permanent organization of command."[8] Despite his poor treatment by Richmond, and Davis bypassing him for a full generalship and giving it to Kirby Smith, Longstreet decided to stay on: "A soldier's honor is his all, and of that they would rob him and degrade him in the eyes of his troops. The occasion seemed to demand resignation, but that would have been unsoldierly conduct. Dispassionate judgment suggested, as the proper rounding of the soldier's life, to stay and go down with faithful comrades of long and arduous service."[9]

McLaws's and Robertson's court-martials were set for January 16, 1864, at Russellville, Tennessee, Longstreet's headquarters, by Seddon but the trials did not begin until February 12 in Morristown. The first case was the trial of Jerome Robertson. Testimony was given and Longstreet granted Robertson permission to go to Richmond and "await there the promulgation of the sentence." Nothing ever came of it; Davis and Seddon dismissed the charges and, in June, Robertson was ordered to take command of the "reserve forces of the State of Texas," his home state. Nevertheless, Longstreet was rid of him. In a letter to his mother dated January 22, 1864, L. M. Brackford said of Robertson, he was not "considered a good officer."

The case of General McLaws was to be heard on February 13 but was adjourned until March 15. Longstreet had begun a movement against Knoxville and he "shall need not only the witnesses that your court wants, but the members of the court who belong with us." Longstreet had no desire to pursue a court-martial against General McLaws, a personal friend, and had sent a message to General Cooper concerning McLaws on December 30, 1863, when he reluctantly pressed charges: "General McLaws was not arrested when he was relieved from duty, for the reason that it was supposed that his services might be important to the Government in some other position. If such is the case, I have no desire that he should be kept from that service or that his usefulness should be impaired in any way by a trial." Before going to Augusta, Georgia, McLaws had confronted Longstreet as to why he was relieved of command and wanted formal charges lodged, asking Cooper to order a court-martial; Longstreet's answer to McLaws, remembered in a postwar letter, was: "I had not co-operated cordially with him & he was afraid that my influence would extend to the troops that one of us must go, that he could not & therefore I must & could."[10] It was not until May 4, 1864 at Richmond that the court found McLaws not guilty of the first two specifications but guilty of the third; he was suspended from rank and command for 60 days. General Cooper disapproved and overturned the findings and sentence of the court, citing technical grounds; McLaws was to return to duty with his command and the court dissolved. Instead, McLaws was assigned to the Department of South Carolina, Georgia, and Florida at the end of May, although he had appealed to the War Department for restoration to his former command.

The Impossible Position That I Held

Longstreet wrote McLaws a letter on July 25, 1873, in which he stated he had relieved McLaws "in an unguarded moment." Longstreet continued: "I know as well as you that Mr. Davis would be pleased to have you make charges against me, and that Gen. Bragg would be more than pleased to join you, and I will say frankly that I would rather have had you make charges against me than to be obliged to make them against you. I was anxious to be rid of the impossible position that I held."[11]

General Robertson was replaced by "an excellent officer, General Gregg, had been sent to report, and was assigned the Texas brigade," but more than anything, Longstreet wanted to promote Micah Jenkins, whom he considered very competent, to retain command of Hood's division. To succeed to McLaws's division, Longstreet wanted to advance Major General Joseph B. Kershaw, "a lawyer from South Carolina" whom Sorrel described,

> was one of the most distinguished and efficient officers of the Virginia army. His service had been long and uninterrupted. Coming out with a fine South Carolina regiment among the first to be sent to Virginia, his abilities soon made him a colonel. He served long in that rank, his steady courage and military aptitude invariably showing handsomely in the arduous service of the regiment [Second South Carolina]. It was one of those forming the South Carolina Brigade of McLaws's division. Longstreet was quick to perceive Kershaw's merit and recommended him for promotion. It was sometime coming. But when he was brigadier-general and placed in command of the brigade he maintained his high reputation fully. In 1864 he was promoted to be major-general, and continuing his service with Longstreet's corps, his conduct and abilities were conspicuous until the very end of hostilities. General Kershaw was of most attractive appearance, soldierly and handsome, of medium size, well set up, light hair and moustache, with clean-cut, high-bred features.[12]

Instead of consulting Longstreet as to his preferences for division commanders, the War Department, for reasons of its own, thwarted Longstreet's wishes by Special Orders No. 36 on February 12, 1864: "Brig. Gen. C. W. Field, Provisional Army, C. S., will proceed without delay to Morristown, Tenn., and report to Lieut. Gen, J. Longstreet, commanding, for assignment to duty with the division lately commanded by Lieut. Gen. J. B. Hood."[13] The very day this order was issued, Charles W. Field, a 35-year-old Kentuckian, was promoted to major general. He had graduated from West Point, class of 1849. He had been seriously wounded in the leg at Second Manassas while leading a brigade of A. P. Hill's "Light Division"; it was feared the mangled leg would require amputation, but it was saved by the doctors. For one year, Field recuperated, moving on crutches, but he never fully recovered, while convalescent Field served as Superintendent of the Bureau of Conscription from

May 1863. His appearance was stocky and his personality was congenial and full of humor. Sorrel declared he "was to prove an active and capable commander."

Longstreet saw a way to work around this directive and tried a different arrangement by placing Simon Buckner who was on temporary duty with Longstreet and who had always served in the Mississippi Valley and was unlikely to go to Virginia, in charge of Hood's division and assign Field to Buckner's troops. That way when Buckner was called to a different post, Jenkins would be promoted to command Hood's division. After making these appointments, on February 25, 1864, Longstreet reported by letter to Cooper:

> I have thought it best to assign General Buckner to the command of the division recently commanded by General Hood and to assign General Field to the division lately commanded by General Buckner. In consequence of the badly crippled condition of General Field; it is thought the interest of the service will be advanced, inasmuch as General Hood's old division is the largest that I have, and will therefore require the most active and energetic officer that I have. General Buckner's old division is very small, composed of but two brigades at present. It will therefore better suit General Field's condition, for the present at least.
>
> I have felt the less hesitation in this as General Lee suggested such assignment of General Buckner.[14]

Upon receiving the letter on March 4, 1864, Cooper telegraphed rejection of this setup: "Your assignment of General Buckner to Hood's old division not approved. The order from this office assigning General Field to that division will be carried into effect." Longstreet was persistent and not going to take no for an answer. He tried a different tack to attain his goal for Jenkins, sending a telegram in the form of a question on March 4: "Would it meet the views of the Department to assign Major-General Field to the division formerly commanded by Major-General McLaws?" But Davis and Cooper would not give an inch to accommodate the commanding general and shot back by telegraph the same day: "It does not suit the views of the president to assign Major-General Field to the division lately commanded by Major-General McLaws. He is to take the division to which he was assigned in orders from this office."[15]

Flagrant disregard by the president of his selections to lead his divisions rankled Longstreet. He vented those feelings in a letter on March 20, in which he asked as to "the distinguished services rendered by this officer [Field] and the high recommendations of his commanding generals which have induced the Government to make this unusual promotion and assignment." Cooper discharged a scathing reprimand on April 2:

> The advice you have asked as to [Field's qualifications] is considered highly insubordinate and demands rebuke. It is also a reflection upon a gallant and meritorious officer, who has been severely wounded in battle in the cause of the Confederate States, and is deemed unbecoming the high position and dignity of the officer who thus makes the reflection. The regulations of the Army, with which you should be familiar, prescribes that appointments of general officers

are made by selection-selection by whom? Of course by the Executive, by whom appointments are made under the Constitution.

The regulations referred to do not require the recommendation of general officers for the procurement of such appointments, and your inquiry is a direct reflection upon the Executive.[16]

Resolution of Thanks for Longstreet's Service by the Confederate Congress

In contrast the Congress showed appreciation for Longstreet's contributions in a joint resolution, making a commentary upon the shabby treatment he received from the executive offices:

> No. 78
> Thanks of the Confederate Congress to Lieut. Gen. James Longstreet and his command.
> No. 43-JOINT RESOLUTIONS of thanks to Lieutenant-General Longstreet and the officers and men of his command.
>
> Resolved by the Congress of the Confederate States of America,
> That the thanks of the Congress are due, and hereby cordially tendered, to Lieut. Gen. James Longstreet and the officers and men of his command, for their patriotic services and brilliant achievements in the present war, sharing as they have the arduous fatigues and privations of many campaigns in Virginia, Maryland, Pennsylvania, Georgia, and Tennessee, and participating in nearly every great battle fought in those States, the commanding general ever displaying great ability, skill, and prudence in command, and the officers and men the most heroic bravery, fortitude, and energy, in every duty they have been called upon to perform.
> Resolved, That the President be requested to transmit copy of the foregoing resolution to Lieutenant-General Longstreet for publication to his command.
>
> Approved February 17, 1864.[17]

The Union High Command wanted Longstreet expelled from East Tennessee. Hallock urged Grant to drive Longstreet out. Grant had visited Knoxville on December 31, remaining till January 7 to ascertain why Foster had not pressed Longstreet. He found Foster was as bad off as Longstreet, lacking supplies, clothing, and shoes. Grant ordered up the necessities and commanded Foster to advance on Longstreet.

After being adequately reinforced and equipped, Foster started a movement on January 14 and 15 toward Dandridge, which is 30 miles from Knoxville on the right bank of the French Broad River. General Foster stayed behind at Knoxville, incapacitated by an old wound. He was superseded by Major General Gordon Granger. Longstreet met this threat by cleverly attacking with Brigadier General William Martin's cavalrymen, driving Granger's cavalry through the town. Longstreet personally led a charge by one of Martin's brigades. Longstreet told the War Department he had improved the cavalry's usefulness: "The cavalry is doing good service, and has learned more of its duties since I came here than in all its previous service."[18] Longstreet rode into Dandridge as Granger withdrew:

While yet on the streets of Dandridge, giving directions for such pursuit as we could make, a lady came out upon the sidewalk and invited us into her parlors. When the orders for pursuit were given, I dismounted, and with some members of my staff walked in. After compliments of the season were passed, we were asked to be seated, and she told us something of General Granger during the night before. She had never heard a person swear about another as General Granger did about me. Some of the officers proposed to stop and make a battle, but General Granger swore and said it "was no use to stop and fight Longstreet. You can't whip him. It don't make any difference whether he has one man or a hundred thousand." Presently she bought out a flask that General Granger had forgotten, and thought that I should have it. It had about two refreshing inches left in it. Though not left with compliments, it was accepted. Although the weather had moderated, it was very wet and nasty, and we had taken our coffee at three o'clock, it was resolved to call it noon and divide the spoils. Colonel Fairfax, who knew how to enjoy good things, thought the occasion called for sentiment, and offered, "General Granger—may his shadow never grow less."[19]

General Joseph Johnston warned Longstreet that trains loaded with troops were leaving Chattanooga for Loudon to advance against him. Longstreet asked for an additional 10,000 troops to overcome the Union build-up and Lee proposed sending Pickett's division to him. Longstreet was thinking in terms of another offensive against Knoxville, augmented by the additional troops who would be used to sever the railroad and bridges between Chattanooga and Knoxville so that he could starve the Federals into submission at Knoxville. Longstreet telegraphed his old friend and former commander, General Joseph E. Johnston, inquiring if the Army of Tennessee could assist him: "It was thought," Longstreet conjectured,

that the army at Chattanooga could not afford sufficient detachments to drive me from that work without exposing that position to danger from General Johnston at Dalton, but upon inquiry of General Johnston if he could avail himself of such opportunity, he replied that he was ordered to reinforce General Polk, who was operating in Mississippi in front of General Sherman [Sherman had advanced from Vicksburg with 35,000 men occupying Jackson then Meridian; Polk's Army of Mississippi had less than ten thousand infantry and cavalry to oppose them]. Instead of reinforcing General Polk, the latter should have been ordered to General Johnston. That would have drawn General Sherman to General Thomas, but Polk, having interior lines of transit, could have been in time for Johnston to strike and break up the road and bridge behind Thomas before Sherman could reach him. The break could have forced Thomas to care for his own position, and the want of the bridge behind him might have forced him to abandon it, in search of safe communications with his supplies. But the authorities could not be induced to abandon the policy of placing detachments to defend points to which the enemy chose to call us. We had troops enough in Tennessee, Georgia, Alabama, and Mississippi, if allowed to use them in co-operative combination, to break the entire front of the Federal forces and force them back into Kentucky before the opening of the spring campaign, when we might have found opportunity to "dictate" their campaign. The enemy was in no condition for backward move at the time of my advance upon Knoxville, so simultaneous advance of our many columns could have given him serious trouble, if not confusion.[20]

On February 19, 1864, President Jefferson Davis telegrammed Longstreet that the reinforcement was not forthcoming and directing him to send Martin's cavalry to Johnston's army, informing him that Johnston needed the cavalry more than he did. Without Martin's cavalry, Longstreet was left with only 1,300 effective troopers. He had to fall back to a line behind Bull's Gap with his right on the Holston River and his left on the Nolichucky River to lessen his exposed flanks.[21] The position was covered by a spur of the mountains, and Longstreet had his men use picks and shovels in the defiles to make the line unassailable. However, he had so little cavalry that he could not take the offensive. There, Longstreet's troops rested for the winter, undisturbed. The enemy's cavalry was worn down by severe winter service. The medical inspector of the Cis-Mississippi District visited Longstreet's troops and found the soldiers healthier and in better spirits than other armies in the district.

Raid into Kentucky

Longstreet realized the "strategic importance of the field" he occupied in East Tennessee. It was near the gateway to Kentucky and by seizing the Louisville and Nashville Railroad, he would cut supplies to the Union armies in Middle Tennessee, thus forcing them to retire. The line he occupied also guarded the approaches to Virginia. On February 21, 1864, Longstreet proposed a raid into Kentucky to General Lee:

> General Johnston and I-with two armies between us; this army entirely helpless, except the enemy comes up and attacks me in front. The enemy can concentrate both armies upon General Johnston, without the chance of a counter move by me against this portion of his line. You will readily see my difficulties as well as those of General Johnston. Under the circumstances, I can see no great hope of doing more than check the enemy occasionally on this road, unless he is bold enough to come out and attack me. This he will not do, as he can always throw me back by turning my flanks by his superior numbers and excess of cavalry.
>
> It seems to me that the only thing left for me is to mount the command and move into Kentucky. If I can get on the railroad between Louisville and Nashville I can hold Kentucky, I think. At all events, I can hold it long enough to force the enemy to quit Tennessee and allow General Johnston to advance and regain it. The only way to mount us is by sending us 5,000 mules from Virginia, 2,500 from Georgia, and 2,000 from South Carolina; I have 5,000. Of these I can get along with about half, by taking no wagons except for ammunition; we will be able to get enough for other purposes from the enemy. We have no time to spare, and the whole thing should be kept from other parties.[22]

Lee was enthusiastic about the plan and started to procure equipment and mules and horses for such an expedition.

Longstreet sent the same proposal to Secretary of War Seddon the next day— February 22, 1864—elaborating on the details needed to carry it out:

> I am moving my command back, and propose to occupy a range of hills extending from the Nola Chucky across to the Holston as our principal line, and the two streams just mentioned as our flanks. This position, I think, could be held until the roads are so good as to allow the enemy to turn it by passing up the Holston toward Bristol.

The enemy, having two armies between General Johnston and myself can concentrate his entire force against either of us, and can certainly crush mine unless I get out of the way. General Johnston has just telegraphed me that the enemy has concentrated his main force in my front, near Knoxville. My information is to the same effect, and that he is pushing his forces forward from Kentucky through Nashville; that he has stopped granting furloughs, and that his men are refusing in every instance to re-enlist.

The concentration in my front had induced me to retire to the line above mentioned. I had given orders for the retrograde movement in consequence of a telegram received from the President to send Martin's cavalry to General Johnston, and as everything was ready to move when I received his second dispatch, and as this heavy force was concentrated in my front, I thought it best to retire. A similar move on the part of the enemy must continue to throw me back as often as he makes it, unless my force is considerably augmented.

In view of our difficulties, and the general situation, I propose to endeavor to mount my entire command and move it across the mountains into Kentucky. It seems to be almost impossible for me to overcome the distance and the difficulties of supplying troops with forage and subsistence on the route into Kentucky. If the troops march in, and if we should get there with this small force of infantry, we might be obliged to return without accomplishing a great deal. But if we can go into Kentucky as mounted infantry we can get possession of the railroad there and hold it long enough to force the enemy to leave Tennessee, and we can remain in Kentucky until General Johnston can come up and join us.

It seems almost impossible to get animals enough to mount the entire command, but by extra energy I hope that it may be done by the middle of April, and that we could by that time set out for Kentucky. I have written General Lee upon this subject, and hope that he may be able to aid us in furnishing a large number of horses and mules. I believe that about a third of the men can furnish their own horses or mules. I have 5,000 mules. I propose to take half of these, using wagons only for ammunition, and hoping to capture enough in Kentucky for our supply trains. If General Lee can let me have 3,000 or 4,000, General Beauregard 2,000 or 3,000, and General Johnston 1,000 or 2,000, I shall be able to go into Kentucky and remain. We will require many horse and mule shoes, many saddles and bridles and spurs, and a large depot of corn at Abingdon or Bristol to start upon.

Other movements of cavalry by General Forrest and General Wheeler should follow mine, so as to cut the enemy's communication in rear of Chattanooga and occupy the cavalry of that army whilst I am getting some few supplies in Kentucky on my arrival there. Then the cavalry in Western Virginia should co-operate in the general move. I have merely mentioned the general points of the grand move.

I take the liberty of sending this directly to you, in order that it may be as secret as possible. If you think well of the proposition, please take great pains not to let it go beyond the President and yourself, as it will be a partial success if the enemy ever gets an intimation of it.

P. S.-If the views are adopted we should go to work with great energy immediately. Please telegraph me with your approval or disapproval, that I may know whether to go to work at the plans.[23]

When Longstreet asked President Davis on February 29 whether he should begin preparations to execute his plan, Cooper snapped back with a curt reply: "The Department cannot determine the propriety of your movements; that rests in your discretion."[24] Longstreet's plan was given the brush off by the War Department who seemed more interested in when General McLaws's trial would assemble than with winning the war. Longstreet needed the Department's support to implement his offensive.

Nonetheless, events were taking place that would impel the Southern War Department to examine its strategic situation in light of recent developments. Ulysses S. Grant was raised to the rank of lieutenant general and assigned as commander in chief of half a million men in the Union armies. He was an aggressive campaigner and the South knew he would be organizing combinations for the Confederacy's demise. Longstreet gave a summation of the strategic picture:

> The armies under General Lee in Virginia and General Johnston in Georgia were in defensive positions, with little prospect of striking by their right or left flanks in search of a way to break their bounds, and the army in East Tennessee had been called back to the defensive for want of cavalry, but the latter still covered gate-ways through the mountains that offered routes to Kentucky for strategic manoeuvres. The Trans-Mississippi was an open field of vast opportunities but was lying fallow.[25]

Military Conference

On March 8, 1864, Longstreet left his command to travel to Richmond for a conference "for plans or suggestions that could anticipate the movements of the enemy, disconcert his plans, and move him to new combinations."[26] Attending this conference were Secretary of War Seddon, President Davis, General Lee, General Longstreet, and Davis's new military advisor, General Bragg, serving in a capacity similar to Robert E. Lee prior to his taking command of the Army of Northern Virginia. President Davis brought Bragg to Richmond and named him his military advisor, charging him "with the conduct of military operations in the armies of the Confederacy" on February 24, 1864.

The conference took place on March 14, 1864, to discuss military options. "Forced to extremities, the Richmond authorities began to realize the importance of finding a way out of our pent-up borders before the Union commander could complete his extensive arrangements to press on with his columns," Longstreet accurately considered.

> In front of General Lee and on his right and left the country had been so often foraged by both Union and Confederate armies that it was denuded of supplies. Besides, a forced advance of Lee's army could only put the enemy back a few miles to his works about Washington. General Johnston's opportunities were no better, and in addition to other difficulties, he was working under the avowed displeasure of the authorities, more trying than his trouble with the enemy.[27]

During the discussions, Davis pushed a plan supposably devised by Bragg but borrowed from Beauregard for joint operations by Johnston and Longstreet in Middle Tennessee. Longstreet had received a verbal message from President Davis through General Alexander and sent Johnston a letter on March 5, asking whether Johnston believed such a juncture was feasible. Johnston thought the venture fool hardy—it was to take place in the winter when there would be no grass for the horses and mules through an area thoroughly foraged, sparsely populated, and poor in agricultural products. Johnston thought "food for man and beast for at least ten days" would be required. Longstreet had to depend on Johnston for transport and supplies. The enemy forces were closer to each other and connected by railroad, while Johnston and Longstreet were in rugged country further separated from each other than to the enemy. The enemy, situated on their flank, could easily concentrate against either one and crush them one at a time. Besides, the enemy could march unopposed to seize Johnston's base at Atlanta and fortify it, thereby cutting Johnston off from the all-important railroad. Longstreet advised Johnston against this plan on March 5 for this very reason:

> There is one serious objection to the move, or so it looks to me. If the enemy should slip in behind you and fortify strongly, both armies (yours and mine) will be obliged to disperse in the mountains and many of us perish, or surrender to the enemy without a fight. It may be that this would be sport to some people, but I confess that I should not enjoy it at all. It does not look very inviting to me, and from here it looks very much less so to you.[28]

Apparently, Bragg and Davis did not consider the value of the railroad as a vital artery for men and supplies or how their plan would expose Atlanta. Johnston wanted to concentrate Polk's army in Mississippi, Longstreet's army in East Tennessee, and whatever troops could be spared throughout the Confederacy at Dalton, Georgia, to defeat the Federal offensive in the spring, then counterattack and push them back through Tennessee—a very wise idea.

Longstreet's strategic vision had ripened into a more extensive plan:

> I was under the impression that we could collect an army of twenty thousand men in South Carolina by stripping our forts and positions of all men not essential for defence; that that army could be quietly moved north by rail through Greenville to the borders of North Carolina, and promptly marched by Abingdon, Virginia, through the mountain passes, while my command covered the move by its position in East Tennessee. That army passing the mountains, my command could drop off by the left to its rear and follow into Kentucky,-the whole to march against the enemy's only line of railway from Louisville, and force him to loose his hold against General Johnston's front, and give the latter opportunity to advance his army and call all of his troops in Alabama and Mississippi to like advance, the grand junction of all of the columns to be made on or near the Ohio River,-General Beauregard to command the leading column, with orders not to make or accept battle until the grand junction was made. That General Johnston should have like orders against battle until he became satisfied of fruitful issues. The supplies and transportation for Beauregard to be collected at the head of the railroad, in advance of the movement of troops, under the ostensible purpose of hauling for my command. The arrangements perfected, the commander of the leading column to put his troops on the rail at or near Charleston and march with them as they arrived at the head of the road.[29]

His game plan had both military and political objectives which he astutely perceived as a means to end the conflict. Longstreet laid out the political aspect in a letter to Brigadier General Thomas Jordan on March 25, 1864:

> The political opponents of Mr. Lincoln can furnish no reason at this late day against the war so long as it is successful with him, and thus far it has certainly been as successful as any one

could reasonably expect. If, however, his opponents were to find at the end of three years that we held Kentucky and were as well to do as at the beginning of the war, it would be a powerful argument against Lincoln and against the war. Lincoln's re-election seems to depend upon the result of our efforts during the present year. If he is re-elected, the war must continue, and I see no way of defeating his re-election except by military success.[30]

But the most attractive thing about Longstreet's design was that it left Johnston's Army of Tennessee in place on the railroad, guarding Atlanta. It avoided a direct confrontation in pitched battle to achieve the objectives but rather involved a grand turning movement aimed at the enemy's communications to force a retrograde movement. Longstreet recognized the importance of the railroad to bring reinforcements from throughout the Confederacy for a quick concentration to accomplish military operations. He was heedful that by threatening the vital railroad communications of the enemy, he could induce them to pull back and relinquish territory and disrupt their designs.

Longstreet arrived in Virginia and met with General Lee:

> With this proposition I went to Virginia and submitted it to General Lee. He approved, and asked me to take it to the Richmond authorities. I objected that the mere fact of its coming from me would be enough to cause its rejection, and asked, if he approved, that he would take it and submit it as his own. He took me with him to Richmond, but went alone next morning to see the President. He met, besides the President, the Secretary of War and General Bragg. Conference was held during the fore-noon, but was not conclusive. In the afternoon he called me with him for further deliberation.
>
> At the opening of the afternoon council it appeared that General Bragg had offered a plan for early spring campaign, and that it had received the approval of the President, -viz.:
>
> "General Johnston to march his army through the mountains of Georgia and East Tennessee to the head-waters of Little Tennessee River; my command to march through the mountains east of Knoxville to join General Johnston. The commands united, to march west, cross the river into Middle Tennessee, and march for the enemy's line of supplies about Nashville."
>
> When asked an opinion of this, I inquired as to General Johnston's attitude towards it, and was told that he objected; that he thought the sparsely-settled country of the mountains through which he would move could not supply his army; that he would consume all that he could haul before turning westward for the middle country, and would be forced to active foraging from his first step between two armies of the enemy.
>
> General Lee inquired if General Johnston had maturely considered the matter. I thought that he had, and that the objections of the officer who was to conduct the campaign were, of themselves, reasons for overruling it; but its advocates were not ready to accept a summary disposal of their plans, and it began to transpire that the President had serious objections to General Beauregard as a commander for the field.
>
> But General Lee called us back to business by asking if there was anything more to be added than General Johnston's objections. I called attention to General Bragg's official account of the battle of Chickamauga' in which he reported that a similar move had been proposed for him through Middle Tennessee towards the enemy's line of communication at Nashville early on the morning after the battle; that he rejected it, reported it "visionary"; said that it would leave his rear open to the enemy, and alluded to the country through which the march was proposed as "affording no subsistence to men or animals." This at harvest season, too! the enemy demoralized by the late battle, and the Confederates in the vigor of success! Now, after

a winter of foraging by the Union armies, the country could not be so plethoric of supplies as to support us, while an active army was on each flank, better prepared to dispute our march.

General Lee wore his beard full, but neatly trimmed. He pulled at it nervously, and more vigorously as time and silence grew, until at last his suppressed emotion was conquered. The profound quiet of a minute or more seemed an hour. When he spoke, it was of other matters, but the air was troubled by his efforts to surrender hopeful anticipations to the caprice of empirics. He rose to take leave of the august presence, gave his hand to the President, and bowed himself out of the council chamber. His assistant went through the same forms, and no one approached the door to offer parting courtesy.

I had seen the general under severe trial before, especially on his Pennsylvania campaign when he found the cavalry under General Imboden had halted for rest at Hancock, at the opening of an aggressive movement. My similar experience with the President in the all-day talk, on Missionary Ridge, six months before, had better prepared me for the ordeal, and I drew some comfort from the reflection that others had their trials. General Lee took the next train for his army on the Rapidan, and I that by the direct route to my command by the Southside Railway.[31]

The Conference Ended Without Reaching a Conclusion

While at Petersburg, Longstreet wrote a lengthy letter to President Davis on March 16, explaining his stratagem to try and capture Knoxville a second time and to persuade Davis to consider his plan to invade Kentucky. He felt Davis might still be inclined to favor it, swaying him to accept General Beauregard for field service and pointing out the folly of Bragg's scheme:

Early in February the railroad was finished and all of our men were tolerably comfortable with their winter clothing; the army was therefore advanced as far as Strawberry Plains. General Martin's cavalry was advanced on the south side of the French Broad, and his pickets were posted so as to keep the enemy under the protection of his fortifications. Our pickets on the northside of the Holston were also advanced and the enemy's stronghold reconnoitered from both sides of the river. The strength of the fortifications was greatly increased since the last siege, and many other works and improvements had been added to the general system of defenses. But the enemy had no provisions on hand, and I determined to ask for 10,000 men to aid me against any succoring army in the reduction of the garrison at Knoxville. I telegraphed General Johnston at the same time, asking him to cut communication between Chattanooga and Knoxville, so as to keep back any succoring force.

Failing to get the re-enforcements and co-operation both, it seemed to be useless to lay siege to Knoxville again with an almost certainty of being obliged to raise it again before the enemy could be starved out. The advantage in taking Knoxville would have been very considerable, I think, inasmuch as we should have captured an army of 12,000 to 15,000 men and our loss would have been small, as we should have taken it by starving the enemy out. He was much demoralized and had no supplies in depot except meal. It would have given us a very strong point, too, for future operations against the enemy's line of communication in Middle Tennessee.

My proposition to mount my infantry for the purpose of throwing it upon the enemy's line of communication in Kentucky would be attended with much difficulty, but I am inclined to believe that it might be accomplished. Three-fourths of our men claim to be able to mount themselves. I presume that nearly half of them could. I could mount a third in case of emergency, and I thought it probable that I might get animals from elsewhere for the balance by reducing transportation to the lowest possible limit.

This force mounted and in Kentucky could destroy any mounted force that the enemy could bring against us, and it could avoid any infantry force that might be too strong for us. If obliged to avoid one point of the enemy's railroad it could move around and occupy others, and finally force the enemy to retreat from Tennessee, and probably to the northern part of Kentucky. In this position mounted we could hardly be farther from the other armies than we are at present, inasmuch as the greater rapidity of our movements would enable us to co-operate as readily as we now can.

Longstreet rejected Bragg's scheme for a juncture with Johnston's army:

The proposition to unite the army of General Johnston with my forces at Maryville, East Tenn., for the purpose of moving into Middle Tennessee, via Sparta, I apprehend some difficulty, however, in making the move so as to effect a junction of the forces in good time. The two armies are about 200 miles apart, with the enemy holding all of the country between us. As soon as either army starts to move, the enemy must get advised of it. He occupying the railroad will have great facilities for concentrating his forces against one or the other of these armies, and he would cripple the one that he might encounter so badly as to prevent the further progress of the campaign. This we must assume that he will do at all hazards, as there are no supplies in the country through which our armies would pass. The enemy might depend upon delaying us by occupying the mountain passes until our supplies are consumed and force us to retreat in that way. Both armies would be compelled to have everything in the way of forage, subsistence, ammunition, &c., from the moment of starting out, and in such quantities as to last them until they reached Sparta, without them the certainty of reaching these articles in any considerable quantities. My information leads me to fear that at Sparta we would find a great scarcity of supplies-that is, for any large army.

It occurs to me that a better plan for making a campaign into Middle Tennessee would be to re-enforce General Johnston in his present position by throwing the Mississippi troops and those from General Beauregard's department and my own to that point.

The shortest practicable route by which I could join him must be a little over 200 miles, and this through a very rough, mountainous country, and at a season of the year when we may expect some delays from the mountain streams. It would probably be better, therefore, to take a quicker route and march from my present position to Greenville, S.C., and take the railroad thence to Atlanta and march up from Atlanta.

As there are two routes of railway to Atlanta I have supposed that one can be used for the speedy transportation of troops while the other is occupied in transporting provisions, &c. This move may be made, if it is begun very soon, in time to enable us to take the initiative in the approaching campaign.

Our strongest and most effective move, however, is to concentrate an army near Abingdon, Va., and throw it into Kentucky upon the enemy's line of communication. This can be done best by moving General Beauregard up via Greenville, S.C., to unite with my troops and march through Pound Gap.

General Beauregard could collect his transportation and supplies at Greenville, S.C., for the purpose ostensibly of supplying my army, which could be advertised as about to march by that route for General Johnston's army. Having his supplies and transportation ready, he could throw his troops up by rail and put them on the march as rapidly as they could arrive. We could thus mask the move so completely that our own people would not suspect it before the troops were well on the march for Kentucky.

If General Beauregard could start on his march from Morganton, N.C., he would have some 60 miles less than if he sets out from Greenville or Spartanburg, S.C. The move itself would not surprise the enemy, of course, but the strength of it would, and we should in all probability encounter a force of his which could not stand before us.

If the enemy is obliged to abandon his present line he must give up nearly, if not all, of Tennessee south of the Cumberland. This of itself will be equal to a great victory for us. If he moves his entire force to the rear for the purpose of attacking General Beauregard with his concentrated forces, General B., if he sees fit, can avoid him, and our armies, Johnston's and Beauregard's, can unite in Tennessee and then advance into Kentucky, or if we only hold Tennessee without a fight we shall have accomplished great moral advantages.

But there can scarcely be a doubt but we can advance into Kentucky and hold that State if we are once united. I presume that nearly all of General Beauregard's troops could be spared from his department by drawing off General Loring's division from Mississippi and General Maury's at Mobile, and replacing the troops drawn from General Beauregard's department by one of these commands, and placing one at Atlanta to re-enforce Charleston, Savannah, Mobile, or Dalton.

General Longstreet envisioned a strategic turning movement into Kentucky by forces under General Beauregard which would combine with his command, utilizing the railroad for rapid movement. Longstreet felt that this was the Confederacy's best play. This combined operation would fall upon the enemy's communications, forcing them to pull back from Tennessee to Kentucky to meet this threat. General Johnston could leisurely advance from Dalton, Georgia, to join them. The Confederates would take the initiative and recover Tennessee and Kentucky by these extensive combinations. The result would have significant effect upon the morale of the North, with political ramifications—possibly, ending the war. The plan was a design of broad scope, making use of the new technology of the railroad.

This last position would only be necessary as a temporary precaution, of course, as the enemy will be entirely occupied by the move into Kentucky as soon as he begins to feel us upon his rear. This move would leave our own positions as securely covered as they now are, at the same time gives us the opportunity to strike a vital blow at the enemy. It can be made much sooner than any other; promises much greater results than any other without such difficult and complicated maneuvers as the move into Middle Tennessee; it gives us the certain means of getting provisions for our troops, and if entirely successful will put an end to the war.

It has the objection that there may be some difficulty in joining the armies of General Johnston and General Beauregard, it is more probable that these two armies would be able to unite without serious trouble. After the enemy has been thrown back into Kentucky, and whilst in the confusion and trouble attending his speedy retreat [sic], than that two armies starting from the two-ends of the enemy's lines to effect a junction at an intermediate point would be able to join and have an opportunity to get a blow at the enemy. There would be no necessity that General Johnston should pursue the enemy rapidly, so as to expose himself to the enemy.

He could throw the cavalry under Generals Lee (S. D.), Forrest, Roddey, and Wheeler upon the enemy's rear, and damage him so much during the retreat that he would hardly be prepared to give us battle in Kentucky when he reached there. If we should fight him in Kentucky with General Beauregard's army alone, there can be no great doubt but we can greatly cripple him without any great injury to ourselves, and then move back and join General Johnston at our leisure.

My troops can start out upon this or any other move in three days. General Beauregard could not prepare, however, sooner than the 1st of April. If we can get the troops in motion by that time we shall be able to take the initiative, as the enemy will not be prepared to move before the 1st of May. He may, and probably will, make a diversion in Virginia before that time for the purpose of trying to draw my troops from the West, and thus put a stop to this campaign. He seems already in some concern about our position and movements.

These ideas are given under the supposition that, if they are thought worthy to be adopted, it will be done with a determination to execute the movements with such undivided vigor as to insure great results. In order that there may be as little delay as possible, I have hurriedly given my views. In my hurry I fear that I may not have made myself as well understood as I would like, and I may have failed to make the suggestions as much in detail as you would like.[32]

Longstreet wrote to General Beauregard on March 15 asking him to evaluate his plan for a junction of their forces for a proposed move into Kentucky via Pound Gap, touching upon the political aspect: "The enemy in Tennessee, as elsewhere, is much discouraged, not to say demoralized, and any effective move against his rear must have a powerful effect upon his troops and upon political affairs, which would in all probability result in a settlement of our troubles by negotiation and treaties of peace."[33]

Longstreet's letter to Davis (above), was sent to Lee on March 16 to present to the president that it might carry more weight:

I have delayed at this place [Petersburg, Va]. to answer the letter of the President, which you read to me in his presence on Monday. I send you a copy of the letter as the readiest means of explaining my appreciation of our position. I fear that my views may not be regarded by the President and General Bragg as worthy of much attention; as I have a better hope of calm consideration from you, I send them to you. The move of Beauregard's and my forces will, if as strong as it should be made, say even 40,000 men (infantry and artillery), be the beginning of the end of the war. It can be made, and therefore should be made, even if it costs us some little inconvenience elsewhere. It can be made an entire success. Your influence with the President, and your prestige as a great leader, will enable you to cause its adoption and successful execution.

You complain of my excess of confidence, but I think that it is based upon good judgment and a proper appreciation of our difficulties. I have entire confidence if our affairs are properly managed, but I have none if they are not well managed. Hence my great anxiety and concern at our present inaction[34]

In the letter, Longstreet hoped Lee would join and lead the advance into Kentucky.

Beauregard responded on March 18, giving his insufficient wagons, horses, and saddles as a reason for not assisting, and he wanted to know how Longstreet would get supplies and ammunition if the enemy closed the Cumberland Mountain gaps behind him: "The true maxims of war require us never to abandon our communications, but act on those of the enemy without exposing our own." It did not occur to Beauregard that his plan would require Johnston to relinquish the railroad to his base at Atlanta nor did he understand the concept of a raid which Grant used quite effectively.[35]

President Davis's letter arrived on March 25, in which he rejected Longstreet's plan: "To furnish you the troops you require in your proposed plan, from General Beauregard, and to re-enforce General Johnston from Mobile and the West, would expose all of our productive country and the principal cities of the South." Also cited as another reason not to support the invasion was the lack of and demand for mules and horses by other Southern armies, so none could be spared. He would not contemplate allowing Longstreet to move his troops by the railroad at Greenville, S. C. to reinforce General Johnston, since the transport would be over a line used to bring corn from Georgia to the Army of Northern Virginia and he claimed it would be overtaxed to bring supplies in addition to shifting troops. Davis did not see the big picture and was still trying to defend every area of the South, reducing its war effort to a policy of reacting to every Northern threat; he would not envisage any disruption in materiel or defensive measures in his departmental system for the greater benefit, as Longstreet saw it, to gain the strategic initiative, upset the North's designs, and bring about a favorable end to the war in the November elections of 1864.[36]

CHAPTER 15

The Old Warhorse Is Up at Last!

The Wilderness

On March 31, 1864, Longstreet informed Lee that the Ninth Army Corps had left Knoxville, heading east. Longstreet had no striking power left; his animals were short of forage. This information culminated a vast flow of intelligence that Grant was preparing a great effort in Virginia and had issued a directive that his headquarters was with the Army of the Potomac. Lee asked Davis that Longstreet be thrown into the Shenandoah Valley so that Lee and Longstreet could unite much more easily.

Longstreet received orders to march:

> On the 7th of April I was ordered, with the part of my command that had originally served with the Army of Northern Virginia, back to service with General Lee on the Rapidan. The move was made as soon as cars could be had to haul the troops, halting under orders at Charlotteville to meet a grand flanking move then anticipated. On the 22d we were ordered down as far as Mechanicsville, five miles west of Gordonsville, watching there for a lesser flank move. On the 29th, General Lee came out and reviewed the command.[1]

Longstreet was about to embark upon his greatest battle, the battle of the Wilderness. He would display his consummate skill as a master tactician; it would be his shining moment and the worst tragedy of his military career.

After arriving, Longstreet had discussions with Lee on the coming campaign:

> After reporting the return of my command to service with the Army of Northern Virginia, I took the earliest opportunity to suggest that the preliminaries of the campaign should be carefully confined to strategic manoeuvre until we could show better generalship. That accomplished I argued, the enemy's forces would lose confidence in the superiority of their leader's skill and prowess; that both armies were composed of intelligent, experienced veterans, who were as quick to discover the better handling of their ranks as trained generals; that by such successful manoeuvres the Confederates would gain confidence and power as the enemy began to lose prestige; that then we could begin to look for a favorable opportunity to call the enemy to aggressive work, while immediate aggression from us against greater numbers must make our labors heavy and more or less doubtful; that we should first show that the power of battle is in generalship more than in the number of soldiers, which properly illustrated, would make the weaker numbers of the contention the stronger force.
>
> In this connection I refer to the policy of attrition which became a prominent feature during part of the campaign, and showed that the enemy put his faith in numbers more than in superior skill and generalship.[2]

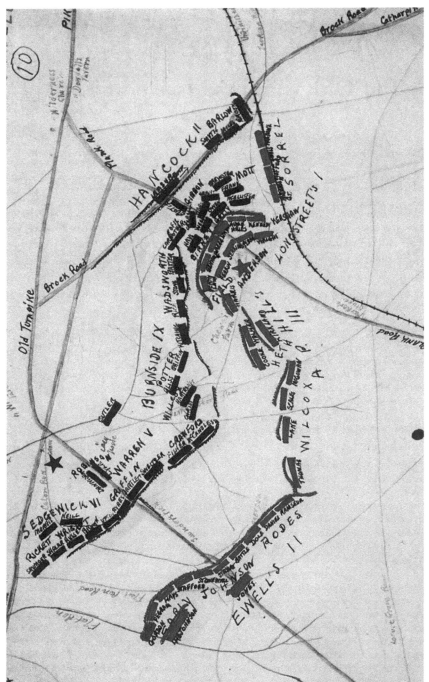

The Wilderness

Policy of Attrition

Grant's aim and policy was to overwhelm the Confederates:

> From an early period in the rebellion I had been impressed with the idea that active and continuous operations of all the troops that could be brought into the field, regardless of season and weather, were necessary to a speedy termination of the war. The resources of the enemy and his numerical strength were far inferior to ours; but as an offset to this, we had a vast territory, with a population hostile to the Government, to garrison, and long lines of river and railroad communications to protect, to enable us to supply the operating armies.
>
> The armies in the East and West acted independently and without concert, like a balky team, no two ever pulling together, enabling the enemy to use to great advantage his interior lines of communication for transporting troops from east to west, re-enforcing the army most vigorously pressed, and to furlough large numbers, during seasons of inactivity on our part, to go to their homes and do the work of producing for the support of their armies. It was a question of whether our numerical strength and resources were not more than balanced by these disadvantages and the enemy's superior position.
>
> From the first, I was firm in the conviction that no peace could be had that would be stable and conducive to the happiness of the people, both North and South, until the military power of the rebellion was entirely broken. I therefore determined, first, to use the greatest number of troops practicable against the armed force of the enemy, preventing him from using the same force at different seasons against first one and then another of our armies, and the possibility of repose for refitting and producing necessary supplies for carrying on resistance; second, to hammer continuously against the armed force of the enemy and his resources, until by mere attrition, if in no other way, there should be nothing left of him but an equal submission.
>
> With no exchange of prisoners, and the South without any means of recruiting her shattered ranks, while the armies of the North were being constantly augmented from her ample resources both at home and abroad, it was only a matter of time as to who should succeed.[3]

Grant's primary objective was to subdue the two main armies the South fielded in the two principal positions, commanded by the two best generals: Robert E. Lee's Army of Northern Virginia and Joseph E. Johnston's Army of Tennessee at Dalton, Georgia. Grant was now with the Army of the Potomac and had placed General Sherman in command of 100,000 troops below Chattanooga, facing Johnston. "He was to go for Lee and I was to go for Joe Johnston. That was the plan," summarized Sherman after meeting with Grant in Cincinnati.[4]

In Virginia, Grant had decided on four major objectives, utilizing four strike forces: (1) the Army of the Potomac was to engage Lee's forces; (2) the Army of the James was to threaten Richmond and Petersburg; (3) a column under Sigel was to invade the Shenandoah Valley, depriving Lee of food and closing this avenue of invasion; (4) a second column under Crook, stationed in West Virginia, was to join Sigel at Staunton, destroying railroads and saltworks as it went, then head toward the rail junction at Lynchburg.

Alexander provided this assessment of Grant's campaign:

> The campaign against us was practically to be one of extermination, and was conducted by four separate armies and as much of the navy as could be used in the James River.

There were no returns of Longstreet's corps after his return from E. Tenn., but he gives as a "liberal estimate," 10,000 men. The return of the rest of the Army of Northern Virginia, on April 20, was as follows:

Ewell's Corps…….. 17,079
Hill's Corps …….. 22,199
Artillery …….. 4,854
Cavalry …….. 8,497
Miscellaneous…….. 1,355 Total ……. 53,984

Adding 10,000 for Longstreet's, Lee's total force was about 64,000, and he had about 274 guns. Against the armies of Sigel and Crook, Breckenridge was able to muster in the Valley and in the S. W. Va., about 9000 men and 24 guns.

To meet Butler, Beauregard brought to Petersburg, from various points in the South, troops which he organized into four divisions, comprising about 22,000 infantry, 2000 cavalry, and about 50 guns. These included Pickett's division of Longstreet's corps, say 5000 men, which rejoined Longstreet about June 1, and Johnson's brigade of Early's division, which was returned to the division on May 6.

To recapitulate, the forces under Grant's command were about 156,000 men and those under Lee's were about 95,000.[5]

"The numerical strength of armies should not be considered as of exclusive bearing upon the merits of the campaign," Longstreet asserted. "The commanders had chosen their battle after mature deliberation. They knew of each other's numbers and resources before they laid their plans, and they had even known each other personally for more than twenty years. Each had the undivided support and confidence of his government and his army."[6]

A Prussian observer, Justus Scheibert, made this chess analogy: "Grant can be said to prefer the rook. By never swerving from the rook's way, he intended to dominate the game and end it. Lacking the power of numbers, Lee took the more elegant and graceful way of the knight and bishop."[7]

Atop Clark's Mountain, a high ridge with an elevation of some 600 feet, Lee met with his three corps and eight division commanders on May 2 at the signal station. Longstreet arrived with his new division heads, Field and Kershaw. Ewell came up with Early, Johnson, and Rodes, and the frail Hill was accompanied by Wilcox, Heth, and Anderson; Lee raised his field glasses and studied the campsites of the Army of the Potomac on the far bank of the Rapidan River and stated Meade would move his army around the Confederate right flank, downstream by either Germanna or Ely's Ford or both. Although Lee believed logic dictated a move around his right, he wanted to be prepared in case Grant decided to strike his left instead or both flanks at the same time. Lee had to wait upon his adversary. He could not launch his own offensive: the Army of Northern Virginia lacked sufficient mules and horses; what they had were debilitated due to a deficiency of fodder. Food and clothing were inadequate and the manpower pool had reached the bottom of the barrel.

The Army of the Potomac had been consolidated into three large corps and was encamped in an inverted V-shaped stretch of land between the Rappahannock and Rapidan Rivers; the 5th Corps under Gouverneur Warren, with his headquarters at Culpeper, had its divisions in close proximity to the town. On Cole's Hill, a low, round acclivity was carpeted by Major General Winfield S. Hancock's 2nd Corps, covering an area from Stevensburg north toward Brandy Station. From Brandy Station to the Rappahannock was John Sedgwick's 6th Corps, and Burnside's 9th Corps, just arriving from Annapolis, was on Meade's right flank at Manassas Junction protecting the Orange and Alexandria Railroad—Meade's vital supply line; Meade's headquarters was at Brandy Station. Burnside reported directly to Grant. Meade's cavalry commanded by General Philip Sheridan patrolled the Rapidan and its fords.

Lee had positioned Ewell's Second Corps east of Clark's Mountain behind Mine Run. Hill's Third Corps was downstream next to Ewell, near Orange Court House where the Orange Turnpike and Orange Plank Road intersected, and Longstreet's 1st Corps was close to Gordonsville, a vital railroad junction between the Orange and Alexandria Railroad and the Virginia Central Railroad, from which he could quickly move reinforcements to Richmond or to the Shenandoah Valley and still be available to support the Rapidan Line on the left flank. Lee's cavalry guarded from Mine Run to Fredericksburg.

Although Lee had a strong back-up line on the North Anna River, he was reluctant to give up the heavily fortified Rapidan Line easily; he wanted a deep buffer between the Army of the Potomac and Richmond so he could maneuver and catch the Federals off guard.

There were strong indications that Burnside's army was moving around the Confederate left. On May 1, 1864, Longstreet sent General Field's division toward Liberty Mills, just west of Orange Court House. He asked Venable to have Pickett's division returned to him. Certainly, the return of Pickett's division would have enhanced the power of the Army of Northern Virginia; this was the main event in Grant's campaign. On April 30 and, more forcefully, on May 4, Lee asked Davis to have all his troops returned to his army:

> You will already have learned that the army of Genl Meade is in motion, and is crossing the Rapidan on our right, whether with the intention of attacking, or moving towards Fredericksburg, I am not able to say. But it is apparent that the long threatened effort to take Richmond has begun, and that the enemy has collected all his available force to accomplish it. The column on the Peninsula if not already moving, will doubtless now cooperate with Genl Meade, and we may assume it is as strong as the enemy can make it. Under these circumstances I regret that there is to be any further delay in concentrating our own troops. I fully appreciate the advantages of capturing New Berne, but they will not compensate us for a disaster in Virginia or Georgia. Success in resisting the chief armies of the enemy will enable us more easily to recover the country now occupied by him, if indeed he does not voluntarily relinquish it. We are inferior in numbers, and as I have before stated to Your Excellency the absence of the troops belonging to this army weakens it more than by the mere number of men. I would recommend that the troops in North Carolina belonging to this army be at once returned to

it, and that Genl Beauregard with all the force available for the purpose, be brought without delay to Richmond. Your opportunities of deciding this question are superior to my own, my advice being based upon such lights as I possess. It seems to me that the great efforts of the enemy here and in Georgia have begun, and that the necessity of our concentration at both points is immediate and imperative.

I submit my views with great deference to the better judgment of Your Excellency, and am satisfied that you will do what the best interests of the country require.[8]

Apparently, though the fate of the Confederacy hung in the balance, His Excellency did not deem the crisis important enough and did not comply with Lee's wishes until May 4 when he telegraphed Beauregard to send troops to Lee.

The movement Lee was referring to was the advance of the Army of the Potomac soon after midnight on May 3 and 4, over the Rapidan. It was nicely detailed in Longstreet's memoirs:

At midnight of the 3d of May, 1864, the Army of the Potomac took its line of march for the lower crossings of the Rapidan River at Germania and Ely's Fords, the Fifth and Sixth Corps for the former, the Second for the latter, Wilson's division of cavalry leading the first, Gregg's the second column. The cavalry was to secure the crossings and lay bridges for the columns as they came up. Wilson's cavalry crossed at Germania Ford, drove off the Confederate outpost, and began the construction of a bridge at daylight. Gregg also was successful, and the bridges were ready when the solid columns came. Warren's (Fifth Corps) crossed after Wilson's cavalry, marching westward as far as Wilderness Tavern. Sedgwick's corps followed and pitched camp near the crossing. Hancock's corps followed Gregg's cavalry, and made camp at Chancellorsville. Generals Grant and Meade went over after Warren's column and established head-quarters near the crossing. General Grant despatched for Burnside's corps to come and join him by night march. Sheridan was expected to engage Stuart's cavalry at Hamilton's Crossing near Fredericksburg.[9]

Grant's Options

Grant had a number of options on how to approach Lee. Grant decided against a direct approach upon Richmond by the James River, up the Peninsula, where the Rebels had well-prepared earthworks and Lee would be able to hold him there with part of his army and threaten Washington with the remainder. The Rapidan earthworks were too strong to attack directly and Grant realized he would have to sweep around them. If Grant went around Lee's left, he could rely on the Orange and Alexandria Railroad for supplies and, at the same time, shield Washington. However, the Federals would have to march 40 miles in full view, and a low set of hills called Southwest Mountain along the rail line could be turned into defensive works by the Rebels. Swinging around Lee's right would place the Army of the Potomac between Lee and Richmond and closer to Butler and supplies brought in on the tidal rivers from Chesapeake Bay, but Grant would have to have a large train of vulnerable, slow wagons to bring rations and ammunition by that route and would have to traverse the Wilderness. Grant decided to cross downriver which necessitated a train of 4,300 wagons, smartly assembled by Grant's longtime friend Brigadier General Rufus Ingalls: "There never was a corps better organized than was the quartermaster's corps with the Army of the Potomac in 1864," Grant recorded in his personal memoirs:

> With a wagontrain that would have extended from the Rapidan to Richmond, stretched along in single file and separated as the teams necessarily would be when moving, we could still carry only three day's forage and about ten to twelve days' rations, besides a supply of ammunition. To overcome all difficulties, the chief quartermaster, General Rufus Ingalls, had marked on each wagon the corps badge with the division color and the number of the brigade. At a glance, the particular brigade to which any wagon belonged could be told. The wagons were also marked to show the contents: if ammunition, whether for artillery or infantry; if forage, whether grain or hay; if rations, whether bread, pork, beans, rice, sugar, coffee, or whatever it might be. Empty wagons were never allowed to follow the army or stay in camp. As soon as a wagon was empty it would return to the base of supply for a load of precisely the same article that had been taken from it. Empty trains were obliged to leave the road free for loaded ones. Arriving near the army they would be parked in fields nearest to the brigades they belonged to. Issues, except ammunition, were made at night in all cases. By this system the hauling of forage for the supply train was almost wholly dispensed with. They consumed theirs at the depots.[10]

Additionally, Ingalls had 835 ambulances and a herd of cattle for slaughter.

Longstreet received reports of the Union movements across the Rapidan and deliberated on the strategic situation, as Lee did, if they were turning east or west. He sent a dispatch to Lee at 10:30am on May 4: "I fear that the enemy is trying to draw us down to Fredericksburg. Can't we threaten his rear, so as to stop his move? Fredericksburg will not be a strong position, with the flank and rear exposed to a force at West Point. We should keep away from there, unless we can put out a force to hold any force at West Point in check."[11] However, Grant had made Lee his objective: "Major-General Meade was instructed that Lee's army would be his objective point; that wherever Lee went he would go also."[12] Thus Grant became enmeshed in the Wilderness.

By 9:00am on May 4, Lee knew that Grant was on the move and at 11:00am Lee ordered his corps commanders to advance. Ewell's Second Corps of three divisions—less Stephen Ramseur's brigade of Rodes's division with three regiments from each of the other divisions that were left behind to picket the Rapidan—took the Orange Turnpike or "old stone road" close to and parallel with the Rapidan, having an 18-mile march to reach Grant's route. Hill's Third Corps with two divisions traveled on the Orange Plank Road, several miles south of the turnpike; it would have 28 miles to go. Ewell was to regulate his march to Hill and both were instructed not to bring on a general engagement until Longstreet came up. Longstreet's First Corps, the furthest away, had some 42 miles to traverse over country roads; Longstreet was to follow Hill but obtained a modification on his route:

> We were ordered forward by the Plank Road to Parker's Store; the order was received after one o'clock, and sent out for information of the commanders, who were ordered to prepare and march. But I asked for and received authority to march by a shorter route that would at the same time relieve the Plank Road of pressure of troops and trains (for we had been crowded off the road once before by putting too many troops upon a single track). By the same despatch I asked and subsequently obtained leave to go on the Brock Road, where we could look for and

hope to intercept the enemy's march, and cause him to develop plans before he could get out of the Wilderness. We marched at four o'clock by the Lawyer's Road. Our chief quartermaster, Colonel Taylor, whose home was between Orange Court-House and the Wilderness, had been ordered to secure the services of the most competent guide to be found. We halted at Brock's Bridge for rest, and there Colonel Taylor brought up our guide, James Robinson, who had been for several years the sheriff of the county, and whose whole life had been spent in the Wilderness. The march was resumed, and continued with swinging step, until we reached Richard's Shops, at five P. M. of the 5th. There we overtook Rosser's cavalry, engaged in severe encounter with part of Sheridan's. The enemy abandoned the contest and rode away, leaving his dead with some of ours on the field.

The distance of march was twenty-eight miles. Soon after my arrival at the shops, Colonel Venable, of general head-quarters staff, came with orders for a change of direction of the column through the wood to unite with the troops of the Third Corps on the Plank Road. The rear of my column closed up after dark, and orders were sent to prepare to resume march at twelve o'clock. The accounts we had of the day's work were favorable to the Confederates; but the change of direction of our march was not reassuring.[13]

Venable's new orders were disconcerting to Longstreet, what happened was this.

Ewell moved out along the Orange Turnpike. By nightfall he had made camp at Locust Grove, some five miles west of Wilderness Tavern. Hill, accompanied by Lee, having 10 extra miles to cover, reached the hamlet of New Verdiersville (the soldiers dubbed it "My Dearsville") before dark and encamped, but Hill was still some three miles behind Ewell and 12 miles from Wilderness Tavern.

Lee wanted Grant entangled in the Wilderness where his greater numbers would be negated, his superior artillery neutralized, and his better armed cavalry's role diminished, while the 4,300 wagons would encumber Grant's army and slow its march, which is why Lee did not challenge Grant at the fords of the Rapidan. Lee could hit the Union flank if Grant went south; if Grant headed east toward Fredericksburg, Lee would attack his rear, or Lee could take a strong defensive position, perhaps at Mine Run if Grant headed his way.

Lee pitched his tent in the woods opposite the Rhodes's house and had Colonel Walter H. Taylor write General Ewell at 8:00pm:

> He [General Lee] wishes you to be ready to move on early in the morning. If the enemy moves down the river, he wishes to push on after him. If he comes this way, we will take our old line. The general's desire is to bring him to battle as soon now as possible. General Hill is on this road. Heth has passed this place. Wilcox near here. Longstreet is on our right, moving up. The cavalry in your front has been instructed to keep you informed of all movements of the enemy.[14]

About 8:00am the next morning, Ewell sent Major Campbell Brown of his staff to General Lee to get instructions. Lee repeated his directive for Ewell to fix his progress to Hill's by the sound of the fighting and not to bring on a general engagement until Longstreet arrived. About 11:00am Ewell sent Lieutenant Colonel "Sandie" Pendleton to Lee, reporting sighting a column of Federal troops crossing the turnpike from the Germanna Ford, heading toward Orange Plank Road. Ewell halted his corps and to Pendleton, Lee reiterated the previous instructions given to Campbell Brown. Ewell set to work constructing a defensive line on the turnpike at Saunders's Field.

Allegheny Johnson's division formed on the left, extending north toward the Rapidan with Brigadier General John M. Jones's Virginia brigade on elevated ground to the right of the turnpike. Battle's brigade of Rodes's division was placed behind Jones in support with Doles's brigade on Battle's right, trailing south by Daniel's brigade. "They were instructed not to allow themselves to become involved," commented Ewell, "but to fall back slowly if pressed."[15] Early's division, consisting of the brigades of Pegram, Hays, and Gordon were in reserve. As a Confederate officer observed: "The position of Ewell's troops, so near the flank of the Federal line of march, was anything but favorable to a preservation of the peace, and a collision soon occurred which opened the campaign in earnest."[16]

Grant and Meade believed Lee would "fight behind Mine Run" and collaborated with Meade's chief of staff, Brigadier General Andrew A. Humphreys, a small, humorless, bow-legged, and profane man considered a military genius, planning to get out of the Wilderness quickly and executing a turning movement around Lee's right to flush him out of the Mine Run entrenchments.

General Lee, aggressive as always, hoped to pin Meade in the Wilderness with Ewell's and Hill's corps and have Longstreet proceed on the Catharpin Road for a flank attack on the Federal left very similar to Jackson's flanking maneuver on the same road during the Chancellorsville campaign.

By 10:15am May 5, Meade had received intelligence of Ewell's movements on the Orange Turnpike. Meade decided to push Warren's and Sedgwick's corps to meet him. Meade believed that this was a deception as he stated to Warren, Sedgwick, and others nearby: "They (the enemy) have left a division to fool us here, while they concentrate and prepare a position towards the North Anna; and what I want is to prevent those fellows from getting back to Mine Run."[17] "Push forward a heavy line of skirmishers followed by your line of battle, attack the enemy at once and push him," Warren directed his division commanders at 10:30am.[18] Sedgwick's 6th Corps was coming up on Warren's right. Warren's Fifth Corps had 24,000, together with over half of the Sixth (about 12,000) confronting Ewell's 17,000.

Warren's corps swarmed out of the foliage, falling upon Ewell's line. Jones's brigade, flanked on the right while engaged in front, was driven back in confusion, causing panic in Battle's brigade. Jones's left flank was anchored on Maryland Steuart's brigade but on its right was a light skirmish line of dismounted cavalry. Just behind the line, Jones was deliberating with Ewell, Early, and Rodes. Jones and his aide, Captain Robert D. Early, Jubal Early's nephew, mounted their horses and rushed to the scene but were killed trying to rally the troops.

"Major, you will find Gordon a short distance up the pike. Ride to him as fast as you can and tell him to bring up his brigade as quick as possible," Early told his aide, Major John W. Daniel. Daniel found Gordon and rode up to him, delivering Early's message. "Major, do me a favor," Gordon answered. "Give the instructions yourself to each of my regimental commanders while I ride to the front and see the situation and prepare for the charge." Daniel replied, "Certainly,

General"[19] Gordon's brigade of Early's division, concurrently with Daniel's brigade of Rodes's division, drove the enemy back, regaining the lost ground. "Dear, glorious, old, one-legged Ewell, with his bald head, & his big bright eyes, & his long nose (like a wood cock's as Dick Taylor said)" (Alexander's description of him) dug in and was able to repulse all Union attacks and check the Union probes for his flank throughout the battle. He even counter-attacked with Steuart's and Battle's brigades, capturing a lot of prisoners and two 24-pounder howitzers, which were brought off after dark. Early's division had been sent to Ewell's left to meet Sedgwick's flanking attack. In the evening of May 5, General Ramseur arrived with his brigade and the three regiments on picket duty, which were returned to their brigades. Ramseur's brigade was assigned to the extreme right of Ewell's line, which was heavily intrenched during the night.[20]

Lieutenant General Ambrose Powell Hill was heading down Orange Plank Road with his two butternut divisions as Ewell was becoming hotly engaged on the turnpike. He was encountering some resistance from the 5th New York cavalry with their repeating carbines under Lieutenant Colonel John Hammond. Hammond was fighting a delaying action at Parker's Store at 8:00am and was pushed back by Heth's men within an hour. Hill was now within three miles of the junction of the Orange Turnpike and Brock Road—a crucial intersection, since Brock Road was the Federal's main north–south route and holding it would cut Grant's army in two, cutting off Hancock's II Corps from the rest of the Army of the Potomac. Hancock had marched past the Orange Plank Road and was halted at Todd's Tavern awaiting Meade's further orders. By mid-morning, near 10:00am, Meade learned of this development and at 10:30 he dispatched from Sedgwick's corps Brigadier General Richard Getty with his division of 6,000 seasoned veterans to hold Brock Crossing and await Hancock's corps, which was countermarching by Meade's orders to the important crossroads.

Riding ahead, Getty and his staff reached the center of the intersection around 11:30am, just as Hammond's battered troopers were dispersed. They defiantly held their ground while Rebel bullets flew around them until their men came up. Getty's men pushed back Heth's skirmishers, threw up some rude defensive works, and brought up artillery to command the intersection.

General Lee established his headquarters at the Widow Tapp farm and evaluated the changing battle conditions. He was worried about the two-mile gulf in his center, as the turnpike and the Plank Road diverted from each other, separating Ewell's corps from Hill's and leaving an opening Grant and Meade could exploit to hit their flanks. Lee ordered Cadmus Marcellus Wilcox's division to bridge the gap. At the same time, Lee, contemplating a full-scale assault on the crossroads and hoping it was lightly defended, sent a staff officer to Heth asking him to occupy the intersection "without bringing on a general engagement." Heth had received reports from his skirmishers that the Federals were there in strength: "Say to the general that the enemy are holding the Brock Road with a strong force. Whether I can drive them from the Brock Road or not can only be determined by my attacking with my entire division, but I cannot tell if my attack will bring on a general engagement or not. I am ready to try if he says attack."[21] Heth had his men deploy on a thickly wooded rise athwart the Orange Plank Road overlooking a swampy hollow, with both flanks resting on marshes; light breastworks were put together. Heth never got the chance to test the Brock Road defenses.

Grant had established his headquarters near the Lacy house by the Orange Turnpike; he wanted the Army of the Potomac to attack. At 4:00pm Meade sent word that he expected a Union assault on the Orange Plank Road. Getty's lone division was to be the first wave. Hancock had arrived at the crossroad at 2:00pm but had spent two hours having his men strengthen the entrenchments, with crude log breastworks to fall back on in case of a setback, wary of the ever-aggressive A. P. Hill.

Getty's push down the Orange Plank Road was met with a "tremendous volley" from Cooke's and Walker's Confederate veterans that staggered the Yankee line as they worked themselves within 100 yards of Heth's position. The Federals returned the fire, shooting volleys breast high, but the Rebels lay prone to the ground behind cover while the blue-clad soldiers, standing erect, had nothing but foliage to protect them. "So many were at once shot down that it became plain that to advance was simply destruction. The men dropped again. They could not advance, but there was no thought of retreat," reported one Union brigade's historian. Colonel Lewis A. Grant, commanding one of the Union brigades, later reported: "The rebels had the advantage of position inasmuch as the line was partially protected by a slight swell of ground, while ours was on nearly level ground."[22] Just as Getty's attack was stalled, Hancock threw in some of his divisions (Mott's and Birney's) but still the blue assault was bogged down. Lee became apprehensive and had Wilcox's division brought back and posted on Heth's left flank. Two of Wilcox's brigades, commanded by Brigadier Generals Samuel McGowan and Alfred M. Scales, charged into the woods routing the Yankees only to be pushed back. Hancock threw in part of Gibbon's and Barlow's divisions, which shook Hill's line but did not break it. Hill's two divisions (Heth's and Wilcox's) held with but 7,000 each, while Hancock had at his disposal the whole of the 2nd Corps (28,000) and the smaller half of the 6th Corps (around 10,000 men). The vegetation was so thick as to prevent sighting the adversary: "We could seldom see the enemy's battle line because of the denseness of the foliage but powder flashes from the opposing lines often told that they were but a few yards apart," a soldier from the Orange Blossom Regiment commented.[23]

The Wilderness

William Swinton, a *New York Times* correspondent, made vivid the terrain in which the battle was fought:

> The field where the first encounter of the armies had taken place, and where it was now decreed the battle should be fought, was that region known as "The Wilderness." I have already touched on some of the characteristic features of this region; but it is necessary

that these should be fully realized in order to gain a just appreciation of this singular and terrible combat. It is impossible to conceive a field worse adapted to the movement of a grand army. The whole face of the country is thickly wooded with only an occasional opening, and intersected by a few narrow wood-roads. But the woods of the Wilderness have not the ordinary features of a forest. The region rests on a belt of mineral rocks, and, for above a hundred years, extensive mining has here been carried on. To feed the mines the timber of the country for many miles around has been cut down, and in its place there had arisen a dense undergrowth of low-limbed and scraggy pines, stiff and bristling chinkapins, scrub-oaks, and hazel. It is a region of gloom and the shadow of death. Manoeuvring here was necessarily out of the question, and only Indian tactics told. The troops could only receive direction by a point of the compass; for not only were the lines of the battle entirely hidden from the sight of the commander, but no officer could see ten files on each side of him. Artillery was wholly ruled out of use; the massive concentration of three hundred guns stood silent, and only an occasional piece or section could be brought into play in the road-sides. Cavalry was still more useless. But in that horrid thicket there lurked two hundred thousand men, and through it lurid fires played; and, though no array of battle could be seen, there came out of its depths the crackle and roll of musketry like the noisy boiling of some hell-cauldron that told the dread story of death. Such was the field of the battle of the Wilderness.[24]

Alexander gave this account of the fierce fighting:

There never was more desperate fighting than now ensued & continued until darkness put an end to it. The Wilderness hid our small numbers from the enemy & their great numbers from our men. When Wilcox's men came to Hill's support they, at first, passed in front, & made some attacks, but finally fell back pretty much in the same line. There they generally laid flat on the ground & fired through the thicket & the enemy failed whenever they attempted to advance in the face of that fire. But night did not terminate the fighting any sooner than Hill needed it. His men were exhausted, his ammunition low, his lines disarranged & ragged, sometimes disconnected, & sometimes facing in different directions. Fresh brigades of the enemy were making their way around him, & if Hancock could have recalled the daylight he had wasted, even the force he had at hand would probably have wrought disaster to the two gallant divisions in spite of their glorious resistance.

But besides this ruin impending on their front & right, a regular dead-fall was being set over them on their left. Gen. Warren, while fighting Ewell & hunting around his flank, had discovered Wilcox's division in its temporary location, & he also saw its withdrawal to go to Heth's assistance. He at once prepared a strong force to move in that direction & attack Heth in flank & rear, sending Wadsworth's division, & Baxter's brigade, probably 8,000 men. Darkness overtook Wadsworth within a hundred yards of Hill's flank, & his whole command bivouaced where they halted, ready to move on in the morning.[25]

A courier had reached Hill, warning that a large Union force (Wadsworth's) was approaching his left where Wilcox had been. Hill rose to the emergency sending the 5th Alabama battalion of 125 soldiers—they were held back to guard the host of prisoners but were replaced by any non-combatants or wounded soldiers available—into the woods at the Union host in a widespread skirmish line, screaming the Rebel yell and firing as fast as they could, giving the impression that a large Rebel command was coming at them, halting Wadsworth's troops in their path just at nightfall.

Heth and Wilcox were deeply concerned at the condition of their battle line. Wilcox stated: "About nine o'clock General Wilcox, from a partial examination made under difficulties-thick woods and darkness of the night-but mainly from the reports of his officers, learned that his line was very irregular and much broken and required to be re-arranged." Heth put it: "Wilcox's troops and my own were terribly mixed up."[26] In the language of Colonel William H. Palmer, Hill's adjutant general, "They were like a worm fence, at every angle."[27] Wilcox and Heth went to Hill's tent where they found him sitting on his campstool by the fire feeling sick. Hill extended a hand to Heth as he came near and said: "Your division has done splendidly today; its magnificent fighting is the theme of the entire army." Heth retorted: "Yes, the division has done splendid fighting, but we have other matters to attend to just now." Describing the intermingling of his and Wilcox's troops sprawled "at every angle," Heth made a request to realign their troops: "Let me take one side of the road and form a line of battle, and Wilcox the other side and do the same, we are so mixed, and lying at every conceivable angle, that we cannot fire a shot without firing into each other. A skirmish line could drive both my division and Wilcox's, situated as we are now. We shall certainly be attacked early in the morning." By Heth's account of the conversation, Hill responded: "Longstreet will be up in a few hours. He will form in your front. I don't propose that your division shall do any fighting tomorrow, the men have been marching and fighting all day and are tired. I do not wish them disturbed." Wilcox was not satisfied with Hill's answer and went to see Lee, giving the following narrative of Lee's reaction:

> He [Wilcox] repaired to General Lee's tent, intending to report the condition of his front, and to suggest that a skirmish line be left where the front then was, the troops be retired a short distance, and the line rectified. General Lee, at the time, was not over two hundred yards from the point General Wilcox had fixed for his headquarters during the night, and was not over four hundred yards from where the battle has been fought. As General Wilcox entered the tent, General Lee remarked that he had made a complimentary report of the conduct of the two division on the plank road, and that he had received a note (holding it in his hand) from General Anderson, stating that he would bivouac at Verdierville for the night; but, he continued, "he has been instructed to move forward; he and Longstreet will be up, and the two divisions that have been so actively engaged will be relieved before day." General Wilcox, hearing this, made no suggestions about the line, as he was to be relieved before day.

Heth went to see Hill twice more and on the third attempt, Hill shouted, "Damn it Heth, I don't want to hear any more about it! I don't want them disturbed!" Apprehensive, Heth rode away from the last conference with Hill "agitated by an anxiety such as he had never felt before or afterwards." "The only excuse I can make for Hill is that he was sick," complained Heth.[28]

When Colonel Charles S. Venable found Longstreet at Richard's Shop, Longstreet's veterans had covered 32 miles in 24 hours, a remarkable march, and had settled into bivouac. In a postwar letter, Venable refreshed Longstreet's memory of the meeting;

"My message to you was to reach General Lee's position as soon as practicable on the morning of the 6th. 'By daylight,' was the order as I remember it."[29] Alexander gave this account of the First Corps progress:

> Our corps should have been where it could come in, promptly upon the Brock Road, & take in flank the forces fighting Hill & cut off those fighting Ewell. The Wilderness was our favorite fighting ground. The enemy's enormous force of artillery was there only in his way. Never was a better chance offered Gen. Lee, & never was a chance more quickly snapped at. But the one trouble was that we were so many miles away. It took longer for the orders to reach us, & we were only able to start about 4 P. M. with about 42 miles to go by the road used. It was 6 miles shorter by Orange Courthouse & the Plank Road, but we had to leave that road to Hill.
>
> At four o'clock [May 4] everything was on the road with orders to march all night, & until stopped on the road during the next day, only halting for such rest & feed as necessary to keep the horses from being broken down. Between midnight & daylight my staff & myself turned out into a wood & laid down under the trees & slept. Then the march was resumed & kept up until about 4 P.M. when the whole corps went into bivouac. We were then near Craig's Meeting house, (Alexander had started this sentence, "As well as I can locate the spot we were then at Richard's Shop."), on the Catharpin Road, about 36 miles from Mechanicsville by the roads we had come. Just before we went into bivouac we passed a few bodies of Federal cavalrymen, freshly killed, showing that the enemy was, now, not very far away. We were ordered to cook, eat, & rest until 1 A. M., when we were again to march, having a very fair late risen moon-& our destination, I understood, was to be Todd's Tavern. But my recollection is that before we started orders were received from Gen. Lee directing us to strike across to the Plank Road at Parker's Store & come in behind Hill's corps. At any rate we took that route, and, at some place where there was a fork in the road, the leading division took the wrong road for a little ways & thus lost about its length in distance while the rear division lost none. It resulted that when we finally got out in the broad straight Plank Road at Parker's Store at daylight the heads of the marching flanks were right abreast of each other, & the two sets of fours gave a front of 8 men to the column, which between dawn & sunrise came swinging fast down the road. I was at the front with Gen. Longstreet & the different battalions were some in & some behind the column.[30]

"About eleven o'clock in the night the guide reported from General Lee to conduct my command through the wood across to the Plank Road, and at one o'clock the march was resumed," explained Longstreet:

> The road was overgrown by the bushes, except the side-tracks made by the draft animals and the ruts of wheels which marked occasional lines in its course. After a time the wood became less dense, and the unused road was more difficult to follow, and presently the guide found that there was no road under him; but no time was lost, as, by ordering the lines of the divisions doubled, they were ready when the trail was found, and the march continued in double line. At daylight we entered the Plank Road, and filed down towards the field of strife of the afternoon of the 5th and daylight of the 6th.[31]

General Lee was becoming anxious as the evening wore on. Lee conveyed his concern to Stuart, who sent his chief of staff, Major Henry B. McClellan, to inform Longstreet "about the condition of things and the importance of getting up to us at the earliest possible hour in the morning." McClellan rode out about 7:00pm and found General Field's camp. Field was seated at a table and had just finished his dinner. McClellan explained that Lee wanted him to start at once to relieve Hill. Although he complained that his men needed rest, Field began preparations to move immediately. But a half an hour later, Field summoned McClellan, saying he had received another order from Longstreet directing him to start at 1:00am. Over 10 years later, McClellan wrote, "General Field's reply has never escaped memory. It was, I prefer to obey General Longstreet's order." Highly indignant, Major McClellan rode back and three hours later reported to Lee the rude reception he received from Field, instead of seeking out Longstreet whose headquarters was three miles farther back. Realizing the gravity of the situation, McClellan wanted to ride back with written orders but Lee demurred: "No. major, it is now past ten, and by the time you could return to General Field and he could put his division in motion, it would be one o'clock, and at that hour he will move." However, a little later, Lee changed his mind and sent a third courier, Catlett C. Taliaferro, to Longstreet: "and urge him to use the utmost diligence in coming to his assistance." Taliaferro found Longstreet and delivered Lee's directive. Longstreet told Taliaferro: "Go back to General Lee and tell him that I shall be with him at daylight and do anything he wants done." Before leaving, Taliaferro warned: "The Yankees are on this road and you had better be careful." Longstreet responded: "You be off, sir, and give my message to General Lee. I will take care of any Yankees on this road."[32]

Hancock could not throw in all his divisions in the morning attack due to a rumor. A Confederate staff officer imparted:

> Grant had been misled into a serious blunder by false information, curiously like what had been imposed upon Hooker in the Chancellorsville campaign. By the stories of prisoners he was led to believe, just as Hooker had been, that Pickett's division had arrived, and he ordered Hancock to withdraw Barlow's division from the force about to attack Heth, and post it on his left, on the Brock road, in anticipation of Pickett's expected appearance. There happened to be near that point the grading of an unfinished railroad, designed to run from Fredericksburg to Orange C. H., and nearly parallel to the Plank Road. It offered a great opportunity to turn the flank of either of the lines about to be engaged near the road. Fortunately for us, Barlow did not utilize it, but left the opportunity to Longstreet.[33]

Apparently, even absent Pickett has some effect. Hancock had his men replenish their ammunition and work during the night, strengthening their position, while Lee, for some unexplained reason, did nothing. Longstreet was astonished:

> The divisions of Heth and Wilcox rested during the night of the 5th where the battle of that day ceased, but did not prepare ammunition nor strengthen their lines for defence, because informed that they were to be relieved from the front. Both the division commanders claim that they were to be relieved, and that they were ordered not to intrench or replenish supplies. So it seems that they were all night within hearing of the voices of Hancock's men, not even reorganizing their lines so as to offer a front line of battle! General Heth has stated that he proposed to arrange for battle, but was ordered to give his men rest. While Hancock was sending men to his advanced line during the night and intrenching there and on his second line, the Confederates were all night idle.[34]

General Lee had pushed his luck too far; if he had Hill's corps fallen back and intrenched, it would have made Longstreet's task easier and prevented much unnecessary loss of life. As morning broke, the Confederate lines were assaulted as Longstreet's division approached. Alexander, who was in Longstreet's vanguard, gave this account of the action:

Grant had ordered his lines everywhere to assault at 5 A. M. At that time we were just about turning into the Plank Road at Parker's Store & very soon we began to hear from the front & left those grand roars of musketry & quick thunders of artillery which announce that the god or demon of war is about to hold one of his great carnivals.

As to what took place on the left, I can make a very short story of all the morning. Gen. Ewell was attacked by Sedgwick and Warren fiercely & frequently from 5 A. M. until about 11 A. M. He had improved his lines during the night, & gotten in more artillery, & he repelled every attack without any trouble & with severe loss to the enemy. By 11 o'clock all the fight was taken out of them, & Grant ordered them to give it up. But they were ordered to set to work & strengthen their own breastworks, so that a portion of their forces could be withdrawn & used elsewhere, & to help in this a brigade of engineer troops was sent to assist them.

But there is a different story to tell of what happened to Hill's two divisions while we were marching the three miles, on the Plank Road, which separated us from them at dawn. Not only was the Wadsworth dead fall sprung upon their left flank at five o'clock, but their right flank was also far over lapped by Hancock's assaulting columns. The fight that they made was desperate, but it was not of long duration. The two extreme flanks, being taken in reverse, were soon rolled up toward the centre, & the men, appreciating that their position was no longer tenable, fell back from both sides into the Plank Road & came pouring past the Tapp house, & Gen. Lee & Poague's guns which were among the small pines. That was, I think the most critical moment which Gen. Lee's fortunes had yet known. Gen. McGowan afterward told me of an interview which he had with the general as he passed. Gen. Lee rode up to him & said, "My God! Gen. McGowan is this splendid brigade of yours running like a flock of geese?"

McGowan answered, "No, General! The men are not whipped. They just want a place to form and they are ready to fight as well as ever." And, indeed, the bearing of the men fully confirmed McGowan's statement, that they were not whipped out of their positions, only flanked out.

For now I may resume my narrative & tell what I saw of the retreat of Heth's & Wilcox's divisions as I rode with Gen. Longstreet's staff at the head of the double column. When we still had, perhaps, a half mile to go I noted that we seemed to be passing some troops being marched in the opposite direction. Our two divisions, marching 8 abreast & file closers & mounted officers on the sides, nearly filled the road, & the troops going west were crowded to each side along the edge of the woods. But they went along nonchalantly & in such apparent order that I, & those about me, supposed them to be, perhaps, reinforcements being sent to Ewell.

After awhile, we saw an excited officer on horse back, apparently trying to stop some of them. Jos. Haskell, who had the useful faculty of knowing every man whom he had seen before, said, "Major, what's the matter. Are not those men being marched back?" "No! God, damn 'em!" swore the major. "They are running." They were, indeed, the men of Heth's and Wilcox's divisions, not running but now so mixed up as to be aware that they could be of no use until they had an opportunity to sort themselves out again into their respective commands. We could now tell too that the firing was approaching the Tapp field, particularly in the woods on the right flank, & as we approached the Tapp field, of small pines and broom grass, on the left, bullets began to whistle from the woods on the right, square across the road, & some also seemed to come directly from the front. Two or three guns among the pines (I could not see exactly how many) were firing square to their front. The head of our infantry column took the double quick, & soon after commands were shouted, "Forward into Line!" & Kershaw on the right & Fields on the left began to form their leading brigades in line of battle. We had arrived on time but it was a pretty close call.[35]

General Wilcox had a far different perspective as his men received Hancock's assault:

The struggle was renewed early in the morning of the 6th by Ewell striking the enemy on his extreme right flank (Seymour's Brigade), and involving the whole of the right two divisions, Wright's and Rickett's, of the Sixth Corps. This attack was followed soon by Hancock advancing a heavy force on the plank road. On this the Confederates were in no condition either to advance or resist an attack. Wilcox, in front, was in an irregular and broken line; Heth's men had slept close in rear, without regard to order. The corps commander had informed General Heth that the two divisions would be relieved before day, and hence this unfortunate condition of affairs at this critical moment. The tree-tops were already tinged with the early rays of the rising sun, but the enemy lay quiet; at length the sun itself was seen between the boughs and foliage of the heavy forest, and on the plank road of the Confederates, eager to catch at straws in their unprepared state, began to have hopes that the Federals would not advance; but these were soon dispelled. A few shots were heard on Wilcox's right, and the firing extended rapidly along to the left, to the road and across this, and around to his extreme left, which was considerably in rear of his line on the right of the road. The musketry increased rapidly in volume, and was soon of the heaviest kind. Heth's men hurried to the rear, preparatory to re-forming line; the badly formed line of Wilcox received, unaided, this powerful column, which soon enveloped its flank. The fighting was severe as long as it lasted. Swinton says of it, "an hour's severe fighting."

While the firing was severe on the flank, a dense mass of Federals poured into the road from the thickets on either side, and the Confederates began to yield. Wilcox rode back rapidly to General Lee, found him where he had been the night before, and reported the condition of his command. His response was, "Longstreet must be here; go bring him up." Galloping to the road, the head of his corps, Kershaw's division was met, and ordered to file at once to the right and get into line as quickly as possible, for fear his division would be forced back on it while forming. Less than a brigade had left the road when Longstreet in person arrived. He was informed where General Lee would be found-within one hundred and fifty yards. In the open space-old field-where General Lee's tent was at 9 P. M., and where he reappeared so early in the morning, was artillery-one or two batteries-on a gentle swell of the surface, in front descending, and open for several hundred yards; the enemy were not within one hundred and fifty or two hundred yards of these guns. When Wilcox's men had fallen to the rear sufficiently to enable the guns to be used, they were directed into the woods, obliquely across the plank road; the enemy on the road could not see the guns. Wilcox's men, while Kershaw was uncovering the plank road, and before Field's Division formed on the left of it, filed off the plank road and took position a half mile to the left, between Ewell's right and the troops on the plank road, filling up in part this long intervening unoccupied space. Later, Heth's Division took position on his right.[36]

The guns Wilcox was referring to were 16 guns posted by A. P. Hill in the large field of the Tapp farm, on a slight rise under William Poague and David McIntosh. When a staff officer told Hill there was no adequate road to bring the guns out if the Federals broke through, Hill replied in an irritated manner, "I know this. In battle the guns must take their chances of capture. They will help hold the line if such an emergency occurs."[37]

As Longstreet arrived in person, Colonel William H. Palmer, a member of Hill's staff who had known the old War Horse for several years, grasped his hand: "Ah,

General, we have been looking for you since twelve o'clock last night." Longstreet disregarded the remark: "My troops are not up. I have ridden ahead ..." The rest was inaudible due to the crash of musketry.[38]

Sorrel rode with Longstreet's staff as they drew near the battle on Lee's right:

> Longstreet had moved at 1 A. M., the march being difficult and slow in the dense forest by side tracks and deep furrowed roadways. At daylight he was on the Plank Road and in close touch with Lee when Hancock struck the two unprepared divisions. The situation when we came on the scene, that of May 6th, was appalling. Fugitives from the broken lines of the Third Corps were pouring back in disorder and it looked as if things were past mending. But not so to James Longstreet; never did his great qualities as a tenacious, fighting soldier shine forth in better light. He instantly took charge of the battle, and threw two divisions across the Plank Road, Kershaw on the right, Field on the left. None but seasoned soldiers like the First Corps could have done even that much. I have always thought that in its entire splendid history the simple act of forming line in that dense undergrowth, under heavy fire and with the Third Corps men pushing to the rear through the ranks, was perhaps its greatest performance for steadiness and inflexible courage and discipline. Hill's men were prompt to collect and reform in our rear and soon were ready for better work.[39]

Private William Dame of the Richmond Howitzers watched as the First Corps arrived, and later commented: "Like a fine lady at a party, Longstreet was often late in his arrival at the ball. But he always made a sensation and that of delight, when he got in, with the grand old First Corps sweeping behind him as his train." The men of the Richmond Howitzers had fought under Longstreet earlier in the war and raised a cry as they spotted Longstreet's column, which Dame remembered years later: "Look out down the road. Here they come! Here's Longstreet. The old War Horse is up at last. It's all right now."[40] "In perfect order, ranks well closed, and no stragglers, those splendid troops came on," described an onlooker, "regardless of the confusion on every side, pushing their steady way onward like 'a river in the sea' of confused and troubled human waves around them."[41] One of Longstreet's artillerymen, John Cheves Haskell, recalled how Longstreet handled his troops: "Longstreet, always grand in battle, never shone as he did here." The general "rode up and down the lines, encouraging, exhorting, and steadying the men, with an effect on them that no other leader I ever saw had on his troops."[42] Colonel C. S. Venable of General Lee's staff, in his address before the Southern Historical Society, remembered Longstreet's conduct:

> General Longstreet rode forward with the imperturbable coolness which always characterized him in times of perilous action, and began to put them in position on the right and left of the road. His men came to the front of the disordered battle with a steadiness unexampled even among veterans, and with an elan that presaged restoration of our position and certain victory. When they arrived the bullets of the enemy on our right flank had begun to sweep the field in the rear of the artillery-pits on the left of the road, where General Lee was giving directions and assisting General Hill in rallying and re-forming his troops.[43]

Longstreet's first task was to blunt the impetus of Hancock's assault. Longstreet ordered the men into line on each side of the road; Field's division took the left of the road (Gregg, Benning, and Law), while Kershaw's division (Kennedy, Humphreys, and Bryan) took the right. The First Corps was hidden from the enemy by the slight rise Poague's guns were mounted on. A counterstroke assembled as Field explained Longstreet's order was to "charge with any front I could make." As the Texas Brigade formed behind the blazing guns, Longstreet rode his horse at a walk down the line addressing the men: "Keep cool, men. We will straighten this out in a short time-keep cool." Hearing Longstreet repeat these lines, Colonel William H. Palmer, Hill's chief of staff, noted: "In the midst of the confusion, his coolness and manner was inspiring."[44]

General Lee was near Poague's guns and had sent his adjutant, Colonel W. H. Taylor, to prepare the trains for movement to the rear. He was directing the fire of the guns and assisting in rallying Hill's troops as Gregg's Texans swept past the batteries. General Lee rode over next to Gregg and shouted, "General, what brigade is this?" "The Texas Brigade," (Hood's Texans) Gregg answered. "I am glad to see it," Lee exclaimed. "When you go in there, I wish you to give those men the cold steel. They will stand and fight all day, and never move unless you charge them."

"That is my experience," answered Gregg.

To encourage the troops, Lee added, "The Texas brigade always has driven the enemy, and I want them to do it now. And tell them, General, that they will fight today under my eye-I will watch their conduct. I want every man of them to know I am here with them."

"Attention, Texas Brigade," Gregg shouted. "The eyes of General Lee are upon you. Forward. March!"

A tall Texan on the left lifted his hat and called for Lee to go back. The cry was taken up by the others. Gregg remonstrated for Lee to go to a place of safety. Lee raised his hat, waving it in the air as to salute the Texans, shouting: "Texans always move them!" Then he said: "Well then, I will go back." Pointing to the Old War Horse, Venable cried: "General, you've been looking for General Longstreet. There he is, over yonder."[45]

Lee conferred with Longstreet briefly, then moved off a little way. Colonel Venable whispered to Longstreet that he had great difficulty in persuading Lee to get out of harm's way; Longstreet requested Venable to convey a message to Lee: "I asked that he would say, with my compliments, that his line would be recovered in an hour if he would permit me to handle the troops, but if my services were not needed, I would like to ride to some place of safety, as it was not quite comfortable where we were."[46] Lee moved further to the rear, leaving Longstreet to handle the fighting.

Left to his own devices Longstreet's tactical brilliance shone forth. His two divisions were massed in columns on each side of the Orange Plank Road. Then each brigade smashed into the Union lines with hammer-like blows. The brunt of the action was bore by Gregg's Texans, followed by Benning's Georgia brigade. "The ground over which Field's troops were advancing was open for a short distance, and fringed on its farther edge with scattered pines, beyond which began the Wilderness," recalled a Rebel participant:

> The Federals [Webb's brigade of Hancock's corps] were advancing through the pines with apparently resistless forces, when Gregg's eight hundred Texans, regardless of numbers, flanks, or supports, dashed directly upon them. There was a terrible crash, mingled with wild yells, which settled down into a steady roar of musketry. In less than ten minutes one-half of that devoted eight hundred were lying upon the field dead or wounded; but they had delivered a staggering blow and broken the force of the Federal advance. Benning's and Law's brigades came promptly to their support, and the whole swept forward together. The tide was flowing the other way.[47]

Longstreet had brought Hancock's advance to a halt and almost drove it back to its starting place. Meade's aide, Lieutenant Colonel Theodore Lyman, sent a dispatch to Meade: "The left of our assault has struck Longstreet. We about hold our own against Longstreet and many regiments are tired and shattered." Of the 800 soldiers in the Texas Brigade, only 250 returned unscathed; Gregg was nearly killed and Benning was severely wounded. As Law's Alabama Brigade moved up, Lee took notice. Lee asked, "What troops are these?" A private in the 15th Alabama called back, "Law's Alabama brigade." Lee exclaimed, "God bless the Alabamans, Alabama soldiers, all I ask of you is to keep up with the Texans." A soldier in the ranks watched Lee and had this impression: Lee "appeared to be very much perturbed over his misfortune, and the only time I ever saw him excited."[48]

As the fighting moved into the Wilderness, Longstreet changed his tactics to suit this harsh terrain, using a very unconventional formation:

> As full lines of battle could not be handled through the thick wood, I ordered the advance of the six brigades by heavy skirmish lines, to be followed by stronger supporting lines. Hancock's lines, thinned by their push through the wood, and somewhat by the fire of the disordered divisions, weaker than my line of fresh and more lively skirmishers, were checked by our first steady, rolling fire, and after a brisk fusillade were pushed back into their intrenched line, when the fight became steady and very firm, occasionally swinging parts of my line back and compelling the reserves to move forward and recover it.[49]

This loose-order formation allowed the Confederates to slip through the woods and still deliver an effective firepower, developing the enemy's line while being difficult targets to hit. At eight o'clock, Anderson's division arrived and General Lee ordered Anderson to report to Longstreet. Lee and Hill re-formed the Third Corps and they were now prepared to fight again. Lee desperately wanted Hill to fill the gap between Ewell's Second Corps and Longstreet's First Corps. Hill dispatched his adjutant general, Colonel William H. Palmer, to request one of Anderson's brigades. General Lee told Palmer to "see Longstreet about it." Magnanimously, Longstreet offered: "Certainly, Colonel, which one will you take?" "The leading one," Palmer replied and brought the brigade to Hill. In a postwar letter to a friend, Palmer described how Longstreet's arrival impacted the battle: "In a short time he was master of the field and everybody felt that way about it." Palmer felt that Hill's soldiers were humiliated at their condition as the First Corps came up: "After putting up such a battle the day before, to have been found by Longstreet's troops retiring, and in more or less confusion was dreadful. They [Longstreet's soldiers] only knew that with a conspicuous courage and steadiness they had redeemed a losing battle, and saved the Army of Northern Virginia from disaster."[50] As Heth's troops fell back through the ranks of Kershaw's division, they were chided: "Do you belong to Lee's army? You don't look like the men we left here. You're worse than Bragg's men."[51]

Brigadier General Martin Luther Smith, Lee's chief engineer, arrived with Anderson's division. Smith had graduated from West Point in 1842 and was a classmate of James Longstreet. he was born in Danby, New York, but had married a Georgia belle in 1846, raising a family there. When Georgia seceded, he sided with the Confederacy. He was in charge of constructing the defenses of Vicksburg in May 1863. After Vicksburg fell in July 1863, he was a prisoner of war for seven months until exchanged in early 1864. He was head of the Engineer Corps for the entire Confederate army from March until April, then was appointed chief engineer for the Army of Northern Virginia.

Longstreet aspired to win a victory rather than settle for a stalemate. He desired to find an opening for a flank on Grant's left as originally intended: "General Lee sent General M. L. Smith, of the engineers, to report to me. He was ordered through the wood on my right to the unfinished railroad to find a way around the left of the enemy's line, while we engaged his front."[52] Longstreet had high regards for Smith: "He was a splendid tactician as well as a skillful engineer, and gallant withal." Sure enough, Smith reported to Longstreet that he had found an avenue to approach Hancock's unprotected flank undetected:

> About 10 o'clock Maj. Gen. M. L. Smith and the other officers sent out to examine the enemy's position, reported that the left of the enemy's line extended but a short distance beyond the plank road. Special directions were given to Lieutenant-Colonel Sorrel to conduct the brigades of Generals Mahone, G. T. Anderson, and Wofford beyond the enemy's left, and to attack him on his left and rear-I have since heard that the brigade of General Davis formed a part of this flanking force-the flank movement to be followed by a general advance.[53]

General Longstreet quickly seized the opportunity to strike into the flank and rear of the enemy, his keen tactical skills and superb generalship were displayed in his battle plan and the handling of his troops to effectuate the desired outcome—the rout of the Federals. His flanking tactics minimized his casualties with a maximized effect on the enemy.

Sorrel recorded the events and his conversation with Longstreet:

> Gen, M. L. Smith, an engineer from General Headquarters, had reported to Longstreet and examined the situation on our right, where he discovered the enemy's left somewhat exposed and inviting attack; and now came our turn. General Longstreet, calling me, said: "Colonel, there is a fine chance of a great attack by our right. If you will quickly get into those woods, some brigades will be found much scattered from the fight. Collect them and take charge. Form

a good line and then move, your right pushed forward and turning as much as possible to the left. Hit hard when you start, but don't start until you have everything ready. I shall be waiting for your gun fire, and be on hand with fresh troops for further advance."

No greater opportunity could be given to an aspiring young staff officer, and I was quickly at work. The brigades of Anderson, Mahone, and Wofford were lined up in fair order and in touch with each other. It was difficult to assemble them in that horrid Wilderness, but in an hour we were ready. The word was given, and then with heavy firing and ringing yells we were upon Hancock's exposed left, the brigades being ably commanded by their respective officers. It was rolled back line after line. I was well mounted, and despite the tangled growth could keep with our troops in conspicuous sight of them, riding most of the charge with Mahone's men and the Eighteenth Virginia. A stand was attempted by a reserve line of Hancock's, but it was swept off its feet in the tumultuous rush of our troops, and finally we struck the Plank Road lower down. On the other side of it was Wadsworth's corps in disorder. (I had last seen him under flag of truce at Fredericksburg.) Though the old General was doing all possible to fight it, his men would not stay. A volley from our pursuing troops brought down the gallant New Yorker, killing both rider and horse.

There was still some life left in the General, and every care was given him by our surgeon.

We were then so disorganized by the chase through the woods that a halt was necessary to reform, and I hastened back to General Longstreet to press for fresh troops. There was no need with him. He had heard our guns, knew what was up, and was already marching, happy at the success, to finish it with the eager men at his heels.[54]

G. B. (Tige) Anderson's brigade of Field's division had been held in reserve, while Gregg, Benning, and Perry ground Hancock's forward momentum to a halt; Wofford's Georgians of Kershaw's division had just arrived from Parker's Store with the First Corps supply trains. Finally, Mahone's Virginia brigade came from R. H. Anderson's division. On the way, Sorrel picked up the diminished brigade of Brigadier General Joseph R. Davis of Heth's division made up of a mix of men from Mississippi and North Carolina, now under the command of Colonel John M. Stone, as Davis was absent. The brigade was keen to join the flanking column. In the words of Alexander:

> Sorrel moved the four brigades by the flank to the unfinished railroad, where they faced to the left, and, about 11 A. M., they advanced upon the Federal line, striking it in flank and rear. The success of the movement was complete. Brigade after brigade was routed and rolled up. Hancock, noted for his power and influence with his men on such occasions, endeavored in vain to stay the panic, but was unable to do so, and consulting with Birney, he decided to abandon all in front and endeavor to reestablish his line upon the Brock Road. Here he had, the day before, sacrificed valuable time to intrench a line which might now serve him as a refuge. The panic had extended even across the Plank Road where Wadsworth had been killed and Baxter wounded, when their troops were routed.
>
> This was Longstreet's great opportunity. Nearly the whole of Grant's army had been first fought to a standstill, and now four brigades, with little loss by a lucky movement, had utterly routed about two full corps in the Wilderness, where it was almost impossible to rally broken troops. Longstreet, with five more fresh brigades, was close at hand, fully prepared to join the victorious four and be aided by the brigades which had relieved Heth and Wilcox in the morning in a supreme effort to follow up the fugitives, and drive them into the Rapidan. When Smith had directed Sorrel's column on its turning expedition, he had been given a small party and directed to find a way across the Brock Road which would turn Hancock's extreme left.

He had now returned and reported one found. He was asked to conduct the flanking brigades and handle them as the ranking officer.[55]

This evaluation of Longstreet's tactics was given by a Confederate officer: "Forming at right angles to it, they attacked in flank and rear, while a general advance was made in front. So far the fight had been one of anvil and hammer. But this first display of tactics at once changed the face of the field. The Federal left wing was rolled up in confusion toward the Plank Road and then back upon the Brock road."[56] In his report, General Mahone said: "The three brigades in imposing order and with a step that meant to conquer, were now rapidly descending upon the enemy's left. The movement was a success, complete as it was brilliant."[57] Some years after the event, Hancock confessed to Longstreet: "You rolled me up like a wet blanket, and it was some hours before I could reorganize for battle."[58] The Confederates seemed "like an army of ghosts rising out of the earth," as a Federal officer depicted it, adding "such an apparition will unsettle the stoutest nerves."[59]

Longstreet had fresh brigades to throw into the fray and was in firm control of the engagement; he sent General Smith on a second reconnaissance with the task of turning Hancock's breastworks on the Brock Road, culminating the ruin of the Union left:

> As soon as the troops struck Hancock his line began to break, first slowly, then rapidly. Somehow, as they retreated, a fire was accidentally started in the dry leaves, and began to spread as the Confederates advanced. Mahone's brigade approached the burning leaves and part of it broke off a little to get around, but the Twelfth Virginia was not obstructed by the blaze and moved directly on. At the Plank Road Colonel Sorrel rode back to join us. All of the enemy's battle on the right of the Plank Road was broken up, and General Field was fighting severely with his three brigades on the left against Wadsworth and Stevenson, pushing them a little.
>
> The Twelfth Virginia Regiment got to the Plank Road some little time before the other regiments of the brigade, and, viewing the contention on the farther side between Field's and Wadsworth's divisions, dashed across and struck the left of Wadsworth's line. This relieved Field a little, and, under this concentrating push and fire, Wadsworth fell mortally wounded. In a little while followed the general break of the Union battle. The break of his left had relieved Kershaw's troops, and he was waiting for the time to advance, and Jenkin's brigade that had been held in reserve and that part of R. H. Anderson's division not in use were ready and anxious for opportunity to engage, and followed as our battle line pushed forward.
>
> General Smith then came and reported a way across the Brock Road that would turn Hancock's extreme left. He was asked to conduct the flanking brigades and handle them as the ranking officer.[60]

General Smith took the brigades of Mahone, Anderson, Davis, and Wofford by inversion from their position facing the Brock Road to strike Hancock's intrenched line in the left rear on the Brock Road—pulling Wofford's brigade, the right element of the initial alignment, to move left and rear and establish the left of the resulting formation, while the other brigades moved in succession to the right of Wofford.

Longstreet Detested Frontal Assaults

Longstreet's approach was described by one historian:

> No one was better aware of the realities of this situation than Longstreet himself. A tactician of consummate ability, with a profound distrust of the doctrine of wholesale attack, or, as more elegantly styled by its European proponents, la offensive a outrance, Longstreet abhorred the practice-all too frequently indulged during the War of American Secession-of staking the decision of battle on brutal and violent frontal attacks, unrelieved by a skillfully coordinated flanking maneuver. These deep convictions brought him to the verge of mutiny on the battlefield of Gettysburg. To him, Pickett's charge was little short of a crime.[61]

Brigadier General Micah Jenkins's brigade was to spearhead an attack up the Orange Plank Road upon Hancock's earthworks on the Brock Road as Smith's four brigades struck flank and rear. Kershaw, as indicated in his official report, was to coordinate in the attack with Jenkins:

> We met the lieutenant-general commanding coming to the front almost within musket range of the Brock Road. Exchanging hasty congratulations upon the success of the morning, the lieutenant-general rapidly planned and directed an attack to be made by Brigadier-General Jenkins and myself upon the position of the enemy upon the Brock Road before he could recover from his disaster. The order to me was to break their line and push all to the right of the road toward Fredericksburg. Jenkins' brigade was put in motion by a flank in the plank road, my division in the woods to the right. I rode with General Jenkins at the head of his command, arranging with him the details of our combined attack.[62]

Jenkins spoke of his mission with his longtime friend Colonel Asbury Coward, of the 5th South Carolina: "Old man, we are in for it today. We are to break the enemy's line where the Brock Road cuts across the pike. The point lies just over there, I think," he said, extending his arm in the direction. "Your regiment is the battalion of direction. Tell your men that South Carolina is looking for every man to do his duty to her this day." On assignment, Porter Alexander came upon Jenkins:

> Gen. Longstreet directed me to go in person & find Gen. Stuart's cavalry, out on our right flank, & confer with him, & see if there was an opportunity for me to get a position for guns in that quarter. As I started on this errand I passed Jenkins's brigade halted in the road, & loading their muskets. I shook hands with Jenkins & said, "Old man, I hope you will win that next grade this morning." "Well," he said, turning towards his men, "we are going to fight or old South Carolina today, aren't we boys?"[63]

Longstreet was moving to the front to take charge in a cavalcade of Generals and their staffs at the head of Jenkins's brigade on the Orange Plank Road. Longstreet rode over to General Field and seized his hands: "He congratulated me in warm terms on the fighting of my troops and the result of the assault," Field recalled. Sorrel, Longstreet's assistant adjutant general, had returned and was with Longstreet as the column moved up:

> There was quite a party of mounted officers and men riding with him-Generals Kershaw and Jenkins, the staff and orderlies. Jenkins, always enthusiastic, had thrown his arm about my

shoulder, with, "Sorrel, it was splendid; we shall smash them now." And turning back I was riding by Longstreet's side, my horse's head at his crupper, when firing broke out from our own men on the roadside in the dense tangle.

Longstreet was severely wounded and without his leadership the attack was stymied.

The Lieutenant-General was struck. He was a heavy man, with a very firm seat in the saddle, but he was actually lifted straight up and came down hard. Then the lead-torn coat, the orifice close to the right shoulder pointed to the passage of the heavy bullet of those days. His staff immediately dismounted him, at foot of a branching tree, bleeding profusely.

The shot had entered near the throat and he was almost choked with blood. Doctor Cullen, his medical director, was quickly on the spot. Even then the battle was in the leader's mind, and he sent word to Major-General Field to go straight on. He directed me to hasten to General Lee, report what had been accomplished, and urge him to continue the movement he was engaged on; the troops being all ready, success would surely follow, and Grant, he firmly believed, be driven back across the Rapidan. I rode immediately to General Lee, and did not again see my chief until his return to duty in October. The fatal firing that brought him down also killed General Jenkins, Captain Foley and several orderlies. Jenkins was a loss to the army-brave, ardent, experienced and highly trained, there was much to expect of him.[64]

Longstreet had been warned by his aide, Andrew Dunn, not to expose himself at the head of the column. "That is our business," replied Longstreet, as if to say it was part of their vocation, soldiering.

Longstreet presented his viewpoint as to the unfortunate events that brought him down and with it any hope of a complete victory in the Wilderness:

I rode at the head of the column, Jenkins, Kershaw, and the staff with me. After discussing the dispositions of their troops for reopening the battle, Jenkins rode closer to offer congratulations, saying, "I am happy; I have felt despair of the cause for some months, but am relieved, and feel assured that we will put the enemy back across the Rapidan before night." Little did he or I think these sanguine words were the last he would utter.

When Wadsworth fell the Union battle broke up in hasty retreat. Field's brigade closed to fresh ranks, the flanking brigades drew into line near the Plank road, and with them the other regiments of Mahone's brigade; but the Twelfth Regiment, some distance in advance of the others, had crossed the road to strike at Wadsworth's left before the other regiments were in sight, and was returning to find its place in line. The order for the flanking brigades to resume march by their left had not moved those brigades of the right. As the Twelfth Regiment marched back to find its place on the other side of the Plank road, it was mistaken, in the wood, for an advance of the enemy, and fire was opened on it from the other regiments of the brigade. The men threw themselves to the ground to let the fire pass. Just then our party of officers was up and rode under the fire. General Jenkins had not finished the expressions of joyful congratulations which I have quoted when he fell mortally wounded.

Captain Doby and the orderly, Bowen of Kershaw's staff, were killed. General Kershaw turned to quiet the troops, when Jenkins's brigade with leveled guns were in the act of returning the fire of the supposed enemy concealed in the wood, but as Kershaw's clear voice called out "F-r-i-e-n-d-s!" the arms were recovered, without a shot in return, and the men threw themselves down upon their faces.

At the moment that Jenkins fell I received a severe shock from a minie ball passing through my throat and right shoulder. The blow lifted me from the saddle, and my right arm dropped to my side, but I settled back to my seat, and started to ride on, when in a minute the flow of blood admonished me that my work for the day was done. As I turned to ride back, members of the staff, seeing me about to fall, dismounted and lifted me to the ground.

Orders were given General Field, the senior officer present, to push on before the enemy could have time to rally. The two lines marching along the Plank road, southward, in pursuit, and the flanking brigades to move in the other direction, were, for the moment, a little perplexing, as he was not accurately advised of the combinations, but he grasped the situation. Before he was prepared, however, General R. H. Anderson, came into command as senior, and then General Lee came up. The plans, orders, and opportunity were explained to him, but the woods conceled everything except the lines of troops alongside the road. General Lee did not care to handle the troops in broken lines, and ordered formation in a general line for parallel battle. The change in the forest tangle consumed several hours of precious time, and gave General Hancock time to collect his men into battle order, post his heavy reinforcements, and improve his intrenchments.[65]

General Longstreet and his entourage were caught in a cross-fire on the Orange Plank Road. The 12th Virginia regiment had its path blocked by fires ignited by burning powder from the incessant musketry and had become separated from the other regiments in Mahone's brigade, crossing the Plank Road alone. The officers realized that the regiment was isolated, turned it around to rejoin their brigade, and moved along the northside of the Plank Road in an area one Union officer described as "so dense that one could distinguish nothing." The four remaining regiments of Mahone's brigade were "lying down or kneeling," south of the Orange Plank Road, waiting to join with Smith's flanking movement on Hancock's Brock Road defenses. Suddenly, shadowy figures appeared north of the road and Mahone's men fired on them, believing they were Yankees; shots were exchanged across the road. George Bernard wrote in his diary for May 7 that the deadly fire came from the 41st Virginia: "and I hear also part of the 61st regiment." Colonel David A. Weisiger of the 12th Virginia informed his wife on May 7 that the 41st "mistook us for the enemy" and fired the fatal shots.

Longstreet was lowered from his horse by three of his staff members—Sorrel, Peyton Manning, and Francis Dawson—carried to the roadside and propped against a tree. With bloody foam forming in his mouth, he ordered Colonel Fairfax: "Tell General Field to take command and move forward with the whole force and gain the Brock Road." When General Field arrived at Longstreet's side, Longstreet told him: "Assume command of the corps. Press the enemy." The Old War Horse was lifted onto a litter and carried to an ambulance, with his hat placed over his face to protect it from the sun. Word spread among the soldiers that their commander was dead and this rumor was murmured by the men as Longstreet passed: "As my litter was borne to the rear my hat was placed over my face, and soldiers by the roadside said, 'He is dead, and they are telling us he is only wounded.' Hearing this repeated from time to time, I raised my hat with my left hand, when the burst of voices and the flying of hats in the air eased my pains somewhat." Longstreet wanted to maintain the morale of the troops. Longstreet was placed in an ambulance to be moved to the field hospitals at Parker's Store;

his staff accompanied the hospital wagon. Passing by to find a place for his guns, an artillery major witnessed the scene:

> I had been sent forward, perhaps to look for some place where we might get into the fight, when I observed an excited gathering some distance back of the lines, and pressing toward it I heard that General Longstreet had just been shot down and was being put into an ambulance. I could not learn anything definite as to the character of his wound, but only that it was serious—some said he was dead. When the ambulance moved off, I followed it a little way, being anxious for trustworthy news of the General. The members of his staff surrounded the vehicle, some riding in front, some on one side and some on the other, and never on any occasion during the four years of the war saw a group of officers and gentlemen more deeply disturbed. They were literally bowed down with grief. One, I remember, stood upon the rear step of the ambulance, seeming to desire to be as near him as possible. All of them were in tears. One, by whose side I rode for some distance, was himself severely hurt, but made no allusion to his wound, and I do not believe he felt it. It was not alone the general they admired who had been shot down-it was rather, the man they loved.

Although he was not particularly acquainted with Longstreet, the artilleryman wanted to look in the ambulance to see his status:

> I rode up to the ambulance and looked in. They had taken off Longstreet's hat and coat and boots. The blood had paled out of his face and its somewhat gross aspect was gone. I noticed how white and dome-like his great forehead looked and, with scarcely less reverent admiration, how spotless white his socks and his fine gauze undervest, save where the black red gore from his breast and shoulder had stained it. While I gazed at his massive frame, lying so still except when it rocked inertly with the lurch of the vehicle, his eyelids frayed apart till I could see a delicate line of blue between them, and then he very quietly moved his unwounded arm and, with his thumb and two fingers, carefully lifted the saturated undershirt from his chest, holding it up a moment, and heaved a deep sigh. He is not dead, I said to myself, and he is calm and entirely master of the situation. He is both greater and more attractive than I have heretofore thought him.

Francis Dawson was with Longstreet's ambulance and watched General Lee when he looked inside: "I shall not soon forget the sadness in his face, and the almost despairing movement of his hands, when he was told Longstreet had fallen." After Longstreet reached the Confederate field hospital, his wound was diagnosed as "not necessarily fatal" by Dr. Cullen and three other surgeons (Barksdale, Wood, and Guild).[66]

E. Porter Alexander complained of Lee's tactics when he took over:

> At any rate, nothing was done until about four o'clock, & than it seemed more like an apology for the attack that Longstreet was conducting, than anything really calculated to produce results. Only Field's & Anderson's divisions took part, & Law was absent from Field's, & Perry from Anderson's. The enemy had now had several hours of rest & quiet. And yet, in spite of all that, & of their excellent intrenchments, & of some artillery that they brought up, poor Jenkins's South Carolina boys, who had been loading their guns in the morning, & whom Longstreet was leading to the attack when he & Jenkins were shot, actually carried the breastworks in front of them & planted their colors & held them for

quite a while, although no good was to be accomplished by it. They were led in this charge by my great personal friend, Gen, Bratton, who succeeded Jenkins in their command. This attack ought never, never to have been made. It was sending a boy on a man's errand. It was wasting good soldiers whom we could not spare. It was discouraging pluck & spirit by setting it an impossible task.[67]

Colonel Walter H. Taylor, Lee's chief of staff, believed that but for the fall of Longstreet the battle of the Wilderness would have been a Confederate victory:

General Longstreet immediately made dispositions to move again against the enemy's left in his new position. Jenkins's brigade of Kershaw's division, which had been held in reserve, and Kershaw's other brigades now released, and all of Anderson's division not engaged, were available for the movement. The leading brigades had already moved off in the advance, and General Longstreet, accompanied by Generals Kershaw and Jenkins, was riding along the Plank Road, when, owing to some misapprehension, there was a volley fired by our own men across the Plank Road just as this body of officers rode along, when General Jenkins was killed and General Longstreet so seriously wounded as to be compelled to leave the field. It required some time to recover from this catastrophe, and in the interval opportunity was given the enemy in which to rally his troops, put in reinforcements, and greatly strengthen that portion of his line, so that, when our troops advanced, although they captured a portion of the intrenched line of the enemy, they were unable to hold it. I have always thought that had General Longstreet not been wounded, he would have rolled back that wing of General Grant's army in such a manner as to have forced the Federals to recross the Rapidan.[68]

Longstreet did not return to the First Corps until Lee was besieged in Richmond and stayed until the final surrender at Appomattox.

General Longstreet perceived the political facet in the war: "If we break up the enemy's arrangements early, and through him back, he will not be able to recover his position nor his morale until the Presidential election is over, and we shall then have a new President to treat with."[69] On the morning of the battle of the Wilderness, when President Lincoln was asked about the best thing that could happen to the Union that day, he was quoted: "To kill Longstreet."

The Federal casualties in the battle were 2,246 killed, 12,037 wounded, and 3,383 missing, for a total of 18,366. Confederate returns were inaccurate but it is estimated they lost 8,000 all told.

Epilogue

General Longstreet's Strategy and Tactics

Technological changes prior to the American Civil War from 1840 to 1860 had a tremendous impact on the battlefields and the course of the war. The introduction of the infantryman's muzzle-loading rifled musket as standard armament, concurrent with the invention of the "Minie Ball" in 1849, drove the cavalry and artillery from the open field of battle and made it extremely hazardous for infantry to take the offensive in a frontal assault. Previously, the rifle had been too slow to load. However, Captain Claude A. Minie of the French Army perfected on the invention of a cylindroconoidal bullet by Captain Norton of the British army. Minie's bullet, smaller in diameter than the bore, could easily be dropped down the muzzle of the rifle, making for efficient loading. As the hollow base expanded on firing, to fit the spiral grooves of the barrel, it produced a horizontal spin, which resulted in long-range accuracy, higher velocity, and greater penetrating power. With the introduction of the rifled muzzleloader, the defense, especially behind field fortifications, had at least three times the strength of the offense. Lieutenant General James Longstreet was well aware of the impact of this new technology—the rifled musket and cannon—on the battlefield and was a strong proponent of defensive tactics. Longstreet favored the use of intrenchments and terrain to shield his troops from exposure to the enhanced long-range accuracy of the improved weaponry. He preferred turning and flanking movements to frontal assaults. He did not believe in fighting battles unless there was a fruitful outcome with a minimal loss of life to his troops. This is evident again and again in his advice and recommendations on the conduct of battlefield tactics and strategy.

Prior to the battle of Chancellorsville, Longstreet had discussed strategy with General Lee in case Hooker advanced against the Army of Northern Virginia while Longstreet's divisions of Hood and Pickett were gathering provisions around Suffolk. The plan was for Lee to strengthen and improve his existing trenches on interior lines, which would make his army of 60,000 on par with Hooker's 113,000. That would have provided time for Longstreet to return to Lee with his two divisions; Hooker would be compelled to attack or retreat. Longstreet was surprised that

General Lee went on the offensive, losing 21 percent of his forces while inflicting only 15 percent casualties on Hooker in desperate fighting. Longstreet felt that the South had to conserve its manpower and resources to win the war against the North who had a much larger manpower pool and industrial capacity. He believed that battles like Chancellorsville would so bleed the South that it would not be able to field armies to meet the Northern incursions.

In May 1863, after Chancellorsville, General Longstreet advanced a grand strategic plan to Secretary of War Seddon who was trying to cope with General Grant's moves against General Pemberton's army at Vicksburg. Longstreet advocated a strategy that utilized the new technology of the railroad to shift troops in space and time by rapid transit, to concentrate an overwhelming force in Tennessee, utilizing interior lines, to oppose Union General Rosecrans's army. The telegraph, another technological achievement, would ease connections in the movement. This would have been an invasion, with the railroad providing logistical support. Longstreet revealed his plan to General Lee, but Lee wanted to invade Maryland and Pennsylvania. General Lee prevailed and started a campaign, which would lead him to Gettysburg. General Lee's proposition was little more than a raid depending upon animal-drawn conveyance rather than a railroad and could not be sustained for any length of time. Confederate General Edward Porter Alexander supported Longstreet's proposal: "I want to point out a variation which we might have played; & which Longstreet claims that he urged upon President Davis; & which, I think must be pronounced by all military critics to have been much our safest play." Alexander continued:

> Our forces & resources were far inferior to those of the enemy upon the whole, but the one single advantage which we possessed was that of the interior lines. We could reasonably hope to transfer a large force from our Army of Northern Virginia to our Army of Tennessee, or vice-versa, much sooner than the enemy could discover & transfer an equivalent force to meet us. Such a manouvre, by the axioms of the game, was our best hold.[1]

With the defeat of Rosecrans's army, the Confederates could have marched to the Ohio River, which would have protracted the war and diminished Union morale, with a possible political outcome in the elections.

As General Lee's army reorganized and refitted for its march northward into Pennsylvania, Generals Longstreet and Lee deliberated about strategy and tactics "almost every day from the 10th of May 63 until the Battle (of Gettysburg)" according to a letter written by James Longstreet to Lafayette McLaws on July 25, 1873. They analyzed previous campaigns, especially where the Confederates were the aggressors, in Longstreet's words, "concluded even victories such as these were consuming us, and would eventually destroy us." Longstreet thought there was an understanding as to the "the ruling idea of the campaign" that "under no circumstances were we to give battle, but exhaust our skill in trying to force the enemy to do so in a position of our own choosing. The 1st Corps to receive the attack and fight the battle. The other corps to then fall upon and try to destroy the Army of the Potomac." In his letter to McLaws, Longstreet expressed his tactical view that the Confederacy could not continue to squander its manpower in offensive operations: "Our losses were so heavy when we attacked that our army must soon be depleted to such extent that we should not be able to hold a force in the field sufficient to meet our adversary."

The two armies collided on Wednesday, July 1, west of Gettysburg where Lee's infantry routed two Union corps who retreated to a strong position atop Cemetery Hill. Longstreet surveyed the Federal position and saw a great opportunity to fulfill his strategic and tactical views, suggesting that the Confederate army "file around his left and secure good ground between him and his capital." Longstreet "was not a little surprised" when General Lee asserted that he wanted to attack. In his postwar letter to Lafayette McLaws, Longstreet expounded: "Lord will not understand my surprise at finding all of our previously arranged plans so unexpectedly changed, and why I might wish and hope to get the Gen. to consider our former arrangements." General Longstreet rejoined Lee on Seminary Ridge in the pre-dawn darkness on July 2 and again proposed a turning movement around the Federal left, and once again General Lee rejected the idea. General Lee was adamant that an assault on the Union position was to be carried out by Hood's and McLaws's divisions of Longstreet's First Corps, supported by his artillery batteries along the Emmitsburg Road. Hill's and Ewell's corps were to coordinate their attacks with Longstreet's but the whole affair was disorganized and failed. Things went from bad to worse for on July 3, General Lee decided to attack the left center of the Union position, with Pickett's division supported by some of Hill's Third Corps. The column advanced over open ground, some 1,400 yards with not a stick of cover, under concentrated battery fire and long-range rifle fire during the entire assault which ended in a repulse and much useless slaughter. This frontal assault was in the Napoleonic tradition but the introduction of the new long-range, highly accurate weaponry doomed it to failure, which Longstreet had surmised and was opposed to the attack.

After the battle of Gettysburg, Longstreet's thoughts returned to conditions in the west. With his superior armies, General Rosecrans was maneuvering General Bragg out of his lines in Tennessee and advancing on the northern borders of Georgia. Again, Longstreet advanced his strategic plan to employ the railroad to concentrate a superior force against Rosecrans by skillful use of interior lines. This time it was approved and Longstreet had his two divisions, McLaws's and Hood's, plus Alexander's batteries, transported to Tennessee; the battle of Chickamauga was fought with a decided Confederate victory.

However, General Bragg failed to gather the fruits of victory and let them slip through his hands. He took no part in directing the battle other than ordering an attack on the Union lines by frontal assault, causing massive casualties, which the South could not afford. General Longstreet succeeded in the battle by his masterful use of the wooded terrain but would have preferred to fight the battle in a flanking movement, interposing on the enemy's communications. General Bragg asked Longstreet's advice on strategy after the battle but never followed it up and settled for a siege of Chattanooga. Clearly, General Longstreet should have been placed in command of Bragg's Army of Tennessee prior to the conflict. General Alexander commented on Longstreet's strategic plan: "We actually did make the play in September, after our return from Gettysburg, & with very fair success even then, although the circumstances were much less favorable than those prevailing in May."[2]

General Longstreet was sent to subdue General Burnside before he reached Knoxville, Tennessee. However, the campaign ended with a repulse of the Confederate attack on Burnside's fortifications around Knoxville. Longstreet wintered his men in East Tennessee. While there, he proposed a raid into Kentucky by mounting his infantry. He wanted to disrupt the vital and essential railroad, bringing supplies to Union forces facing General Johnston at Dalton, Georgia. This would have caused them great discomfort and broke up their plans but the strategy was not approved by the government. Leaving East Tennessee, he reunited his First Corps with the Army of Northern Virginia, which was completed by April 21, 1864.

In the meantime, Ulysses S. Grant was appointed as lieutenant general and commander in chief of the field forces of the United States on March 9, 1864, and established his headquarters with the Army of the Potomac in Virginia. Grant made his objective Lee's army his objective and commenced crossing over pontoon bridges laid at Germanna and Ely's Ford on the morning of May 4. Grant's army became entangled in an area termed the Wilderness, a dense thicket of second-growth trees some 15 miles square along the south bank of the Rapidan River. The terrain of the Wilderness minimized the effectiveness of Grant's superior artillery, powerful cavalry, and the great disparity in numerical strength Grant enjoyed. The two armies collided and, after some intense fighting, the Union forces routed Hill's corps. Just then, Longstreet's troops arrived and stabilized the situation. Showing superior generalship, Longstreet used creative tactics, employing a strong skirmish line followed by stronger supporting lines to check the Union advance, as a full line of battle would be unwieldy in the heavily wooded terrain of the Wilderness. Longstreet was able to find a way around the Union left and launched an attack on the enemy's flank and rear, which broke the Union lines. Unfortunately, as Longstreet was setting up another flanking movement, he was wounded by his own men and had to be removed from the field of battle. Had this not happened, Grant's army might have been driven back across the Rapidan River.

After the war, Longstreet moved his family to New Orleans where he entered into the cotton-brokerage business and was elected president of an insurance company; he also served as president of the Southern Hospital Association. Longstreet became affiliated with the Republican Party and supported his friend Grant's campaign for President of the United States. On June 24, 1868, he received a federal pardon and became free from political disabilities due to Grant's intervention. After Grant was elected, Longstreet received a number of lucrative political offices from the Grant administration and the Republican Louisiana state government. These included surveyor of customs of the port of New Orleans; levee board commissioner of engineers for Louisiana; adjutant general of the state of Louisiana on May 13, 1870; and commander of the Louisiana state militia with the rank of major general. Longstreet was made president of the New Orleans and Northeastern Railroad. In 1875, for health reasons, Longstreet decided to leave Louisiana and take up residence in Gainesville, Georgia, where his brother William was living. On June 14, 1880, Longstreet was confirmed by the Senate as United States minister to Turkey but left the post in 1881 for the appointment as United States marshall for Georgia but lost the position in 1885. On January 22, 1898, Longstreet was appointed Commissioner of Railways for four years by President McKinley and confirmed by the Senate. Longstreet died at 6:00pm on January 2, 1904, and was laid to rest in the Alta Vista Cemetery in the suburbs of Gainesville.

Longstreet's advice, based on sound strategy and tactics in response to the technological changes which had taken place prior to the conflict, should have been given more weight. The Confederate government and military leaders tried offensive tactics and failed to use the railroad adequately to take advantage of their interior lines. They spread their limited manpower throughout the country to defend every piece of territory rather than concentrate their forces. To the Confederacy's detriment, Confederate leaders adhered to outdated military concepts and policies, which caused them to lose the war.

Notes

Chapter 1

1 Edward Alexander, *Military Memoirs of a Confederate* (Dayton: Morningside Bookshop, 1977), 38.
2 Ibid, 8.
3 Grady McWhiney and Perry Jamieson, *Attack and Die* (Alabama: University of Alabama Press, 1982), 161.
4 Alexander, *Military Memoirs of a Confederate*, 53-4.
5 Henry Commager, *The Blue and the Gray*, (New York: The Bobbs-Merrill Company, Inc., 1950), 65-6.

Chapter 2

1 Jeffry Wert, *General James Longstreet* (New York: Simon and Schuster, 1994), 131.
2 Moxley Sorrel, *Recollections of a Confederate Staff Officer* (Dayton: Morningside Bookshop, 1978), 76.
3 James Longstreet, *From Manassas to Appomattox* (Secaucus: The Blue and Grey Press, 1984), 329-30.
4 John Jones, *A Rebel War Clerk's Diary*, Volume I, (Philadelphia: J. B. Lippincott & Co., 1866), 292-3.

Chapter 3

1 Longstreet, *From Manassas to Appomattox*, 327-8.
2 Alexander K. McClure, ed., *Annals of the War*, "General James Longstreet, Lee in Pennsylvania" (Dayton, Ohio: Morningside Bookshop, 1988), 416.
3 Ibid, 416.
4 James Longstreet to Louis T. Wigfall, May 13, 1863, Wigfall Papers, Library of Congress.
5 Official Records, Volume 25, Part II, 790.
6 Shelby Foote, *The Civil War A Narrative: Fredericksburg to Meridian* (New York: Random House, 1963), 431.
7 Walter Taylor, *General Lee 1861-1865* (Dayton: Morningside Bookshop, 1975), 180.
8 Longstreet, *From Manassas to Appomattox*, 158-9.
9 McClure, *Annals of the War*, "General James Longstreet, Lee in Pennsylvania," 416-17.
10 Alexander, *Military Memoirs of a Confederate*, 364-5, 222.
11 Taylor, *General Lee 1861-1865*, 179-80.
12 Johnson and Buel, Battles and Leaders of the Civil War, Volume III, p. 246-7

13 William Garrett Piston, *Lee's Tarnished Lieutenant* (Athens, Georgia; The University of Georgia Press, 1987), 40

Chapter 4

1   William Swinton, *Campaigns of the Army of the Potomac* (New York: Charles B. Richardson, 1866), 312.
2   Comte de Paris, *History of the Civil War in America*, Volume III, 460.
3   McClure, *Annals of the War*, General James Longstreet, Lee in Pennsylvania, 418.
4   Swinton, *Campaigns of the Army of the Potomac*, 315–16.
5   Comte de Paris, *History of the Civil War in America*, 470.
6   Gary Gallagher, *Fighting for the Confederacy* (Chapel Hill: University of North Carolina Press, 1989), 222.
7   Longstreet, *From Manassas to Appomattox*, 336–337; Official Records: Volume 27, Part III, Lee to President Davis, June 23, 1863, 924–5.
8   Champ Clark, *The Civil War, Gettysburg: The Confederate High Tide* (Alexandria, Virginia: Time-Life Books, 1985), 25.
9   Longstreet, *From Manassas to Appomattox*, 343.
10 McClure, *Annals of the War*, "General James Longstreet, Lee in Pennsylvania," 418–19.
11 Robert Underwood Johnson and Clarence Clough Buel, eds, *Battles and Leaders of the Civil War*, Volume III (Secaucus, New Jersey: Castle, 1982), 249–50.
12 Sorrel, *Recollections of a Confederate Staff Officer*, 164.
13 Ibid, 156–7.
14 Longstreet, *From Manassas to Appomattox*, 348.
15 Frederick Maurice, ed., *An Aide-de-Camp of Lee* (Boston: Little, Brown and Company, 1927), 218–20.
16 Official Records, Volume 27, Part II, 637.
17 Stephen Sears, *Gettysburg* (Boston: Houghton Mifflin Company, 2003), 136.
18 Douglas Freeman, *Lee's Lieutenants*, Volume III (New York: Charles Scribner's Sons, 1944), 78.
19 Official Records: Volume 27, Part II, 607.

Chapter 5

1   Alexander, *Military Memoirs of a Confederate*, 381.
2   Official Records: Volume 27, Part II, 637.
3   Alexander, *Military Memoirs of a Confederate*, 382.
4   Arthur Fremantle, *Three Months in the Southern States* (Boston: Applewood Books, 2008), 198.
5   Longstreet, *From Manassas to Appomattox*, 351–2.
6   Fremantle, *Three Months in the Southern States*, 202.
7   Longstreet, *From Manassas to Appomattox*, 352.
8   Ibid, 350.
9   Fremantle, *Three Months in the Southern States*, 203.
10 Foote, *The Civil War A Narrative: Fredericksburg to Meridian*, 445–6.
11 Longstreet, *From Manassas to Appomattox*, 357–8.
12 McClure, *Annals of the War*, "General James Longstreet, Lee in Pennsylvania," 420–1.
13 A. L. Long, *Memoirs of Robert E. Lee* (Secaucus, New Jersey: The Blue and Grey Press, 1983), 276–7.

Chapter 6

1   Official Records: Volume 27, Part II, 318.
2   Longstreet, *From Manassas to Appomattox*, 357.
3   Gallagher, *Fighting for the Confederacy*, 233-4.
4   Comte de Paris, *History of the Civil War in America*, Volume III, 94.
5   Taylor, General Lee 1861–1865, 190.
6   Sears, Gettysburg, 227.
7   Alexander, *Military Memoirs of a Confederate*, 387-8.
8   Gallagher, *Fighting for the Confederacy*, 234.
9   Official Records: Volume 27, Part II, 446.
10 Alexander, *Military Memoirs of a Confederate*, 386.
11 McClure, *Annals of the War*, "General James Longstreet, Lee in Pennsylvania, Dr. Cullen's Letter to Longstreet," 439.
12 Longstreet, *From Manassas to Appomattox*, 362.
13 Fremantle, *Three Months in the Southern States*, 205-6.
14 Johnson and Buel, *Battles and Leaders of the Civil War*, Volume III, 340.
15 Sears, *Gettysburg*, 236; Noah Trudeau, *Gettysburg*, (New York: HarperCollins Publishers, Inc., 2003), 284.
16 McClure, *Annals of the War*: General James Longstreet, Lee in Pennsylvania, 422.
17 Ibid, 438.
18 Harry Pfanz, *Gettysburg the Second Day* (Chapel Hill: The University of North Carolina Press, 1987), 112.
19 Sorrel, *Recollections of a Confederate Staff Officer*, 166-7.
20 Long, *Memoirs of Robert E. Lee*, 281.
21 McClure, *Annals of the War*, "General James Longstreet, Lee in Pennsylvania," 422.
22 Longstreet, *From Manassas to Appomattox*, 365.
23 Alexander, *Military Memoirs of a Confederate*, 391-2.
24 McClure, *Annals of the War*, "General James Longstreet, Lee in Pennsylvania," 422-3.
25 Foote, *The Civil War A Narrative, Fredericksburg to Meridian*, 492.
26 Sorrel, *Recollections of a Confederate Staff Officer*, 168.
27 John Bell Hood, *Advance and Retreat*, (Edison, NJ: The Blue and Grey Press, 1985) 57-9.
28 Longstreet, *From Manassas to Appomattox*, 367-9.
29 Gallagher, *Fighting for the Confederacy*, 239.
30 Alexander, *Military Memoirs of a Confederate*, 395.
31 Longstreet, *From Manassas to Appomattox*, 370.
32 Official Records: Volume 27, Part II, 318-19.
33 Fremantle, *Three Months in the Southern States*, 208.
34 Alexander, *Military Memoirs of a Confederate*, 393.
35 McClure, *Annals of the War*, "General James Longstreet, Lee in Pennsylvania," 424-6.
36 Pfanz, *Gettysburg the Second Day*, 349.
37 Trudeau, *Gettysburg*, 332.
38 Freeman, *Lee's Lieutenants*, Volume III, 140.
39 Alexander, *Military Memoirs of a Confederate*, 394.
40 Comte de Paris, *History of the Civil War in America*, Volume III, 642.
41 Alexander, Military Memoirs of a Confederate, 393.
42 Longstreet, *From Manassas to Appomattox*, 373.
43 Alexander, *Military Memoirs of a Confederate*, 405-6.

44 Robertson, *General A. P. Hill*, 219; Pfanz, *Gettysburg the Second Day*, 386.

45 Trudeau, *Gettysburg*, 394.

46 Alexander, *Military Memoirs of a Confederate*, 401.

47 Ibid, 408–413; Official Records: Volume 27, Part II, 556.

48 McClure, *Annals of the War*, "General James Longstreet, Lee in Pennsylvania," 428.

49 Fremantle, *Three Months in the Southern States*, 208-9.

50 Sears, *Gettysburg*, 306.

51 Long, *Memoirs of Robert E. Lee*, 286.

52 Longstreet, *From Manassas to Appomattox*, 382.

53 Gallagher, *Fighting for the Confederacy*, 244.

54 Tradeau, *Gettysburg*, 412.

Chapter 7

1 Official Records: Volume 27, Part II, 320.

2 Gallagher, *Fighting for the Confederacy*, 246-7.

3 Longstreet, *From Manassas to Appomattox*, 385-6.

4 McClure, *Annals of the War*, "General James Longstreet, Lee in Pennsylvania," 429.

5 Official Records: Volume 27, Part II, 320.

6 Alexander, *Military Memoirs of a Confederate*, 370.

7 McClure, *Annals of the War*, "General James Longstreet, Lee in Pennsylvania," 429-30.

8 Longstreet, *From Manassas to Appomattox*, 335.

9 Alexander, *Military Memoirs of a Confederate*, 415.

10 Long, *Memoirs of Robert E. Lee*, 286-8.

11 Official Records: Volume 27, Part II, 359.

12 Alexander, *Military Memoirs of a Confederate*, 416.

13 Johnson and Buel, *Battles and Leaders of the Civil War*, Volume III, 361-2.

14 Ibid, 343.

15 Longstreet, *From Manassas to Appomattox*, 390.

16 McClure, *Annals of the War*, "General James Longstreet, Lee in Pennsylvania," 431-2.

17 Johnson and Buel, *Battles and Leaders of the Civil War*, Volume III, 357.

18 Ibid, 362.

19 Longstreet, *From Manassas to Appomattox*, 390-1.

20 Alexander, *Military Memoirs of a Confederate*, 420-1.

21 Gallagher, *Fighting for the Confederacy*, 255.

22 Alexander, *Military Memoirs of a Confederate*, 420, 421, 422-3.

23 McClure, *Annals of the War*, "General James Longstreet, Lee in Pennsylvania," 430-1.

24 Gallagher, *Fighting for the Confederacy*, 258-9, 261.

25 Alexander, *Military Memoirs of a Confederate*, 424.

26 Gallagher, *Fighting for the Confederacy*, 261-2.

27 Longstreet, *From Manassas to Appomattox*, 391.

28 Gallagher, *Fighting for the Confederacy*, 248.

29 Trudeau, *Gettysburg*, 452.

30 Johnson and Buel, *Battles and Leaders of the Civil War*, Volume III, 372.

31 Longstreet, *From Manassas to Appomattox*, 393-4.

32 Johnson and Buel, *Battles and Leaders of the Civil War*, Volume III, 345-7.

33 Fremantle, *Three Months in the Southern States*, 210-16.

34 Alexander, *Military Memoirs of a Confederate*, 425.
35 McClure, *Annals of the War*, "General James Longstreet, Lee in Pennsylvania," 431.
36 Wert, *General James Longstreet*, 292.
37 Longstreet, *From Manassas to Appomattox*, 396.
38 Fremantle, *Three Months in the Southern States*, 217.

Chapter 8

1 Fremantle, *Three Months in the Southern States*, 217–18, 300.
2 Alexander, *Military Memoirs of a Confederate*, 435.
3 Sears, *Gettysburg*, 470.
4 Owen, *In Camp and Battle with the Washington Artillery*, 255.
5 Fremantle, *Three Months in the Southern States*, 219.
6 Trudeau, *Gettysburg*, 541–2.
7 Johnson and Buel, *Battles and Leaders of the Civil War*, Volume III, 423.
8 Gallagher, *Fighting for the Confederacy*, 270.
9 Alexander, *Military Memoirs of a Confederate*, 439.
10 Gallagher, *Fighting for the Confederacy*, 270–1.
11 Ibid, 272.
12 Longstreet, From Manassas to Appomattox, 429.
13 Fremantle, *Three Months in the Southern States*, 229.

Chapter 9

1 Alexander, *Military Memoirs of a Confederate*, 374.
2 McClure, *Annals of the War*, "General James Longstreet, Lee in Pennsylvania," 435.
3 Ibid, 433.
4 Gallagher, *Fighting for the Confederacy*, 237.
5 McClure, *Annals of the War*, "General James Longstreet, Lee in Pennsylvania," 435–6.
6 *Civil War Times*, Vol. XLIV, No. 3 August, 2005, 31.
7 Johnson and Buel, *Battles and Leaders of the Civil War*, Volume III, 358.
8 Ibid, 349–50.
9 Gallagher, *Fighting for the Confederacy*, 234–5.
10 Johnson and Buel, *Battles and Leaders of the Civil War*, Volume III, 341.
11 McClure, *Annals of the War*, "General James Longstreet, Lee in Pennsylvania," 434.
12 Gallagher, *Fighting for the Confederacy*, 252.
13 Alexander, *Military Memoirs of a Confederate*, 416–18.
14 Gallagher, *Fighting for the Confederacy*, 251.
15 Sears, *Gettysburg*, 377
16 Official Records: Volume 27, Part II, 321.
17 Gallagher, *Fighting for the Confederacy*, 283, 236
18 Ibid, 277–8.
19 McClure, *Annals of the War*, "General James Longstreet, Lee in Pennsylvania," 430.
20 Longstreet, *From Manassas to Appomattox*, 384.
21 Gallagher, *Fighting for the Confederacy*, 92.
22 Johnson and Buel, *Battles and Leaders of the Civil War*, Volume III, 428.

23 Longstreet, *From Manassas to Appomattox*, 400; Thomas Cutrer, *Longstreet's Aide*, Charlottesville: (University Press of Virginia, 1995), 158 (Letter to General James Longstreet from Thomas J. Goree, May 17, 1875).
24 Ibid, 400.
25 McClure, *Annals of the War*, "General James Longstreet, Lee in Pennsylvania," 432.
26 *Washington Post*, June 11, 1893.
27 *Charleston Mercury*, July 22, 30, 1863.
28 Piston, *Lee's Tarnished Lieutenant*, 65.
29 Longstreet, *From Manassas to Appomattox*, 432.
30 *New York Times*, June 4, 1893.

Chapter 10

1   Johnson and Buel, *Battles and Leaders of the Civil War*, Volume III, 350.
2   Alexander, *Military Memoirs of a Confederate*, 447.
3   Official Records: Volume 29, Part II, 693-4.
4   Longstreet, *From Manassas to Appomattox*, 433-4.
5   Alexander, *Military Memoirs of a Confederate*, 448.
6   Longstreet to Louis T. Wigfall, August 18, 1863, Wigfall Papers, Library of Congress.
7   Longstreet, *From Manassas to Appomattox*, 434; Official Records: Volume 29, Part II, 701; Colonel John W. Fairfax to General Longstreet, April 16, 1898, Fairfax Papers.
8   Official Records: Volume 29, Part II, 699.
9   Alexander, *Military Memoirs of a Confederate*, 447-8.
10 Longstreet, *From Manassas to Appomattox*, 436.
11 Longstreet to Louis T. Wigfall, September 12, 1863, Wigfall Papers, Library of Congress.
12 Official Records: Volume 29, Part II, 711-12.
13 Ibid, 713-14.
14 Longstreet, *From Manassas to Appomattox*, 437.
15 Taylor, *General Lee 1861-1865*, 223.
16 Longstreet, *From Manassas to Appomattox*, 436-7.
17 Alexander, *Military Memoirs of a Confederate*, 449.
18 Sorrel, *Recollections of a Confederate Staff Officer*, 189.
19 Ibid, 192-3.
20 Fremantle, *Three Months in the Southern States*, 115.
21 Baird, *David Wendel Yandell*, 50.
22 Johnson and Buel, *Battles and Leaders of the Civil War*, Volume III, 652.
23 Alexander, *Military Memoirs of a Confederate*, 451-3.
24 Johnson and Buel, *Battles and Leaders of the Civil War*, Volume III, 640, 644, 645-6.

Chapter 11

1   Longstreet, *From Manassas to Appomattox*, 440.
2   DiNardo and Nofi, *James Longstreet*, 112, 157.
3   Hood, *Advance and Retreat*, 62.
4   Ibid, 62-3.
5   Longstreet, *From Manassas to Appomattox*, 447.
6   Korn, *The Fight for Chattanooga, Chickamauga to Missionary Ridge*, Time-Life Books, 56.

7   Cozzens, *This Terrible Sound*, 363.
8   Alexander, *Military Memoirs of a Confederate*, 460-1.
9   Cozzens, *This Terrible Sound*, 393.
10   Longstreet, *From Manassas to Appomattox*, 448.
11   Hood, *Advance and Retreat*, 64.
12   Cozzens, *This Terrible Sound*, 376.
13   Owen, *In Camp and Battle with the Washington Artillery*, 288.
14   Wert, *General James Longstreet*, 314.
15   Cozzens, *This Terrible Sound*, 426.
16   Tucker, *Chickamauga*, 330.
17   Longstreet, *From Manassas to Appomattox*, 450.
18   DiNardo and Nofi, *James Longstreet*, 125.
19   Longstreet, *From Manassas to Appomattox*, 450-1.
20   Ibid, p. 451-2.
21   Johnson and Buel, *Battles and Leaders of the Civil War*, Volume III, 659.
22   Longstreet, *From Manassas to Appomattox*, 452-3.
23   Johnson and Buel, *Battles and Leaders of the Civil War*, Volume III, 660.
24   Official Records: Volume 30, Part II, 289.
25   Longstreet, *From Manassas to Appomattox*, 452.
26   Sorrel, *Recollections of a Confederate Staff Officer*, 201-2.
27   Johnson and Buel, *Battles and Leaders of the Civil War*, Volume III, 661.
28   Kean, *Inside the Confederate Government*, 115-16.
29   Connelly, *Autumn of Glory*, 227-8.
30   Johnson and Buel, *Battles and Leaders of the Civil War*, Volume III, 659.
31   Cozzens, This Terrible Sound, 514.
32   Foote, *The Civil War A Narrative, Fredericksburg to Meridian*, 758.
33   Official Records: Volume 30, Part II, 289.

Chapter 12

1   Official Records: Volume 30, Part II, 289-90.
2   Cozzens, *This Terrible Sound*, 519-20; Korn, Time-Life Books, *The Fight for Chattanooga*, 72-3.
3   Longstreet, *From Manassas to Appomattox*, 462.
4   Official Records: Volume 30, Part II, 37.
5   Longstreet, *From Manassas to Appomattox*, 463.
6   Ibid, 464.
7   Kean, *Inside the Confederate Government*, 106-7.
8   Woodward, *Mary Chesnut's Civil* War, 469.
9   Cozzens, *This Terrible Sound*, 530.
10   Wert, *General James Longstreet*, 324.
11   Official Records: Volume 30, Part IV, 705-6.
12   Kean, *Inside the Confederate Government*, 108-9.
13   Official Records: Volume 52, Part II, 549-50.
14   Wert, *General James Longstreet*, 326-7.
15   Official Records: Volume 52, Part II, 538.
16   Jones, *A Rebel War Clerk's Diary*, Volume II, 70.
17   Official Records: Volume 30, Part IV, 742.
18   Longstreet, *From Manassas to Appomattox*, 465-6.

19 Wert, General James Longstreet, 327.
20 Official Records: Volume 30, Part IV, 742.
21 Sorrel, Recollections of a Confederate Staff Officer, 200-1.
22 Gallagher, Fighting for the Confederacy, 307.
23 Longstreet, From Manassas to Appomattox, 466-8.
24 Gallagher, Fighting for the Confederacy, 307-8.
25 Sanger and Hay, James Longstreet, 407.
26 Cozzens, This Terrible Sound, 533.
27 Wert, General James Longstreet, 329.
28 Cozzens, This Terrible Sound, 533.
29 Longstreet, From Manassas to Appomattox, 468-9.
30 Ibid, 471.
31 Ibid, 473-4.
32 Alexander, Military Memoirs of a Confederate, 467-9.
33 Longstreet, From Manassas to Appomattox, 480-1.
34 Ibid, 481-2.
35 Comte de Paris, History of the Civil War in America, Volume IV, 224.
36 Kean, Inside the Confederate Government, 115-16.

Chapter 13

1   Alexander, Military Memoirs of a Confederate, 472-3.
2   Longstreet, From Manassas to Appomattox, 484-485; Official Records: Volume 52, Part II, 559-61.
3   Sorrel, Recollections of a Confederate Staff Officer, 210.
4   Longstreet, From Manassas to Appomattox, 478-9.
5   Gallagher, Fighting for the Confederacy, 296.
6   Official Records: Volume 52, Part II, 557.
7   Ibid, 554-5.
8   Official Records: Volume 31, Part I, 476.
9   Official Records: Volume 31, Part III, 686-7.
10 Ibid, 680.
11 Longstreet, From Manassas to Appomattox, 487-8.
12 Ibid, 486.
13 Battles and Leaders of the Civil War, Volume II, 695.
14 Sanger, James Longstreet, 223; Comte de Paris, History of the Civil War in America, Volume IV, 234.
15 Longstreet, From Manassas to Appomattox, 488.
16 Sorrel, Recollections of a Confederate Staff Officer, 210-11.
17 Longstreet, From Manassas to Appomattox, 490.
18 Ibid, 457
19 Korn, The Civil War: Chickamauga to Missionary Ridge, Time-Life Books, 107-8.
20 Longstreet, From Manassas to Appomattox, 493.
21 Ibid, 493.
22 Official Records: Volume 31, Part I, 526.
23 Longstreet, From Manassas to Appomattox, 499.
24 Official Records: Volume 31, Part III, 736-8.
25 Alexander, Military Memoirs of a Confederate, 485.
26 Gallagher, Fighting for the Confederacy, 324.

27 Ibid, 325–6.
28 Official Records: Volume 31, Part III, 756.
29 Gallagher, *Fighting for the Confederacy*, 326–327.
30 Official Records: Volume 31, Part III, 757.
31 Gallagher, *Fighting for the Confederacy*, 327.
32 Johnson and Buel, *Battles and Leaders of the Civil War*, Volume III, 743.
33 Korn, *The Civil War: The Fight for Chattanooga*, Time-Life Books, 114.
34 Johnson and Buel, *Battles and Leaders of the Civil War*, Volume III, 749.
35 Longstreet, *From Manassas to Appomattox*, 505–6.
36 Johnson and Buel, *Battles and Leaders of the Civil War*, Volume III, 750.
37 Sorrel, *Recollections of a Confederate Staff Officer*, 215.
38 Johnson and Buel, *Battles and Leaders of the Civil War*, Volume III, 744.
39 Sorrel, *Recollections of a Confederate Staff*, Officer, 215.

Chapter 14

1   Sorrel, *Recollections of a Confederate Staff Officer*, 217.
2   Longstreet, *From Manassas to Appomattox*, 514.
3   Ibid, 520–1.
4   Sorrel, *Recollections of a Confederate Staff Officer*, 220.
5   Longstreet, *From Manassas to Appomattox*, 524.
6   Freeman, *Lee's Lieutenants*, Volume III, 306.
7   Official Records: Volume 33, 1075.
8   Official Records: Volume 32, Part II, 681–2.
9   Longstreet, *From Manassas to Appomattox*, 524–5.
10 Wert, *General James Longstreet*, 361–2; Official Records: Volume 31, Part I, 503.
11 Ibid, 365.
12 Sorrel, *Recollections of a Confederate Staff Officer*, 238.
13 Official Records: Volume 32, Part II, 726.
14 Ibid, 801–2.
15 Official Records: Volume 32, Part III, 583.
16 Ibid, 738.
17 Official Records: Volume 31, Part I, 549–50.
18 Official Records: Volume 31, Part II, 597.
19 Longstreet, *From Manassas to Appomattox*, 529–30.
20 Ibid, 539–40
21 Official Records: Volume 32, Part II, 772.
22 Ibid, 789–90.
23 Ibid, 791–2.
24 Ibid, 818.
25 Longstreet, *From Manassas to Appomattox*, 542–3.
26 Ibid, 542.
27 Ibid, 543.
28 Official Records: Volume 52, Part II, 634.
29 Longstreet, *From Manassas to Appomattox*, 544.
30 Official Records: Volume 32, Part III, 679–80.
31 Longstreet, *From Manassas to Appomattox*, 544–6.
32 Official Records: Volume 32, Part III, 637–41.

33 Ibid, 627–8.
34 Ibid, 641–2.
35 Ibid, 649; Connelly and Jones, *Politics of Command*, 142–50.
36 Ibid, 674–6.

Chapter 15

1 Longstreet, *From Manassas to Appomattox*, 547–8.
2 Ibid, 551.
3 Official Records: Volume 36, Part I, 12–13; Rhea, *The Battle of the Wilderness*, 46.
4 Jaynes, *The Civil War: Wilderness to Cold Harbor*, Time-Life Books, 26.
5 Alexander, *Military Memoirs of a Confederate*, 496–7.
6 Longstreet, *From Manassas to Appomattox*, 554.
7 Trautmann, *A Prussian Observes the American Civil War*, 31.
8 Dowdey and Manarin, *The Wartime Papers of R. E. Lee*, 708, 720.
9 Longstreet, *From Manassas to Appomattox*, 555.
10 Grant, *Personal Memoirs of U. S. Grant*, 423–4.
11 Official Records: Volume 36, Part II, 947.
12 Official Records: Volume 36, Part I, 15.
13 Longstreet, *From Manassas to Appomattox*, 556–7.
14 Official Records: Volume 36, Part II, 948.
15 Official Records: Volume 36, Part I, 1070.
16 Johnson and Buel, *Battles and Leaders of the Civil War*, Volume IV, 121
17 Swinton, *Campaigns of the Army of the Potomac*, 420–1.
18 Rhea, *The Battle of the Wilderness*, 133.
19 Ibid, 159.
20 Official Records: Volume 36, Part I, 1070–1071; Gallagher, *Fighting for the Confederacy*, 353.
21 Ibid, 194–5.
22 Ibid, 195–6.
23 Ibid, 200.
24 Swinton, *Campaigns of the Army of the Potomac*, 428–9.
25 Gallagher, *Fighting for the Confederacy*, 354–5.
26 McClure, *Annals of the War*, "General Wilcox, Lee and Grant in the Wilderness," 494; Rhea, *The Battle of the Wilderness*, 276.
27 Freeman, *R. E. Lee*, Volume III, 281.
28 Rhea, *The Battle of the Wilderness*, 277, 279.
29 Ibid, 273.
30 Gallagher, *Fighting for the Confederacy*, 350.
31 Longstreet, *From Manassas to Appomattox*, 559.
32 Rhea, *The Battle of the Wilderness*, 278.
33 Alexander, *Military Memoirs of a Confederate*, 502.
34 Longstreet, *From Manassas to Appomattox*, 560.
35 Gallagher, *Fighting for the Confederacy*, 356–8.
36 McClure, *Annals of the War*, "General Wilcox, Lee and Grant in the Wilderness," 495–6.
37 Robertson, *General A. P. Hill*, 255.
38 Ibid, 263.
39 Sorrel, *Recollections of a Confederate Staff Officer*, 240.
40 Rhea, *The Battle of the Wilderness*, 295–7.

41 Johnson and Buel, *Battles and Leaders of the Civil War*, Volume IV, 124.
42 Rhea, *The Battle of the Wilderness*, 298-9.
43 Long, *Memoirs of Robert E. Lee*, 330.
44 Steere, *The Wilderness Campaign*, 345.
45 Freeman, *Lee's Lieutenants*, Volume III, 357-8; Foote, *The Civil War A Narrative: Red River to Appomattox*, 170.
46 Longstreet, *From Manassas to Appomattox*, 560-1.
47 Johnson and Buel, *Battles and Leaders of the Civil War*, Volume IV, 125.
48 Rhea, *The Battle of the Wilderness*, 304.
49 Longstreet, *From Manassas to Appomattox*, 561.
50 Rhea, *The Battle of the Wilderness*, 316.
51 Foote, *The Civil War A Narrative, Red River to Appomattox*, 170.
52 Longstreet, *From Manassas to Appomattox*, 561.
53 Official Records: Volume 36, Part I, 1055.
54 Sorrel, *Recollections of a Confederate Staff Officer*, 241-3.
55 Alexander, *Military Memoirs of a Confederate*, 505.
56 Johnson and Buel, *Battles and Leaders of the Civil War*, Volume IV, 125-6.
57 Taylor, *General Lee 1861-1865*, 235.
58 Longstreet, *From Manassas to Appomattox*, 568.
59 Rhea, *The Battle of the Wilderness*, 359.
60 Longstreet, *From Manassas to Appomattox*, 562-3.
61 Steere, *The Wilderness Campaign*, 388.
62 Official Records: Volume 36, Part I, 1062.
63 Gallagher, *Fighting for the Confederacy*, 359.
64 Sorrel, *Recollections of a Confederate Staff Officer*, 243-4.
65 Longstreet, *From Manassas to Appomattox*, 563-5.
66 Rhea, *The Battle of the Wilderness*, 370-373; Official Records: Volume 51, Part II, 893; Longstreet, *From Manassas to Appomattox*, 562-5.
67 Gallagher, *Fighting for the Confederacy*, 362-3.
68 Taylor, *General Lee 1861-1865*, 236.
69 Official Records: Volume 32, Part III, 588.

Epilogue

1 Gallagher, *Fighting for the Confederacy*, 219-20.
2 Ibid, 219.

Bibliography

Books

Alexander, E. P. *Military Memoirs of a Confederate*, Reprint Edition. Dayton, Ohio: Morningside Bookshop, 1977.

Baird, Nancy Disher. *David Wendel Yandell: Physician of Old Louisville*. Lexington: The University Press of Kentucky, 1978.

Clark Jr, John E. *Railroads in the Civil War*. Baton Rouge: Louisiana State University Press, 2001.

Commager, Henry Steele. *The Blue and the Gray*. New York: The Bobbs-Merrill Company, Inc., 1950.

Comte De Paris. *History of the Civil War in America*. Four Volumes. Philadelphia, Pennsylvania: Porter & Coates, 1888.

Connelly, Thomas Lawrence. *Autumn of Glory: The Army of Tennessee 1862–1865*. Baton Rouge: Louisiana State University Press, 1971.

Connelly, Thomas Lawrence and Jones, Archer. *The Politics of Command: Factions and Ideas in Confederate Strategy*. Baton Rouge: Louisiana State University Press, 1973.

Cooper Jr, William J. *Jefferson Davis and The Civil War Era*. Baton Rouge: Louisiana State University Press, 2008.

Cozzens, Peter. *This Terrible Sound: The Battle of Chickamauga*. Chicago: University of Illinois Press, 1992.

Cutrer, Thomas W., ed., *Longstreet's Aide: The Civil War Letters of Major Thomas J. Goree*. Charlottesville: University Press of Virginia, 1995.

DiNardo, R. L. and Albert A. Nofi, eds, *James Longstreet: The Man, the Soldier, the Controversy*. Conshohocken, Pennsylvania, Combined Publishing, 1998.

Dowdey, Clifford and Louis H. Manarin, eds, *The Wartime Papers of R. E. Lee*. Boston: Little Brown and Company, 1961.

Eckenrode, H. J. and Bryan Conrad. *James Longstreet: Lee's War Horse*. Chapel Hill: The University of North Carolina Press, 1986.

Freeman, Douglas Southall, Ed. *Lee's Lieutenants: A Study in Command*. Three Volumes. New York: Charles Scribner's Sons, 1944

Freeman, Douglas Southall. *R. E. Lee: A Biography*. Four Volumes. New York: Charles Scribner's Sons, 1949.

Gallagher, Gary W., ed., *Fighting for the Confederacy: The Personal Recollections of General Edward Porter Alexander*. Chapel Hill: University of North Carolina Press, 1989.

Gallagher, Gary W., ed., *The Wilderness Campaign*. Chapel Hill: University of North Carolina Press, 1997.

Hagerman, Edward, *The American Civil War and the Origins of Modern Warfare: Ideas, Organization, and Field Command*. Indianapolis: Indiana University Press, 1988.

Hood, John Bell, Advance and Retreat. Edison, New Jersey: The Blue and Grey Press, 1985.

Jones, Archer. *Civil War Command and Strategy: The Process of Victory and Defeat*. New York: The Free Press, 1992.

Jones, John B. *A Rebel War Clerk's Diary*. Two Volumes. Philadelphia: J. B. Lippincott & Co., 1866.

Knudsen, Harold M., LTC. *General James Longstreet: The Confederacy's Most Modern General*. Girard, Illinois: USA Publishing Services, 2007.

Long, A. L. *Memoirs of Robert E. Lee: His Military and Personal History*. Secaucus, New Jersey: The Blue and Grey Press, 1983.

Longstreet, Helen D. *Lee and Longstreet at High Tide: Gettysburg in the Light of the Official Records*. Wilmington, North Carolina: Broadfoot Publishing Co., 1989.

Longstreet, James. *From Manassas to Appomattox: Memoirs of the Civil War in America*. Secaucus, New Jersey: The Blue and Grey Press, 1984.

Longstreet Papers, Duke University.

Lord, Walter, Ed. *The Fremantle Diary*. Boston: Little, Brown and Company, 1954.

Maurice, Frederick, ed., *An Aide de Camp of Lee: Being the Papers of Colonel Charles Marshall, Assistant Adjutant General on the Staff of Robert E. Lee 1862–1865*. Boston: Little, Brown and Company, 1927.

McClure, Alexander K., ed., *Annals of the War Written by Leading Participants North and South*. Reprint Edition. Dayton, Ohio: Morningside Bookshop, 1988.

McWhiney, Grady and Perry D. Jamieson. *Attack and Die: Civil War Military Tactics and Southern Heritage*. Alabama: University of Alabama Press, 1982.

Owen, William Miller. *In Camp and Battle with the Washington Artillery*. Boston: Ticknor and Company, 1885.

Pfanz, Harry W. *Gettysburg: The First Day*. Chapel Hill: The University of North Carolina Press, 2001.

Pfanz, Harry W. *Gettysburg: The Second Day*. Chapel Hill: The University of North Carolina Press, 1987.

Piston, William Garrett, *Lee's Tarnished Lieutenant: James Longstreet and His Place in Southern History*. Athens, Georgia: The University of Georgia Press, 1987.

Rhea, Gordon C. *The Battle of the Wilderness: May 5–6, 1864*. Baton Rouge: Louisiana State University Press, 1994.

Sanger, Donald Bridgmen and Thomas Robson Hay. *James Longstreet: I. Soldier, II. Politician, Officeholder, and Writer*. Baton Rouge: Louisiana State University Press, 1952.

Sears, Stephen W. *Gettysburg*. Boston: Houghton Mifflin Company, 2003.

Sorrel, G. Moxley. *Recollections of a Confederate Staff Officer*. Reprint Edition. Dayton, Ohio: Morningside Bookshop, 1978.

Steere, Edward. *The Wilderness Campaign*. Mechanicsburg, Pennsylvania: Stackpole Books, 1960.

Swinton, William. *Campaigns of the Army of the Potomac*. New York: Charles B. Richardson, 1866.

Taylor, Walter H. *Four Years with General Lee*. New York: B. Appleton and Company, 1878.

Taylor, Walter H. *General Lee: His Campaigns in Virginia 1861–1865*. Reprint Edition. Dayton, Ohio: Morningside Bookshop, 1975.

Time-Life Books, Inc. *The Civil War*. 28 Volumes. Alexandria, Virginia: Time-Life Books, 1985.

Trautmann, Frederic, ed., *A Prussian Observes the American Civil War: The Military Studies of Justus Scheibert*. Columbia: University of Missouri Press, 2001.

Trudeau, Noah Andre. *Gettysburg: A Testing of Courage*. New York: HarperCollins Publishers, Inc., 2003.

Tucker, Glenn. *High Tide at Gettysburg: The Campaign in Pennsylvania*. New York: Charter Books, 1964.

Tucker, Glenn. *Lee and Longstreet at Gettysburg*. Indianapolis, Indiana: The Bobbs-Merrill Company, Inc., 1968.

Johnson, Robert Underwood and Buel, Clarence Clough, eds, *Battles and Leaders of the Civil War*. "The Century War Series." Four Volumes. Secaucus, New Jersey: Castle, 1982.

U. S. War Department. *The War of the Rebellion: A Compilation of the Official Records of the Union and Confederate Armies*. 128 Volumes. The Government Printing Office, Washington, D.C., 1891.

Wert, Jeffry D. *General James Longstreet: The Confederacy's Most Controversial Soldier*. New York: Simon and Schuster, 1994.

Wigfall Papers, Library of Congress.
Woodward, C. Vann, ed., *Mary Chesnut's Civil War*. New Haven, Connecticut: Yale University Press, 1981.
Younger, Edward, ed., *Inside the Confederate Government: The Diary of Robert Garlick Hill Kean*. New York: Oxford University Press, 1957.

Newspapers

Charleston Mercury
New York Times
Washington Post

Magazines

Civil War Times Illustrated

Index